IRANIANS IN MUGHAL POLITICS AND SOCIETY 1606-1658

IRANIANS IN MUGHAL POLITICS AND SOCIETY 1606-1658

DR. ABOLGHASEM DADVAR

GYAN

GYAN PUBLISHING HOUSE

NEW DELHI-110002

IRANIANS IN MUGHAL POLITICS AND SOCIETY (1606-1658)

(History)

ISBN: 81-212-0639-1

Published in 1999 in India by
Gyan Publishing House
5, Ansari Road
New Delhi-110002
Lesser Typeset at: Ellite Art New Delhi-110002
Printed at: Mehra Offest Press New Delhi-110002

In the name of Allah

Dedicated to my wife Fazileh

and

my children Farzaneh and Fatimeh

Contents

Acknowledgements 9

Abbreviations of References 11

Abbreviations of Tables and Graphs 12

Abbreviations of Reasons and Contexts of Migration 13

System of Transliteration 14

List of Tables 15

List of Graphs 17

List of Maps 19

Introduction 21

1. Relations between the Mughal Rulers and the Safavids 33
2. Iranians in Mughal Politics and Administration 71
3. Poets as Administrators 137
4. Scholars, Artists and Physicians in Administration 171
5. Iranian Poets in Mughal Culture 203
6. Scholars, *Sufis* and *Darvishes* 239
7. Artists, Craftsmen and People with Diverse Skills 291
8. Iranian Traders and Iranian Travellers 329

Conclusion 369

Appendix 393

Bibliography 403

Index *421*

Acknowledgements

Several friends' help has gone into the making of this humble work. It is my pleasant duty to express my gratitude to Professor Muzaffar Alam. The completion of this work could not have been possible without his consistent encouragement and advice. His detailed and critical comments as also his suggestions at each and every stage of the preparation of this study have indeed been of immense value.

From Dr. Zia-ud-Din Dasai, Dr Ahmad Golchin Maani, Professor Sharif Husain Qasemi, Dr. Yunes Jafari, Professor S. Jamaluddin, Dr. Seema Alavi, Professor Harbans Mukhia and Professor B.D. Chattopadhyaya I have received advice and suggestions regarding the issues relevant sources and secondary works related to this work. I take this opportunity to express my sincere thanks to them for their help and cooperation.

I must acknowledge my deep gratitude to my wife and companion, Dr. Fazileh, for preparing the maps and for her indulgence and patience during the writing of this book.

I would also like to put on record my gratitude to the helpful staffs of various libraries and archival depositories mainly the Jawaharlal Nehru University Library, New Delhi, Jamia Millia, Hamdard and Delhi Universities, New Delhi, Indian Council of Historical Research, New Delhi, Iran Culture House at New Delhi, National Museum, Nehru Memorial Museum Library, National Archives, Archaelogical Survey of India, New Delhi, Maulana Azad Library, Aligarh, Library of Salar Jang Museum, Haidarabad, Libraries of Madras, Bombay, Poona and Ahmadabad

Universities, Central Library of Tehran University, Malik, Majlis and Melli Libraries at Tehran, Library of Firdusi University and Astan-e-Quds Rezavi at Mashhad.

I must also express my deep sense of gratitude to my mother for her constant encouragement and forbearance. Of course, Farzaneh and Fatimeh always provided delightful distractions whenever I was under stress during the preparation of this work.

Needless to say that I am solely responsible for all the errors, omissions and gaps, still remaining in this book.

New Delhi **Abolghasem Dadvar**
1999

Abbreviations of References

A.A.A.	:	*Tarikh-i-Alam Ara-i-Abbasi*
A.N.	:	*Akbar Nama*
Badauni	:	*Muntakhab-ut-Tawarikh*
Bayazid	:	*Tazkira Humayun va Akbar*
C.H.I	:	*Cambridge History of Iran*
E.F.I.	:	*The English Factories of India*
E.I.	:	*Encyclopaedia of Islam*
I.C.	:	*Islamic Culture*
J.B.R.S.	:	*Journal of Bihar Research Society*
J.R.A.S.	:	*Journal of Royal Asiatic Society*
Khafi Khan	:	*Muntakhab-ul-Lubab*
Lahori	:	*Padshah Nama* of Abdul Hamid Lahori
M.U.	:	*Ma'asir-ul-Umara*
Nq.A.	:	*Nuqawat-ul-Asar Fi Zekr-ul-Akhyar*
P.I.H.C	:	*Proceedings of the Indian History Congress*
Qazwini.	:	*Padshah Nama* of Qazwini
T. Auhadi,	:	*Arafat-ul-Ashiqin* of Taqi Auhadi
T.M.	:	*Tazkirat-ul-Mulk* ed. & tr. by Minorskyy
Tuzuk	:	*Tuzuk-i-Jahangiri*
Waris	:	*Padshah Nama* of Muhammad Waris
Z. Kh.	:	*Zakhirat-ul-Khawanin*

Abbreviations of Tables and Graphs

Rg.	Regions
No.	North
WNW	West and North-West
SW	South-West
CP	Central Plateau
SO	South
ENE	East and North-East
SE	South-East
UA	Unclear area
Pr	Period
AK	Akbar
Ja	Jahangir
Sh	Shahjahan
NU	Number
CAT	Categories
PA	Politics and Administration
OA	Poets as Administrators
S	Scholars
AC	Artists and Craftsmen
DO	People with diverse Skills
SW	Scholars, Waqia navis and artists in Administration
PQ	Physicians and *Qazis*
P	Iranian Poets
SS	Iranian Shaikhs, *Sufis* and *Darvishes*
IT	Iranian Traders
IR	Iranian Travellers
IW	Iranian Women

Abbreviations of Reasons and Contexts of Migration

X1	Religious persecution *(Azar va Sakhtgirihai Mazhabi)*
X2	Loss of royal favour
X3	Uzbek attacks on Khorasan
X4	Dissatisfaction with positions in Iran
X5	Rivalry with other poets in Iran
X6	Rivalry with other people in Iran
X7	With Iranian embassy
X8	In the company of relatives
X9	By fate and chance
X10	Encouraged by merchants
X11	In pursuit of wealth
X12	To visit relatives
X13	To visit friends
X14	In search of better opportunities
X15	Service in the *Sarkars* of nobles
X16	Service of the Mughal kings
X17	Legendary fame of the Mughal court
X18	Simply job
X19	Trade
X20	Travelling
X21	To earn fame
X22	Invitation of friends and others
X23	*Sufigari, darvishi* and *qalandari*
X24	Luxury *(Ayyashi)*
X25	As ambassador
X26	Unknown reasons

System of Transliteration

In transliterating Arabic and Persian words in this work, the system adopted is the same as that employed in standard works on oriental subjects, except in the case of Persian names and words that have been spelt according to their accepted and familiar forms in Persian, e.g., the Esfahan Neishabour, *Faqir*, *Darvish*, etc.

The following would explain how some of the Arabic and Persian letters have been denoted.

ت =t	ث =th or s	چ =ch	ح =h
خ =kh	ذ =z	ز =z	س =s
ش =sh	ص =s	ض =z	ط =t
ظ =z	ع =(ʿ)	غ =gh	ق =q
ه =h			

Short vowels: a, i, u

Long vowels: ā, ē, ī, ū

In transliterating Persian and Arabic words, the prevalent subcontinental style has been generally followed. The principle of retaining the well-known, even if somewhat inaccurate spelling, in preference to the lesser known, even if more accurate spelling, has been generally observed. For example, we have preferred *tazkira* rather than *tadhkira*, *Zakhira* instead of *Dhakhira*, Shahjahan instead of Shah-e-Jahan, etc. All translations from the Persian and Arabic have been done by me.

List of Tables

2.1 Iranians in Mughal politics and administration. 77

2.2 Iranians in Mughal politics and administration according to the reasons and contexts of their migration. 121

3.1 Poets as administrators. 141

3.2 Poets as administrators according to the reasons and contexts of their migration. 162

4.1 Scholars and artists in administration. 174

4.2 Scholars and artists in administration according to the reasons and contexts of their migration. 183

4.3 Physicians and *qazis*. 186

4.4 Physicians and *qazis* according to the reasons and contexts of their migration. 195

5.1 Iranian poets. 211

5.2 Iranian poets according to the reasons and contexts of their migration. 233

6.1 Scholars. 242

6.2 Scholars according to the reasons and contexts of their migration. 266

6.3 Iranian Shakhs, *Sufis*, *Qalandars* and *Darvishes*. 270

6.4 Shaikhs, *Sufis*, *Qalandars* and *Darvishes* according to the reasons and contexts of their migration. 280

7.1 Artists and craftsmen. 293

7.2 Artists and craftsmen according to the reasons and contexts of their migration. 316

7.3 People with diverse skills. 319

7.4	People with diverse skills according to the reasons and contexts of their migration.	322
8.1	Iranian traders.	331
8.2	Traders as poets.	332
8.3	Traders as administrators.	334
8.4	Traders according to the reasons and contexts of their migration.	347
8.5	Iranian travellers	350
8.6	Travellers as poets.	353
8.7	Travellers as artists.	359
8.8	Travellers according to the reasons and contexts of their migration.	361
Con. 1	Regions and categories of the migrants.	371
Con. 2	Categories, numbers and periods of the migrants.	377
Con. 3	Total number of the Iranian migrants.	380
Appen. 1	Iranian women.	394
Appen. 2	Women according to the reasons and contexts of their migration.	399

List of Graphs

2.1 Number of Iranians in Mughal politics and administration according to the reasons and contexts of their migration. 122

3.1 Number of poets as administrators according to the reasons and contexts of their migration. 163

4.1 Number of scholars and artists in administration according to the reasons and contexts of their migration. 184

4.2 Number of physicians and *qazis* according to the reasons and contexts of their migration. 196

5.1 Number of poets according to the reasons and contexts of their migration. 234

6.1 Number of scholars according to the reasons and contexts of their migration. 267

6.2 Number of *Sufis* and *darvishes* according to the reasons and contexts of their migration. 281

7.1 Number of artists and craftsmen according to the reasons and contexts of their migration. 317

7.2 Number of people with diverse skills according to the reasons and contexts of their migration. 323

8.1 Number of traders according to the reasons and contexts of their migration. 348

8.2 Number of travellers according to the reasons and contexts of their migration. 362

Con. 1 Number of Iranian migrants in different categories according to the places of their origins. 372-375

Con. 2	Iranians migration in Mughal India according to regions from where the migrants came.	376
Con. 3	Number of Iranian people according to the periods of their migration.	378
Con. 4	Total number of Iranian migrants according to the reasons and contexts of their migration.	381
Appen. 1	Number of women according to the reasons and contexts of their migration.	400

List of Maps

1. India in early seventeenth century (Between pgs) 32-33
2. Iran in Safavid period (Between pgs) 32-33
3. States in modern Iran 69
4. Iranian cities associated with the migrants 70
5. Regional distribution of the Iranian migrants category-wise 388

Introduction

The Mughals had a multi-racial and multi-religious ruling class in which non-Indians occupied a very major place. Commenting on the *mansabdars* listed in the *Ain-i-Akbari*, Moreland noted that just under 70 per cent of the nobles whose origin is known were foreigners belonging to families which had either come to India with Humayun or had arrived at the court after the accession of Akbar.[1] Amongst foreigners the two groups, Turanis and Iranis enjoyed a predominant position in Akbar's nobility. By Turanis we mean persons coming from Central Asia, where the Turkish languages were spoken; and the Iranis were largely the Persian speaking peoples from the country between Herat and Baghdad, i.e. the inhabitants of the whole of the present-day Iran and the Persian-speaking parts of modern Afghanistan and Iraq.

The Mughals came from Central Asia; the Turanis thus occupied special position in Mughal India. But it is also a well-known fact that among the various ethnic groups of the Mughal nobility Iranians had considerable influence on the politics, economy and society of the Mughal empire. They equalled the Turanians in their role in Mughal India. In some respects, they even surpassed them. An accurate and detailed knowledge of these Iranians is, therefore, indispensable for historians interested in any field of Mughal history. At the same time, the question of Iranian migration certainly cannot be overlooked even by those whose main interests remain within the framework of Iranian history. It is necessary to examine the background of that massive emigration for a judicious appreciation of contemporary Iranian society, in the same way as the impact of this migration on Mughal Indian society and culture has to be studied carefully for a proper evolution of the achievements of the Mughal empire.

However, despite the importance of such a study, there has not been, to my knowledge, any comprehensive work focusing on and around this theme. Historians of Iran have, over a long period, been interested in understanding the process of this migration. Several historians saw this just as an inter-court migration. Their analysis virtually begins and ends with the observation that the Indian rulers offered better opportunities than those available at Esfahan to scholars, administrators, poets, painters, calligraphers and litterateurs. Many historian have sought to see in the migration just an assertion of 'age-old connections', or the result and extension of the presence of the Iranians already in India.[2] The subject thus has not been investigated systematically and no modern historian in Iran has done any significant work in this field.

In India, however, some modern historians have examined some aspects of this theme as a part of their study of the Mughal nobility. But in these works many a relevant question has not even been asked. These works, in more than one respect, or at least for our purpose, are just incomplete. Among the early writers who worked around this theme was K.P. Khosala. His work entitled *Mughal Kingship and Nobility* which was written in 1934, is primarily on Mughal administration. The author has discussed only the elementary but by no means insignificant, considering the time when it was just published, aspects of the institution of nobility under the Mughals. There is little in Khosala's work about many Iranians and Turanians who, at one or other level, formed the Mughal polity. Khosala is also least concerned with the internal conditions of the countries whence people came in Mughal India. Thus while he does take into account the Iranians' presence in Mughal administration, a number of crucial issues for our purpose have escaped his attention.

The best recent work on the Mughal nobility is by Professor M. Athar Ali. His works are the *Mughal Nobility under Aurangzeb* and *The Apparatus of Empire: Awards of Ranks, Offices and Titles to the Mughal Nobility (1574-1658)*. The second work is of greater interest for our purpose. Athar Ali's study in this book covers the periods of Akbar, Jahangir and Shahjahan. Principal, rather exclusive, emphasis here is on awards of *mansab* during these periods, which he classifies into three: the highest (5,000 and above in rank), high (1,000 to 4,500) and medium (500 to 900). Professor Athar Ali has just prepared a list of nobles, *mansabdars* and *amirs* their official posts and positions, including those of the Iranians. He has not mentioned anything about many Iranians who at first sight appeared to be of no consequence for Mughal state service. Besides, Athar Ali pays little heed to the Iranians who, even as they were on the fringe of administration, contributed significantly in many ways to the prevalent Mughal lifestyle and culture. Among such people were a large number of the Iranian scholars, shaikhs, *sufis, darvishes*, qalandars, physicians, *qazis*, artists and craftsmen and poets, for example. Further, Athar Ali does not identify the places from where these Iranians came to India. Again, he has mentioned only 133 Iranians in Jahangir's reign, whereas I have shown that 256 Iranians in different areas of work and activity lived in India during the reign of Jahangir.

Thus, even though several historians have taken into account the Iranians' presence in 17th century India in the context of their valuable studies of the Mughal state and its apparatus, they do not examine in depth the Iranians' share in the formation of this apparatus. Many key questions remain unclarified, such as the region of Iran they came from, the type of people who migrated to India, their status and occupations before coming to India, the reasons and context of their migration and the place where they finally settled to live and die. The purpose of this study is to examine some of these issues. The period under our review is principally the first half of the 17th century. I have drawn for information very largely if not exclusively on the contemporary Iranian and Mughal Indian Persian sources, both published and unpublished. My prime concern in the present work has been as follows: First, what were the reasons and factors that determined the Iranians' migration to India? Second, why did Iranian people migrate to India, why not, for instance to Central Asia? Third, what were the factors which influenced and shaped the Mughal policy towards the Iranian nobility? Was it guided by the interests of the Mughal state? If yes, to what extent? Fourth, did religion exert any influence on the migration of Iranians into India, and or on their relationship with the Indian Mughal rulers?

Before we go ahead, it is also my duty to be clear of certain delicate problems, unavoidable when dealing with the inter-country relations of the period under discussion. The first concerns the definition of Iran, and, more particularly, who the Iranian people were. Of course, Iran did not exist as a state as it is defined today. In the *Zakhirat-ul-Khawanin* and *Ma,asir-ul-Umara,* people from what is geographically Iran today are usually described as either men of Khurasan or men of Iraq. I need not emphasize that the notion of Iran as a state is a very modern one.

A further problem is that the Safavid territory was not always fixed. In Khurasan in the east and in Azarbaijan in the west especially, the borders changed a number of times. I am thus constrained to identify in this study those people as Iranians who came to India during the 17th century from the areas within the modern political boundaries. Besides the regions of modern Iran, the cities of Herat and Qandahar have also been taken as parts of the country of the then Iranians. Our narrative is divided along the following lines of the regions and cities of the origins of the migrants:

1. North (Mazandaran and Gilan provinces).
2. West and North-West (Azarbaijan-i-Sharqi, Azarbaijan-i-Gharbi, Ardabil, Kordestan, Hamadan, Kermanshah, Lorestan and Ilam provinces).
3. South-West (Chahar Mahal Bakhtiyari, Kohkiluyeh va Buyer Ahmad and Khuzestan).
4. Central plateau (Markazi, Qazwin, Zanjan, Semnan, Qom, Tehran, Esfahan, Yazd and Kerman).
5. South (Fars, Bushehr and Hormuzgan).
6. East and North-East (Khurasan).
7. South-East (Sistan va Baluchistan).

The chapters are arranged accordingly into different sections to show the geographical distribution of the migrants throughout Iran. There are a considerable number of these migrants about whose places of origin our sources help us very little. In the tables and graphs I have listed them as migrants from unclear or unidentified areas.

In terms of reasons and contexts, these migrants could be broadly divided into two categories. In one category were the people who fled to India as a consequence of the Uzbeks' attacks in East or the Ottoman raids in West; and or the people who were accused of adhering to Sunni and Nuqtavi creeds; or the people who just lost royal favour. India became for them a kind of political asylum. This was in a measure forced migration, and in this case most of the migrants did not return to Iran.[3]

In such cases also the push factors are located in Iran itself. In the second category were the people who moved to India of their own free will. Unable to get enough opportunities to prosper in Safavid society, they moved to India of their accord. Many a such migrant returned to Iran as well, or at least they kept in touch with their friends and relatives in Iran.[4] There were then strong pull factors in these migrations as well. Indian rulers offered better opportunities than those available in Iran to poets, scholars, artists and craftsmen, etc. Attempt has been made to locate such pull factors in the regions which the migrants visited and where they stayed. Our attempt is to tabulate and also to show through graphs these reasons and the contexts. We have identified 26 reasons in all.

We will notice that many *sardars* and great men of Lur, Turkman, Taklu and Afshar tribes of Safavid Iran moved to Mughal India. Some of these Iranian immigrants joined their relatives and friends who were already in India possessing important posts and *mansabs*. Still others came to India for trade, travelling and among them were also adventurers and fortune-seekers. The Nuqtavis, the Sunnis and those Shias who dissented from the Safavid brand of Shiim were also among the important Iranian migrants in Mughal India. The history of the Nuqtavis has not been dealt with adequately. They were also called Pasikhanis after the name of their leader Mahmud Pasikhani Gilani.

In India for these immigrants there were ample opportunities and plenty of suitable positions in Mughal India. They received encouragement and high honours from the Mughal kings and the Mughal nobles. The fact of the matter that the India of Akbar, Jahangir and Shahjahan was much more affluent and richer than Safavid Iran and that the Safavid resources of patronage of poets were evidently inadequate compared to the resources of the Mughals for the purpose. A sojourn in India, whether permanent or temporary, ensured ample fortunes to a considerable cross-section of the Persian elite, including the men of pen and administrative acumen.[5] In the oft-quoted Persian verse it is this reality which was narrated:

Nist dar Iran zamin saman-e tahsil-e kamal

Ta nayamad sū-ye Hindostan ḥena rangin na shud

(The means of acquiring perfection do not exist in Iran

The henna does not acquire colour till it comes to India).

In addition, the religious persecution, political sectarianism and Safavid rulers' excesses also contributed to this process. But all this, for whatever reasons, evidently enriched the Mughal culture, reinforced the bases of the Mughal state and added new dimensions to Mughal administration in India.

My work has been divided into chapters which are as follows. Each chapter, excepting Chapter I, comprises of the biographical details of the emigrants. Summed up also are the tables and the graphs. The chapters begin with a brief description of the arrangement of the information contained therein.

Chapter I briefly describes the relations between the Mughal rulers and the Safavids. The relations of the Mughal empire with Persia underwent various phases of friendship and amity as well as of tension and conflict. Their relations covered politics, diplomacy, culture, literature, trade, commerce and religion. There was often misunderstanding and friction about Qandahar. Further, the attitude of the Mughal emperors towards the Shia state of the Deccan was not acceptable to their Persian allies. But there was also the memory of friendship and political alliance between Babur and Ismail I and Tahmasp's help to Humayun. Besides, most of the Timorids in India though Sunnis were non-sectarian, also some of them had leanings towards Shia doctrines and consequently they had no difficulties in being closely allied to Persia. This was in sharp contrast to the other Sunni powers of Central Asia. An obvious explanation of this could be found in the peculiar Mughal Indian religious and political culture.[6] The Mughal emperors were also tied to the Safavids by matrimonial bonds. Many Safavid princesses were married to Mughal princes. I have examined the events which cemented the relations between the two and those which caused cleavage in the light of both the Indian and the Iranian contemporary accounts.

Chapter II, a bit long, takes care of the Iranians who held high, medium or low positions in Mughal politics and administration. The Iranians comprised one of the two most important groups of the nobles in Mughal India. But they occupied not simply high offices; their presence was pronounced at almost all levels of Mughal administration. Many Iranians (54) are to be found in positions of prominence in the Mughal kingdom, and in point of fact the Mughal historiography has considered at some length the issue of the power of this faction in relation to others like the Turanis, Rajputs and Indian Muslims. Mughal historians have posited, in particular, the growth in Irani power under Akbar, as a reaction to revolts of Turani nobles in the early period of his rule. The result of this trend could be seen in the Iranian domination in the subsequent period. Almost all of Jahangir's important ministers were Iranis, including all three of his *Wakils,* six of his *Divans,* all his *Mir Bakhshis* and *Mir Samans* with only the post of *Sadr* remaining free of Irani control. In this chapter we have tried to identify the Iranians who had enjoyed some status in Iran before their departure for India. We will also see how they maintained their relations/ties with their homelands. As stated earlier, we will first give brief description of some of the noted Iranians, then subsequent to tabulated information the chapter will attempt at some biographical details arranged according to the regions of Iran they came from. To show this we have prepared tables, graphs and maps, with information and identification of people, the reasons and context of their migration, jobs and position both in Iran and India.

The following two chapters are virtually an extension of Chapter II. Since for Chapter II we had enormous information, unwieldy and unmanageable in a single chapter, we selected information regarding those administrators and officials who were either poets or scholars in two separate chapters. In the first of these, are noticed those Iranians in Mughal state service who had some pretension of being poets and versifiers as well, while the following Chapter IV, enumerates the scholars in politics. There were many Iranians coming direct from Iran in search of administrative employment, since they were forced to leave their own country due to the growing political instability and Uzbek and Ottoman pressures. Quite a few of them belonged to the reputed and eminent families whose members had been in the service of important Safavid officials, while some others were themselves in possession of high offices in Iran. As regards the persons of rank, our list shows that many of the immigrants or their ancestors held important offices under their previous masters too in Iran or in the Deccan, before joining the Mughal service.

In Chapter III are described 28 such Iranians who excelled in administration at various levels and were also known in their time as reasonably good versifiers and poets. Of course here also we have illustrated and summed up our information in different tables, graphs and a map.

In Chapter IV, in the category of administrators who were scholars, *Waqianavis* and artists, physicians and *Qazis*, and who earned from the Mughal emperors varied ranks, offices and awards, we have identified twenty (20) persons. The most important among these people of scholarly merit were Baqir Khan Najm-i-sani, Mir Abdul Karim Mamuri Esfahani and Khwaja Jahan Khafi. In this chapter again, we try first to identify the emigrants and also mention if they had any positions in Iran before their departure for India and whether they continued their connections with their homelands. What was the nature of this connection? Did anyone of them return to Iran? Are also some other questions that the chapter is concerned with. At least nine of such emigrants were physicians and theologians or *qazis*. We have a separate section for information about such people.

Chapter V is intended to highlight the role of the Iranians in Mughal culture during the 17th century with special reference to the poets. During the seventeenth century there was a large influx of poets from Safavid Iran to Mughal India and the Deccan. Persian poetry blossomed in India rather than in its birthplace in Iran and central Asia. The attitudes of the Safavid immigrant poets to India range from enthusiastic nostalgia to bitter dislike. Usually they came full of hope and expectation.

Appreciation of poetry was one of the pre-eminent cultural occupations of a Mughal noble. A large number of the nobles and higher *mansabdars* had poets in their entourage. Patronage of poets was a status symbol, and the expense incurred was well-justified in a noble's view. Since his *mansab* and estate was not hereditary, he tried to spend his wealth as lavishly and as elegantly as possible during his lifetime. Some of the higher nobles of the Mughal court stand out as generous patrons of poets. Most outstanding of the patrons of poets among the Mughal nobles, was Abdur-Rahim Khan-i-Khanan, himself a poet in three languages. His generosity was princely. However, a large number of Persian poets migrated to India either permanently or temporarily. Our tables would show that 201 Iranian poets came to India in later days of Akbar and during the periods of Jahangir and Shahjahan. Among them were the brilliant 16th-17th century poets like Muhammad Salim Tehrani, Talib Amuli, Zuhuri, Saib Tabrizi, Mir Ilai Hamadani, etc. Abu Talib

Kalim Kashani and Haji Muhammad Jan Qudsi Mashhadi both became poet-laureates at the court of Shahjahan. In this chapter we have attended also to lesser poets who have not been mentioned in any modern books. There are several studies and books about poets. On the whole they are rich and valuable, but they neglected to mention all Iranian poets who had came to India. To show this we have prepared tables and graphs with information and identification of these poets, the regions where they came from, reasons and context of their migration and their position both in Iran and India. Since most of the big poets have been noted in modern writings. I have refrained in this chapter to give the known details.

Chapter VI is also concerned with the Iranians' contribution to the Mughal culture, with reference to the scholars, *sufis*, shaikhs, *darvishes* and *qalandars*. The Mughal court generously patronized the Persian scholars from Iran. In Mughal India both Persian prose and poetry flourished. According to our major sources, in the 17th century there were at least 37 such Iranians whose prime identity was the one of a scholar. In addition to these scholars a very significant group of Persian immigrants were *sufis*, shaikhs, *darvishes* and *qalandars*. Many of them were motivated by a lust to wander and the quest of new spiritual or emotional experiences. But some of them also came fleeing from the tortures, humiliations and indignities to which they were subjected in Iran. In 1614-15/1023-24 Shah Abbas ordered the massacre of the *sufis*, when he feared that their resistance to the new policy may jeopardize his position. Therefore, some of them migrated to India to take asylum here. According to our tables 19 Iranian shaikhs, *sufis, darvishes* and *qalandars* came to India during the period under review.

From Chapter VII, which mentions the Iranian artists and craftsmen and the Iranians with diverse skills, we move in a measure from the domain of culture to the material world, to the world where we notice the manifest marks of the Iranian craft and skill. Mughal empire was a place where the wishes of aspiring artists were fulfilled with unmatched generosity. Large number of people of excellence and quality, artists, calligraphers, skilled artisans, and people of other pursuits from various cities of Iran as well as from other parts of world visited the imperial court, the nobles' establishments with expectations and hopes. In this chapter we try to identify those Iranian artists and craftsmen who came to India in the period under our review either to live here permanently or just to make fortunes and then return. There were 47 such Iranians, most of whom came as adventurers in search of better opportunities, knowing that the Mughal court was open to talented people, where by merit they might be able to achieve distinct positions and *mansabs* in the Mughal government. Besides these 47, we have also mentioned five others with diverse skills, who were also in India in the period to look for better prospects.

Chapter VIII mentions Iranian traders and Iranian travellers. A significant number of Iranians (24) migrated to India and settled in various cities of India for trade. The Indian people also settled in Iran for trade and business, but no person of Indian origin is known to have attained high position at the Safavid court. At the same time, however, it must not be forgotten that the migration was always one way, from Iran to India.

In Jahangir's period some Iranians such as Touri and Johari Tabrizi, Ami Esfahani and Amin Kashani came to India for trade. In Shahjahan's reign also we notice traders like Kazim Savoji, Qutrati and Nasib-i-Esfahani who were involved in trade in India. Some Iranian nobles also took keen interest in trade. Mir Muhammad mentions Mir Jumla Ardestani as one such eminent Irani in trade. He spent his early life in Esfahan. In the Deccan, he acquired an interest in jewelry trading and eventually managed to use the profits from the diamond trade to buy a high position in the Golkonda administration by way of revenue farming. By the mid-1650s he entered Mughal service and received the title of Muazzam Khan, paid his respects to the Emperor of Delhi and received the rank of 6000 *zat* with 6000 *sawar*. His reasons for leaving Iran are stated to have been first to make his living easy, secondly to remit money to aged and infirm members of his family who had remained in Iran and thirdly to escape the *zulm* and the grasping instinct of the Persian *Shaikh-ul-Islam* with regard to the property of the orphans and the poor.

In this chapter we will try to identify a number of other Iranians who like Mir Jumla visited India as merchants, then earned not simply enormous fortunes but also respectable positions in politics. Besides, in a section of this chapter we will survey the Iranian tourists and travellers, their brief biography and also the cities they had travelled and visited in the subcontinent.

In sum, our attempt by giving details in these chapters has been to see how in the seventeenth century there existed, culturally and economically, a loosely unified area which included Iran, Afghanistan and central India. A number of Iranian people possessing sophisticated Persian culture migrated from Iran to India seeking honour and fortune, while many Indian merchants moved from India to Iran looking for economic profit.

REFERENCES

1. W.H. Moreland, *India at the death of Akbar,* Delhi, 1974, pp. 69-70.

2 Iqtidar Alam Khan, 'The Nobility under Akbar and the Development of his religious policy', 1560-80, *Journal of the Royal Asiatic Society* (1968), p. 29-36; M. Athar Ali, *Mughal Nobility under Aurangzeb,* Bombay, 1970; Afzal Husain, 'Growth of Irani element in Akbar's nobility' in: *Indian History Congress*, Aligarh, 1975, pp. 166-79; Athar Abbas Rizvi also examined Iranian *mansab* holders under Akbar based on the *Ain-i-Akbari. A Socio-Intellectual History of the Isna Ashari Shiais in India,* 2nd Vol., Canberra, 1986, Vol. I, pp. 235-41.

3. See, Chapter II, 'Iranians in Mughal Politics and Administration'.

4. In this connection see: Chapters V, VI, 'Iranian Poets and Scholars'.

5. For a recent review of the issues around this theme, see: Muzaffar Alam, 'The Pursuit of Persian: Language in Mughal Politics', *Modern Asian Studies,* Cambridge, June, 1998.

6. For some discussion on this question see: M. Alam, 'State Building under the Mughals: Religion, Culture and Politics', in *Cahiers D'Asie Centrale,* No. 3-4, 1997.

1

Relations between the Mughal Rulers and the Safavids

The Mughal Empire and the Safavid monarchy were among the four leading Muslim powers of the 16th and 17th centuries. The Ottomans and the Uzbeks of Central Asia were other powers which constantly competed with the Safavids for the control of the regions and the peoples on west, north-west and north-east borders of Iran. At times the Uzbeks sought help from the Mughals, on occasion the Ottomans and the Uzbeks coordinated their moves against the Safavids. Diplomatic contacts subsisted at various other levels between all these four great powers. The princes of the one empire would cultivate relations with the sovereigns of the other. Dignitaries of the one would correspond with those of the other. As regards the Mughals, while the Safavids had close links with them, there were also certain regions in the subcontinent of India with which Persian authorities maintained direct diplomatic and trade contacts. There were two regions of the subcontinent with which Persia maintained such links, in particular, the Deccan, and the north-west frontier provinces, namely Kashmir, Kabul, Lahore, Multan and Qandahar. The last of these, Qandahar, remained alternatively in Persian and Mughal hands and changed hands several times during the two centuries. Then under the Mughals, its governor would maintain contacts with Persia, and when under Persian occupation, its governor would do likewise with Mughal authorities[1].

The Mughal empire and Safavid Persia had enough in common regarding faiths and, cultural and territorial interests to encourage long periods of peace, although the main territorial issue between them was for the control of Qandahar. During the 17th century, the Deccan kingdoms, with their political and Shi'ite religious affinity to Persia, also caused tension in Mughal-Safavid relations.

The rise of the Safavids in Persia and the Mughals in Hindustan were almost synchronous. The military assistance of Ismail Safavid proved to be of great moral value to Babur in central Asia.[2] The diplomatic relations were first established by Ismail I who, after the conquest of Merv in 1510, and the death of Shaibani Khan treated Babur's sister Khanzada Begum[3], one of the captives with great respect and sent her along with his ambassador to her brother. Babur received the embassy at Qunduz, where he had come at the invitation of Khan Mirza, and he in return sent an emissary to thank the Shah.[4]

In 1524, Shah Ismail died and was succeeded by his eldest son Tahmasp. Two years after this, Babur conquered Delhi and Agra in 1526,[5] and became the emperor of Hindustan. He used this occasion to display his instinct of generosity and bestowed rewards on all and sundry. He also sent presents to some people in Khurasan and Iraq (Western Persia).[6]

Humayun and Shah Tahmasp

After the death of Babur, his son Nasiruddin Muhammad Humayun was enthroned in the year 1530. Kamran Mirza, Humayun's brother, who was the governor of Kabul and Qandahar during their father's reign, rebelled and conquered Lahore and expanded his realm. Thus, he physically stood between the governments of Delhi and Qazvin. Therefore, during the first 13 years of the reign of Humayun there were no contacts between Humayun and Shah Tahmasp and no ambassadors were exchanged.

The two defeats that Humayun suffered at the hands of Sher Shah Suri at the battles of Chausa and Qannauj forced him to seek refuge in Iran[7] on the recommendation of Bairam Beg, Khan-i-Khanan, along with fifty of his followers.[8]

The story of Humayun's one year stay in Persia (1544 including some three months' stay with the Shah), and the accounts of the receptions, festivities and banquets held in Humayun's honour make interesting reading, but the details need not detain us here. Two things, however, stand out: that it was with the unexpectedly extensive military help of Tahmasp that it was possible for Humayun to recover Qandahar, which in turn became the stepping stone for the recovery of Kabul and later, of Delhi. Secondly, Humayun's fine sensibility in the matter of art and calligraphy[9] could not fail to impress the Persians; and several outstanding Persian artists, including Mir Sayyid Ali and Khwaja Abd-ul-Samad, joined Humayun's service and eventually became instrumental in founding the Mughal school of painting at Delhi.[10]

On the way of comeback to India, after capturing Bust,[11] Humayun marched to Qandahar. Humayun's seizure of Qandahar from the Persians did not interrupt his friendly and cordial relations with Shah Tahmasp. After Humayun had conquered Kabul and established himself there, several embassadors were exchanged between the two kings. Shah Tahmasp sent Walad Beg Taklu as his ambassador to greet him for his victory. This ambassador reached Kabul in the year 1546. He participated in the battle which Humayun had undertaken at Badakhshan along with Iranian soldiers. These soldiers who were the combat troop of Shah Tahmasp, displayed great valour in this battle.[12]

In the year 1548, Humayun appointed Khwaja Jalal-ud-din Mahmud, his Mir Saman, as his ambassador to the court of Shah Tahmasp, but this ambassador, for reasons not known, remained in Qandahar and thereafter returned to Kabul. A year later, Humayun appointed Ghazi Shaikh Ali as his ambassador. This ambassador carried a letter from Humayun to Tahmasp in which Humayun complained of the mutinies of Kamran Mirza. In reply Shah Tahmasp advised Humayun not to be soft with his brother and offered military aid. In the year 1551, Humayun sent another ambassador, Khwaja Ghazi to Tahmasp. This, ambassador remained in Iran for two years. During this period Humayun sent a short letter to Tahmasp in which he informed him of Kamran Mirza's revolts and his failures.

At the time when Humayun was gathering his forces in Kabul for the attack on India, an ambassador; Ulugh Beg came from Tahmasp to his court. This ambassador brought precious gifts for Humayun and Bairam Khan.[13] Ulugh Beg was the last ambassador of Tahmasp to the court of Humayun.

Relations between Akbar and Tahmasp

In the years 1556, Humayun died in Delhi and his son Jalal-ud-din Muhammad Akbar succeeded him at the age of 14. Tahmasp attacked and conquered Qandahar which was at one time promised to him by Humayun.[14] This act offended Akbar and culminated in a course of dissension between the two courts. In the year 1562, Tahmasp designated

Sayyid Beg Safavid, son of Masum Beg one of his relatives, as ambassador to Akbar's court.This ambassador carried a letter to Akbar conveying the condolences of Tahmasp on the death of Humayun and felicitations to the new emperor. In this letter Tahmasp referred to his friendship with Humayun and the diplomatic mission of Khan Khanan, ambassador of Humayun.[15] As Khafi Khan related in *Muntakhab-ul-Lubab,* the purpose of this letter was to mollify the offence taken by Akbar on the occupation of Qandahar by Tahmasp. This ambassador also carried some presents to Akbar. Akbar in return bestowed upon the ambassador Rs.200,000, a richly caparisoned horse and a costly robe of honour.[16]

In the year 1564, Sultan Mahmud of Bhakkar sent a letter with some gifts to the court of Shah Tahmasp. He requested that the Shah of Iran recommend him to Akbar to grant him the designation of Khan-i-Khanan.[17] Upon receipt of this request Shah Tahmasp wrote a letter to Akbar and recommended him. Based on this recommendation Akbar granted Sultan Mahmud with the title of 'Etibar Khan' and wrote a letter to Shah Tahmasp informing him to this effect and also of the future favours that he was planning for Sultan Mahmud.

Akbar and Shah Ismail II

In the year 1576, Shah Tahmasp died and his son Shah Ismail II succeeded him.[18] During his short reign Shah Ismail had no diplomatic relations with Akbar, but wrote a letter to Mirza Hakim, Akbar's brother, who was the governor of Kabul. In this letter Shah Ismail called Mirza Hakim 'the king', and asked him to send his diplomatic envoys to Iran. He also informed Mirza Hakim that the Haj pilgrims of Kabul could travel by the Iranian routes.

Akbar and Khudabanda

After the death of Shah Ismail II, in the year 1577, his blind brother Sultan Muhammad Khudabanda[19] was enthroned. Khudabanda, the eldest son of Shah Tahmasp, when he was the viceroy in Khurasan, in the year 1572, sent Yar Ali Beg to Akbar's court as his diplomatic envoy.[20] Following this, several diplomatic and cultural envoys were exchanged. At that time the internal situation of the country was in chaos and due to the disarray of the central government,[21] the Ottomans incited the Turks on the western borders who began attacking Iran in the west.[22] Under these unpleasant circumstances Khudabanda dispatched Sultan Quli Chandan Oghli to Hindustan and requested Akbar's aid. Akbar had in mind to send one of his sons to Iran to assist in curbing the disorder. He even had a plan to come personally to Khurasan in order to fight the Turks.[23]

While Iran was struggling along with these disasters, a new and graver danger presented itself. Abdullah Khan Uzbek, who had already captured Balkh in the year 1573, occupied Badakhshan in 1584, invaded Khurasan and occupied a part of that province.[24] Abdullah Khan sent ambassadors to Akbar and suggested that together they attack Iran, so that the rule of the impious (Shias) should end and the road be opened to pilgrims to Mecca and Medina. He also suggested that Qandahar should once again be a part of Hindustan's territory.[25] In his reply to Abdullah, Akbar stated that the Safavids were the descendants of the Prophet and therefore were not impious.[26] He told Abdullah that by conquest of Gujarat by him (Akbar) the sea route was open to pilgrims and that the Turks could use this route.[27] In regard to the return of Qandahar to Hindustan, Akbar wrote to Abdullah that since the governors of Qandahar were on friendly terms with him and had not molested Hindustani caravans, he could see no reason to attack Iran and take Qandahar back. Thus, with this firm and noble attitude, he rejected all the proposals of Abdullah.[28]

Akbar and Shah Abbas I

Shah Abbas formally ascended the Iranian throne in 1588. He was in a difficult position with pressure from the Ottoman Turks in the west and with the Uzbeks in occupation of Khurasan. He sent Yadagar Sultan Rumlu[29] as his ambassador to the court of Akbar (1591), principally for the purpose of seeking Mughal support against the Uzbeks; Abdullah Khan Uzbek's occupation of Khurasan and Uzbek's activity in the Mughal frontier region, were no less worrying for Akbar, who stayed for about fourteen years in the Punjab to keep a watch on the frontier. Placed thus, Akbar had to conduct his foreign relations cautiously. Hence for a good while he discouraged Abdullah Khan Uzbek's proposal for a joint Mughal-Uzbek invasion of Persia (985/1577), and when later, he signed agreement (994/1586), he did so to keep the Khan humoured fully knowing that the contingency of such a Mughal-Uzbek invasion was hardly ever likely to occur.[30]

Akbar's real interest was in the recovery of Qandahar, for which he awaited a suitable opportunity.[31] Finding that they could not save it from the burgeoning Uzbek power and losing hope of support from the Shah in distant Qazvin, the Persian governor of the fort Rustam Mirza and Muzaffar Husain Mirza,[32] sons of Sultan Husain Mirza Safavid gladly handed it over to Akbar's men and accepted high *mansabs* for themselves in the Mughal court.[33] Akbar had detained the envoy of Shah Abbas, Yadgar Sultan Rumlu for more than four years.[34] It is significant that the envoy was not given leave to go back till the acquisition of Qandahar had become a certainty. Along with this ambassador Akbar dispatched Mirza Zia-ud-din Kashi, as his ambassador to Iran.[35] In return Shah Abbas dispatched Manoucher Beg, *Eshik Aqasi Bashi*[36] to India bearing precious gifts.[37] This emissary arrived at the court of Akbar in Lahore in the year 1598 and was warmly welcomed.[38] As requested by Akbar, Shah Abbas in his letter informed him in detail of the complicated status of Iran, the disputes among the Qizilbash tribes and the attacks in the western zones of Iran by the Ottoman Emperor.

During the stay of this ambassador in India, fortune favoured Shah Abbas. Both Abdullah Khan Uzbek and his son Abdul Mumin Khan Uzbek died.[39] Their deaths paved the way for Iran to regain the occupied parts of Khorasan. In the year 1598 Shah Abbas conquered Herat,[40] and he wrote a letter to Akbar giving details of his victory and also expressed the hope for the return of Qandahar to Iran.[41]

Manoucher Beg, the Iranian ambassador returned to Iran in the year 1602, with gifts for the Shah and Rs. 10000 for himself.[42] During the siege of Irevan, Mir Masum Behkari,[43] a prominent scholar, was sent by Akbar in 1602[44] to Iran with precious gifts. Shah Abbas received this ambassador warmly at the battlefield.[45] In the letter that Mir Masum brought, Akbar lauded Shah Abbas for his victories over the Ottomans in the west and the Uzbeks in the east. Meanwhile, he informed the Shah of Iran of his own victories at Asirgarh and in the South of India.[46]

Mir Masum returned to the Mughal court in early 1605 (1013). He brought with him a letter from the Shah for Akbar, describing the Persian victories at Irevan and elsewhere. Mir Masum also brought a letter from the Shah's aunt to Akbar's mother, Maryam Makan Begum (Hamida Bano Begum).[47]

Jahangir and Shah Abbas I

As a prince, Jahangir had been on very friendly terms with Shah Abbas through envoys, letters and messages. But his reign opened with an attempt by the Iranians to occupy Qandahar and this created a deterioration in the relationship between the two empires.[48] The death of Akbar and the revolt of Khusrau gave Shah Abbas the opportunity of instigating the chiefs of Khurasan to attack Qandahar; but Shah Beg Khan, the Indian governor of the fortress, put up a stout defence. Early in 1607, Jahangir sent reinforcement under Mirza Ghazi Tarkan.[49] The Persians were struck with terror, raised the siege and retreated to Khurasan. Foiled in this business Shah Abbas disclaimed knowledge of the invasion, rebuked the Khurasani nobles and apologized to Jahangir. He wrote to explain that the restless border tribes had committed the mischief of their own accord and that he had punished them for their foolish audacity.[50] Shah Abbas sent Husain Beg to Jahangir, in order to clarify the Qandahar incident.[51] In the reply which Jahangir sent by Husain Beg to Shah Abbas he complained of delay on the part of the Shah in opening regular diplomatic relations and noted that the dispatch of a major Persian ambassador had been further postponed.[52] It was in the 6th year of the reign of Jahangir (in 1610) that the first formal ambassador of Iran, Yadgar Sultan Ali Talish, a former governor of Baghdad and an eminent scholar, was sent to India.[53] Shah Abbas in his letter to Jahangir, which was carried by this ambassador, expressed his condolences on the death of Akbar and added his congratulations on Jahangir's ascending the throne of India.[54] The royal letter cited the campaigns of the Shah in the western provinces as an excuse for delay in sending a regular ambassador.[55] He returned with honours and rewards in August 1613 to accompany the Mughal envoy, Khan Alam to Persia.[56] During the two and a half years stay of Yadgar Sultan Ali in India, there were further diplomatic exchanges between the two monarchs.[57] In one of these, the Shah sent a note recommending one Salamullah Arab for promotion. Jahangir at once increased his *mansab* and *jagir*.[58]

The pattern of subsequent diplomatic relations is an almost one-sided succession of envoys and emissaries from Persia to India. Jahangir sent only one major emissary, but the Shah dispatched two major (besides that of Yadgar Sultan) and numerous minor envoys. The purpose of these numerous missions was to allay all apprehensions on the score of Persian interest in Qandahar and to build up a relationship of confidence and trust with Jahangir.[59]

Besides political relation between Jahangir and Shah Abbas, there were commercial and trade connections between them. The first mission of this kind was sent by Jahangir some years before his accession. His agent was a trader, Khwaja Burj Ali Nakh Chiwani, with the title of Zubdatul Tujjar. Shah Abbas intervened and supplied his requirements from the royal stores, and wrote a letter to Jahangir (i.e., the then prince Salim) complaining why he should have entrusted his needs to traders rather than have written to him directly. Shah Abbas sent this letter through Khwaja Muhammad Baqir, an Indian trader who seems to have been in Persia for trade purposes.[60] In the year 1613, Jahangir decided to send a connoisseur of jewels, Muhammad Hussain Chalabi, to Turkey to buy certain jewels. Since he had to go to Turkey via Iran he brought a letter and some gifts for Shah Abbas. When Shah Abbas saw the list of the jewel requirements of Jahangir he assigned Uwaisi Beg Topchi to procure these articles and later on sent him with these and a letter to India. Muhammad Husain Chalabi's mission is referred to at length in the Shah's letter brought by Muhammad Reza in 1025/1616 and recorded by Jahangir in his memoirs.[61] One of the articles (says the letter) on Chalabi's list was a set of jewels one of which was engraved with the names of Jahangir's ancestors. According to religious endowments these rubies belong to the Shrine of Najaf. However, the rubies under question were taken back following a request by the religious leaders. "Since the jewel box", the letter mentions, "prepared by Chalabi was not worthy of your Majesty. Shah Abbas ordered his artisans to prepare a jewel box deserving Your Majesty's dignity. Insha-Allah, after its completion, I will send the rubies to you in this box."[62]

At Jahangir's request, the Shah also sent the original astrolabe of Ulugh Beg, the celebrated Timurid prince,[63] keeping for himself only a copy. In 1615, he dispatched Khwaja Abdul Karim Gilani, a Persian trader, with a letter and with certain rarities asked for by Jahangir. The Khwaja is described therein as a trusted servant of the court, and Jahangir is requested to appoint his own agents to assist the Khwaja. Another Persian trader, Muhammad Qasim Beg came, probably with the Persian ambassador Muhammad Reza Beg, on a commission from the Shah.[64]

It may be added here that prince Shahjahan also sent purchasing agents to Persia, Turkey and the Middle East. These agents catered almost exclusively for royal requirements, most of which in the nature of rarities; horses of superior quality for display purposes were also in demand at the Mughal court. Apart from the venture of royal agents some private traders also received royal patronage. One Haji Rafiq, for instance, went to Persia a number of times and made himself known to Shah Abbas I. Appreciating his initiative and tact, Jahangir conferred on him the title of Malikut Tujjar. Haji Rafiq carried letters between the Shah and Jahangir.[66]

The Great Ambassador of India

Jahangir assigned Mirza Barkhordar Khan, whose title was Khan Alam, from the famous tribe of Barlas and one of his close relatives, as his first ambassador and sent him to Iran in the year 1618 with a variety of precious gifts.[67]

The embassy of Khan Alam is a very important landmark in the history of Mughal diplomacy, for never before or later was a more splendidly equipped mission sent out.[68] Khan Alam was much cherished by Jahangir, who addressed him as brother. He was the most important envoy sent to the court of the Safavids. This ambassador stayed in Herat, later at Qom before coming to Qazvin. The embassy was meant to strike the imagination of the Persians, but was also aimed at impressing Abbas with the wealth of India as well as the warmth of feeling Jahangir entertained for him. The impression it created in Persia is recorded by Eskandar Beg Munshi, Pietro Della Valle, Italian traveller, Shah Husain Malik Ghiyathuddin Muhammad, nobleman of Sistan and author of the *Ihyaul Muluk*, who witnessed its entry into Qazvin and Esfahan.[69] Eskandar Beg says that no embassy like this had ever come to Safavid court since the foundation of the dynasty. Besides at least a thousand servants, a number of painters such as Bishan Das,[70] Kheirat Khan and Likraj were also members of the Indian ambassador's cortege.They came to Iran to paint the portraits of Shah Abbas and his courtiers.A number of these portraits which are extant today are the masterpieces of the works of these painters. Mohsen Fani Kashmiri, a great writer, also came with Khan Alam to Esfahan in the capacity of a chronicler. He used to prepare the news of Shah Abbas' court and despatch it to India.

In the year 1620, after a two year sojourn in Iran, the Indian diplomatic mission returned to its country. Khan Alam with his excellent behaviour made a very favourable impression on Shah Abbos which prompted the Shah of Iran to call him 'Jan Alam'[71] (Spirit of the World). This ambassador successfully completed his mission and upon his return to India was warmly welcomed by Jahangir and was rewarded by being promoted to 5000 *zat* and 3000 *sawar*, and in 1621 appointed him governor of Allahabad.[72]

Missions from Persia

When Khan Alam was in Iran, several envoys were dispatched to India by Shah Abbas. Robert Sherley was the first envoy who came to India. He was the Englishman, who strangely spent thirty years of his life in the service of the Persian king. He came to Jahangir's court in 1614, on his return from a round of diplomatic visits to the Christian princes of Europe, and was well received and set on his way with two elephants and eight antelopes as presents to the Shah.[73] The second envoy of Shah Abbas to India was Mustafa Beg in the year 1615. He carried a letter from Shah Abbas to Jahangir which contained a report of the victories of the Shah of Iran over Georgia. Among the presents sent with Mustafa Beg were several European hunting dogs that Jahangir had wanted. After a few months' stay in India he returned to Iran with Jahangir's letter and presents.[74] A few months after Mustafa Beg's departure, another ambassador Muhammad Reza Beg Shamlu arrived in November 1616, with presents and a letter from the Shah.[75] Sir Thomas Roe, English envoy at the Mughal court, has recorded an interesting and detailed account of this ambassador.[76]

It is not clear as to whether the embassy of Muhammad Reza had any special purpose, apart from those stated in Shah Abbas's letter. Roe heard reports that the envoy had ostensibly come only to ensure peace between the two empires on account of the Deccan but that his real aim was to obtain monetary aid for his master in his wars against the Turks.[77] Beni Prasad thinks that Muhammad Reza's embassy had something to do with Qandahar.[78] But no reference to this question was made by the Shah till after Khan Alam's return to India. He was despatched at Mandu with ample rewards on the 3rd Rabi I A.H. 1026 (April/1617).[79] On his way Muhammad Reza[80] died at Agra and Jahangir ordered all his goods to be handed over to Muhammad Qasim Beg, a Persian merchant.[81]

Jahangir had sent a cup for Shah Abbas with Muhammad Reza, and the Shah Abbas in return sent a crystal goblet and a letter giving an account of recent Persian victories with Sayyid Husain on the 27th Rabi I 1027 A.H. (March 1618).[82] Shah Abbas, who was always desirous of designating an ambassador to India bearing equal standing and dignity of Khan Alam, appointed Zainal Beg[83] and dispatched him to India with gifts from himself and other Iranian nobles.[84] He reached Lahore in the summer of 1622,[85] when Jahangir was away in Kashmir.[86] Jahangir on learning of his arrival, sent Mir Hisam-ud-din, son of Mir Aziz-ud-din, to Lahore to meet Zainal, and gave orders to the governor to bear all the expense of the ambassador. Zainal Beg presented his credentials in November,[87] when Jahangir returned to Lahore. Besides gifts, the ambassador also presented two gentlemen of his entourage. Wisal Beg and Haji Niamat, who were courtiers of the Shah.[88] The mission of Zainal Beg coincided with the dispute regarding Qandahar. He continued to press his point about Qandahar with the Mughal authorities but without success. According to *Alam Ara*, Zainal Beg was unbending at the Mughal court and firmly refused to offer court salutation in the Mughal custom.[89] While Zainal Beg was in India five other envoys were dispatched by Shah Abbas to India with letters and presents.[90] The first envoys were Aqa Beg and Muhibb Ali.[91] Among the presents they brought was a ruby from the collection of Mirza Shah-Rukh bin Amir Timur. Ulugh Beg's name was engraved on this ruby, and the Shah also had his name[92] engraved in a corner. As this was a precious heirloom, it was much appreciated. It seems that Gilan horses and some ornaments and clothes were sent by the Shah.[93]

While this mission was still in India, another embassy under Haji Beg and Fazl Beg arrived with a letter and presents from Shah Abbas I. These envoys were dismissed in the end of Rabi I, 1030 (1621).[94]

Scarcely had these four envoys departed, when another envoy, Qasim Beg appeared with letter and presents from the Shah. The Shah had asked for some birds, which were sent with the ambassador when he was dismissed in January, 1622. While these ambassadors came and went, Zainal Beg continued to reside at the court.[95]

Jahangir, on coming to know of Shah Abbas's request for Qandahar, consulted his advisers. The chroniclers during the reign of Shahjahan claim for him the credit of advising Jahangir to reject the Persian request.[96] In any event, the opinion that finally prevailed was that the surrender of Qandahar would be regarded as a sign of weakness. This is confirmed by the Persian sources as well, for they say that a group of mischief-makers at Jahangir's court prevented the settlement of the issue in accordance with the Shah's desire.[97] Zainal Beg, then at the Mughal court, kept the Shah informed of the position.[98] He sent also reports of movement of troops, especially the dispatch of large Mughal forces to the Deccan under Shahjahan to deal with renewed trouble organized by Malik Ambar.[99] It can safely be presumed that his reports also covered the internal political situation of the empire and the factious intrigues at the court. There can be little doubt the news of that internal political position of India reached Shah Abbas I regularly through his ambassador and frequent emissaries as well as through other informants, and encouraged him to decide on marching to Qandahar and choose his own time for it.[100]

In the year 1622, Shah Abbas conquered Qandahar.[101] Jahangir's attempt to form an alliance with the Uzbeks and his plans to send an expedition under prince Shahjahan for the recovery of the fort, all came to nought.[102]

After the conquest of Qandahar, Shah Abbas sent Haidar Beg and Wali Beg Dharogha Shotor Khan as emissaries to India, in order to clarify any misunderstanding and check offence on the part of Jahangir.[103]

The Shah's defence of his action agrees with that recorded in the *Alam Ara Abbasi*. When his frequent request to cede Qandahar was repeatedly ignored, he decided to pay a friendly visit to the fort to demonstrate to the world the complete accord of the two empires, but on the stupid refusal of the commander of the fort to admit him as an honoured guest, he had no choice left but to force an entry and take the fort forcibly. The letter closes with the remark that their mutual friendship was too firmly founded to be affected by minor events.[104]

Jahangir sent a reply to Shah Abbas with the retiring Persian envoys. He indicated his surprise at the hasty action by Shah Abbas in conquering Qandahar. He pointed out that Shah Abbas should have awaited the return of Zainal Beg.[106] However, in this letter Jahangir stated that the friendship between the two rulers is much stronger than to allow a matter such as Qandahar to injure it.[107] Shah Abbas made every effort to conciliate Jahangir and to assuage the legacy of bitterness over Qandahar. So he wrote to this effect to other influential personage like prince Shahjahan, Nur Jahan and Khan Alam.[108]

While Shah Abbas was still at Qandahar, prince Shahjahan's ambassador Zahid Beg appeared with letters[109] and presents—an act which cannot be explained in any way, for so far Jahangir had taken no action against Shahjahan. The Shah treated the ambassador very kindly and dismissed him with a reply to the letter he had brought.[110]

Another letter was sent by prince Shahjahan to Shah Abbas with Khwaja Haji[111] at the time of his retreat to the Deccan in 1622. This was an open appeal for help, for he says, "I too have like my forefathers turned to you for help with hope that you will give me proper aid at the proper time". But the Shah, whatever encouragement he might have given to Zahid Beg now advised Shahjahan to be loyal to his father, and said: "I am sending an ambassador to Jahangir to recommend your case."[112] One letter was also sent by Shah Abbas to the prince Shahjahan[113] with Ishaq Beg Yazdi,[114] *Mir Saman* of Mumtaz Mahal in 1627. In this letter Shah says: The supreme thing in life is love and affection.The relation of love between the father and the son has been resorted, expressing joy and gratitude at this and hopes that the prince will persevere in seeking his father's pleasure.

In the year 1624, Aqa Muhammad *Mustaufi-i-Ghulaman*[115] was sent to India with a letter[116] from Shah Abbas in which he reported his victory over Baghdad.[117] Some of the booty from Baghdad was sent to Jahangir also. This ambassador was received by Jahangir in Lahore in October, 1625. Aqa Muhammad, after six months' stay in India brought an amicable letter and precious gifts from Jahangir for Shah Abbas.[118]

In the year 1627, Shah Abbas intended to send Takhta Beg Yuzbashi Ustajlu[119] to India to convey his condolences to Jahangir on the death of his son, prince Parviz,[120] on 17 Safar 1036/18th, Oct., 1626. It was planned that this envoy carry four letters for Jahangir, his son and Nur-i-Jahan.[121] But news of the death of Jahangir[122] (on 27 Safar 1037/28th Oct., 1627) negated this mission.

The Relations among Iran, the Deccan and the Mughals

Besides Qandahar and the frontier tracts, the Deccan was another area where Mughal and Persian interests collided; the conflict was both political and sectarian. The Mughals never recognised Deccan governors as independent rulers and in the Mughals state papers and official chronicles, they are described as Adil Khans, Qutbul Mulks and Nizamul Mulks respectively. These Muslim kingdom of the Deccan were targets of Mughal ambitions from the days of Akbar. Looking around for support, they saw in Persia the nearest great power which could counterbalance the constant Mughal pressure upon them. Another tie which bound them to the Safavids was their common religious denomination. The Adil-Shahs of Bijapur and the Qutb-Shahis of Golkonda were already Shia before the advent of the Chaghatai Mughals into India, and the Nizam Shahis of Ahmadnagar adopted Shism in 944/1537-8, and that the Nizam Shah was converted to Shism by a distinguished Persian émigré, Shah Tahir Hussain. This Shah Tahir was indeed the Shiite apostle of South India and played a leading role in the spread of Shia beliefs there.[123] Shah Tahir also maintained active contact with the Safavid court.[124]

From the beginning of the Safavid period there were close relationships between the governors of three important districts of the Deccan: Golkonda, Bijapur and Ahmadnagar.[125] Shah Tahmasp and Shah Ismail II continued these contacts[126]. In Ahmadnagar the name of Shah Abbas was mentioned in the Friday sermons. This started from the time of Shah Ismail. Shah Abbas I greatly strengthened these relations by frequent exchange of envoys; he also arranged for a matrimonial alliance with the Qutb-Shahi family.[127] Persians were much honoured at the Deccan courts and some of them became highly influential in the royal councils.[128]

The Mughals regarded with suspicion and displeasure any ties between the Deccan kingdoms and the Safavids, and they strongly objected to the inclusion of the name of the ruling Safavid in *Khutba* in Golkonda, a practice which the Qutab Shahs had adopted soon after the rise of Shah Ismail in Iran.[129]

Though mainly preoccupied with the affairs of northern India, neither Babur nor Humayun were oblivious of the Deccan. They were in correspondence with Buhan Nizam Shah of Ahmadnagar. Humayun occupied Gujarat, though only for a short period, and was interested in Khandesh as well.[130] From 1573 onwards, Akbar sent a series of missions to the various Deccan kingdoms. Khandesh (where Faizi, the famous poet, had been sent as Mughal envoy) was the first Deccan kingdom to accept Mughal paramountcy. The other states—Ahmadnagar in particular—resisted Mughal pressure. Finally, by the end of Akbar's reign, the Mughals were already a Deccan power.[131]

Coming to Jahangir's reign, Mughal pressure on the Deccan increased during the years 1608-17. Abdur Rahim Khan-i-Khanan and prince Shahjahan, one after the other, launched large scale offensives on Ahmadnagar and Bijapur.[132] Deccan rulers asked Shah Abbas I to intercede. In 1613 Mir Khalilullah Khushnavis, a Persian 'emigre, was sent to the court of Shah Abbas by Ibrahim Adil Shah II, the ruler of Bijapur. The rulers of Golkonda and Ahmadnagar also sent envoys to the court of Shah Abbas, but the names of them are not known.[133] The Shah dismissed them in 1614 and wrote a letter[134] to Jahangir, recommended his blessings of these rulers, and also reciprocated the gesture by sending an envoy to each of the Sultans of Deccan.

In 1617, when Jahangir was at Mandu, Husain Beg Quaichaji Tabrizi, the retiring Persian ambassador to Golkonda, and Shaikh Muhammad Khatun, the Qutb-Shahi envoy to Persia, presented themselves at the court. This suggests lenience towards the Deccan kingdoms as well as condemnation of their accord with Persia.[135] In 1620, while dismissing Shaikh Muhammad Khatun and other Deccan envoys, Shah Abbas sent three envoys to Bijapur, Golkonda and Ahmadnagar, respectively. Qasim Beg, commander of Mazandaran was envoy to Qutab Shah with Shaikh Muhammad Khatun envoy of Sultan Muhammad Qutab Shah, the ruler of Golkonda.[136] With Qasim Beg, Shah Abbas sent a letter[137] for Jahangir to be delivered to him in Agra on his way to the Deccan. In this letter Shah Abbas expressed his appreciation for the kindness shown by Jahangir to the rulers of the Deccan upon his recommendation.

The second envoy Shah Abbas sent was Talib Beg Awaghli with Mir Khalilullah Khushnavis to Ibrahim Adil Shah II, the ruler of Bijapur.[138] The third envoy sent was Darvish Beg[139] to Murtaza Nizam Shah, the ruler of Ahmadnagar.[140] In 1621, another envoy, Habsh Khan, arrived at the Persian court from Nizam Shah. This ambassador remained in Persia for some time and accompanied Shah Abbas in his Qandahar expedition in 1622.[141]

S.M.R. Naqvi says: The immediate purpose of the Deccan missions to Persian court, therefore, seems to be, as referred to both by the Persian chroniclers[142] and Shah Abbas himself in his letter to Jahangir, was to utilize the services of their old ally for a compromise. They did succeed in their mission by securing a recommendation to the Mughal Emperor for a considerate solution of their conflict.[143] R. Islam says: In spite of Shah Abbas's letter's of thanks to Jahangir, and the claim of the *Alam Ara-i-Abbasi* that the Mughal emperor called off his Deccan campaign at the Shah's request (which in any case is chronologically inadmissible,[144] Shah's remark had no effect on the Mughal policy in the Deccan. His intercession on behalf of the Deccan kingdoms must have been unwelcome to Jahangir, and that is why, it seems, he omits all mention of it in the *Tuzuk*.[145]

Shah Abbas and Shahjahan

Towards the end of Jahangir's reign we have seen that relations with Persia were not maintained, although the Shah seemed anxious to renew them. After the loss of Qandahar, Jahangir had a justly resentment against an old friend who had not only deprived him of a rich province, but had instigated against him the rulers of the Deccan and possibly Shahjahan. The Shah, however, kept on sending ambassadors, but no one was sent in return from India.[146] Shahjahan had been in active correspondence before his accession with Shah Abbas I[147] and the two had started calling each other uncle and nephew respectively. When Shahjahan ascended the throne, Shah Abbas sent Bahri Beg with a letter congratulating him, offering his help if he needed it.[148] The envoy was received outside Agra by Mutaqid Khan, and was admitted to audience[149] on July 5, 1629.

Shah Safi and Shahjahan

While Bahri Beg was on his way to India Shah Abbas I died in Mazandaran in January, 1629.[150] He was succeeded by his grandson Sam Mirza, son of the unfortunate Safi Mirza. The new king after his accession adopted the title of his father, and is known to history as Shah Safi.[151] After death of Shah Abbas I Bahri Beg continued his trip to India. He was dismissed on the 13th Rabi I 1039/1629 with further reward, an elephant, a robe of honour and a jewelled dagger.[152] In the year 1629 Shahjahan appointed Mir Barka to proceed to Iran to convey his condolences on the death of Shah Abbas and felicitations on the enthroning of the new Shah. He was given a robe of honour, a letter, a studded dagger, an elephant and Rs. 50,000. The letter is very long and is full of all sorts of advice for the young Shah.[153] It closes with a word of praise for Mir Barka, a request for his early dismissal, and a promise of a regular embassy in the near future.[154] Mir Bakar was received warmly at the court of Shah Safi. After a few months he was granted permission to return to India. Kambu says: Mir Barka arrived back to the Mughal court in Dhul-Hiji 1041/May-June, 1632.[155]

Shah Safi continued the policy of his father in maintaining amicable friendship with the Mughal court and appointed Muhammad Ali Beg one of his eminent courtiers, as his envoy to India. He sent with this envoy letters,[156] gifts consisting of horses, camels and valuable products of Iran worth 300,000. Near Burhanpur he was welcomed by Afzal Khan and Sadiq Khan, and when he was admitted to audience he handed to the Mughal Emperor the letter of the Shah. Shahjahan was very lavish in his bounty to the Persian envoy, and let no occasion pass without presenting him with some gift of value to impress his dignity on him. He was dismissed on the 30th June, 1632.[157]

Shahjahan had three main objectives in foreign policy each of which was related to Persia directly or indirectly. He wanted to recover Qandahar, to re-establish the power of his monarchy in his ancestral lands in Turan, and to assert his suzerainty over the Deccan kingdoms and destroy their alliance with Persia. It was naturally his aim to preserve friendship with Turan when striking at Qandahar and to keep Persia neutral when invading Turan.[158] So he proceeded energetically to establish relations with both sides. A major embassy was sent to the Safavid court.

On the 25th of Shawal 1042/April/1633, Shahjahan selected Khwaja Qasim otherwise known as Safdar Khan from among other learned courtiers as his envoy to convey his greetings to Shah Safi. About four lakhs of rupees worth of gifts was sent to the Shah of Iran through this ambassador. The majority of the presents consisted of finely wrought jewellery and other fancy articles manufactured in the royal factories of Ahmadabad, Patna, Benares and Malda. The letter[160] to the Shah was drafted by Afzal Khan,[161] and in it Shahjahan acknowledged the embassy of Muhammad Ali Beg, pointed out to the Shah the need of cherishing able men, explained the duties of a king and concluded with reference to the suppression of Khan Jahan's rebellion, the submission of Qutbul Mulk, the campaign against the Adil Shah, the capture of Hugli and the extirpation of the Portuguese.[162]

Shah Safi assigned Yadgar Beg as his ambassador and sent him along with Safdar Khan to India. The letter that was carried by Yadgar Beg from Shah Safi to Shahjahan contained the news of the seizure of Iravan by Shah Safi. He also took gifts from Shah Safi to Shahjahan. Yadgar Beg was granted three audiences with Shah Jahan and was bestowed with gifts worth Rs. 90,000, together with a studded dagger and other presents.[163] The main purpose of Yadgar Beg's mission[164] was to ascertain Delhi's attitude towards Qandahar, but a month before he reached India, Qandahar fell into the hands of the Indian army. The loss of Qandahar offended the Shah of Iran and thereafter Shah Safi did not dispatch any other envoy to India.

According to *Khuld-i-Barin,* the Shah Safi conferred further favours on Safdar Khan and finally dismissed him in early 10471/mid 1637.[165] Safdar Khan, it appears, moved slowly in order to keep in touch with affairs in Persia. He reached Qandahar late in 1638, after the Mughals had seized it.[166]

In the year 1637, while Safdar Khan was still in Iran, Shahjahan sent Mir Husain to Iran with a letter to Shah Safi. But when this ambassador reached Iran, Safdar Khan had already left. However, Mir Husain returned to India in Rajab 1048/November 1638 without delivering the letter of Shahjahan to Shah Safi.[167] Because it was to be delivered to the Shah through Safdar Khan, but as the latter had left by this time, the message could not be delivered and its purport is not known.[168] It is quite likely that it had something to do with Qandahar.

Shahjahan, the Safavid Rulers and Qandahar

Owing to its strategic situation and commercial importance Qandahar as we noticed above, was a bone of contention between Persia and Mughal India. Our details have shown that Qandahar occupied a position of great importance in the defence systems and or the caravans of India and Iran. It was a gateway to India and a natural base of operations for a Persian or Central Asian invader of India. The fort was one of the strongest in the east. It has a fertile hinterland and a plentiful supply of water. A comparatively small force under an able determined commander could hold out for a long time. Its commercial importance was no less great. Here gathered merchants from India, Persia, Turkey and Central Asia, and it connected the principal trade routes from India to Central Asia, and the countries of Europe. The rare occasions when the stronghold appears to have been seized by force were attended by exceptional circumstances. The possession of Qandahar was essential for the security of Kabul as well as Khurasan.

We saw above how Qandahar was lost to the Mughals during the last years of Jahangir's reign. Shahjahan naturally was anxious to recover it at the earliest opportunity. In 1041/1632, he had accorded welcome to Sher Khan Afghan of Fushanj, a Persia tributary chief who had rebelled and fled to India. The welcome accorded to him was certainly a hostile act.[169] He instructed Said Khan, Governor of Kabul to send an experienced diplomat to Ali Mardan Khan, the Persian governor of Qandahar, to induce him to join the Mughal service. Said Khan sent Zul Qadr Khan with the utmost secrecy so that no one could know the purpose of the mission.[170] The emissary was to sound Ali Mardan Khan as well as to do the work of military espionage in Qandahar.[171] Zul Qadr Khan was well-received by Ali Mardan Khan. He dismissed the emissary suitably and later sent a message firmly rejecting the Mughal offer.[172]

Ali Mardan Khan was not on good terms with the Persian court as Saru Taqi, the Persian minister, had demanded from him a statement of account of the income and expenditure for his governorship and sent troops to ensure compliance. To evade this Ali Mardan Khan intrigued with the Mughal officers in Kabul and offered to surrender Qandahar to Shahjahan early in 1638, he transferred his services to the Mughal emperor and admitted Indian troops into the fortress.[173] Qilij Khan, governor of Multan was transferred to the governorship of Qandahar. In view of the threat from Siyaush who was encamping only twelve miles away and was in touch with Persians inside the fort, Said-Khan, governor of Kabul, personally came to Qandahar. The pro-Persian party was suppressed.[174]

Shahjahan's name now appeared in the *Khutba* and on the coins in Qandahar. The district of Qandahar was occupied by the Mughal troops without much difficulty.[175] Ali Mardan was richly rewarded and later appointed governor of Kashmir and then Kabul.[176]

After the occupation of Qandahar and other forts, Shahjahan sent a letter to Shah Safi (with Yadgar Beg),[177] expressing the hope that recent events would not cloud mutual relations and offering to pay every year a sum equal to the revenues of Qandahar.[178]

By Jumada I 1049/ September, 1639, Shah Safi had made peace with the Ottomans at the cost of Baghdad and soon after ordered elaborate preparations for an expedition to Qandahar. After two years of preparations, he set out from Esfahan but fell ill on the way and died at Kahsan on 12 Safar 1052/2 May, 1642. Shahjahan expressed his condolences at his death, and ascribing it to the good fortune of Dara Shukoh, who had been entrusted with the defence of Qandahar, conferred on the latter the little of Shahzada Buland Iqbal or Prince of High Fortune. The Shahjahan chronicles indeed make highly uncharitable references to Shah Safi after his death.[179]

Meanwhile Shahjahan had launched his expedition to Turan. The motives for this were sentimental according to some historians. Some other historians identify realistic objectives like defining the borders to be the aim of this campaign.[180] Though successful at the outset, the plan inevitably failed, and the Mughals had to beat a costly retreat after only fifteen month's occupation of Balkh.[181] This is also disputed for according to one opinion the Mughals made some gains subsequent to this expedition. At any rate the Mughal retreat from Balkh paved the way for a Persian advance on Qandahar.

Shah Abbas II and Shahjahan

Shah Safi was succeeded by Shah Abbas II in the year 1642 at the age of eleven years at the time of his accession.[182] During his minority the administration was carried on by Saru Taqi. Shahjahan dispatched Jan Nisar Khan on March 26, 1646,[183] as his envoy to Persia. This mission , the first after the death of Shah Safi indicated a desire on the part of Shahjahan to resume the friendly relations with the Shah which had been broken after the occupation of Qandahar. The pretext adopted for sending the envoy was to congratulate Shah Abbas II on his accession. On the face of it, it was absurd. Jan Nisar Khan carried a very lengthy letter for the Shah. From the point of view of contemporary diplomacy it is very interesting. In it we come across a strong mixture of condolence and congratulations, advice and apology and also offers him only help he needed to strengthen his rule.[184]

When Nazr Muhammad Khan escaped to Persia Shahjahan immediately sent two ambassadors, Mir Aziz and Arsalan Beg to Persia.[185] Mir Aziz carried a letter from Shahjahan to Nazr Muhammad Khan who had come to Iran to seek assistance after the loss of Balkh. However, Shah Abbas II did not deem it advisable that this letter be given to Nazr Muhammad Khan.[186] Arsalan Beg brought a letter from Shahjahan for Shah Abbas II, which contained news of his victory in Uzbekistan. The purpose of their mission is plainly described in the Safavid sources as securing Persian neutrality in the current Indo-Persian conflict.

All three envoys of India were received warmly in Iran especially Jan Nisar Khan, who was the official ambassador of India. The Shah assured him of Persian neutrality and dismissed him suitably (Dhul-Q.,

1057/December 1647).[187] Autar Khan was appointed to accompany him to India, but for some reason did not proceed. The Shah in a skilfully drafted letter, sent with Arslan Beg, told Shahjahan that out of consideration for the weak condition of the Uzbeks, he had not deemed it proper to interfere in Turan, and that Nazr Muhammad Khan had no intention to proceed to Mecca and had already left for Turan.[188]

Shah Abbas II's Capture of Qandahar

The Mughal occupation of Qandahar was a sore wound to Persian pride. During the minority of the Shah Abbas II who was ten years old at his accession in 1052/1642, its recovery was impracticable. The decision to march on Qandahar was taken while the last Mughal ambassador, Jan Nisar Khan was still at the Persian court.[189] The Mughal envoy was however dismissed before active preparations began. Other steps were also taken to prevent leakage of news to India.[190]

Shah Abbas II left Esfahan in Rabi I, 1058/April, 1648, when the Shah reached Bastam, a friendly embassy also arrived from the Ottoman Sultan Ibrahim, thus assuring the Shah of greater security on his western frontiers.[191] Shah Abbas sent Shah Quli Beg to the court of Shahjahan from Bestam. Through him, he sent a polite letter to Shahjahan, praised him for returning Balkh to Nazr Muhammad Khan and hoped for the similar restoration of Qandahar.[192]

The news that Shah Abbas II was intending to recover Qandahar created a great stir in the Mughal court. Shahjahan wished to move immediately to Kabul, and save the situation. But his ministers, who were afraid to face the severities of winter, counselled him against the proposal.[193]

The young Shah Abbas II, undaunted by the weather, reached the outskirts of Qandahar in Dhul-Hijj, 1058/December, 1648.[194] Bust was the first fort to fall,[195] Zamin-Dawar was blockaded but was spared a frontal attack as the commander offered to surrender as soon as Qandahar was taken. Qandahar itself did not resist for long. The garrison under Daulat Khan,[196] its governor, lost heart thinking that no relief from Delhi was likely to arrive in time. Some of the troops in the fortress, anxious to save themselves and their families, opened correspondence with the besiegers and Daulat Khan was not powerful enough to put down the sedition with a strong hand. In fact he himself eventually joined the dispirited garrison and surrendered the fort to the Persians in February, 1649, a month before Aurangzeb was able to reach Kabul on route to Qandahar. Shahjahan was indignant and urged Aurangzeb to hurry up and recover the valuable frontier outpost. The emperor himself advanced to Kabul to hearten the troops by his presence.[197]

From Qandahar the victorious Shah Abbas II sent an envoy, Shah Verdi Beg, with a letter offering an explanation of his invasion and expressing the hope that this would not affect mutual amity and also he explained the reasons for his attack and capture of Qandahar. Shah Verdi Beg arrived in Rajab 1059/July 1649 at the Mughal court when it was on its way to Kabul. Shahjahan, unhappy at the turn of events, received Shah Verdi Beg coldly and he was not granted an audience and his letter was not accepted.[198] He was given a verbal message for his master and was dismissed with an escort. Muhammad Quli Beg (who had been sent by the Shah earlier from Bastam) was permitted to return without being granted an audience.[199]

The second siege of Qandahar in 1652 accrued again out of the Emperor's anxiety and Aurangzeb's determination to retrieve his pride. This time the Mughal forces were accompanied by matching powerful cannons. Aurangzeb, ably assisted by Sadullah Khan and Rustam Khan began the siege in May, 1652. The Persians, however once again proved superior in the skilful use of artillery. The Mughals suffered heavy casualties. The second siege lasting for over two months also proved futile and was abandoned in spite of Aurangzeb's assurance to win against all odds. Shahjahan lost confidence in Aurangzeb and shifted him to Deccan. Dara was now put incharge of Kabul.

The third siege of Qandahar was led by Dara in 1653, who, in order to humiliate Aurangzeb, was determined to secure victory. The Mughals attacked the fort four times. Each time they were confidently resisted by the Persians. Once again the Mughals suffered heavy losses and the futile siege continued for over seven months.

The three sieges of Qandahar (1649, 1652 and 1653) sapped the resources of the empire. They cost about 12 crores of rupees without any compensating advantage. Not an inch of territory was added to the imperial dominions. In fact, the empire lost not only the impregnable fortress of Qandahar, but also a large extent of territory around it. Quite a large number of men and beasts of burden perished in the enterprise. The political and military prestige of the empire suffered greatly and revealed the inefficiency of Shahjahan's military organization.[200] The conquest of Qandahar created a coldness and in the relationship between the two countries and no other ambassadors were exchanged until the end of lifetime of Shahjahan in 1657. Shahjahan himself remarked to one of the last Persian envoys, diplomatic exchange were pointless under the circumstances.[201] Shahjahan now tried to improve relations with the Uzbeks and Ottoman Turks, but his attempts were fruitless.

Shahjahan, the Safavids and the Deccan

Jahangir's continuation of Akbar's aggressive policy in the Deccan was stultified by weak leadership and the Mughal frontiers remained unchanged. Shahjahan pursued a more determined and forward policy in the Deccan. The Deccan kingdoms continued to look to Persia for protection and for diplomatic support against Mughal aggression. Abdullah Qutb Shah sent Khairat Khan, a highly placed noble of Persian birth, as envoy to Persia. Muhammad Quli Beg, son of Qasim Beg, the deceased Persian ambassador,[202] was given leave to join Khairat Khan.[203] When they arrived at Surat, they received a summons from Shah Abbas I and dismissed them (August, 1628). Khairat Khan and Muhammad Quli Beg arrived at Bandar Abbas (February, 1629) to learn of the great Shah's death. Khairat Khan's embassy was given a magnificent reception by Shah Safi, full details of which are recorded by both Safavid and Deccan chronicles.[204]

He was dismissed some years later and Imam Quli was appointed to accompany him as Persian ambassador. The two envoys saw Shahjahan in Ramazan 1043/March 1634, handed him a letter from Shah Safi and proceeded on their way to Golkonda, where they arrived about a year later. The Safavid envoy was received in Golkonda with elaborate magnificence.[205]

By 1633, the Mughals had extinguished the Ahmadnagar kingdom, which weakened the position of the two remaining Deccan powers, Golkonda and Bijapur. Shahjahan did not like the political independence of the two kingdoms and he particularly objected to the inclusion of the name of the Shah of Persia in the *Khutba* that was recited at Golkonda in the Shia fashion. In 1045/1636 Shahjahan sent *farmans* to

Qutb Shah and Adil Shah. The *farmans* to Qutb Shah demanded the replacement of the name of the Shah of Iran by that of Shahjahan and recitation of the *Khutba* in the Sunni fashion.[206] The *Khutba* was read for the first time in the Sunni *fashion* and Shahjahan's name replaced that of the Shah. News of Shahjahan's victories in the Deccan is reported in letter by Mir Husaini to Shah Safi.[207]

In late 1046/early 1637, Shah Safi appointed Ahmad Beg Qurchi to proceed on mission to Muhammad Adil Shah.[208] Shah Safi also gave an early conge to the Adil Shah's envoy, Rahim Muhammad, and entrusted him with a letter.[209]

In 1051/1641, Hakimul Mulk, an envoy from the court of Abdullah Qutb Shah, arrived in Persia along with Imam Quli Beg, the retiring Persian ambassador.[210] Shah Safi also sent traders on royal purchasing missions to Golkonda with letters addressed to Abdullah Qutb Shah.[211] The Mughal authorities suspected that these diplomatic exchanges were directed against them, and they strongly objected to the despatch of Hakimul Mulk's embassy.As a result no further mission was sent to Persia for some years. Thus neither of the Deccan powers could send the usual congratulatory embassy on Shah Abbas II's accession.[212] In 1650, however, a Persian envoy came to Golkonda on an English boat.[213] The previous year Shah Abbas had captured Qandahar and he now stood in a better position to offer the Deccan kingdoms moral support, if nothing else.[214]

The Iranian Mughal relations, as we saw above began right from the time of the foundation of the dynasty. Babur was assisted against the Uzbeks by Shah Ismail Safavi, so was his son Humayun when he was hunted out of India by Sher Shah Sur. It was with the help of Iranian troops at the command of Shah Ismail's son, Shah Tahmasp that Humayun in 1555 regained the throne of Delhi. Here was a rare instance of a Mughal Indian father and son being assisted by an Iranian father and son, and the concord so established between the royal dynasties led to progressive relations between Mughal India and Safavid Iran.

The protege and patron relationship between the Mughals of India and the Safavids of Persia entered upon a new phase with the consolidation of the empire under Akbar. Akbar's tolerance and far treatment of his subjects raised the prestige of the dynasty abroad. A close diplomatic contact was then established between Agra and Esfahan which soon extended far beyond the portals of the royal palaces. This contact did not simply draw the bureaucracy and the *mansabdars* from Iran, it penetrated the deepest aspects of life. The cultural relationship thus established between the Mughal rulers and the Safavid monarchs brought about regular intercourse and, of course, exchange of envoys. It is true that there was often misunderstanding and friction about Qandahar. In the Qandahar province the frequent changes of government between India and Persia fomented dissension and intrigue. But on the whole, the Mughal-Safavid relations were cordial, constantly nourished by the memory of Babur's alliance with Shah Ismail, and Shah Tahmasp's help to Humayun. Between 1556 and 1666 seven Indian embassies went to Persia and twenty three Persian envoys came to India. As a result of this diplomatic intercourse was reinforced by a continuous flow in Mughal India of Iranian administrators, scholars, poets, artists and craftsmen. They all contributed to the development of Mughal culture and refinement. We will see in the following chapters the details of these migrations.

REFERENCES

1. R. Islam, 'Iran and the Mughal Frontier Provinces' in : *Farhang-i-Iran Zamin*; Vol. XXI, Nos.1-4, Tehran, 1976, p. 110.
2. J.N Sarkar, 'Correspondence between the Deccani sultanates and Mir Jumla with the court of Iran', in : *J.B.O.R.S*, March, 1942, p. 65, Vol. XXVIII.
3. A. Rahim, Mughal relations with Persia, in: *Islamic Culture*, Vol. VII, 1934, p. 463. Quoted from *Babur's Memoirs*, pp. 15,19 and Tarikh-i-Rashidi, pp. 175, 186.
4. *Ibid.*, p. 463.
5. J.L. Nehru, *The Discovery of India*, Calcutta, 1946, p.162; A.A Jorfi, 'Iran and India, Age-old friendship in: *India Quarterly;* Vol. 1, No. 41994, p.77.
6. Allami-Abul Fazl, *Akbar Nama*, Vol. I, Bib.Indica, Calcutta, 1877-78, p. 99; Bakhshi, Khwaja Nizamuddin Ahmad, *Tabaqat-i-Akbari*, Bib.Indica, Vol. II, Calcutta, 1931, p.17; Badauni, Abdul Qadir b. Muluk Shah, *Muntakhab-ut-Tawarikh*, Bib. Indica, Vol. I, Calcutta, 1868, p.337.
7. About Humayun in Persia: see, *A.A.A. op. cit*, 1334/1955, Vol. II, pp. 96-100 and also see: Wali Quli Shamliu, *Qisasul Khaqani*, edited by

Hasan Sadat Nasiri, Part-I, Tehran, 1992, pp. 67-71.

8. For details See. *Akbar Nama*, pp.163-69.
9. For details, see: Bayat Bayazid, *Tazkira Humayun va Akbar*; Bib. Indica; Calcutta, 1941, pp. 68-69.
10. R. Islam, 1970, *op. cit.*, p. 166; p. Brown, *Indian painting under the Mughals*, Oxford, 1924, pp. 53-54.
11. Bayazid, 1941, p. 39 See also; *Akbar Nama*, Vol. I, p.227.
12. Bayazid, 1941, pp. 64-65 ; *Akbar Nama*, Vol.I, pp. 249, 252, 259.
13. Bayazid, 1941, pp.173-175 See also: *Akbar Nama, op. cit*, Vol. I p. 335.
14. *A.A.A.*1955, p. 92.
15. Badauni, Vol. II, pp. 40-41 and also see; Abdur Rahim; 'Mughal relations with Persia' in; *Islamic Culture*, Vol.VIII, 1934, p. 466.
16. M.H. Khafi Khan; *Muntakhab-ul-Lubab*, Bib. Indica, Calcutta, 1909-25, Vol. I, p.143.
17. S.S.D. Shah Nawaz Khan, and Abdul Hayy, *Maasir-ul-Umara* Bib. Indica, Calcutta, 1885-95,Vol. III, pp. 240-45.
18. *A.A.A.* 1332/1955, - pp. 213-214 and also see: N. Falsafi; Tehran, 1334/ 1955, Vol. I, pp. 20-33.
19. The Enc Islam (New edn.) p. 8, ascribes (Inaccurately the blinding of Khudabanda to Abbas, CF. *A.A.A.. op.cit,* p.126 which says he became blind during his boyhood.
20. *Akbar Nama,* II, p. 8 and also see: S.H. Elliot and J. Dowson, *History of India as told by its own Historians*, Vol. .V, London, 1867-75, p. 342.
21. *A.A.A.* 1334/1955, pp. 222-28 and also see: Falsafi, 1955, Vol. I, p. 53.
22. *A.A.A.* 1334/1955 - , pp. 230-35 and also: N. Falsafi, 1995, p. 147.
23. R. Islam, 1970, p. 51.
24. See: Sir H.H. Howorth, *History of Mongols*; London, 1876-1927.
25. *Akbar Nama, op.cit.* Vol. II, p. 368. Tr., by H. Beveridge, p. 534.
26. *Ibid.*, Vol. III, p. 297,
27. R. Islam, 1970, p. 52 quoted it is a matter of curious interest to recall Mulla Badauni's story that *Makhdumaul Mulk, Akbar's Shaik-ul-Islam* gave a legal injunction against proceeding on pilgrimage to Mecca through Persia on the ground of that country being in Shiite hands. Badauni, II, p. 203.
28. R. Islam, *op.cit.*, 29.
29. Also called Shamlu, *A.A.A*, 1055, p. 314, p. 291 ; N. Falsafi, 1955, Vol. I, p. 218.
30. *Encyclopaedia of Islam*, 1993, Vol. VII, p. 317.
31. *A.N*, Vol. III, p. 117.

32. See: notices of their careers in; *M.U.* Vol. III. p. 296, 434.
33. *A.N.*, Vol. III, pp. 645-46, 669, see: *Tabaqat-i-Akbari,* Vol. II, p. 423.
34. R. Islam, 1970, p. 61 quoted in *Akbar Nama,* III, p. 588. According to *A.N.* the Persian envoy arrived at the Mughal court in 999 and left in 1003, the *Alam Ara,* 1314/1935, p. 361, says that he left Persian in 999 and arrived back in 1005.
35. *Ibid.*, quoted in *A.N.* Vol. III, p. 656, names them Ziyaul Mulk and Abu Nasr, the *Alam Ara*, 1314/1935, p. 361, calls them Ziyauddin Kashi and Abu Nasr Khwafi, and notes that both were Persian; see. Abdur Rahim, *Islamic Culture*, Vol. VIII, 1934, pp. 471-72.
36. Grand Usher, or Lord of the Gate.
37. For details see, N. Falsafi, 1955, Vol. I, pp. 232-34 and also see: *A.A.A.*, 1334/1955, Part I, pp. 543-44.
38. *A.N.*, Vol. III, p. 745.
39. *A.A.A.*, 1334/1955, Part. I, pp. 553-58.
40. *A.A.A.*, 1334/1995, Part. I, pp. 569-70.
41. *A.A.A.*, 1314/1935, Part. I, pp. 405, 683, and also; *A.N.*, Vol. III, p. 749 makes no mention of the request for the restoration of Qandahar.
42. *A.N.*, Vol. III, pp. 787, 815.
43. For Mir Masum, see: *M.U.*, III, p. 326.
44. *A.N.*, Vol. III, p. 825-27 Azar, 47th R.Y. of Shah Abbas I the author of *Alam Ara* says that Mir Masum arrived with Minchihr. But the A.N.s. careful chronology makes this unlikely. (See: *A.A.A.*, p. 448).
45. *Ibid.*, 1314/1935, pp. 448, 455.
46. For regarding the entertainment of Shah Abbas to Mir Masum see; *A.A.A., op. cit,* pp. 647-48.
47. Abdur Rahim, Mughal relations with Persia' in: *Islamic Culture,* Vol. VIII, 1934, pp. 472-73 and also see: R. Islam, 1970, p. 111 quoted in *A.N.*, Vol. III, p. 836.
48. Jahangir, *Tuzuk-i-Jahangiri*, Aligarh, 1281/1869, p. 349.
49. About relationship between Mirza Ghazi and Shah Abbas I, see: Sayyid Mir Muhammad, *Tarkhan Nama,* ed., S. Hasamud-din Rashdli, Hyderabad, 1965, pp. 91-92.
50. A.L. Srivastava, 1989, p. 260; B. Prasad, 1962, pp. 147-48, see also, *Islamic Culture*, 1934, pp. 649-50.
51. *A.A.A.*, 1935, p. 693, *Tuzuk*, p. 53.
52. R. Islam, 1970, p. 70, quoted from Bhag Chand Munshi : *Jami-ul-Insha;* B.M. or 1702, ff. 230b-32b.
53. *A.A.A.*, 1334/1955, p. 782.
54. *Ibid.*, about gifts of Shah Abbas to Jahangir by Sultan Ali Talish, See; *Ibid.*, p. 783.

55 R. Islam, *Ibid.*, 1970, p. 70, quoted in *Tuzuk*, *op. cit.*, pp. 94-95, this letter is purely congratulatory, a condolatory letter given in the *Munsha'at-i-Tusi*, ff. 158a-59b, and claimed by the compiler as his own composition, was also brought by the same envoy, this second letter is also given in Abul Qasim Haidar Beg Iwaghli, *Nuskhai Jamia Murasilat-ul-Albab*, A collection of letters to and from the Shahs of Persia.B.M. Add, 7688, also or 3482, f. 214ab.

56. *A.A.A.*, 1334/1955, p. 939.

57. This refers to the missions of Chalabi Beg from India and Uwaisi Beg from Persia.

58. *Tuzuk*, p. 117, and *Tuzuk*, trans. by Rogers and Beweridge, London, 1909-14, Vol. I, pp.158, 448.

59. R. Islam, in the *Encyclopaedia of Islam*, Vol. VII, 1993, p. 317.

60. R. Islam, 1970, p.71.

61. *Tuzuk*, pp.165-66.

62. N. Falsafi, 1961, Vol. IV, p. 87.

63. Ulugh Beg, Timurid, prince and astronomer, died 853/1449, was son of Shah Rukh, Timur's son and successor.

64. R. Islam, 1970, p. 72, quoted in *Tuzuk*, p.166.Qasim Beg was a brother of Muhammad Husain Chalabi.

65. R. Islam, 1970, p. 73, quoted in Lahori, Vol. II, pp. 184-88, gives a detailed account, the agent's *Nama* was Mir Zarif; another, Mir Humai was sent to Persia to purchase horses.

66. *Ibid.*, quoted in *Tuzuk*, p. 223 and also N. Falsafi, 1960, Vol. IV, p. 295.

67. *Tuzuk*, *op.cit.*, p. 121.

68. *M.U.* text, Vol. I, p.782.

69. For details about reception of Khan Alam in Iran see; *A.A.A.*, 1334/1955, pp. 939-40, 951, Pietro Della Vella, Vol. IV, pp. 243-47 quoted from N. Falsafi, 1960, Vol. III, pp. 278-80, *Ihyaul Muluk*, ff. 213b-15a, N. Falsafi, 1939, pp. 56-61. M.U., text Vol. I, p. 737.

70. For Bishan Das see: P. Brown, 1924, pp. 82, 126.

71. *M.U.*, text Vol. I, p. 734; Khafi Khan, II, p. 202.

72. *Iqbal Nama Jahangiri*, p. 134, see also: *M.U.*, text Vol. I, p. 735.

73. Clara Cary Edwards, Relations of Shah Abbas the Great of Persia, with the Mughal Emperors, Akbar and Jahangir, in *J. of the American Oriental Society*, Vol. 35, No. 1.3, 1915, p.155; and also see N. Falsafi, 1939, p. 42.

74. Adur Rahim: 'Mughal Relations with Persia: *Islamic Culture*, op.cit., 1934, p. 655; Hadi Hassan, *Collection of Articles*, Hyderabad Deccan, 1954, p.40.

75. *Islamic Culture*, 1934, p. 655-56; quoted *Jamia'a-i-Murasilat*, ff. 217, for the letter.
76. Sir Thomas Roe, *The Embassy of Sir Thomas Roe*, edited by Sir W. Foster, O.U.P., 1926, pp. 258-60, 300-01, 350-51.
77. S.T. Roe, 1926, pp. 258-59.
78. B. Prasad, 1962, p. 345, see also: *Iqbalanama*, pp. 89-90.
79. Roe, *ibid.*, 1926, pp. 363, 64 About gifts and rewards see: *J. A.O.S*, 1915, pp. 256-57.
80. For details about Muhammad Reza Beg see: Herbert Moris, *Muhammad Reza Travellers*, Trans. by Abdul Husain Vojdani, Tehran, 1362/1983.
81. R. Islam, 1970, p. 77 qouted from *Tuzuk*, *op.cit*, p. 197.
82. *Islamic Culture*, 1934, p. 656 but R. Islam has mentioned Sayyid Hasan in *Shawwal* 1026/October 1617, see: R. Islam, 1970, p. 77.
83. Zainal seem to be the correct form of the *Nama;* see: *A.A.A.*, 1334/1955, pp. 950, 993 and see also, N. Falsafi, *op.cit.*, p. 109. It has been written as Zambil in the *Tuzuk*, pp. 289.
84. *A.A.A.*, 1334/1955, p. 951.
85. Tuzuk, p. 315.
86. *A.A.A.*, 1334/1955, p. 993.
87. About gifts of Shah to Jahangir see: *A.A.A.*, 1334/1955, p. 951.
88. A.Rahim, 'Mughal relations with Persia' in: *Islamic Culture*, 1934, p. 658 quoted from, *Tuzuk*, Vol. II, p. 186.
89. *A.A.A.*, 1334/1955, p. 994.
90. These envoys have not been mentioned in *Alam Ara Abbasi*.
91. R. Islam, *A Calendar of documents on Indo-Persian Relations*, Vol. I, Karachi, 1979, p.202.
92. *Banda Shah Wilayat.*
93. 'A.Rahim : 'Mughal relations with Persia' in: *Islamic Culture*, 1934, p. 658, for the account of this embassy see Saqi *Mustaid Khan, Maasir-i-Alamgiri*, Bib. Indica, Calcutta, 1947, : ff. 143.
94. *Ibid.*, ff. 147.
95. *Tuzuk*, (Rogers trans.), Vol. II, p. 211.
96. R. Islam, 1970, p. 81, quoted from, A. Lahori, *Padshah Nama*, Bib. Indica, Calcutta, 1867, Vol. II, p. 25 and also see Khafi Khans, Vol. I, p. 325-6, 343, Khafi Khan's statement that Nur Jahan and Asaf Khan advised acceptance of the Shah's request, lacks confirmation; earlier sources, C.F. *Maasir-i-Jahangiri*, ff.1736.
97. *A.A.A.*, 1334/1955, p. 961.
98. *A.A.A.*, 1314/1935, p. 700.

99. R. Islam, 1970, p. 81 quoted from Lahori, II, p. 26, For details, see: *Tuzuk*, p.322.

100. R. Islam, 1970, pp. 81-82.

101. *A.A.A.*, 1334/1955, p. 973; for details about conquer of Qandahar by Abbas I see: *Ibid.*, pp. 970-78.

102. *Tuzuk*, pp. 352, 345; *Maasir-i-Jahangiri*, ff. 173b.

103. *A.A.A.*, 1334/1955, p. 994 and also see: Dh. Thabitiyan, *Asnad Va Namaha-i-Tarikhi, Daura-i-Safaviya*, Tehran, 1343/1964; p.312.

104. R. Islam, 1970, p. 83; For Shah's letter and Jahangir's reply see: *Tuzuk*, pp. 348-52. It refers to the keys of the kingdom of Iran being sent to Jahangir which is also mentioned in *Alam Ara*, 1314/1935, p. 686, lines 9-10. For details of letter see; R. Islam, *ibid.*, 1979, Vol. I, pp.205-209.

105. R. Islam, 1970, p. 83 and N. Falsafi, *ibid.*, Vol. IV, Tehran, p.105, of the dismissal of Zainal Beg, the principal Persian envoy, there seems to be no clear mention in the *Tuzuk-i-Jahangiri* which merely says (p. 348) that all the envoys that had come from Shah Abbas at short intervals were given robes and expenses (*Khilat wa Kharchi*) and were dismissed at Lahore on Azar, 17th r.y. (the month and the year corresponding to November-December, 1632). Zamal Beg was evidently one of them. The *Alam Ara-Abbasi*, p. 994, says that Jahangir became angry with Zainal Beg on account of Qandahar affair, but later suitably dismissed him along with the other Persian envoys.

106. *Tuzuk*, pp. 350-52 and also R. Islam, 1979, Calendar No. J.91.

107. *A.A.A.*, 1314/1935, p. 700.

108. R. Islam, 1970, p. 84.

109. For letters of prince Shahjahan to Shah Abbas see: *Majmua*, Tehran University Central Library, MS 2591, pp. 89-90. For second letter see: *Ibid*, MS 2591, f(p) 87 for reply from Abbas to prince see: *Ibid.*, MS 2591, p. 90.

110. For details see: *A.A.A.* 1334/1955; pp. 976-77.

111. For letter of prince Khurram to Shah Abbas by Khwaja Haji see: N. Falsafi, 1960 Vol. IV, pp.110-11 for reply of letter from Abbas to Khurram by Khwaja Haji in 1032/1623 see: *Ibid.*, pp.112-13.

112. For details see; A.A.A. 1334/1955, pp.1015-16.

113. About letter see: Muhammad Salih, *Majmua-i Makatib-i Mukhtalifa*, Majlis library (Tehran) Ms; 2247 Cat. X, 333497 p. 248-49.

114. For Ishaq Beg Yazdi see: A.Lahori, vol: I, p.393, Those letters (Three abovementioned) have not been indicated by Riazul Islam in *Indo-Persian relations*.

115. About embassy of *Mustaufi-i-Ghulaman* see: *A.A.A.*, 1334/1955, p. 1012-14.

116. For letter of Shah Abbas to Jahangir see: *A.A.A.*, and also see: Dh. Thabityan, 1964 pp.317-19.

117. For conquest of Baghdad by Abbas see: *A.A.A.*, 1955 986-87 and also see; *Tuzuk*, p. 399.

118. *Iqbal Nama Jahangiri*, p. 252 For letter of Jahangir to Abbas see: *Majmua*, Tehran University Central Library; Ms. 2591, p. 254.

119. *A.A.A.*, 1314/ 1935, p. 1012.

120. Beni Prasad, 1962, p. 398.

121. The first letter, making a reference to Jahangir's enquiries about his (Shah's) welfare gives an account of his recent prosperous affairs. (See; R. Islam, Vol. I, 1979, p. 218, Calendar No. J.96) Another was a formal letter of condolence to Jahangir. (see: *Ibid.*, p. 219, no. J.97). But the most interesting was the third despatch which was addressed to Nur Jahan (See: R. Islam, 1970, p. 86 and R. Islam , 1979, p. 220). This letter makes a brief mention of recent Persian victories against the Turks, condoles Parwez's demise and finally making a reference to his (Shah's) close friendship with Jahangir, says, if Your Majesty were to consider this house (i.e., dynasty or state) as your own and were to assign to servants of this dynasty and business at this end it would further augment mutual amity and union. This is unique, being addressed by a king to a foreign queen the only one of its kind in Indo-Persian state correspondence.The letter also indicates Shah Abbas's understanding of Nur Jahan's dominant position in the Mughal empire.(For Nur Jahan's dominance, see: B. Prasad , 1962, p. 194 and Chapter XIV) The fourth letter was addressed to prince Shahryar, youngest son of Jahangir and son-in-law of Nur Jahan (see : R.Islam, 1979, p. 221).

122. *A.A.A*, 1334/1955, pp. 1066-68.

123. R.Islam, 1970, p. 92.

124. For Shah Tahir relation and correspondence with Shah Tahmasp see: Abdul Husain Nawai, *Shah Tahmasb Safavi* (documents); Tehran, 1350/ 1971, pp.69-72,78-79.

125. For details see: Sadiq Naqvi, *The Iran-Deccan relations*, Hyderabad,1994, pp. 29-65.

126. *A.A.A.*, 1314/1935, pp. 89, 148.

127. R. Islam, *op. cit.*, 1970, p.93.

128. E.g, Shaikh Muhammad Khatun, *A.A.A.* 1314/1935, p. 663; 'Mir Muhammad Mumin, Firshta, II, p.341; Muhammad Amin Mir Jumla and etc.

129. Firshta, II, p. 329-30.

130. R. Islam, *op.cit.*

131. R. Islam, p. 94, for an excellent modern account of Akbar's intervention

in the Deccan, see: R.P. Tripathi, Rise and Fall of the Mughal Empire, Allahabad, 1956, Chapter XV.

132. B. Prasad, 1962, pp. 262-83.

133. *A.A.A.* 1334/1955, p. 951.

134. For letter see: Majlis Library, Tehran, Catalogue X, MS, No. 3455, p. 135 and MS 2247, Catalogue X, 3349, p. 33-34.

135. R. Islam, 1970, p. 95.

136. *A.A.A.* 1334/1955, p. 951.

137. About letters of Shah Abbas to Jahangir by Qasim Beg see: N. Falsafi, 1961, Vol. IV, pp. 302-3.

138. *A.A.A.* 1334/1955, p. 51.

139. Darvish Beg died at Shiraz and Muhammadi Beg was appointed in his place. It written as Muhammad Beg in : *Islamic Culture*, 1934, p. 659.

140. *A.A..A*, 1334/1955, p. 951; Sayyid Muhammad Reza Naqvi (in his article, *Shah Abbas and the conflict-between Jahangir and the Deccan States* in : Medieval India I., A miscellany Vol. I, A.M.U. 1969, p. 272) has quoted from *Alam Ara Abbasi* (the other copy, 1314/1897, p. 612 about envoys of Bijapur, Golkonda and Ahmadnagar, but he was not written who accompanied them from to Deccan. CF. *Alam Ara Abbasi*, 1334/1955, p. 951.

141. *A.A.A., ibid.*, 1334/1955, p. 964.

142. *A.A.A.*, 1314/1935, p. 612.

143. S.M.R.Naqvi. *Shah Abbas and the conflict between Jahangir and the Decean states,* in: 'Medieval India', I., A Miscellany Vol. I, A.M.U., 1969, p. 276.

144. R.Islam, 1970, p. 96 quoted from : *A.A.A,* 1314/1935, p.612 and Muhammad Yusuf Walih, *Khuld-i-Barin,* Cambridge University, G. 14(19); and B.M. or, 3481, IV, F-4136, claim this credit in the account of the year 1022, while the Mughal campaign continued for another four years.

145. R. Islam, 1970, p. 96.

146. A. Rahim; Mughala relations with Persia' in: *Islamic Culture;* 1935, Vol. 9, p.113.

147. About correspondence between Prince Shahjahan and Shah Abbas see: *Majmua,* Majlis Library: Tehran, catalogue VIII, MS, NO. 2665, ff (P), 444-45, and N. Falsafi, IV, pp. 110-11.

148. For letter see: R. Islam, 1979, p. 214.

149. B. Prasad Saksena, 1932, p. 211, quoted from *Jamaiul-Morasilat*, F.229, Qazvini, FF.1766-77.

150. *A.A.A.*, 1334/1955; p. 1077.

151. *Favayidul-Safaviya*; 1988, p.48, see also: Wali Quli Shamlu, *Qisasul-Khaqani,* ed., Sayyid Hasan Sadat Nasiri, Tehran 1371/1992, p. 208.
152. Kambu Lahori, Muhammad Salih, *Amal-i-Salih,* Bib. Indica, Calcutta, 1912-39, Vol. I, pp. 333, 335.
153. For letter see: Dh.Thabitiyan, 1964, pp. 325-32 and see: Lahori, Vol. I, pp. 282-86.
154. A. Rahim, 'Mughal relations with Persia' in: *Islamic Culture*; 1935, p.114.
155. *Amal-i-Salih*, Vol. I, p. 492.
156. About letters see: R. Islam, 1979, Part. I, pp. 239-42.
157. For details see; B. Prasad Saksena, 1933, pp. 212-13, quoted from, Lahori, Vol. I, p. 441 and also see: Qazvini, ff. 249-50.
158. R.Islam, 1970, p.99.
159. *Amal-i-Salih,* Vol. I, p.550; Lahori, Vol. I, pp. 477-86.
160. About latter see: Dh.Thabitiyan, 1964, pp. 222-35, see also: *Majmua,* Tehran University, Central Library, MS, No. 2591, p. 231.
161. For Afzal Khan see: Lahori, Vol. I, p. 478.
162. B. Prasad Saksena, 1932, p. 214 and also see: A.Rahim, Mughal relations with Persian in: *Islamic Culture*, 1935, pp. 115-16.
163. Khafi Khan, *Muntakhab-ul-Albab*, Karachi, Vol. II, pp.76-80 and also see. Khuld-i-Barin, ff, 90 and 107.
164. For urgent mission of Yadgar Beg to India, see: Wali Quli Shamlu, 137 1992, p. 241.
165. R.Islam, 1970, p.1101 quoted from Khuld Barin, Vol. V, ff. 649.
166. R.Islam, *op.cit,* quoted from Lahori; Vol. II, p. 49.
167. *Amal-i-salihil*, Lahore, 1967, Vol. I, pp. 457-58, See : *Favyidul-Safaviya* 1988,
168. For letter See: Dh. Thabitiyan, 1964, pp. 344-46.
169. B.P. Saksena, 1932, p. 213.
170. Wali-Quli Khan Shamlu, 1371/1992, pp. 241-42.
171. Lahori, II, p. 23.
172. R. Islam, 1970, p. 103.
173. For details see: W.Q. Shamlu, 1371/1992, pp.242-50 also see: B.P. Saksena 1932, pp. 216-19; see: *Islamic Culture*; 1935, pp.117-119; see: R Burn, 1963, Vol. IV, p. 19 See also : H.K Shamlu, *Munshaat Hasan Khan Shamlu,* edited by Riazul Islam, Karachi, 1971, pp. 1-2.
174. Lahori, Vol. II, pp. 24-25, See; *Amal-i-Salih*, Vol. II, pp. 272-76.
175. A.L. Srivastava, 1989, p. 305
176. *Amal-i-Salih,* Vol. II, p. 304.

177. *Ibid.*
178. *Favayidul-Safaviya,* 1988, pp. 58-59.
179. R.Islam, 1970, p. 105; Quoted from Khafi Khan, Vol. I, pp. 589-91 *Khuld Barin*, Vol. V, ff. 78a-80. English Factories, 1642 - 5, p. 83. Safi died there (at Kashan) unworthily, whilst drinking excessively and other ryots hastened his end.
180. See; M.Athar Ali : Objectives behind the Balkh and Badakhshan Expeditions; *PIHC.*
181. For details on the subject of Mughal invasion of Turan see: B.P. Saksena, 1932. pp. 189-91; Lahori, Vol. II, pp. 435-56
182. W.Q. Shamlu, 1371/1992, pp. 266-7 and also see: *Favayidul-Safaviya*, 1367/1988, pp. 61-62.
183. The author of *Amal-i-Salih* has written; 1645, Vol. II, p. 389. About envoy of Jan Nisar Khan to Iran see: *Favayidul-Safaviya*, 1367/1988, p. 64.
184. For comment of letter see: R. Islam, 1979, Part I, pp. 291-92.
185. See: *Favayidul-Safaviya*, 1367/1988, p. 69.
186. *Amal-i-Salih*, Vol. II, p. 415.
187. V.Q. Shamlu, 1371/1992, p. 305.
188. For comment of letter see : Muhammand Salih, *Majmua-i-Makatibt-i-Mukhtalifa;* Majlis Library, Tehran, Ms, 2247 Cat-X, 3349, p. 423-25.
189. R. Islam, 1970, p. III.
190. *Amal-i-Salih,* 1939, p. 66.
191. M.T. Wahid Qazvini, *Abbas Nama*, edit. Ibrahim Dhakhan, Arak, 1329/1950, p. 97.
192. Ibid, pp. 98-102 also see: *Favayidul-Safaviya,* 1988, p. 65; W.Q. Shamlu, *Ibid*, pp. 313, 318-19; see also *Amal-i-Salih,* 1939, p. 66; For comment of letter see: Dh: Thabitiyan, 1964; pp. 347-52.
193. B.P. Saksena, 1932, p. 224 quoted from Waris, pp. 411-13.
194. Waris, *op. cit,* p. 912.
195. For conquest of Bust by Shah Abbas see: W.Q. Shamlu, p. 345, 352-9.
196. For Shah Abbas's *raqam* to Daulat Khan see: *Abbas Nama,* 1329/1950. pp. 119-24.
197. The campaign has been described in great detail by the Safavid sources: *Abbas Nama;* 1950, pp. 92-124; W.Q. Shamlu, 1371/1992, pp. 249 - 352 In India sources see: *Amal-i-Salih;* Vol. III, pp. 70-81 M.H. Kafi Khan, Vol. I, pp. 688-90; B.P. Saksena, 1932, pp. 223-27.
198. For details about letter of Shah Abbas II to Shahjahan by Shah Verdi

Beg see: W.Q. Shamlu , 1992, pp. 418-420 and also see: *Abbas Nama*, 1950, pp. 125-127; According to Khafi Khan (I, p. 693) the present letter was not accepted at the Mughal court for Shah Verdi Beg's mission see: Kambu III, p. 99.

199. See: *Abbas Nama*, 1950, p. 129 also for his letter see: Dh. Thabitiyan, 1964, pp. 347-52 for his arrival to Shahjahan's court see: *Amal-i-Salih*, Vol. III, p. 66 for his dismissal see: *Ibid*, p. 94.

200. For details about three campaigns between Iran and India for Qandahar in this period see: W.Q. Shamlu. pp. 345-47, 372-76, 435-47; see also: *Favayidul-Safaviya*. pp. 65-79, also see; *Abbas Nama*, 1950, pp.132 -38, 150-52, 162-67 sources : *Amal-i-Salih*, III, pp. 70-92, Khafi Khan, I, pp. 690-700, 708-311, S.R. Raychoudhary, *op.cit*, pp. 227-239. A.L Srivastava, 1989; pp: 309-311, S.C. Raychoudhary, 1988, pp. 159-160 See also, M. Singh, 1978, pp. 313-14.

201. *Amal-i-Salih*, Vol. III, pp. 93-94.

202. *Ibid.*

203. For the letter to Shah Abbas I carred by Khairat Khan see; R. Islam, 1979, Part II, p. 148, also see; *Favayidul-Safaviya*, 1988, p. 53.

204. R.Islam, 1970, p.116.

205. R. Islam, *op.cit.*, 1970, p.116, quoted from Lahori, I, II, 2, 8; see also; *Amal-i-Salih*, Vol. II, pp.1-2.

206. *Amal-i-Salih*, Vol. II, pp. 148-50; Lahori; I, II, pp. 130-33 and also see : Abdul Majeed Siddiqui, *History of Golkonda*, Hyderabad Deccan, 1956, pp. 159-61.

207. Dh. Thabitiyan, 1964, pp. 344-46.

208. R. Islam, 1970, p.118 quoted from *Khuld-i-Barin*, Vol. V, p. 63b.

209. R. Islam, *op.cit.*, and also see : R. Islam, 1979, Part II, p. 154.

210. *Favayidul-Safaviya*, 1367/1988, p. 53.

211 . For letters see; *Majmua*, Tehran University Central Library, MS. 2592, p. 112 and also see; Muhammad Salih, *Majmua-i-Makatibt-i-Mukhtalifa*, Majlis Library, Cat-X-MS 3349, pp.377-78.

212. Mir Jumla's letter to the Persian *Wazir*, *Khalifa Sultan;* For a summarized translation of this letter, see, *Journal of Bihar and Orissa Research Society*, Vol. XXVIII, Part III, June 1942, pp. 193-6, trans. by Jagdish Narayan Sarkar.

213. R. Islam, 1970, pp. 118-19, quoted from English Factories, 1651-4, p. 73.

214. R. Islam, 1970, p. 119.

A Sketch Map
of
STATES IN MODERN IRAN

LEGEND

City Centres

—— International Boundary

– – – State Boundary

—— Water Bodies

Map No. 3

A Sketch Map of Iranian Cities Associated with the Migrants

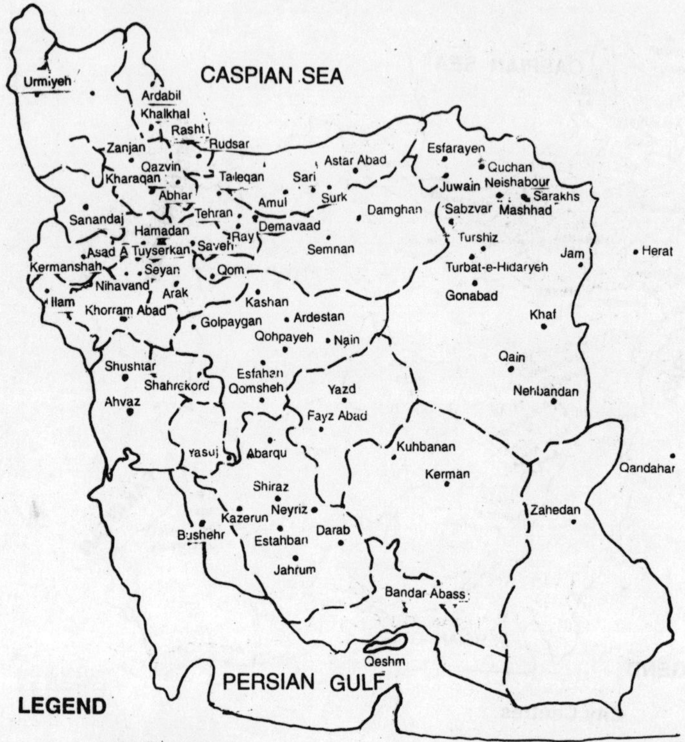

LEGEND

City Centres

International Boundary

State Boundary

Water Bodies

Map No. 4

2

Iranians in Mughal Politics and Administration

Many Iranis occupied positions of prominence in Mughal politics and administration. Mughal historiography has considered at some length the issue of the power of this group in relation to others like the Turanis, Rajputs and Indian Muslims. In this chapter we try to identify the Iranians who had enjoyed some status in Iran before their departure for India. We will also see how they maintained their relations/ties with their homelands. As stated earlier, we will first give brief description of some of the noted Iranians, then subsequent to a tabulated information, the chapter will attempt at some biographical details, arranged according to the regions of Iran they came from. Among such Iranians who held some position of significance in their homelands two groups are to be particularly noted. In the first, there were many Iranians coming directly from Iran in search of employment in administration, since they were forced to leave their own country due to the growing political instability and Uzbek pressure. Quite a few of them belonged to the reputed and eminent families whose members had been in the service of Safavid rulers holding important positions, while some others were themselves in possession of high offices in Iran. In addition to these two groups a number of important Iranian immigrants who had been serving in the Deccan kingdoms also joined the Mughal service during the period.

As regards the persons of rank, our list shows that many of the immigrants or their ancestors held important offices under their previous masters too in Iran or in the Deccan, before joining the Mughal service. To show this we have prepared tables, with information and identification of people, their jobs and position in Iran and in India.

As regards the Iranian territories these immigrants came from out of 54 mentioned in our sources, 5 came from regions in the west and north-west such as Tabriz and Lurestan while most of them (26) belonged to central regions such as Qazwin, Kashan, Tehran and Esfahan. A very limited number (2) came from the southern regions; 7 people came from regions in the east and north-east such as Mashhad and Turbat, while about hometowns of the remaining fourteen our sources are unclear.

Among the 5 people who came from regions in the west and north-west, Mustafa Turkman migrated to India during Akbar's reign because he lost favour with the Safavid Shah. At that time Shah Abbas decided to break the Turkman leader's monopoly of military power by creating a new army. The policy as a result reduced the number of powerful Qizilbash provincial governors who acted like petty princes in the areas under their jurisdiction and enhanced the prestige of the Ghulams. Therefore, many tribal people left for India. Probably Mahmud Beg Turkman also left Iran under similar circumstances. The remaining three of these five arrived in India during Shahjahan's period in the company of their fathers.

Among the 26 Iranis who came from central regions, 13 came during Akbar's reign, 8 in the reign of Jahangir and 5 during the Shah Jahan's reign. The most important of them was Naqib Khan Qazwini who hailed from the family of the Saifi Sayyids of Qazwin. His father Abdul Latif was the first person known to have come to India because of religious persecution in Iran. He was known in Iran as a noted member of the Sunni community. Abdul Latif's father Mir Yahya Saifi was a famous philosopher and theologian of Iran.[1] He enjoyed the patronage of Shah Tahmasp who used to call him Yahya Masum. He was so favourably treated by the Shah that his enemies, envious of his good fortunes, reported to the Shah that Mir Yahya and his son Abdul Latif were the leading members of the Sunni sect. Thereupon, Shah Tahmasp who was then on the borders of Azarbaijan ordered Mir Yahya and his son Abdul Latif to be imprisoned. Alau'd-daula Qazwini, the second son of Mir Yahya being too old remained there but Abdul Latif along with his son Khwaja Ghiyas-ud-din fled to Gilan and then at the invitation of Humayun proceeded to India. However, he reached Delhi after the death of Humayun.[2] Mir Yahya was imprisoned in Esfahan where he died at the age of seventy after a year and nine months in prison in 1555.[3]

After the arrival of Mir Abdul Latif and Ghiyas-ud-din Naqib Khan other members of the family such as Shah Ghazi Khan, a cousin of Ghiyas-ud-din Naqib Khan, Ala-ud-daula Qazwini and Qazi Isa who had served as Qazi of Iran for a very long period came to India and were taken in service. The family of Abdul Latif was very highly respected by the Mughal Emperor. Fahmi Qazwini also migrated to India under similar circumstances.

In order to avoid punishments and persecutions at the hand of the court a large number of leading nobles of the Safavid empire migrated to India. Sultan Afshar, Ali Mardan Khan and his sons came to India under such circumstances. Amongst the direct Iranian immigrants the best known was Ali Mardan Khan Zig, a Kurd by origin. His father Ganj Ali Khan Zig was a confidential officer of Shah Abbas I who called him Arjumand Babai and appointed him governor of Kerman and Qandahar. After his father's death Ali Mardan Khan was appointed governor of Qandahar and was called Babai Sani by the Shah.[4] When he was charged with serious offences by Shah Safi he made over the fort of Qandahar to Shahjahan in 1638 and came to India where he was awarded the rank of 6000/6000 and the titles of *Amir-ul-Umara* and *Yar-i-Wafadar.*[5] He was also appointed *subadar* of Kashmir and subsequently of Lahore and Kabul; his rank was raised to 7000 *zat* with 7000 *sawar.*[6]

Among those immigrants who came from the Deccan to Mughal court, was Yehya Qomi. Mir Abdur-Razzaq Mamuri and Rahmat Khan Kashani left Iran at the instance of relatives already settled in India. The author of *Maasir-ul-Umara* states that Abdur-Razzaq was a true Sayyid of Mamurabad village in the holy locality of Najaf. The translator of the *Maasir-ul-Umara* says that the place of origin of the Ma'muris was a place called Ma'mura near Kabul.[8] No place called Ma'murabad is mentioned in *Haft Iqlim* or the *Rauzat-us-Safa*, a history of Iran, nor is it mentioned in Le Strong. The lands of the Eastern Caliphate, Mamuri—a village in the city of Khurram Shahr and a village of the same name in the city of Neishabour are mentioned in *Farhang-i-Jughrafiya-i-Iran,* vols: 689 respectively.[9] The modern author of the *The Caravan of India* says, Mir Abdur Razzaq and Mir Abdul Karim belonged to Sadat Mamuri family of Esfahan,[10] and this is a more reasonable ascription of their native place. The *Maasir-ul-Umara* mentions that his ancestors had already migrated to India.[11] Mir Abdur Razzaq came to India in the later half of Akbar's reign and he was appointed as *Bakhshi* of *Suba* Bihar.[12] In 1592, he was appointed as *Bakhshi* of Gujarat.[13] Jahangir granted him the title of Muzaffar

Khan.[14] During the last days of Jahangir's reign he was appointed *Subadar* of Malwa.[15]

Mulla Shafia-i-Yazdi, who was given the title of Danishmand Khan, was a learned scholar of Iran. When he came to the notice of Shahjahan, he was awarded the rank of 1000 *zat* and 100 *sawar*[16], and subsequently promoted to 3000 *zat* and 800 *sawar.*[17] He is known to us also through Bernier, who was employed by him during his sojourn at Delhi, and from whom he wished to learn European sciences.[18]

In addition to these specific types of immigrants, a large number of Iranis came to India during the 17th century to try their luck or as adventurers in search of better opportunities. They knew that the Mughal court was open to talented people, where by merit they might be able to achieve distinct position and high *mansabs* in the Central *Government.* The most important of them were Khwaja Ghiyas Itimad-ud-daula Tehrani and Asaf Khan Tehrani. Khwaja Ghiyas was the son of Khwaja Muhammad Sharif who served as Chief Minister of Tatar Khan, son of Muhammad Khan Sharaf-ud-din Ughlu Taklu the *Beglar Begi* of Khurasan and after his death under Qazaq Khan. After Qazaq khan's death Shah Tahmasp first made him *wazir* of Yazd and after that *wazir* of Esfahan. He had two brothers; *Khwaja* Ahmad was Kalantar of Ray and also incharge of *Khalissa* and Khwajgi Khwaja, a master of eloquence. His two sons were Aqa Mulla Tahir and Ghiyas Beg.[19] Muhammad Sharif died in 1576 and after his death Ghiyas Beg as a result of unfortunate circumstances started for India as a fugitive along with his two sons and a daughter. His coming to India may be seen in the context of the death of his father followed by the change of regime which might have adversely affected the fortunes of the family.[20]

Mirza Abul-Hasan (Asaf Khan) was the son of Itimad-ud-daula and elder brother of Nur Jahan. He came to India in the company of his father. At the time of the political crisis in 1627 after the death of Jahangir, Asaf Khan played a very important role in winning the succession for Shahjahan.[21] After his accession Shahjahan promoted Asaf Khan to the highest rank of 9000 *zat* and 9000 *sawar*, and confirmed him in the post of *wakil*[22] which he held till his death in 1641. It is significant to note that after the death of Asaf Khan, Shahjahan did not fill the post of *wakil.*[23]

Two people came from the southern region; Mahabat Khan and Afzal Khan Shirazi. Interesting information on the personal life of Mahabat Khan is available both in the *Maasir-ul-Umara*[24] and the *Zakhira-t-ul-khawanin.*[25] Mahabat Khan's father Ghayur Beg was a Razavi Sayyid of Shiraz. He came to Kabul in his youth and entered Mirza Hakim's service. After the death of that prince, Ghayur Beg came to India and joined Akbar's service, but he could not rise to a high position and apparently failed to get a *mansab*. His son Zaman Beg during the Jahangir's reign was appointed governor of Kabul, Ajmer, Deccan and Malwa. He was also promoted to the rank of 6000 *zat* and 5000 *sawar*. After the accession of Shahjahan to throne, he was granted the title of Khan-i-Khanan, *sipahsalar*, and the rank of 7000 *zat* and 7000 *sawar.*[26] Mulla Shukr Ullah Shirazi, a learned man of Shiraz intended to migrate to the Deccan and reached Surat. There he was entertained by Abdur Rahim Khan-i-Khanan who himself was a good scholar and patron of learning. He took the Mulla into his service. Later on Mulla Shukr Ullah was appointed *Arz-i-Mukarrar* by Jahangir.[27]

Among the 7 people who came from the east and north-east regions, Ali Turkman Khurasani, Saf Shikan Khan and Khwaja Abul Hasan Turbati migrated during Akbar's reign and the other 4 people came during the reign of Jahangir. Ali Turkman Khurasani left Iran because creation of a new military corps of the Ghulam's Qullars and reduced the power of Qizilbash and Turkman tribes. Saf Shikan Khan, Islam Khan Mashhadi[28] and their two sons migrated in search of better opportunities, while the context of the migration of the other two is unclear.

Among the 14 people who came from the regions which we could not identify six left Iran during Akbar's reign, 5 persons came during the reign of Jahangir and the other 3 came during Shahjahan's time.[29] Khwaja Beg Mirza Safavi and Imam Quli Beg Shamlu migrated to India owing to losing royal favour and dissatisfaction with their position in Iran. The circumstances of Abdur Rahim Farahani's visit is not clear, but Yadgar Ali Sultan[30] came as an ambassador of Shah Abbas I to Jahangir. Sultan Nazr and Saif Khan Mirza Safi left Iran to visit their relatives who were already settled in India. Muhammad Taqi came with the retinue of Shah Safi's ambassador Muhammad Ali. In addition some Iranians moved in search of employment in administration.

A very interesting case of immigration was that of the Mirzas of

Qandahar; Mirza Rustam and Mirza Muzaffar Husain Safavi, great grandsons of Shah Ismail of Persia.[31] Mirza Rustam and Muzaffar Husain held Zamindawar and Qandahar respectively on behalf of Shah Muhammad Khudabanda. But Rustam Mirza was dissatisfied with the resources of Zamindawar. He made several attempts on Qandahar. Having failed to conquer Qandahar he inverted and conquered Farah and Sistan. But soon afterwards he was defeated and expelled from Zamindawar by Jalaludin, son of Malik Mahmud, ruler of Sistan. Therefore, having no place to fall upon in Qandahar he wrote friendly letters to Sharif Khan, the Mughal governor of Ghaznin and expressed his wish to join Akbar's service. In 1593 he came to the court along with his brother Sanjar Mirza, four sons and four hundred Turkmans. Every one of them was exalted with princely favours. He was given the *mansab* of 5000, *suba* of Multan and assigned many *parganas* in Baluchistan which was larger than Qandahar.[32]

After the departure of Mirza Rustam, Mirza Muzaffar could not maintain his position under the pressure of internal strife, Uzbek control of roads and the approaching imperial army from India. He also decided to migrate to India. Abdullah Khan Uzbek wrote him letters to the effect that enmity between the Irani and Turani was of long standing, that he should not trust Akbar and on no account hand over his hereditary country to the Mughals. But the Mirza regarded these letters merely as a clever diplomacy. In 1595 with his four sons and 1000 Qizilbash soldiers he joined Akbar's court. He was addressed by the emperor as *Farzand* and granted the *mansab* of 5000 and assigned Sambal as *jagir*.[33]

Table 2.1
IRANIANS IN MUGHAL POLITICS AND ADMINISTRATION

Name of migrants	Place of birth	Provinces	Regions	Period of migration	Reasons and Contexts of migration	Position in Iran	Position in India	Place of death
Mustafa Turkman	-	Azarbaijan Gharbi	West and North-West	Akbar (1595)	Fear from Shah Abbas I	Government service	1500 rank	India
Mahmud Beg Turkman	-	Lorestan	West and North-West	Jahangir (1606)	Unclear	In the service of Astarabad governor	*Diwan* of Qandahar and governor of Bangash	Unclear
Muklis Husain Tabrizi	Tabriz	Azarbaijan Sharqi	West and North-West	Shah Jahan (1636)	In company of relatives	—	*Wazir* of Bijapur	Unclear
Banda Reza Tabriz	Tabriz	Azarbaijan Sharqi	West and North-West	Shahjahan	In company of relatives	—	*Wazir* of Qutb	Unclear
Kalib Ali Tabrizi	Tabriz	Azarbaijan Sharqi	West and North-West	Shahjahan	In search of employment	—	Manasabdar of Shah-jahan	Unclear
Sultan-i-Afshar	Kerman	Kerman	Central Plateau	Akbar	losing royal favour	His relatives were in the service of Safavids court	*Jagir* of Khandis and Berar	Unclear
Itimad-ud-daula Tehrani	Tehran	Tehran	Central plateau	Akbar 1590	In search of fortune and losing royal favour	High position in Safavid's court	1000 rank and *Diwan Buyutat* in Akbar's reign's *walkil-i-kul-*prime minister and 7000 *zat* and 5000 *sawar* in Jahangir's period	Agra 1620

Table Contd...

Asaf Khan Tehrani	Tehran	Tehran	Central Plateau	Akbar 1590	In company of his father in search of better opportunities	His ancestors had high position in Safavid's court	High *mansab* in Mughal court, such as; governor of Bengal, Punjab, Post of *wakil* and rank of 7000 *zat* and 7000 *sawar*	Lahore 1641
Itiqad Khan Mirza Shapur	Tehran	Tehran	Central Plateau	Akbar 1590	In company of his father in search of better opportunities	His ancestors had high position in Safavid's court	Governor of Kashmir, rank of 5000 *zat* and *sawar* in Jahangir period. Governor of Delhi. *Subadar* of Bihar in Shah-jahan's period.	Bihar 1650
Sadiq Khan Mir Bakhshi	Tehran	Tehran	Central Plateau	In later days of Akbar	In company of his father in search of better opportunities	His ancestor had high position in Safavid's court	Governor of Punjab. Rank of 1000 *zat*, 500 *sawar* in Jahangir's reign. *Bakhshi* and rank of 4000 *zat* at and 4000 *sawar* in Shahjahan's Period	India 1632
Jafar Khan Umdat-ul-Mulk	Tehran	Tehran	Central Plateau	In later days of Akbar	In company of his father in search of better opportunities	His ancestor had high position in Safavid's court	Governor of Punjab and Malwa, rank of 6000 *zat* and 6000 *sawar*	Shah Jahanabad 1670
Mirza Zain-ul-Abidn Qazwini	Qazwin	Qazwin	Central Plateau	Akbar 1577	In company of his father	His ancestor had high position in Safavid's court	Rank of 1500 *zat*, 1500 *sawar* in jahangir's reign	India second year of Shah-jahan's reign

Table Contd...

Table Contd...

Naqib Qazwini	Qazwin	Qazwini	Central Plateau	Akbar	Religious persecution	His ancestor had high position in Safavid's court	Reader of Akbar rank of 1500 *zat* in Jahangir's reign	Ajmer 1614
Adul-Latif Qazwini	Qazwin	Qazwin	Central Plateau	Akbar	Religious persecution	Son of Naqib Qazwini	High position in Mughal court	India
Kaukab	Qazwin	Qazwin	Central plateau	Akbar	Religious persecution	His ancestor had high position in Safavid's court	Army service	India
Muhammad salih	Qazwin	Qazwin	Central plateau	Akbar 1577	Unclear	—	Rank of 1000 *zat* and 800 *sawar*	India
Muqim	Qazwin	Qazwin	Central plateau	Akbar 1577	Unclear	—	Rank of 500 *zat* and 100 *sawar*	India
Mir Abdur-Razzaq Mamuri Esfahani	Esfahan	Esfahan	Central plateau	In later days of Akbar	To visit his relatives	Sadat family of Esfahan	*Bakhshi* of Bihar high *mansab* in Malwa	India
Abdul Qadir Basinani	Esfahan	Esfahan	Central plateau	1603	In search of better his prospects	—	Chancellorship of some lands by Jahangir	Ajmer 1616
Salih Azadani	Azadan	Esfahan	Central plateau	1611	Dissatisfaction of his life	Calligraphist	*Diwan* of Surat	India
Nur-ud-din-Quli Esfahani	Esfahan	Esfahan	Central plateau	Jahangir	Unclear	—	*Kotwal* of Agra during Jahangir's reign	India

Table Contd...

Table Contd...

Mulla Qazwini, Iradat Khan	Qazwin	Qazwin	Central plateau	Jahangir	In search of better his prospects	—	Rank of 1500 *zat* and 600 *sawar* and *Mir Saman*	India
Fahimi Qazwini	Qazwin	Qazwin	Central plateau	Jahangir	Religious persecution	—	Administrator	Unclear
Muhammad Baqir Savoji (Azam Khan)	Saveh	Markazi	Central plateau	Jahangir	In search of better opportunities	Noble Sayyid of Saveh	*Faujdar* of Sialkot, Gujarat and Punjab, governor of Kashmir and different states, rank of 6000 *zat* and 6000 *sawar*	Jaunpur 1649
Ahmad Razi	Ray	Tehran	Central plateau	Jahangir	In search of better opportunities	Treasurer of Shah Abbass' Nawwab	*Diwan* of Patna	Agra 1615
Yehya Qomi	Qom	Qom	Central plateau	Jahangir	Unclear	Sadat family of Qom	*Bakhshi* of Orissa and Kabul	India
Ali Mardan Khan	Kerman	Kerman	Central plateau	Shahjahan (1638)	Fear from Shah Safi and in search of better his prospects	Noble's family; governor of Qandahar	*Amir-ul-Umara Yar-i-Wafadar*, governor of Kashmir, Kabul and etc. rank of 7000 *zat* and 7000 *sawar*.	India
Ibrahim Khan	Kerman	Kerman	Central plateau	Shah jahan (1638)	In company of his father	Son of Ali Mardan Khan	Rank of 4000 *zat* and 3000 *sawar* in Shah Jahan reign	Lahore 1709
Muhammad Ali Beg	Esfahan	Esfahan	Central plateau	Shahjahan	Ambassador	High position in Shah Safi, court	Ambassador	Iran

Table Contd...

Table Contd...

Rahmat Khan Kashani	Khashan	Esfahan	Central plateau	Shahjahan	Invitation of his relatives	Noble family of Kashan	Rank of 2000 *zat* with 300 *sawar*, *diwan* and superintendent of the *Karkirqana* of Ahmadabad	India
Danishmand Khan	Yazd	Yazd	Central plateau	Shahjahan 1650	Notice of Shah Jahan and trade	Scholar and scientist	Rank of 3000 *zat* with 800 *sawar*; *Mir Bakhshi*	India 1670
Mahabat Khan	Shiraz	Shiraz	South	Akbar	In company of his father in search of better opportunities	Razavi Sayyid of Shiraz	Governor of Kabul, rank of 6000 *zat* with 5000 *sawar* in the reign of Jahangir; governor of Ajmer, Deccan and Maiwa, rank of 7000 *zat* with 7000 *sawar* during Shahjahan's reign	India 1634
Afzal Khan Mulla Shukr Ullah	Shiraz	Shiraz	South	Jahangir	In search of better opportunities	Scientist	*Khan-i-Saman* (steward) in Jahangir's period, *Mir Saman* and rank of 7000 *zat* in the reign of Shah-jahan	Lahore 1639
Ali Turkman Khorasani	-	Khorasan	East and North-East	Akbar 1592 C.A.	Fear and displeasure from Shah Abbas 1	In the service of Shah Abbas I	Rank of 700 *zat* in 1615	Burhanpur 1626
Saf Shikan Khan Mirza Lashkari	Mashhad	Khorasan	East and North-East	Akbar	In company of his father in search of better opportunities	Razavi Sayyid of Mashhad	Jagir of Bihar, governor of Kashmir, rank of 15k00 *zat* with 700 *sawar* in the reign of Jahangir; rank of 2500 *zat* with 2000 *sawar* during Shah Jahan's reign	Lahore 1645

Table Contd...

Table Contd...

Khwaja Abdul Hasan Turbati	Turbat	Khorasan	East and North-East	Akbar,	Unclear	--	Rank of 5000 *zat* with Jahangir's reign; rank of 6000 *zat* with 6000 *sawar* in the reign of Shahjahan	India
Islam Khan Mashhadi	Mashhad	Khorasan	East and North-East	Jahangir	In search of better opportunities	--	Governor of various states of India, wakil and Mir *Bakhshi*, rank of 7000 *zat* with 7000 *sawar*	Aurangabad 1647
Abdur Rahim Khan	Mashhad	Khorasan	East and North-East	Jahangir	In company of his father in search of fortune	Son of Islam Khan	Superintendent of the pages (*Darogha-i-Khwassan*)	India 1681
Safi Khan	Mashhad	Khorasan	East and North-East	Jahangir	In company of his father in search of fortune	Son of Islam Khan	Governor of Deccan, rank of 5000 *zat* with 6000 *sawar*	India
Taqi Khurasani	—	Khorasan	East and North-East	Jahangir C 1590	Unclear	--	*Subadar* of Malwa	Unclear
Khwaja Beg Mirza Safavi	Unclear	Unclear	Unclear	Akbar	Losing royal favour	Shah Tahmasp's relatives	Governor of Ahmadnagar and rank of 5000 *zat* in the reign of Jahangir	Ahmadnagar 1617
Mirza Rustam Safavi	Unclear	Unclear	Unclear	Akbar 1593	Uzbek pressure dissatisfaction with the resources on Zamindawar	Great grand son of Shah Ismail; Governor of Zamindawar	Rank of 5000 *zat* with 1500 *sawar* subadar of Multan and governor of Thatta	Agra 1641

Table Contd...

Table Contd...

Murad Safavi (Itifat Khan)	Unclear	Unclear	Unclear	Akbar 1593	In company of his father, Uzbek pressure	Son of Mirza Rustam Safavi	Rank of 2000 *zat* with 800 *sawar*	India
Hasan Safavi	Unclear	Unclear	Unclear	Akbar 1593	In company of his father, Uzbek pressure	Son of Mirza Rustam Safavi	Rank of 1500 *zat* with 700 *sawar* during Jahangir's period; rank of 3000 *zat* with 3000 *sawar* in the reign of Shahjahan	India 1649
Mirza Muzaffar Husain Safavi	Unclear	Unclear	Unclear	Akbar 1593	Uzbek pressure and internal strife	Grandson of Shah Ismail; governor of Qandahar	Rank of 5000 *zat* with 1400 *sawar*, title of *Farzand* by Jahangir	India
Haidar Safavi	Unclear	Unclear	Unclear	Akbar 1593	In company of his father because of Uzbek pressure	Son of Mirza Muzaffdar Husain Safavi	Rank of 500 *zat* with 150 *sawar* in the reign of with 2000 *sawar* during Shahjahan's reign	India
Yadgar Ali Sultan	Unclear	Unclear	Unclear	Jahangir 1018	Ambassador	Administrator of Safavid's kings	As a ambassador	Iran
Saif Khan Mirza Safi	Unclear	Unclear	Unclear	Jahangir	To visit relatives	—	Governor and *diwan* of *Gujarat* rank of 3000 *zat* with 2000 *sawar* in the reign of Jahangir; rank of 4000 *zat* with 4000 *sawar*. governor of Bihar and various states during ShahJahan's reign	Bengal 1639

Table Contd...

Table Contd...

Sultan Nazar	Unclear	Unclear	Unclear	Jahangir	To visit relatives	—	*Bakhshi* and *Waqanavis* of Agra in the reign of Jahangir; rank of 1000 *zat* during Shahjahan's period	India
Abdur Rahim Farahani	Unclear	Unclear	Unclear	Jahangir	Unclear	Wizarat of Kashan	Mansab of Yuzbashi (centurion) and rank of 20 *sawar*	Bengal 1614
Imam Quli Beg Shamlu	Unclear	Unclear	Unclear	Jahangir	Dissatisfaction of his position	Turkman *Yuzbashi* commander of one hundred soldiers	*Amir* and noble of Jahangir's court; rank, *Khilat*, horse and *Inam* from Shahjahan, *Qiladar* of Balaghat	Bengal
Muhammad Taqi	Unclear	Unclear	Unclear	Shahjahan 1630	In company of Muhammad Ali, Shah Safi's ambassador	*Tavildar of tansuqat* (cashier of goods)	—	—
Aqil Khan Inayatullah	Unclear	Unclear	Unclear	Shahjahan	In company of his father to seek employment	—	Rank of 3000 *zat* with 1000 *sawar*, *Mir Saman Waqainavis*, *diwan* of *Buyutat*	India
Mirza Abdul Qasim	Unclear	Unclear	Unclear	Shahjahan	For employment	—	*Diwan* of Kashmir	Kashmir

Table Contd...

WEST AND NORTH-WEST

Mustafa Turkman

Mustafa Khan was the son of Suhrab Khalifa Mosului Turkman, one of the prominent leaders of Qazilbash. According to Baqi Nihavandi Mustafa was associated with Shah Abbas I from childhood until the age of twenty-seven. In the time of Suliman Khalifa's rule, who was Shah Abbas I's brother, Mustafa raised (hoisted) flag of government in some states of Iraq and Khurasan, specially in Gonabad, Tun and Tabas.

The witty people and poets entered in his service and praised him. After death of his brother in the war with Din Muhammad Uzbek in 999/1590, he escaped to Iraq and joined Shah Abbas I, but because of Shah's atrocities and oppression of the Turkman and Takllu tribes Mustafa Khan became apprehensive of his own fate, and finally fled to India in 1005/1596. In India he got access to Akbar through Abdur Rahim Khan-i-Khanan and received a *mansab* of 1500. Later he joined the retinue of prince Parviz during his Deccan campaigns in 1019/1610. Mustafa was also a poet.Several ghazals are ascribed to him. He also composed a *masnavi* about *Yusuf* and *Zolikha.*[34]

Mahmud Beg Turkman

Mahmud Beg belonged to Iranian Turkmen and Chehginian Oimaq. In Iran he was in attendance of Husain Khan Ziyad Oghli Qajar, who was the governor of Astarabad and occupied high position during 995/1586 to 1038/1628. He migrated to India and reached Qandahar in 1015/1606. The reasons of his emigration are unclear.In India he joined the service of Shah Beg Arghun[35] and then was appointed revenue officer (*Diwan*), of some lands. Mahmud, together with the poet, Wasli Shirazi, conducted negotiations with Allah-dad, son of *Jalal-ud-din,* the rebel leader of Raushanaiyah movement in the North-West Frontier Province. His success in conciliating Allah-aad pleased Jahangir. In return he got a raise in rank and was posted as the governor of the Bangash territory. On way from Ajmer to Lahore, the author of *Mai-Khana* accompanied Mahmud and impressed the nobleman by his polished behaviour. Trusting him as a worthy scholar, Mahmud gave his verses to Abdun-Nabi as he himself had no time for their arrangement and publication (1025/1616). Abdun-Nabi's house in Patna caught fire and the verses of Mahmud among his other belongings, were consumed by the flames.[36]

Mukhlis Husain Tabrizi

He was the son of Mulla Kalb Ali Tabrizi. He migrated to India during Shahjahan's reign in the company of his father. During the time of Qasim Khan Juwini, he was *Bakhshi* of Bengal for some time. Prince Aurangzeb dispatched him in the company of his brother Banda-Reza, to Bijapur as a *Hajib* (*wazir* of court) in 1046/1636.[37]

Banda Reza Tabrizi

He was the son of Mulla Kalb Ali and brother of Muklis Tabrizi. He came to India with his father in the reign of Shahjahan. Banda Reza was a *mansabdar* of Shahjahan. In 1046/1636 he was dispatched by prince Aurangzeb to Abdullah Qutb Shah as a *Hajib* (*wazir* of *Darbar*).[38]

Kalb Ali Tabrizi

Mulla Kalb Ali Tabrizi migrated to India during Shahjahan's reign to seek employment. He was one of Shahjahan's *mansabdars.*[39]

SOUTH-WEST

Sultan Afshar

His *Takhallus* was Mehdi Quli. He was the son of Esfandeyar Khan, and the nephew of Khalil Khan Afshar, who was the governor of Kohkiloyeh-va-Boyer Ahmad province. His ancestors and his relatives were in the service of Safavid kings. After the elimination of the important chiefs of the Afshar tribe by Shah Abbas, Mehdi Quli Sultan escaped to India. He joined prince Salim. When Abdur-Rahim Khan-i-Khanan went on campaign to Deccan, Mehdi Quli joined his retinue, with a *Jagir* in Khandesh and Berar. He was also granted high *mansabs*, but Mehdi Quli left the post and *mansab* and chosed a retired life as a *darvish.* He was a skilled musician and knew verification.[40]

CENTRAL PLATEAU

Itimad-ud-daula Jahangir-i-Tehrani

His real name was Mirza Ghiyas-ud-din Muhammad. In early European histories his name was often spelt Ayas, a corruption of Ghiyas, not of Ayaz.[41]

Ghiyas Beg's father was Khwaja Muhammad Sharif, who was a poet and wrote under the assumed name of Hijri. He was *wazir* to Tatar Sultan, son of Muhmmad Khan Sharaf-ud-din Ughlu Takllu, who held the office *Beglar Begi* of Khurasan.[42] After Tatar Sultan's death, the

Khwaja was continued in office by his son Qazaq Khan, and on Qazaq's death, he was made by Shah Tahmasp *wazir* of Yazd,[43] and after that *wazir* of Esfahan.[44] Khwaja Muhammad Sharif is said to have died in 1576. He had two brothers, Khwaja Mirza Ahmad and Khwajagi Khwaja.

The son of Khwaja Mirza Ahmad was the well-known Khwaja Amin Razi (*i.e.*, the town of Ray of which he was *Kalantar*, or magistrate), who travelled a good deal and composed the excellent work entitled *Haft Iqlim* in 1593. Khwajagi Khwaja had a son by the name of Khwaja Shapur, who was likewise a literary man.

Ghiyas Beg was married to the daughter of Mirza Ala-ud-daula, son of Agha Mulla.[45] After the death of his father, Ghiyas Beg decided to migrate, like many others to Hindustan in search of fortune. Ghiyas Beg left Persia for India, accompanied by his two sons Muhammad Sharif and Abdul-Hasan (the future Asaf Khan), his daughter and his pregnant wife.[46] He was plundered on the way, and had only two mules left, upon which the members of the family alternately rode. On his arrival at Qandahar, his wife gave birth to another daughter, who received the name of Mihr-un-Nisa (the son of women) a name which her future title Nur Jahan almost brought into oblivion. In their misfortune, they found a patron in Malik Masud, leader of the caravan, who is said to have been known to Akbar.[47] After his introduction at court in Fatehpur Sikri, Ghiyas Beg rose up to a command of 300 in 1595. He was also placed in charge of the important office of *diwan* of Kabul in the same year. Thus the year proved to be a very lucky one for him. His diligence and ability attracted the notice of the Emperor and he was promoted to a *mansab* of 1000 in course of time and appointed Diwan-i-Buyutat.[48] Towards the end of Akbar's region he was made chief treasurer of the empire. Thus a man who had been almost on the verge of destruction in an arid region where danger lurked at every step, found himself at the helm of affairs in a vast empire within the space of two decades. Ghiyas Beg achieved this splendid feat by his great ability and good fortune.[49]

When Jahangir became the emperor, in the beginning of the reign he gave Mirza Ghiyas Beg the title of Itimad-ud-daula, and made him jointly responsible for the *diwani* with Mirza Jan Beg *wazir-ul-mulk*. In the year 1016/1607 his son Muhammad Sharif foolishly joined others in a plot to deliver Sultan Khusrau from the prison. The plot was soon discovered, and the secrets of the conspiracy fully unravelled. Emperor Jahangir subjected the conspirator to capital punishment.[50] The Mirza was confined in the house of Diyanat Khan,[51] but was released on payment of a fine of two lacs of rupees.[52]

Nur Jahan was married to Jahangir in 1020/1611, Ghiyas, in consequence of the marriage, was made *Wakil-i-kul*, prime-minister, and a commander of 6000 *zat* and 3000 *sawar*. In 1615 the rank of 7000 *zat* and 5000 *sawar* was bestowed on him. He also received a flag and a drum, and was in the 10th year allowed to beat his drum at court, which was a rare privilege.[53] The series of promotions proves conclusively the contention of Dr. Beni Prasad. He would have risen to high office in any circumstance but since he became the emperor's father-in-law his ascent in the hierarchy was extraordinarily rapid.[54] In the 16th year, when Jahangir was on his way to Kashmir, Ghiyas fell ill. The royal couple were recalled from a visit to Kangra fort, and arrived in time to find him on the death bed. Pointing to the emperor, Nur Jahan asked her father whether he recognized him. In answer he quoted a verse from Anwari:

On ke nabinai Madarzad agar hazar shavad; Dar Jabin-e-Alam arayash bebinad mahtari;

"Should one born blind be here,
He would recognize his Majesty in the world-adoring brow."[55]

Ghiyas Beg died after a few hours. The *Tuzuk* (p.339) mentions the 17th Bahman, 1031 (Rabi I, 1031) as the day of his death and says that he died broken-hearted three months and twenty days after his wife, who had died on the 29th Mihr, 1030, i.e. 13th zi qada 1030/1620.[56] Itimad-ud-daula did not compose poetry, but he was a diligent student of the early poets. He was a gifted poet of elegant composition, and wrote in a bold and clear *shikasta* hand.

He also understood business, and was a good writer. He was a pleasant and even-tempered man, and did not cherish hatred even against his enemies. He was devoid of anger; chains, imprisonment, whippings and abuses were not known in his establishment. If anyone deserving capital punishment appeared before him as a supplicant or paid his respects to him for a week, he was pardoned. With all this, however, he was not self-indulgent. All his days were spent in looking into details and writing reports.[57]

Asaf Khan Tehrani

Mirza Abul-Hasan was the son of Itimad-ud-daula and elder brother of Nur Jahan Begum. He came to India during Akbar's time, in consequence of adverse circumstances in Iran and in search of fortune like many others.[58] He was accompanied by his father and family. After Nur Jahan was married to Jahangir, Abul-Hasan received the title of Itiqad Khan[59] and became the *Khan-i-Saman* (steward) in the 7th year of Jahangir, 1020/1611. His daughter Arjomand Banu Begum, is known as Mumtaz Mahal and was married to prince Khurram who was later called Shahjahan. In the 9th year he received the title of Asaf Khan[60] and had a series of promotions, until he obtained the rank of 6000 *zat* and 6000 *sawar.* At the time when relation between Jahangir and prince Shahjahan was strained, intriguers and evil-thinking persons suspected Asaf Khan of favouring the prince, and alienated the mind of the Begum from a brother who was the pillar of the empire:

Chon ghraz amad honar poshida shad; Sad hijab as del ba soye dida shod.

"When self-interest appears, wit goes into hiding.
A hundred veils spread from the heart to the eyes"

In the 18th year, Asaf Khan was appointed governor of Bengal. He was also made governor of the Punjab and had the high office of *wakil* conferred upon him. After that he obtained the rank of 7000 *zat* with 7000 *sawar.*[61]

At the time of the political crisis in 1627, after the death of Jahangir, Asaf Khan played a very important role in securing the succession for Shahjahan.[62] After his accession Shahjahan promoted Asaf Khan to the highest *mansab* of 9000 with 9000 *sawar* (*du-aspa* and *si-aspa* troopers) and confirmed him in the post of *wakil,*[63] which he held till his death in 1051/1641. It is significant that after the death of Asaf Khan Shahjahan did not fill the post of *wakil.*[64]

Asaf received from Shahjahan the titles of Yamin-ud-daula[65] (right hand of the state) and Khan-i-Khanan *sipahsalar,* and was designated in correspondence by the name of uncle (ammu, paternal uncle). Asaf Khan died on the 17th shaban, 1051/1641, and was buried at Lahore, north of Jahangir's tomb. Asaf Khan possessed something of every science. He was also a good accountant and versed in business. He personally examined the accounts of the officers of the exchequer and these of the other departments. He had no need of any guide in this.[66] The author of *Zakhirat-ul-Khawanin* says: Asaf Khan had share of every knowledge, he was particularly an adept in rational sciences and was an expert in accounts. (One who) understood pros and cons of matters, a calligrapher, eloquent; good conversationalist, administrator of the kingdom, and uncomparable in dispensation of affairs and perception and knowledge.[67] Asaf Khan was married to a daughter of Mirza Ghiyas-ud-Din Ali Asaf Khan II.[68]

Asaf Khan's eldest son was the renowned Mirza Abu Talib Shaista Khan, who, as governor of Bengal, is often mentioned in the early history of the East India Company. Shaista was married to a daughter of Irij Shahnawaz Khan,[69] son of Abdur-Rahim Khan-i-Khanan, by whom he had, however, no children. He died at Agra in 1105. His eldest son, Abu Talib,[70] had died before him. His second son was Abul-Fath Khan. One of his daughters was married to Ruhullah I, and another to Zul-Faqar Khan Nusrat-Jang.[71] Asaf Khan's second son, Bahman Yar; was appointed *Amir* in twentieth reignal year of Shahjahan and was honoured with a *mansab* of 2000 *zat* and 200 *sawar*.[72]

Itiqad Khan Mirza Shapur

He was the son of I'timad-ud-daula and brother of Asaf Khan (Asaf Jah Tehrani). He came to India in campaign of his father and his brother in search of fortune. He was the epitome of refined culture of his owe and was known for his pleasantness, brightness, polished manners, taste in dress and food. In the 17th year[73] of Jahangir's reign, he was made governor of Kashmir and ruled there for a long time. Itiqad Khan held the rank of 5,000 *zat* and *sawar*.[74] He was removed from Kashmir in the 5th year of Shahjahan and in the beginning of the 6th year came to the court. In the same year, he was on 17th Shaban appointed to the governorship of the province of Delhi in succession to Lashkar Khan. In the 16th year, he was made *Subadar* of Bihar in succession to Shaista Khan. As the *Zamindar* of Palaun[75] (Palamu) relying on the extensive forests in that province became rebellious, Itiqad Khan sent, Zabardast Khan in the 17th year, with an army against him. He traversed passes and jungles and put the rebels to the sword. Pratap, the *Zamindar* of the area submitted and presented a lac of rupees as *Peshkash* and waited upon Itiqad Khan in Patna every year.

In the 20th year, when prince Muhammad Shuja was recalled from

Bengal, the government of that province, which for population, extent and abundance of produce is equal to a clime (Iqlim), was entrusted to Itiqad Khan. When Bengal was again handed over to Shah Shuja and Itiqad Khan was on his way to the court. He was told that the government of Awadh was made over to him, and an order was issued instructing him to go on this duty from whatever place he had reached. In the 23rd year, 1060/1650 he left Bahraich and came to the court and died.[76]

According to *Zakhirat-ul-Khawanin,* Itiqad Khan was a graceful youngman of neat and tidy household articles and dress. Four persons were celebrated in India for their refined taste in food. One, Mirza Abu Said, grandson of Itimad-ud-daula; second, Yamin-ud-daula Asaf Khan; third, Nawwab Itiqad Khan; fourth, Nawwab Baqir Khan. But if justice is to be given Itiqad Khan used more lavish food than each of the other three. Ultimately, in the reign of Shahjahan, he died a natural death in the year 1060/1650 in Bihar.[77]

Sadiq Khan *Mir Bakhshi*

Mirza Muhammad Sadiq Razi Tehrani was the son of Mirza Muhammad Tahir Wasli,[78] and brother's son and son-in-law of Itimad-ud-Daula of Tehran. He came to India in the company of his father during last days of Akbar. For a time he was, with his father, *Faujdar* of the Punjab. Only in emperor Jahangir's reign he attained a suitable rank.In the 8th year of the reign of Jahangir he received the title of Khan,[79] and in the 9th year was appointed *Bakhshi*, and raised to the 1,000 *zat* and 500 *sawar.* [80] In the 10th year he got a raise of 200 *sawar* and gradually rose higher. In the 18th year he was appointed governor of the Punjab, and was deputed to annex the northern hill country. After accomplishing this work he joined the emperor's entourage with his contingent. Hopeful of royal favour, Jagat Singh, a captive, who for some time had been behaving seditiously in that quarter (the northern hill country), and brought him to the presence.[81]

Jahangir says: On Wednesday, the 27th, I went to the monastery of Shaikh Wajih-ud-din, which was near the palace, and the *fatiha* was read at the head of his shrine, which is in the court of the monastery. Sadiq Khan, who was one of the chief *amirs* of my father, built this monastery.[82]

In the first year of Shahjahan's reign Sadiq Khan presented himself before the three princes, and was graciously received and confirmed in his earlier rank of 4,000 *zat* with 4,000 *sawar* and possession of a flag and drums.[83] As the office of the *Bakhshi* had already been assigned to Iradat Khan, who later at the recommendation of Yamin-ud-daula was made *Wazir*, Sadiq Khan was restored to his office of *Bakhshi* and received a jewelled inkstand.[84] In the 6th year he died a natural death[85] on the 9th Rabi I, 1043/1632. The Emperor, out of consideration for his services, sent prince Muhammad Aurangzeb Bahadur to console his sons. He had four sons, Jafar Khan, Raushan-Zamir Salabat Khan, Abdur-Rahman and Bahram.[86] They will be accounted for separately in the section dealing with Shahjahan's reign.

It is stated that Sadiq Khan was courteous and affable, and tried to treat everyone with kindness, so much so that Mahabat Khan, who was an enemy of his family, regarded him as belonging to his party. He was very fond of horses, and had collected many Iranian (of the Iraqi race) ones. He, however, used every pretext for fining the soldiers for their absence, and so was reviled by them.[87]

Jafar Khan Umadat-ul-Mulk

He was the son of Sadiq Khan Mir Bakhshi,[88] who was the son of Khwaja Muhammad Tahir Wasli Tehrani, and the sister's son and son-in-law (Khwesh) of Yamin-ud-Daula Asaf Khan. Jafar Khan accompanied his father to Hindustan during Jahangir's reign in search of better opportunities. He, however, attained a *mansab* only in the reign of Shahjahan. His wife was Farzana Begum[89] was commonly known as Bibi Jiu. From his early years he enjoyed royal favour, and distinguished himself by devotion and good service. When his father died, Jafar Khan was promoted in the imperial hierarchy from the rank of 1000 *zat*/ 500 *sawar* to position of a *mansabdar* holding 4000 *zat* and 2000 *sawar* rank. Jafar's long and distinguished career record, was decorated with several positions of high status. In the 10th year, he was raised to the rank of 5000 *zat* with 3000 *sawar*. In the 19th year, he was made governor of Punjab. At the end of the 20th year, he was raised to the office of *Mir Bakhshi*. In the 23rd year, he was made governor of the province of Shahjahanabad (Delhi), and, in the 24th year, he was appointed governor of the province of Thatta (Sindh). In the 30th year, he came to the court when Muazzam Khan was removed from the high office of *wazir*. Jafar Khan was exalted, in the 31st year, to the high office of the chief minister, and received the ornamented inkstand. Jafar

Khan was given the governorship of Malwa, and an increase in his *sawar* rank by 1000, both *du-aspa* and *Sih-aspa* (two-horse and three horse troopers), his *mansab* was raised to 6,000 *zat* and 6,000 *sawar*. In the 6th year of Aurangzeb's reign, Jafar Khan was made the chief *diwan* of Kashmir. On his way from Kashmir he paid his respects to the Emperor at Panipat in 1074/1663 and was made Grand *Wazir*. In the 13th year, 1081/1670 he died[90] in Shahjahanabad after a long and severe illness. Jafar Khan was distinguished among the later *mansabdars*. He was promoted for goodness and right mindedness, and was noted for his excellent manners, etc. Everyone is highly understanding.[91]

Mirza Zain-ul-Abidin Qazwini

He was the son of Asaf Khan Mirza Qawamud-din Jafar Beg, who was son of Mirza Badi-uz-Zaman. Zainul-Abidin came to India in the company of his father in 985/1577. He attained the *zat* rank of 1500 along with 1500 *sawars*.[92] He died in the second year of Shahjahan's reign.[93]

Auhadi met him at Ajmer and Mandu in 1025/1616. His pen name was Danish.[94]

According to Nasrabadi, Zainul-Abidin was the son of Asaf Khan. He was poetic by nature, and Nasrabadi mentions some of his verses.[95]

Naqib Qazwini, Mir Ghiyas-ud-Din Ali

Naqib Khan was the title of Mir Ghiyas-ud-Din Ali. His family belonged to the Saifi Sayyids of Qazwin, who were known in Iran for their Sunni tendencies. His grandfather Mir Yahya was a well-known theologian and philosopher, who had acquired such extraordinary proficiency in the knowledge of history, that he was acquainted with the date of every event which had occurred since the inception of Muhammad's religion to his own time.

In the beginning of his career, Mir Yahya was patronized by Shah Tahmasp Safavi, who called him Yahya Masum, and was treated by the king with such distinction, that his enemies, envious of his good fortune, endeavoured to poison his patron's mind against him, by stating that he and his son, Mir Abdul Latif, were the leading men among the Sunnis of Qazwin. They at last prevailed so far as to induce the king, when he was on the borders of Azarbaijan, to order Mir Yahya and his son, together with their families, to be imprisoned at Esfahan. At that time, his second son, Ala-ud-daula, was in Azarbaijan and sent off a special messenger to convey this information to his father. Mir

Yahya, being too old and infirm to flee, accompanied the king's messenger to Esfahan, and died there, after one year and nine months, in 962/1554, at the age of 77 years.[96] Abdul-Latif, however immediately on receipt of his brother's communication fled to Gilan, and afterwards at the invitation of emperor Humayun went to India. He arrived at the court with his family just after Akbar had ascended the throne. Akbar received him with great kindness and consideration, and appointed him in the second year of his reign, as his preceptor. The Mir was a man of great eloquence and of excellent disposition, and so moderate in his religious sentiments,[97] that each party used to revile him for his indifference.

Mir Abdul-Latif died at Sikri on the 5th Rajb, 981/1573, and was buried at Ajmer near the *Dargah* of Mir Sayyid Husain Khing-Suwar.[98]

Abdul-Latif had several sons. The following are mentioned in a contemporary source: 1. Naqib Khan; 2. Qamar Khan; 3. Mir Muhammad Sharif.[99] Consequent to a fall from his horse, while playing polo with the emperor, Mir Muhammad Sharif died in 984/1576 at Fathpur. Mir Ghiyas-ud-Din-Ali (Naqib Khan) was distinguished for his benevolence, good nature and his long service under Akbar, and was a favourite of the king. In the 26th R.Y.[100] he was granted the title of Naqib Khan. Even though he did not rise above the rank of a *Hazari*, he enjoyed great influence in the court.[101] He was Akbar's reader, was very proficient in history, wrote several portions of the *Tarik-i-Alfi* and superintended its translation from Sanskrit into Persian.[102] He also translated some portion from the *Mahabharat.*[103]

On the accession of Jahangir, Naqib was made a commander of 1500. He died in the 9th year of Jahangir's reign (beginning of 1023/1614) at Ajmer, and was buried at the side of his wife within the enclosure of Muin-i-Chishti's tomb.[104] His wife was a daughter of Mir Mahmud, *Munshi-ul-Mamalik* (chief secretary of Akbar), who had been in Akbar's service.[105]

Abdul-Latif Qazwini

He was the son of Naqib Khan Qazwini, who also bore the same name as his grandfather. He came to India in company of his father during Akbar's reign. Abdul-Latif had Sunni proclivities, was a wise and learned man.He was married to the sister of Mirza Yusuf Khan Razavi[106] and had a high rank. But later he became insane and died.[107]

Kaukab

He was son of Qamar Khan,[108] son of Abdul-Latif Qazwini and brother of Naqib Qazwini.[109] He came to India in the company of his father during Akbar's reign. Kaukab, fell into disgrace under Jahangir. He was flogged and imprisoned.[110]

Jahangir, in his account of the twelfth year says: On Tuesday, they caught Kaukab, the son of Qamar Khan. He had put on a Faqir's dress in Burhanpur and went off into the wilds. The brief account of his misadventure in Jahangir's words. He was the grandson of Mir-Abdul-Latif, who was one of the Saifi Sayyids and was attached to this court Kaukab had been appointed to the Deccan army, and had spent some days in poverty and wretchedness. When for a long time he did not get promotion he suspected that I was unfavourable to him and foolishly took the dress of ascetics wandered into wilderness. In course of six months he traversed the whole of the Deccan, including Daulatabad, Bidar, Bijapur, the Karnantic, and Golkonda, and came to the part of Dabul (Dabhol). From there he came by ship to the port of Goga, and after visiting the ports of Surat, Broach, etc. he reached Ahmadabad. In Ahmadabad Zahid, a servant of Shahjahan arrested him and brought him to the court. I ordered them to bring him before me heavily bound. When I saw him I said to him, "considering he obligations of service of your father and grandfather, and your position as a houseborn one, why have you behaved in such an inauspicious manner?"

He replied that he could not tell a lie in the presence of his *qibla* and real teacher, and that the truth was that he had hoped for favours, but as he was unlucky he gone into the wilderness of exile. From the time that he went into exile he had kept a diary showing what he had done, and by examining it, it would be seen how he had conducted himself. These words in raised my compassion for him, and I sent for his papers and read them. It appeared from them that he had encountered great hardship, and that he had spent much time on foot, and that he had suffered from want of food. On this account I felt kindly disposed towards him. Next day I sent for him and ordered them to remove the chains from his arms and legs, and gave him a robe of honour, a horse, and 1000 rupees for his expenses. I also raised his rank by one half, and treated him with such kindness as he had never imagined. He repeated this verse:

"What I see, is it, O God waking or in a trance?
Do I behold myself in such comfort after such torture."[111]

Muhammad Salih and Muqim

The lists of grandees in the Padi Shahnama mention two relations of Asaf Khan Muhammad Salih and Muqim. Muhammad Salih, was the son of Mirza Shahi, brother or nephew of Asaf Khan. He was a *mansab* holder of 1000 *zat* and 800 *sawar* and died in the second year of Shahjahan's reign.

Muqim was *mansab*dar having 500 *zat* and 100 *sawar* rank.[112] Probably they came to India with Asaf Khan in 985/1577.

Mir Abdur-Razzaq Mamuri Esfahani

Mir Abdur-Razzaq entitled Muzaffar Khan belonged to Sadat family of Esfahan. Mir Abdur-Razzaq came to India in the company of his younger brother Mir Abdul-Wahab Khan who had the poetical name of Inayat, towards the last year of Akbar's reign[113] in order to visit his relatives. He held a good position as an eloquent writer, and has a *diwan* to his credit. Jahangir says: when I was prince, Abdur Razzaq Mamuri, had left my service without cause or reason and had gone over to my father, was reinstated as *Bakhshi* and I gave him robe of honour.

Abdur-Razzaq Mamuri, who had been summoned from the Rana's country, was promoted to be *Bakhshi* at headquarters, and it was ordered that in company with Abul-Hasan he should perform this service permanently. The emperor added: I alighted on the night of Thursday, the 2nd Muharram, in the year 1020 (17th March, 1611), at the garden of Abdur-Razzaq Mamuri, which is near, in fact close to the city. On this night many of the servants of the court, such as Khwaja Jahan, Daulat Khan, and a number who had remained in the city, came and waited on me. I stayed in that garden on Friday as well. On that day Abdur-Razzaq presented his own offerings.[114]

In 1027/1618 Muzaffar Khan promoted to the *subadarship* of Thatta (Sind), had the good fortune to kiss the threshold, he was also presented with a dress of honour and an elephant.[115]

The *Maasir-ul-Umara,* contains the following notice of him: Muzaffar Khan Mir Abdur Razzaq Mamuri, was a true Sayyid of Mamurabad, a village in holy Najf (Arabia).[116] His ancestors had migrated to India. The

Mir with regard to his knowledge and ability was among the foremost of his own age. In the reign of Akbar, through his good fortune, he was appointed *Bakhshi* of the Bengal army. At that time Man Singh Kachhwaha, was the governor of the province, he was deputed with prince Sultan Salim on the expedition against Rana Sisodia.Unwisely he left the affairs of that area in the hands of his young grandsons. In the 45th year, the sedition-mongers of the province made the son of Qutlu Lohani—who was one of the leading men of that territory the instrument of strife, and stirred up disturbances. The Raja's men led their forces against them several times, but were defeated Bengal. In the battle of Bengal the Mir was found with a collar round his neck, and chains on his legs and arms. In this condition he was seated on an elephant, and a person had been deputed to kill him in case of a defeat. Suddenly during the tumult, his executioner was shot dead, and the Mir's life was saved.[117] Afterwards, he went to the court, and received royal favours.

As, in the past, the Mir had left the prince's army without permission, and even though he had received favours on arriving at the court, and later been appointed as *Bakhshi* of Bengal, the prince was displeased and even annoyed with him. After Jahangir ascended the throne, he very generously pardoned his offences, and confirmed him in his rank. He granted him the title of Muzaffar Khan, and appointed him the second/deputy *Bakhshi* in Khwaja Jahan's expedition. In this service the Mir gained reputation for his good nature and greatness.

When after the death of Mirza Ghazi Beg Tarkhan the province of Thatta (Sind) came into the royal hands, Mirza Rustam Safavi was appointed governor of the area, and Muzaffar Khan was deputed to make a permanent settlement of its revenue. He by his skill and good judgement fixed the revenue on the basis of the past and current produce, and returned after fixing grants of land for the Mirza and his dependents towards the end of Jahangir's reign he was appointed to the high post of the governor of Malwa. When Shahjahan ascended the throne, the governorship of Malwa in succession to Muzaffar Khan was assigned to Khan Zaman, the son of Mahabat Khan and no favour whatsoever was shown to Muzaffar Khan towards the end of his career. He lived in retirement in the capital, and was included in the reserve detachments. After some time he died.[118]

Abdul Qadir Basinani

Khwaja Abdul Qadir Basinani was from Basinan, a village near

Faridan in district of Esfahan. Indeed he was one of the great men of Esfahan. Depravity of material gains in old age brought him to India in 1012\1603 in order to better his prospects. After twelve years of stay in India he was appointed to chancellorship of some lands by Jahangir. When Basinani was 92 years old, his death occurred in the camp of Jahangir at Ajmer in 1025/1616. He was very soft-spoken and affable person, and has left many verses.[119]

Salih Azadani[120]

Muhammad Salih belonged to great family of Azadan, a village near Esfahan.[121] He came to India during Jahangir's time in order to better his prospects.[122] Muhammad Salih, who held important positions in the reign of Jahangir, served in various capacities of Surat, Burhanpur, Malwa, Allahabad, Jaunpur, Patna, and finally in Bengal.

Muhammad Salih was *diwan* of Surat. He resigned from his *mansab* in 1021/1611, but again he was appointed to this position in 1023/1613. He could write *Shikasta* very well and he also was expert in notation and accounting sciences. Salih Azadani died in 1043/1633. He had four sons. One of them (Muhammad Taqi was in Iran, but the others (Muhammad Said; Muhammad Jafar and Muhammad Sadiq famous to Mina the author of *Shaid-i-Sadiq* and *Subh-i-Sadiq*) were in India.[123]

Nur-ud-Din Quli Esfahani

The reasons for his emigration from Esfahan to Hindustan in the reign of Jahangir are not specific. He was appointed to the prestigious office of *Kotwal* in the capital of Agra. In the 12th year, his rank was advanced to 1,000 *zat* and 300 *sawar*[124] subsequent to Mahabat Khan's display of presumptuous conduct and his flight from the imperial camp, Nur-ul-din was placed in the same army that was sent after him. Nur-ud-din went as far as Ajmer and stayed there.[125] Later, after Jahangir's death, when the standards of Shahjahan reached Ajmer, he did pay homage, and was honoured by reinstatement of his earlier rank of 2000 *zat* with 700 *sawar*. He was deputed along with Khan Jahan Lodi, who was sent for the first time to chastise Jujhar Singh Bundela. In the 3rd year of Shahjahan's R.Y. when the Deccan was the seat of the royal camp, three armies under the command of three officers were deputed to punish Khan Jahan Lodi. The emperor's forces in order to avenge the provocative behaviour of Nizam-ul-Mulk Deccan, who had dared to offer Khan Jahan an asylum there, devastated his territories. Nur-ud-Din was sent with Azam Khan on this campaign. In the 5th year, in

1041/1632 when Nur-ud-din left the *Darbar,* and was going home, Kishan Singh[126] son of Jaswant Rathore, assassinated him to avenge his father's murder at the hands of Nur-ud-din's men during Jahangir's reign. The assassin escaped.[127]

Mulla Qazwini entitled to Iradat Khan

Aqa Mulla, title to Iradat Khan, was the son of Mirza Badi-uz-zaman, and younger brother of Mirza Qawam-ud-din Jafar Asaf Khan Qazwini.

In this account of the year 1016/1607 Jahangir says: I gave Iradat Khan, brother of Asaf Khan, the rank of 1000 *zat* and 500 *sawar* and presenting him with a special robe of honour and a horse, bestowed on him the paymastership of the *suba* of Patna and Hajipur. He also was raised to the rank of *mir-samani* (head butler), in the year of 1017/1608. Iradat Khan received a *mansab* of 1500 *zat* and 600 *sawar.*[128]

According to Auhadi, Iradat Khan died in 1018/1609. He was generous, kind-hearted and peace loving. He also had poetic proclivities.[129]

Fahmi Qazwini

Fahmi Qazwini entitled Amir Muhammad migrated from Qazwin to India because of religious persecution in Iran. He was one of the Jahangir's Darsani.[130] Fahmi was also a poet and has some verses in praise of Jahangir.[131]

Mir Muhammad Baqir Savoji (Azam Khan)

Mir Muhammad Baqir Savaji belonged to the noble Sayyids of Saveh[132] which is one of the old towns of Iraq.[133] He came to India during Jahangir's time in search of better opportunities. Azam Khan was appointed on the post of Asaf Khan Mirza Jafar to be faujdar of Sialkot, Gujarat and Punjab, and afterwards he became *Khan-i-Saman* (steward).[134] In his tenure he showed loyalty and economy due to which he was recipient of the sultan's benevolence, and in the 15th regional year was made governor of Kashmir. From there he was promoted to the court and became *Mir Bakhshi.* After the death of Jahangir he was associated with Yamin-ud-daula in the affair of Shahriyar, and did good service. He waited upon Shahjahan at Agra before Yamin-ud-daula came there from Lahore. Consequent to raise of 500 *zat* and 1000 *sawar* he became a distinguished *mansabdar* of 5000 *zat* and 5000 *sawar.*[135] He was also honoured with a drum and a flag, and was appointed as *Mir Bakhshi.* After that, at the request of Yamin-ud-daula, on 5th Rajab,[136] 2nd March 1623, at the beginning of the reignal year he was made *wazir*. In the following year he was sent to the Deccan.

At beginning of the third year, when Shahjahan visited Burhanpur, Iradat Khan had the honour of paying his respects to Shahjahan and was exalted by the title of Azam Khan conferred on him. He headed an army of 50,000 cavalry to combat with[137] Khan Jahan Lodi and to conquer the territories of the Nizam Shah. Azam Khan and Khan Jahan Lodi contested for a long time. Finally Khan Jahan crept into Daulatabad, and Azam Khan set himself to punish Nizam Shah.

In 1030/1620, he was raised to the rank of 6000 *zat* with 6000 *sawar*. In the 5th year of Shahjahan's reign, after the death of Qasim Khan Juwini he was sent to Bengal. In the 8th year he was made governor of Allahabad, and in the 9th year he was appointed to Gujarat. As the wife[138] of prince Muhammad Shuja, who was the daughter of Muhammad Rustam Safavi, had died, Azam Khan's daughter was married to the prince in the 12th year, 1048/1639-40. Sultan Zainul-Abidin was the fruit of this marriage. After that he was appointed Jagirdar of Islamabad (Mathura) and built a *serai* and quarter (*Pura*) there. Later, he was made governor of Bihar, and in the 21st year he was summoned to take charge of Kashmir. He petitioned to the emperor that he could not stand the cold of that region. The sultan considered his petition and stationed him at Jaunpur in succession of Mirza Hasan Safavi. In the 22nd year 1059/1649, he died after attaining the age of 76. The chronogram of his death is: "Azam Auliya greatest of officers" which indicates the date of death as 1059/1649.He was buried in a garden which he had made before the end of his tenure on the bank of the river[139] Gomti in Jaunpur.[140]

Ahmad Razi

According to Auhadi, Ahmad Beg Lang was the son of Khwaja Mirza Beg. He was native of Ray. He spent most of his life in the leisure of reading. For a while he was incharge of Zargar Khaneh. He was also the treasurer of Shah Abbas Nawwab. Ahmad Razi migrated to India in Jahangir's reign and received the office of the *diwan* of Patna. Jahangir granted high *mansab* to Ahmad Razi as *diwan* of Patna. He died at Agra in 1024/1615.[141]

Yehya Qomi

He was the son of Mir Hashim, a Sayyid Family of Qom. He first migrated to Deccan and then he joined the Mughal service. During Jahangir's reign he was *diwan* and *Bakhshi* of Orissa. After some time he was removed from his *mansab* and was shifted to Patna. Afterwards Yehya went to the court and was appointed as *Bakhshi* of Kabul. He died in India in the early years of Shahjahan's reign.[142]

Ali Mardan Khan

Among the foreign adventures flocking to the Mughal court in Shahjahan's reign to seek their fortune there was a Persian, Ali Mardan Khan, who soon after his arrival emerged as a personality deemed worthy by the emperor to be included among his inner circle of nobles.

His family background is as romantic as that of Itimad-ud-Daula. Ali Mardan Khan was the son of Ganj Ali Khan,[143] who hailed from the nomadic Kurdish clan of Zig[144] inhabiting the hilly region of western Persia.

Ganj Ali Khan Zig was a close confidential officer of Shah Abbas I and had served him in Herat since his childhood. During Shah Abbas' reign he was entrusted with important offices like *Qiladar* of Salamah in Khaf, governor of Kerman and Sistan.[145] He always showed benign qualities of justice and concern for the subjects.[146] In the 36th R.Y. (1031/1612) he was given charge of the administration of Qandahar, the most crucial province of the time which was apparently entrusted to experienced and logical generals. Ganj Ali Khan held Qandahar until he died in 1034/1624, and performed valuable services for his master in beating back the Uzbeks in Khurasan. Shah Abbas I conferred on him the title of Khan and called him Arjumand Babai (honoured father).[147] After his father's death Ali Mardan Khan was appointed governor of Qandahar and was called *Baba-i-Sani* by the Shah.[148] After forty-two years of rule Shah Abbas died on January 6, 1629, and Shah Mirza, succeeded his grandfather to the Persian throne under the title Shah Safi. The inevitable intrigues arising soon afterwards in the Safavid court added fuel to the fire, causing a rift between Shah Safi and Ali Mardan Khan.[149] Shah Safi sent reinforcements to Qandahar and at the same time, at the instigation of some nobles, preferred a charge of embezzlement against Ali Mardan Khan.[150] when charged with serious offences by Shah Safi; Ali Mardan handed over the fort of Qandahar to Shahjahan in 1638 and came to India where he was awarded the rank of 6000/6000 and the titles of *Amir-ul-Umara* and *Yar-i-Wafadar*.[151] He was also appointed *Subadar* of Kashmir and subsequently of Lahore and Kabul. His *mansab* was raised to 7000 *zat*/7000 *sawar.* His total salary amounted to crore dams, the highest salary ever received by any noble after Asaf Khan.[152]

During his governorship of Kabul Ali Mardan Khan was sent against the Uzbeks. In the 18th reignal year 1645, he sent his confidential servants Farhad and Faridun against Tardi Ali Qatghan,[153] who, after a short engagement, took to flight. In 1646 he was sent along with prince Murad Bakhsh, against the Uzbeks to conquer Balkh and Badakhshan. At this time Sultan Khusrau, Bahram Sultan and Subhan Quli Sultan, three sons of Nazr Muhammad Khan came and paid homage to prince Murad while Nazr Muhammad Khan fled to Persia.[154] However, Murad Bakhsh, in spite of Shahjahan's prohibition, returned to Hindustan for which the prince was censured and Sadullah Khan was sent to Balkh. It would seem that normally Ali Mardan Khan have been asked to take over charge of Balkh, but his being an Irani and so a suspected Shia made this impolitic.[155]

During the early period of his governorship of Kashmir Ali Mardan Khan proved his mettle as an able civil administrator.[156] Due to his ability as a wise and understanding administrator, Ali Mardan Khan enjoyed a high status in his province as also at the Mughal court, being rewarded lavishly by the emperor.[157] It was during his tenure as governor of Kashmir and *subedar* of the Punjab that Ali Mardan Khan exhibited authetic facets of his character, reflecting his cultural heritage especially love for natural beauty and passion for the artistic expositions.[158]

An order was given to the Amir-ul-Umaru to punish the rebels of Qanduz and to return to Kabul after the arrival of the governor of Badakhshan. In 1057/1647, prince Aurangzeb was given the charge of Balkh and Badakhshan and was sent there.[159] At this time he had an encounter in Timurabad, with Abdul Aziz, the eldest son of Nazr Muhammad Khan and the governor of Bukhara. Ali Mardan Khan defeated Beg Oghli and Qutluq Muhammad Sultan and Yadgar Tukariya, one after the other in a battle that continued for seven days in which the Uzbek army sustained great losses.[160] Afterwards, when Balkh and Badakhshan were restored to Nazr Muhammad, Ali Mardan Khan came back to Kabul. After some time he was allowed to go to Kashmir, where the climate was more suitable for him.[161]

When the prince Dara Shukoh was appointed to lead an expedition to Qandahar and the province of Kabul was assigned to his eldest son Sulaiman Shukoh in 1653, Ali Mardan Khan was again posted there. Thereafter, he was summoned to court towards the close of 1656. He had an attack dysentery and in the beginning of the 31st R.Y. 1657, while returning to Kashmir he died at Machhiwara (on 16th April, 1657). He was buried in his mother's tomb at Lahore.[162]

Besides being a military commander and a civil administrator Ali Mardan Khan was a great builder. The laying out of a number of gardens, sarais and residential buildings in Kashmir and Lahore are attributed to him.

His buildings can broadly be classified into two types—private buildings such as personal mansions in Kashmir[163] and Peshawar and his own tomb at Lahore and public works like canals, gardens and sarais. Construction of sarais in Kashmir was felt to be necessary by Shahjahan owing to the obstructions of roads by heavy rain and snow fall during winter. Hence, sarais at every stage (*Manzil*) were constructed under the supervision of Ali Mardan Khan in order to provide places of refuge to travellers. In 1639 Naqdi Beg, an employee and apparently an architect of Ali Mardan Khan, was given the charge of repairing and widening roads through Kashmir.[164]

Ali Mardan Khan also constructed a number of gardens both in Kashmir and Lahore. The Ali Abad Garden at village Til Bal in Kashmir was constructed in 1654.[165]

The most important work undertaken by Ali Mardan Khan was the construction of a projected canal designed to bring water to Lahore from the hills at Rajpur near Nurpur, to the length of some 48 1/2 Kurohs. The work was undertaken in 1639 to bring the water for the irrigation of land and Shalimar garden which was then being laid out by Khalil-Ullah Khan. The canal would also provide water to the citizens of Lahore.[166]

Among Ali Mardan Khan's sons, the eldest Muhammad Ali was left in Iran as hostage with Shah Safi. Shahjahan sent a letter to Shah Safi's successor Shah Abbas II to secure his release.[167] But it is not known whether he was ever sent to India. Of the remaining four sons, Abdullah Beg and Ibrahim Beg flourished during the reigns of Shahjahan and Aurangzeb. Ismail Beg and Ishaq Beg both attained moderate *mansabs* of 1500 and 800 respectively and died in the battle of Samugarh.[168]

Ibrahim Khan

He was son of Ali Mardan Khan.[169] He came to India from Qandahar with his father during the rule of Shahjahan. In the 26th year, 1063, he received from Shahjahan the title of Khan as a mark of favour and grace. When his father died in the 31st year, he was granted the rank of 4,000 *zat* with 3000 *sawar*. In the battle of Samugarh, he was in the right wing of Dara Shukoh's army. It is natural, perhaps, for the inexperienced and short-sighted Ibrahim Khan to become a partisan of prince Murad Bakhsh[170] after Dara's defeat at the hands of Aurangzeb. It was during the reign of Aurangzeb that as a reward of his valuable services in the war of succession, he was given rapid promotions and was raised the rank of 6000/6000.[171] He remained *Subadar* of various provinces one after the other (except for a short interval of about four years) during his entire term of fortyeight years' sevice under Aurangzeb. It is also significant that during this period he was appointed *Subadar* of Kashmir thrice.[172] He got a fourth tenure there during the reign of Bahadur Shah. He died at Ibrahimabad Sodhra in Lahore in 1709.

His son was Zabardast Khan. When Ibrahim was governor of Bengal, Zabardast Khan handled an army and fought a severe battle with Rahim Khan, an Afghan, who had raised the head of sedition and called himself Rahim Shah. The latter was completely defeated. In the 42nd year of Aurangzeb he was made the governor of Awadh and had a commission of 3000 *zat* with 2500 *sawar*.[173]

Another son of Ibrahim was Yaqub Khan. In the time of Bahadur Shah he was made the governor of Lahore. After his father's death, he inherited the title of Ibrahim Khan.[174]

Muhammad Ali Beg

Muhammad Ali Beg Afshar came to India as the ambassador of Shah Safi to Shahjahan. Muhammad Ali Esfahani was a loyal and able servant and subsequently rose to a high position. He arrived at Lahore in about zulqada 1039/June 1630. His embassy, being the first from the new Shah, was highly honoured in India. The governor of a province was appointed to conduct him to Burhanpur in the Deccan where the emperor was then encamped. At Burhanpur, he was ushered into royal presence by 'Allami Afzal Khan, the *Wazir*. Shahjahan received him favourably, taking the royal letter[175] personally from his hand, which was special favour. He was amply awarded then and on several subsequent occasions, and his assistants too were not forgotten. In total he is said to have received as reward 3,16,000 rupees in cash and one lac in kind. He was placed, in very high precedence at court ceremonies, and was ceremoniously dismissed in Rabi II 1042/October, 1632.[176]

Rahmat Khan[177] (Dayri Kashani)

His name was Ziya-ud-din, who was the son of Hakim Qutba, brother of Hakim Rukna of Kashan, who was a famous physician, and the most eloquent of men. Ziya-ud-din had married the younger daughter of Talib Amuli, who had been brought up by Sati Khanam[178] who was the wife of Nasira, the brother of Hakim Rukna. Ziya-ud-din was invited by his relatives (Sati Khanam) to come to India. Ziya-ud-din was favoured by Shahjahan, and in the 14th year was appointed superintendent of the *Karkiraq Khana* (furring department), and granted a title[179] and a female elephant. In the 18th year his rank was increased to 1,000 *zat* with 150 *sawars*. In the 22nd year he was made superintendent of Branding (*Dagh*). In the 24th year an additional grant of 100 *Sawars* was made in his rank. In the 27th year on the transfer of *Mir Bakhshi* he was appointed *Divan* and superintendent of the *Karkiraq Khana*[180] of the province of Ahmadabad. In the 29th year his *mansab* was further raised to 1500 *zat* with 400 *sawars*. During the time of Shahjahan's illness, when Murad Baksh assumed[181] sovereignty, and struck coins and had the *Khutba* read in his own name (in Gujarat), Rahmat Khan became his companion. After the prince's arrest he entered the service of Aurangzeb,[182] and was promoted to the rank of 2000 *zat* with 300 *sawars* and was appointed *divan* of Gujarat. When Dara Shukoh arrived at Ahmadabad, though he went with the governor and waited upon him, yet he declined to accompany him. Accordingly when Dara Shukoh fled from near Ajmer, Ziya-ud-din was again an object of favour, and in the 3rd year was appointed *divan* of the emperor's sister, Roshan Rai Begum (Roshan Ara). Afterwards he was promoted to the post of *Divan-i-Buyutat*. In the 8th year he died. Abdur Rahim, his son-in-law, and Muhammad Sadiq, his son received robes of condolence (mourning dresses).[183]

Danishmand Khan

Mulla Shafia entitled as Danishmand Khan belonged to Yazd. For a long time he acquired education in Iran and obtained command over the stages of learning according to ability and potency. After acquiring knowledge, in order to earn a distinguished livelihood as a trader he collected some money from merchants by way of selling their goods for share in the profit. He came to India as a trader which, due to its excessive grandeur, was akin to paradise on earth. In India for some time he engaged himself in trading, buying and selling in the grand army (cantonment).

After collecting the profits he intended to return to his native place. However, when he arrived in the town of Surat, by the action of favourable luck, the degrees of his excellencies and sagacity received notice of Shahjahan.[184] An order was issued directing the officers of the port to send him to the court. The emperor and his *wazir*, said Ullah Khan, were impressed by his learning and conferred on him the rank of 1000 *zat* and 100 *sawar*.[185] Afterwards his *mansabs* was increased, and in the 29th year he was made deputy (mails) *Bakhshi* in succession to Lashkar Khan, and he received the title of Danishmand Khan. An increase of mansab by 500 zat and 200 *sawar* was only appropriate and he ultimately held this position with 2500 *zat* and *sawar*.[186] In the 31st year his rank was raised to 3000 *zat* with 800 *sawars*, and in succession to I'tiqad Khan, he was made *Mir Bakhshi*.[187] In the same year he resigned[188] the office, and lived a retired life in Shahjahanabad (Delhi). In the 2nd year of reign of Aurangzeb he was again encompassed by royal favours and received the rank of 4000 *zat* with 2000 *sawar*. In the beginning of the 7th year his rank was raised to 5000 *zat* and in the 8th year he was *Subadar* and guardian of the fort of Shahjahanabad. In the 10th year he was made Mir Bakhshi in succession to Muhammad Amin Khan, and received a decorated writing case.[189] In the 13th year to Rabi-al awwal 1081, 18 July 1670, he died.[190] This excellent Amir was one of the learned men of the age and was distinguished for his good sense and right thinking. His contemporaries say that when he entered the royal service he was directed to argue and dispute on scientific subjects with Mulla Abdul-Hakim of Sialkot, who surpassed the learning and wisdom of the wise men of his age.[191]

He is known to us also through Bernier, who was employed by him during his sojourn at Delhi, and from whom he wished to learn about European sciences.[192]

SOUTH OF IRAN

Mahabat Khan; Khan-i-Khanan

Interesting information on the personal life of Mahabat Khan is available both in the *Maasir-ul-Umara*[193] and the *Zakhiratul-Khawanian.*[194] The account in the *Maasir* is comparatively brief and is largely based on the *Zakhira*.

Mahabat Khan's name was Zamana Beg, and he was the son of Ghaiyur Beg Kabuli. They were Sayyids of the Razavi family of Shiraz. Ghaiyur Beg came to Kabul in his youth and entered Mirza Hakim's service. After the death of that prince Ghaiyur Beg came to India and joined Akbar's service,[195] but he could not rise to a high position and apparently failed to get a *mansab*. His son Zamana Beg, therefore, had to enter the service of prince Salim as no more than an *Ahadi* or cavalry trooper. Salim was highly impressed by his loyalty and devotion, and gave him the rank of 500 *zat* and the office of the *Bakhshi* of *Shagird Pesha* (ministerial servants).[196] Zamana Beg remained loyal to him even during the period the prince was at Allahabad defying his father when many of his other followers had left him. Upon Salim's instructions he killed Raja of Ujjania who had come to see the prince at the head of a large army.[197]

In the beginning of Jahangir's reign he received the title of Mahabat Khan and the rank of 3000 *zat*,[198] and was appointed to lead the expedition against the Rana of Mewar. In 1615 Mahabat Khan was appointed to serve in the Deccan and was posted there along with Khan-i-Jahan Lodi. On this occasion 700 troopers of his *sawar* rank were converted into *du-aspa, Sih-aspa.*[199]

In the 12th year he was appointed governor of Kabul on the transfer of Shah Beg Khan.[200]

During the years when Mahabat Khan was at Kabul (1620-22), some very significant developments took place in the imperial camp. The release of Khusrau, Shaharyar's marriage with Ladli Begum, departure of Khusrau under the custody of Khurram, and the promotion of Parvez to the rank of 20000 *zat*, 10000 *sawar* took place.[201] These events not only divided the family of Itimad-ud-daula into two groups but, also initiated a serious political crisis in the empire. On account of these developments Mahabat Khan's relation with Nur Jahan seems to have improved. In 1622 when he came to court he was normally received and was styled *Rukn-us-Saltanat*. After a brief stay at the court he returned to Kabul. During the same period his son Aman Ullah was given the *mansab* of 2000 *zat* and 1800 *sawar*.[202] When Khurram rebelled in 1622, Mahabat Khan, whose attitude to Khusrau must have hardened particularly after the murder of Khusrau was summoned to the court. It is significant that the summons should have been sent by Nur Jahan, it was said, at Mahabat Khan's own insistence,[203] that he should be promoted to the rank of 6000 *zat* and 5000 *sawar* and given the command of army against Khurram. After the accession of Shahjahan to thorne the sultan gave him the title of Khan-i-Khanan *Sipahsalar*, and the rank of 7000 *zat* with 7000 *sawar*.[204] He also gave him a present of 4 lacs of rupees, and appointed him governor of Ajmer. In the same year Mahabat Khan was appointed governor of the Deccan, and his son Khan Zaman who had recently been made governor of Malwa was nominated as his deputy. In the 2nd year when Shahjahan went to the Deccan in pursuit of Khan Jahan Lodi, Mahabat Khan was nominated as the governor of Delhi. In the 5th year on the transfer of Azam Khan, he was again appointed governor of the Deccan.[205]

Mahabat Khan died in 1044/1634. The chronograms of his death are, *Zamana aram girift* (Zamana is at rest) and *Sipahsalar raft* (The Commander-in-Chief is gone).[206]

The author of the *Zakhira* is full of praise for the boundless magnanimity and generosity of Mahabat Khan. He was a good judge of men and if he once formed a good opinion about someone he did not easily change it. He was lavish in bestowing gifts and distributing money.[207]

Mahabat Khan was not formally educated, but he was proficient in the study of horoscopes, astronomy, astrology and medicine, the important sciences of the age.[208]

Mahabat Khan was also a man of literary taste and composed verses. One couplet has been quoted in the *Maasir* and *Zakhira*:

Nang-i-delam bod ke bihisht arzu konam; Dozakh nasib-i-man bod-i-arzu mabod.[209]

"My heart's pride longed for paradise; Hell is my lot, may it not be my longing !"

Mahabat Khan was not a religious person nor was he very particular a bout offering prayers or observing fasts. Towards the end of his life he became a follower of Isna-ashari Shiism. But neither the *Zakhira* nor the *Maasir* throws light on the person who influenced him in this respect.

Coming to the question of Indian influences on Mahabat Khan, we know that he was a Razavi Sayyid and his ancestors had come to India from Kabul. His trust in his Indian (Rajput) followers, and in turn their loyalty to him, his liking for Indian food, fondness for elephants, interest in horoscopes, an essentially Hindu practice, in astronomy, astrology and Rajput genealogy, furnish strong evidences of Indian influences on him.[210]

Afzal Khan

His name is Mulla Shukr Ullah, and his birthplace is Shiraz. Having acquired all the degrees of knowledge and accomplishment at the feet of Mir Ibrahim Hamadani and Mir Taqi-ud-din-Muhammad Shirazi, he came to Burhanpur by way of Surat. In order to better his prospects.Afzal Khan enrolled himself in the ranks of the servants of his majesty *Jannat* Makani (Jahangir).[211] Abdur Rahim Khan-i-Khanan chose him as a companion. After that he attached himself to prince Shahjahan, and became the law-officer (*Mir Adil*) of his army. In the affair of the Rana Amar Singh (of Udaipur) he was his secretary and confidant.When by his good council peace was made with the Rana, his reputation increased and he became the prince's *Diwan*. After the campaign was over he received, at the request of prince Shahjahan, the title of Afzal Khan.[212]

In 1035, 1626, Jahangir exalted him by making him his *Khan-i-Saman* (steward) in Lahore, on account of difficulties of the journey and the work connected with the household. In 1037/1628 when Shahjahan ascended the throne, Afzal came from Lahore and paid homage. He was promoted to the office of *Mir Saman* (major-domo) and had an increase in his *mansab* of 500 *zat* and 500 *sawar*, and held the rank of 4000 *zat* and 2000 *sawar.* In the second year he was made Chief *Diwan* (*Diwan-i-Kull*) and was promoted by an addition of 1000 *zat* and 1000 *sawars*.[213] The chronogram is: *Shud Flatun Wazir-i-Iskandar,* Plato became the *wazir* of Alexander (1038/1628-29). In the 11th year his honour was akin to the position of Saturn in the planetary constellation on account of obtaining the *mansab* of 7000 *zat*. In the 12th year, when his age was 70, bodily illness prevailed over him, and the appearance of death was visible in his condition. Shahjahan visited him and showed him kindness. On 12 Ramazan 1048/7th January 1639, in Lahore, he departed from this world. His tomb is on the left bank of the Jumuna between 'Itimad-ud-daulat's tomb and the Taj. He was skilful in astronomy and mathematics and in accounts. It is said that with all his science and learning he never put anything on paper, and that he did not know figures is probably based upon his dignity and indifference.[214] He left no children.[215]

EAST AND NORTH-EAST

Ali Turkman Khurasani

Mirza Ali Quli was the son of Sulaiman Khalifa Turkman, a Qizilbash noble. He lived in Khurasan, and was the governor of Tun and Tabas, and then he received the governorship of Qom. Sulaiman returned to Khurasan in 997/1588. He attained martyrdom in the war between Iranis and Uzbeks in Azqand of Turshiz in 999/1590.[216] His son Ali Quli was born and brought up in Khurasan. After his father's death Ali Quli moved to Esfahan in the company of his relatives and entered in the service of Shah Abbas I. Since Shah Abbas had little respect for Turkman tribesmen; Ali Quli did not expect any patronage from him and shifted to India with his family where he chose to be with *Khan-i-Khanan.* In 1001/1592 he was presented at Akbar's court by Abdur Rahim. In 1019/1610 he was in attendance of Prince Parvez when the latter was despatched to conquer the Deccan. In 1024/1615, through the good offices of *Khan-i-Khanan*, he was appointed to a *mansab* of 700 *zat.* In poetry he followed the style of Maluana Urfi, and his penname was Ali.[217]

According to Auhadi, Ali Quli was *mansabdar* of Jahangir. He was good at composing verses. Auhadi saw him at Burhanpur.[218] The author of *Subh-i-Sadiq* says: Mirza Ali Quli was the son of Sulaiman Khalifa, a great Amir of Shah Tahmasp, who was killed in war with Uzbeks. Mirza Ali Quli had poetic nature. I saw him at Burhanpur in 1036/1626.[219]

Saf Shikan Khan Mirza Lashkari

He was the son of Sayyid Yusuf Khan Razavi. He came to India in the company of his father during Akbar's time in search of better opportunities. After his father's death during Akbar's reign, he worked as the *Thanadar* of Bir in the Deccan. In the beginning of Jahangir's reign he received the title of Safdar Khan, and was granted a *Jagir* in Bihar. In the 5th year he was promoted to the rank of 1500 *zat* and 700 *sawar*.[220] In the 6th year[221] of Jahangir's rule he was appointed governor of Kashmir[222] in place of Hashim Khan who was the son of Qasim Khan Mir Bahr. In the 8th year he was removed[223] from there. In the 21st year Mahabat Khan became presumptuous and fled from the royal presence when news was received that his treasures, which had been brought over from Bengal, had reached near Delhi, Safdar Khan was deputed with a force to confiscate the same. When Safdar Khan reached there, Mahabat Khan's men shut themselves up in an inn (*sarai*), and engaged themselves in fighting with the emperor's men. After the gate of the inn was set on fire they ran away, and he took possession of the treasure.[224] Afterwards, when Shahjahan ascended the throne, he was confirmed in the *mansab* of 2,500 *zat* and 2000 *sawar*, which he had held till the end of Jahangir's reign. When Khwaja Qasim Sayyid Atai was granted the title of Safdar Khan, his title was changed to Saf Shikan Khan.[225] When Bir was taken out of the hands of the officers of *Nizam-ul-Mulk* Deccani, he, according to the old arrangements, was (again) appointed *Thanadar* of the place.[226] He remained there a long time and for some reason he became the object of censure, and was deprived of his rank and *jagir*. A pension of Rs. 12000 a year was assigned to him, and he was told to reside in Lahore. In the 19th year corresponding to 1055/1645 he died.[227]

It is stated that he was of a perverse nature of a careless disposition and a babbler.[228] The author of *Zakhiratul-Khawanin* says: When I was *Diwan, Bakhshi, Amin* and *Waqai-nawis* of Bir Thana, I spent eight years in his company. He was fickle and childish. When he fell from the *mansab* and *jagir*, he received an annuity of 12000 rupees. He died a natural death at Lahore.[229]

Khwaja Abul-Hasan Turbati (Title Rukn-us-Sultanat)

Abul-Hasan belonged to Turbat, a city in Khurasan province. The reason for Abul Hasan's migration to Hindustan during Akbar's reign is not specified. The Khwaja, however, entered the service of prince Danial and was made *diwan* of the Deccan.[230] When Jahangir ascended the throne, the Khwaja was summoned from the Deccan to court, and in the 8th year, 1022/1613 attained the high office of *Mir Bakhshi*. After the death of Itimad-ud-daula, the Khwaja was made Chief *diwan* and held a *mansab* of 5000 *zat* and 5000 *sawar*. In the 19th year he was made governor of Kabul and his son Zafar Khan was sent off from court to be his deputy. In the reign of Shahjahan he attained the rank of 6000 *zat* and 6000 *sawar*. The Khwaja died in the 6th year of Shahjahan's reign 1042/1632-33, at the age of seventy. Talib Kalim (poet-laureate of Shahjahan) composed a chronogram to mark the date of his death: "May he rise with the *Amir-ul-Muminin* (Ali) (1042). The Khwaja was a straightforward and able man but he was of a sour countenance and harsh manner. His heir was Zafar Khan of about whom a special account is being given. Another son was Muhammad Khurshid Nazr.[231]

Islam Khan Mashhadi

His name was Mir Abd-us-salam, and he had the title of Ikhtisas Khan. He came to India during Jahangir's reign in search of better opportunities. At first he did secretary's work. In 1030/1620, the 15th year of Jahangir's reign, when the royal standards went for the second time to redress the affairs of the Deccan, the Mir was made *Wakil* of the *Darbar* (i.e. Shahjahan's agent at his father's court) with a suitable rank and the title of Ikhtisas Khan.[232] When Shahjahan became the king, Ikhtisas Khan waited upon him with a valuable present, and was given the rank of 4000 *zat* with 2000 *sawar*, and the title of Islam Khan, and appointed as the deputy *Bakhshi*. When Shahjahan went to South to put down Khan Jahan Lodi, he was appointed as the governor of Agra. When Sher Khan Tonvar the Nizam of Gujarat died in the 4th reignal year, Islam Khan was made a *mansabdar* of 5,000 *zat* and the governor of that province. In the end of the 6th year, he became *Mir Bakhshi*.[233] In the 8th year, he was appointed governor of the extensive province of Bengal in place of Azam Khan, and there opened wide the gates of victory. In the 11th year, Islam Khan was summoned to the imper'al presence and received charge of the high office of *Wazir*, when Khan Dauran Nusrat Jang,[234] governor of the Deccan was killed. Islam Khan at the New Year's Feast of the 19th year obtained the rank of 6,000 *zat* and *sawar* and the administration of that province. His brother, sons and son-in-law also had suitable increases and accompanied him. In the 20th year, he was raised to the high rank of 70000 *zat* with 7000 *sawars*.

When Islam Khan came to Aurangabad from Burhanpur illness

prevailed over him, and he perceived that it was time for his last journey. He died on 14th Shawwal 1957/12 November 1647, and in accordance with his will he was buried in Aurangabad. The tomb and garden which were made, though old, remain in good condition to this day.[235]

Islam Khan had a full knowledge of the rational and traditional sciences, of elegant compositions, and of calligraphy. In reference to royal business he was jealous, and did not want that anyone should have possession of it. Islam Khan had six sons. Except Mir Abd-ur-Rahman,[236] the others got good *mansabs* during Shahjahan's reign. We will give biographical details about them separately.

Abdur-Rahim Khan

He also was the son of Islam Khan of Mashhad. After his father's death he received a suitable rank, and in the 30th year of Shahjahan's reign he was made superintendent of the pages (*Darogha-i-Khwassan*). In the second year of Aurangzeb he had the title of Khan, and was the *Darogha* of the *Ghusal-Khana*. In the 23rd year he was appointed the third *Bakhshi* and received a jade inkstand. In the 25th year of the sultan corresponding to 1092/1681, he died.[237]

Safi Khan

He was the second son of Islam Khan Mashhadi. In the 19th year of Shahjahan's reign when his father was appointed governor of Deccan, he received a suitable increase in his rank, and went with his father.[238] In the 21st year when his father died, he was promoted to the rank of 1,500 *zat* and 400 *sawar*.[239] In the 23rd year he was deputed as an envoy to Adil Khan at Bijapur.[240] After that he accompanied Sultan Aurangzeb on the Qandahar campaign. In the 26th year on his return from Qandahar he was appointed *Bakhshi* and *Waqai Navis* of the four provinces of the Deccan.[241] In the 27th year he was exalted by the grant of the title of Khan.[242] In the 31st year he was granted an increase of 200 *sawar*, and appointed commandant of the fort of the capital.[243]

During Aurangzeb's reign he was appointed governor of Orissa, Agra, Shahjahanabad (Delhi) and Multan.[244]

In the reign of Muhammad Farukh Siyar he held the post of *Mir Tuzuk*, and also for some time that of second *Bakhshi*. In the reign of

Muhammad Shah he was promoted to the rank of 7,000 *zat.*[245]

Taqi Khurasani

Muhammad Taqi was the son of Khwaja Qasim Khurasani famous to Semsar (dealer in second-hand goods). He migrated to India without any definite purpose during Jahangir's time. Taqi entered in the service of prince Khurram and was granted a good position. Auhadi saw him at Ajmer. In 1029/1619 Taqi was *Subadar* of Malwa[246] and in 1042/1632, he obtained a high *mansab* and *jagir.*[247]

FROM UNKNOWN AREAS

Khwaja Beg Mirza Safavi[248]

Khawaja Beg Mirza was relative of Shah Tahmasp Safavi. He migrated to India in 999/1590, because he feared the displeasure of Safavid kings. He joined Akbar's court by Khan-i-Khanan and received a *mansab* of 5000 *zat.* Jahangir says: "From the date on which the fort of Ahmadnagar, by the efforts of my deceased brother Daniyal, came into the possession of the heads of the victorious state, up till now (1009/1600-1019/1610), the guardianship, and preservation of that place had been entrusted to Khwaja Beg Mirza Safavi, who was a relative of Shah Tahmasp."[249]

The author of *Ma'asir-ul-Umara* says: Khwaja Beg Mirza Safavi, who in the reign of Emperor Jahangir was governor of Ahmadnagar, and had attained the rank of 5,000, died in the 13th year (1027/1617) at Ahmadnagar.[250]

Mirzas of Qandahar: Muzaffar Husain Mirza and Rustam Mirza

The Mirzas of Qandahar belonged to the family of the Safavid rulers of Iran. In India they were known as Qandaharis on account of their having held Qandahar before coming to India. The family came to India with Mirza Rustam Safavi and his elder brother Mirza Muzaffar Husain Safavi. They were the great-grandsons of Shah Ismail Safavi, and their father, Sultan Husain Mirza, was a son of Baharam Mirza, a son of Shah Ismail Safavi. Sultan Husain was governor (*wali*) of Qandahar, Zamindawar and Garmser, which extended up to river Hirmand, during the reign of Shah Tahmasp (1524-76). Later in the reign of Khuda Banda (1577-86) after Sultan Husain's death, Qandahar was assigned to Muzaffar Husain Mirza, while the territory of Zamindawar and Garmser was handed over to Rustam Mirza. The other two brothers Abu Said Mirza and Sanjar Mirza lived with Mirza Rustam at Zamindawar.[251]

Both, the *Akbar Nama* and *Tarikh-i-Alam Arai Abbasi* say that the two brothers, Mirza Muzaffar Husain and Mirza Rustam, did not have cordial relations with each other. As compared to Qandahar, Mirza Rustam's territory of Zamindawar and Garmser did not yield much income. Therefore, he was anxious to annex other territories. This was naturally opposed by Muzaffar Husain Mirza. The brothers fought time and again and both sustained great losses in officers and men. Their situation was further made difficult by the proximity of the Uzbeks, who posed a constant threat to the security of their territories. Finally the approach of the Mughal forces in the terrain made their position almost untenable. Mirza Rustam Safavi was the first to accept Mughal inducements in 1592-93, when he found that during his absence on a hunting expedition, Zamindawar had been seized by Muzaffar Husain Mirza. In 1595, Muzaffar Husain Mirza himself found the combined pressures from the Uzbeks and the Mughals too hard to bear. Preferring to make peace terms with the Mughals, he handed over the possession of Qandahar to them. Both the brothers arrived at Akbar's court with a large retinue. On their arrival they were welcomed and escorted to the emperor by important nobles like Asaf Khan, Abdur Rahim Khan-i-Khanan, Mirza Aziz Koka and Mirza Jani Beg.[252] Mirza Rustam was granted a mansab of 5000 *zat* 1500 *sawar* and Mirza Muzaffar Husain that of 5000 *zat* 400 *sawar*. They were assigned *jagirs* in Multan, Baluchistan and Sambhal. Mirza Rustam was also appointed as *Subadar* of Multan; Mirza Muzaffar Husain was honoured with the title of *Farzand*.[253]

In the last years of his life Muzaffar Husain Mirza was unhappy man. He grieved the loss of his territories and suffered pain on account of bodily hurt. Disappointment with the land of fluid and its envisions only heightened the pathos of Mirza who breathed his last in 1008/1599.

His daughter, called Qandahari Mahal, was in 1018/1609 married to Shahjahan, and gave birth, in 1020/1611, to Nawab Par Pahiz Banu Begum.[254] Of his sons Bahram Mirza, Haidar Mirza and Ismail Mirza were settled in India.[255] Mirza Rustam Safavi was appointed governor of Thatta (Sindh) on the death of Mirza Ghazi Tarkhan in 1021/1612, but was recalled as he ill-treated the Arghuns. After the marriage of his daughter with prince Parwiz, Jahangir raised him to a *mansab* of 6000 *zat* and appointed him governor of Allahabad. In the 21st year, he was appointed governor of Bihar. In the 1st year of Shah Jahangir's reign he was removed from Bihar and came to the court. As he was suffering from gout (*nigris*), and had grown old, he was relieved of service, and granted an annual pension of one lac and twenty thousand rupees so that he might spend his days in peace at Agra. In the 6th year of Shahjahan's reign his daughter was married to prince Shuja. Mirza Rustam died in 1051/1641-42[256] in Agra at the age of 72. As a poet he is known by his penname Fidai. He was a man of the world and understood the spirit of the age. All his sons subsequently held posts of distinction.

His brothers Abu Said Mirza and Sanjar Mirza both died in the year 1005/1596-97.[257]

Murad Safavi (Iltifat Khan)

Mirza Murad[258] was the son of Mirza Rustam Safavi (Qandahari). He came to India in the company of his father in 1002/1593 because of the Uzbek pressure.

Mirza Murad gained his heart's desire (Murad) by marrying the daughter of Abdur Rahim Khan-i-Khanan, and in the reign of Jahangir was exalted with the title of Iltifat Khan, and the *mansab* of 2000 *zat* with 800 *sawar*. He remained in the royal service for a long time even during the reign of Shahjahan. During this time he did not exert himself, and in the 16th year resigned from service, and was granted a pension rupees 40,000 a year. For a long time he lived in tranquillity and comfort in Patna, and his days were spent in ease and freedom from care.[259]

Hasan Safavi

Mirza Hasan Safavi was the son of Mirza Rustam of Qandahar. He came to India along with his father because of the Uzbek pressure in 1002/1593. In Jahangir's time Mirza Hasan attained to the rank of 1,500 *zat* and 700 *sawar*. After Shahjahan's accession he came with his father from Bihar to the court and did homage. In the 2nd year, he was dispatched/sent to Bengal and served there for a long time along with his son, Saf Shikan, among the auxiliaries of that province. In the 19th year, his rank was 3000 *zat* and 2000 *sawar*. He was granted the *jagir* of Fatehpur. In the 20th year he became *Faujdar* of Jaunpur in succession of Shah Nawaz Khan Safavi, his younger brother. In the 21st year he came from Jaunpur with his son, performed homage before the sultan and went to Bengal. In the 22nd year, he was, at Shah Shuja's request, appointed to Kuch (Kuj Bihar), and received an increase of 1,000 *sawar* in the 23rd reignal year, and at the and of 1059/ 11649 he died. He did not accept the title of Khan.[260]

Haidar Safavi

Mirza Haidar was the second son of Mirza Muzaffar Husain Husain Safavi (Qandahari). He came to India in the company of his father in 1002/11593 because of Uzbek turmoil.[261] As Mirza Muzaffar's fortunes did not follow the road of success in the court of the Emperor Akbar, his sons also did not get any high positions. In the reign of Jahangir Mirza Haidar attained the rank of 500 *zat* and 150 *sawars*. When the kingdom was glorified by the accession of Shahjahan to the throne, in view of his being descendant from a noble family, he was granted the rank of 1,000 *zat* and 2000 *sawar*.[262] He died during the fourth reignal year of the Sultan.[263]

Yadgar Ali Sultan

Yadgar Ali Sultan was one of Qazilbash Amir and a learned man. Before Shah Abbas' reign he was governor of Baghdad. In 10181/1609-10, Shah Abbas despatched Yadgar Sultan Ali Talish on a consolatory-cum-congratulatory mission to India.[264] The envoy reached the Mughal court in Muharram 1020 March 1611.[265] Jahangir records his great pleasure on the arrival of the Persian ambassador whom he amply rewarded. The envoy was recipient of various favours at the hands of the Emperor during his two and half years' stay in India.[266] He was dismissed with honours and rewards in August 1613 (A.H.1022) to accompany the Mughal envoy, Khan Alam, to Persia.[267] During the two and a half years that Yadgar Ali Sultan was in India, there were further diplomatic exchanges between the two monarchs.[268] In one of these, the Shah sent a note recommending one Salam Ullah Arab for promotion. Jahangir at once increased his *mansab* and *jagir*.[269]

Saif Khan Mirza Safi

Saif Khan, son of Amanat Khan, came to India during the reign of Jahangir probably, to seek his relative[270] who had been residing in India for some time. In view of th friendly relationship with Asaf Khan Malika Banu, the elder daughter of Asaf Khan, Yamin-ud-daula, was married to him, and he was appointed *diwan* of Gujarat. Mirza Safi, who had never dreamt of such a day, was promoted by the emperor as a reward for this great service from the rank of 700 *zat* and 300 *sawar* to that of 3000 *zat* and 2000 *sawar* given the title of Saif Khan granted a flag and drums ,and was appointed as governor to Gujarat.[271] When Khan Jahan Lodi was deputed with prince Parwiz in place of Mahabat Khan, Saif Khan was reappointed governor of Gujarat. At this time the death of emperor Jahangir occurred. After the accession of Shahjahan, Saif Khan, at the recommendation of the Begum received the *mansab* of 4000 *zat* and *sawar*[272] and was appointed governor of Bihar. He built grand houses in Patna. In the 5th year of Shaih Khan he was transferred as governor to Allahabad,[273] and in the 8th year was nominated as governor of Gujarat.[274] Later he was transferred from there and given the charge of Agra. When in the 12th reignal years Islam Khan the governor of Bengal was summoned to court for appointment as the *Wazir*; and Bengal was taken over by the agents of prince Shuja, an order was issued to Saif Khan to proceed rapidly to that province and to take charge of it till the arrival of the prince who was in Kabul. In the end of the 13th year, 1049/1639, he died in Bengal. He had three sons, Muhammad Yahya, Muhammad Shafi and Abul Qasim.[275] In the 14th year his wife Malika Banu also died.[276]

Sultan Nazar

He was the son of Amanat Khan. Sultan Nazar came to India during the Jahangir's reign with his brothers, Saif Khan and Mirza Safi,[277] to visit his relatives. Sultan Nazar Khan knew by heart the *diwans* of Khaqani and Anwari, and the *masnavi* and *Hadiqa*. At first he was the *Bakhshi* and recorder at Agra. Later, while in Gujarat he quarreled with his brother and joined Khan Jahan Lodi who had been appointed governor. He became intimate with him and received an excellent *Jagir* in the Deccan. During Shahjahan's reign he was awarded a *mansab* of 1000 *zat*.[278]

Abdur Rahim Farahani

Khwaja Abdur Rahim was engaged in clerical work in Shah Abbas' court. After this he received the *wizarat* of Kashan for some years. Afterwards he came to India with unknown reason[279]. In the initial period after his arrival he was attached to prince Jahangir, and later attended upon Khusrau, son of Jahangir and received title of Malik Anwar and the position of *Wazir*.[280] After rebellion of Khusrau he was defeated by Jahangir. Khusrau and his friends were imprisoned. Jahangir has explained these events in his memoirs:

"On Thursday Muharram 3rd, 1015/1606, in Mirza Kamran's garden they brought Khusrau before me with his hands tied and chains on his legs from the left side after the manner and custom of Chingiz Khan. They made Husain Beg stand on his right hand and Abdur-Rahim on his left. Khusrau stood weeping and trembling between them. Husain Beg, with the idea that it might profit him began to speak wildly. When his intention became apparent to me I did not allow him to continue talking, but handed over Khusrau in chains, and ordered these two villains to be put in the skins of an ox and an ass, and that they should be mounted on asses with their faces to the tail and thus taken round the city. As the ox-hide dried more quickly than that of the ass, Husain Beg remained alive for four watches and died from suffocation. Abdur-Rahim, who was in ass's skin and to whom they gave some refreshment from outside, remained alive."[281]

Jahangir has written in 1018/1609: "I gave 1000 rupees to Abdur-Rahim Khan (ass) for expenses on the 14th of the Zil-Hijja of the said year. Having pardoned all the faults of Abdur-Rahim Khan, I promoted him to the *mansab* of *Yuzbashi* (centurion) and 20 *sawars* and ordered him to go to Kashmir along with the *Bakhshi* of that place and hold a muster of the troops of Qilij Khan and all the *Jagirdars* and *Uymaks* in the service and to prepare a list.[282] According to Auhadi, Farahani died some time around 1023/1614 in Bengal.[283]

Imam Quli Beg Shamlu

Imam Quli Beg migrated to India because of dissatisfaction with his position in Iran. He was one the nobles and *amirs* of Jahangir's reign.[284] According to Waris Iman Quli Shamlu and Muhammad Amin Shamlu, who were Yuzbashis (Commander of one hundred soldiers), Iman Quli Shamlu came to India in 1651, and he was granted the rank, *Khilat*, horse and Rs. 5000 *inam*. Later he was appointed *Qiladar* of Zafarnagar Balaghat.[285] He died in Bengal.[286]

Muhammad Taqi

Muhammad Taqi *Tavildar Tansuqat* (cashier of goods) came to India 1040/1630, with Muhammad Ali who was the ambassador of Shah Safi to Shahjahan.[287]

Aqil Khan Inayat Ullah

Aqil Khan was the nephew and adopted son of Afzal Khan Mulla Shukr Ullah.[288] His father's name was Abdul Haq. He came to India in the company of his father during Shahjahan's reign to seek employment. Aqil Khan, in the 12th year of Shahjahan was made *Arz Mukarrar* (reviser of petitions), and after wards received the title of Aqil Khan. In succession to Multafat Khan he was made *Diwan* of the *Buyutat.* In the 15th reignal year his *mansab* was raised to 2000 *zat* and 5000 *sawar* and was appointed as *Mir Saman.* In the 18th year he was recipient of promotion and was given an additional *sawar* of 200 along with the office of *Arz Waqai* of the province. In the 19th year his rank was 2500 *zat* and 800 *sawar*. Afterwards Aqil Khan received a further increase of 200 *sawar* and was made the 2nd *Bakhshi*, and *Arz Waqai* of the provinces. In the 20th year his rank became 3000 *zat* and 1000 *sawars* and he was honoured with gift of a flag. In the end of the 22nd year corresponding to 1059/1649, at the time taken when Kabul was the halting place of the standards of victory, he died unexpectedly. He was well versed in poetry and the science of accounting. The step daughter of Sati[289] Khanam who had charge of the king's harem was married to him.[290]

Table : 2.2

IRANIANS IN MUGHAL POLITICS AND ADMINISTRATION

Rg	Pr	Nu	Reasons and Contexts of Migration																									
			X1	X2	X3	X4	X5	X6	X7	X8	X9	X10	X11	X12	X13	X14	X15	X16	X17	X18	X19	X20	X21	X22	X23	X24	X25	X 26
NO	Ak	0																										
0	Ja	0																										
	Sh	0																										
WNW	Ak	1		1																								
5	Ja	1																										
	Sh	3								2										1								1
SW	Ak	0																										
0	Ja	0																										
	Sh	0																										
CP	Ak	14	3	2						1				1		5												2
26	Ja	7	1			1										3												2
	Sh	5		1						1														2			1	
SO	Ak	1														1												
2	Ja	1														1												
	Sh	0																										
ENE	Ak	3		1												1												1
7	Ja	4								2						1												1
	Sh	0																										
SE	Ak	0																										
0	Ja	0																										
	Sh	0																										
UA	Ak	6		1	5																							
14	Ja	5				1								2													1	1
	Sh	3							1	1										1								
Total		54	4	6	5	2			1	7				3		12				2				2			2	8

Graph : 2.1

Number of Iranians in Mughal Politics and Administration according tothe reasons and contexts of their migration

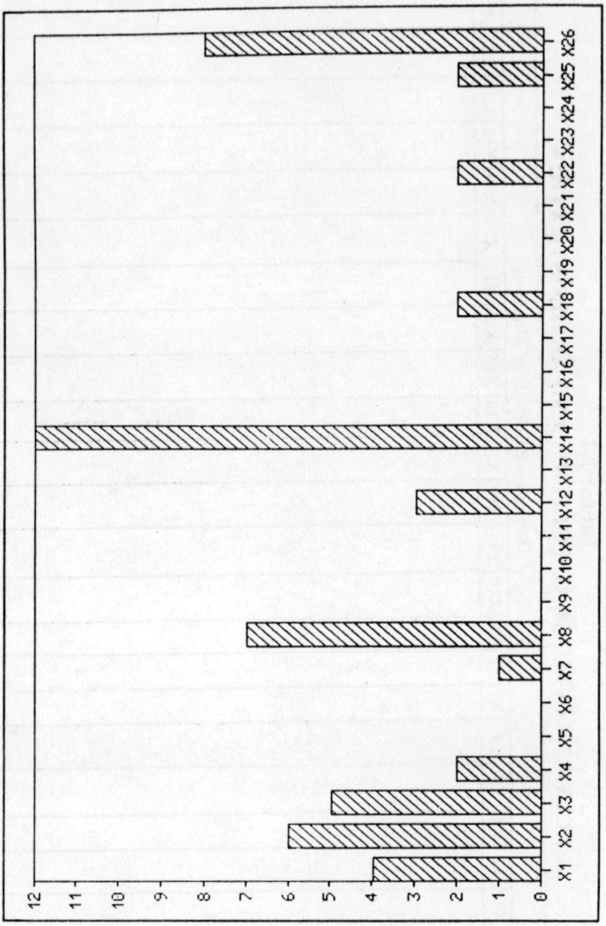

REFERENCES

1. S.A. Arjomand, *The Shadow of God and the Hidden Imam*, University of Chicago, 1984, pp.119-21.
2. Badauni states that Saifi Sayyids were all bigoted Sunnis and Shah Tahmasp deprived them of their estates, thus compelling Mir Abdul Latif to come to India. (see: Badauni;1969; Vol. III, pp. 97-99) Also see; *A.N.* Vol. II, p.19.
3. See: *Ibid*, also see: *M.U.*, text, Vol. II, pp. 381-83.
4. *A.A.A.* Vol. 1955, II, p. 1041.
5. Lahori, Vol. II, pp. 92, 123-26, 222-23.
6. For details see; Above, Chapter I, under his name.
7. *M.U.*, text, Vol. III, p. 376.
8. *M.U.*, Tr. H. Beveridge, Reprint; Patna, 1979, Vol. I, p. 269.
9. Mohd. Afzal Khan, 'The Mamuris.: An Unexplored Clan in the Mughal Nobility', in: *Indian History Congress*, 1981, p. 211, note. I.
10. A.G. Maani, The Caravan of India, 2 vols Mashhad 1369 A.s/1990, Vol. I, p.117 note. 2 and Vol. II, p. 917, also see: *Jahangir Nama,* ed. by Muhammad Hashim, Tehran, 1359 A.S/1980, pp. 48, 207, 209-10.
11. *M.U.* text, Vol. III, p. 376.
12. *A.N.*, Nawal Kishore edition, 1883, Vol. III, p. 328.
13. *Ibid.*, p. 426.
14. *Tuzuk-i-Jahangiri,* ed. Sir Syed Ahmed, Ghazipur, 1863, p. 6.
15. *M.U.*, text; p. 378.
16. *Amal-i-Salih,* Vol. III, pp.388-89.
17. *Ibid.,* also see: *M.U.* Vol. I. Tr. by Beveridge, p. 447.
18. Franvcois Bernier, *Travels in the Mughal Empire,* 1656-1668 Tr. A. Constable, second edition, Delhi, 1968, p. 4.
19. *Afzal Husain;* Growth of Irani Element in Akbar's nobility,' in: *Indian History Congress*, Aligarh, 1975, pp.170-71 cited from Haft Iqlim, Amin Razi, Qutub-ud-din collection Maulana Azad Library, A.M.U. Aligarh, ff. 453b-455a.
20. *M.U.* text, Vol. I, pp. 127-31. About Itimad-ud-daula position see also: table 2.1 and under his name.
21. Lahori, I, pp. 70-71.
22. *Ibid.,* pp.180, 193 see also; *Amal-i-Salih*, Vol. I, p. 284.
23. Ibn Hasan: *The Central Structure of the Mughal Empire*, New Delhi, reprint 1970, p.134.
24. *M.U.,* text, Vol. III, pp. 385-409.
25. *Z.kh,* Vol. II, pp.116-73.

26. See: below under the name of Mahabat Khan.
27. Lahori, Vol. I (a) pp. 257-58; I (b), p. 339; z. Kh. Vol. II, p. 255 where his name is wrongly mentioned as Mulla Abdur Shakur.
28. About Islam-khan Mashhadi, see below under his name.
29. See: table 2.1.
30. About Yadgar Ali Sultan see: above, chapter I, under his name.
31. *M.U.* text, Vol. III, pp. 296, 434, see also; Above, Chapter I.
32. *A.N.* Vol. III, 434-41, see also, *Tabaqat-i-Akbari*, Vol. II, p. 423 see also: M. Q. Fireshta, 1863, Vol. I, p. 511.
33. *A.N.* Vol. I. p. 511, pp. 645-46; 669, 671, *M.U.* text: Vol. III, pp. 296-302.
34. B. Nihavandi, Vol. III, pp. 1608-13.
35. Shah Beg Arghun was the governor of Qandahar in Akbar's time. In 1016/1607 Jahangir appointed him governor of Qandahar and Kabul and gave him title of Khan Dauran. See: *Ain-i-Akbari*. Tr. by Blochmann, Vol. I, p. 328.
36. N. Qazwini, 1926, pp. 563-67.
37. M.S. Mina, *Subh-i-Sadiq*, Aligarah, No. 65415; p. 68; also see: *N.A.* Shirazi, *Hadiqat-ul-Salatin*, Haidarabad Deccan, 1961, p.179.
38. *Ibid.*
39. *Ibid.*, p.179.
40. B. Nihavandi, Vol. III, pp. 1638-42.
41. *Ain-i-Akbari*, Tr. by Blochmann, Vol. I, p. 572.
42. *Ibid;* also see. *M.U.* text, Vol. I, p.127 and *A.N.* Vol. I, p. 432.
43. The Dibacha (Preface) of the *Tuzuk* (p. 20) and the *Iqbal-Nama* (p. 54) agree verbatim.
44. *M.U.* text, Vol. I, p.127.
45. *Ain-i-Akbari*, Tr. By Blochmann, Vol. I, p. 572 and for details see:Irfan Habib: *The family of Nur Jahan during Jahangir's reign: A Political Study*, in : Medieval India, A Miscellany Dept. of History, Aligarh Muslim University, 1969. Vol. I, pp.74-81.
46. *M.U.* text, Vol. I, p.128; Khafi Khan, however, records that Ghiyas Beg was accompanied by two daughters, one son and his wife. He also says: Ghiyas Beg came to India because of hardship and dissatisfaction of his position in Iran. see; Khafi Khan, Vol. I, Calcutta, 1869, p. 263.
47. Blochmann Tr. of *Ain-i-Akbari*, Vol. I, p. 572.
48. Mutamad Khan, *Iqbal Nama-i-Jahangiri*, Calcutta, Bib. Indica, 1865, p. 55, also see: *M.U.* text, Vol. I, p. 128.
49. Ashok Kumar Sarkar, Itimad-ud-daula–'A sketch of his life and career', in: *The Quarterly Review of Historical Studies*, Vol. X, N. 3-1970-71, p.155.

50. *M.U.* tr. by Beveridge Vol. II, Part II, p.1074 and see: *Tuzuk*, Tr. by Rogers and Beveridge, Vol. I, pp.122-23, but the imprisonment and imposition of fine on Ghiyas Beg are not mentioned.
51. See : *M.U.* text, Vol. II, pp. 8, 9.
52. *M.U.* tr. by Beveridge, Vol. II, p. 1074.
53. See: *Tuzuk*, I, pp. 280, 320 and Blochmann. Tr., *Ain-i-Akbari*, Vol. I, p. 573.
54. Beni Prasad, 1939, p.172.
55. S.F. Bhakkari, *Zakhirat-ul-Khawanin*, 3 Vols. Karachi, 1970. Vol. II, p. 15.
56. *Ain-i-Akbari*, tr. by Blochmann, Vol. I, p. 573, *M.U.* tr. by Beveridge, Vol. II, part. II, pp. 1075-76, *Tuzuk*. Tr. by Roger and Beveridge, p. 222, A. K. Sarkar, 1970-71, p.162.
57. *M.U.* tr. by Beveridge, Vol. II, Part. II, p.1076 and see: Blochmann translations of *Ain-i-Akbari*, Vol. I, p. 573 vide see; A. K. Sarkar, 1970-71, pp. 162-63.
58. *M.U*, text; Vol. I, p.128 and also see: *Ain-i-Akbari*, Tr. by Blochmann, Vol. I, p. 572.
59. See: *Tuzuk;* Tr. Rogers, Vol. I, p. 202 also see: *Z. kh*, Vol. II, p. 32.
60. *Jahangir Nama;* 1980, pp. 509-11 and also see: *Tuzuk*, Tr. by Rogers, Vol. I, p. 260.
61. *M.U.* text Vol. I, pp. 151-56 and Beveridge Tr. *M.U.* Vol. I, pp. 288-89
62. Lahori, Vol. I (a) pp.70-71.
63. *Ibid.*, pp. 180, 93 and see; *Amal-i-Salih*, Vol. I, p. 284.
64. *Ibid.*, Hasan, 1971, p. 134.
65. Daula had been in use among the *Khalifas* and the Ghaznavis. Thus Yamin-ud-daula which title Shahjahan bestowed on Abul Hasan Asaf Khan IV, had also been the title of Mahmud of Ghaznavi when Prince. The kings of the Deccan occasionally conferred titles with Daula. This is very likely the reason why Akbar conferred the title of Izud-daula on Mir Fath ullah Shirazi, who had come from the Deccan, the title of Malik, so common among the Pathans, was conferred by the Mughal (Chaghtai) kings of Delhi titles with Jang as Firuzjang, Nusrat Jang, etc. came into fashion with Jahangir. (See: *Ain-i-Akbari*, Tr. By Blochmann, Vol. T, p. 398, note. 2).
66. *M.U.* Beveridge Tr. Vol. I, pp. 293-94.
67. *Z.kh.* Vol. II, p. 33 for details about Asaf Khan see: *Jahangir Nama*, 1980, pp. 509-15 also see: *M.U.* text, Vol. I, pp. 151-60; *Z.kh.* Vol. II, pp. 32-46.
68. About Mirza Ghiyas-ud-din see: *Ain-i-Akbari:* Blochmann Tr. Vol. I, p. 398.

69. See: *Ain-i-Akbari,* Blochmann Tr. Vol. I, pp. 550-51.
70. Also called Muhammad Talib-vide: Lahori, Vol. II, p. 248.
71. Blochmann tr, *Ain,* Vol. I, p. 575.
72. *Ibid.,* cited from Lahori, Vol. II, p. 278.
73. See: *Tuzuk:* Tr. by Rogers, Vol. II, p. 215.
74. *Amal-i-Salih,* Vol. III, p. 451.
75. Palamu in Lahori, Vol. II, pp. 248, pp. 248 and 356, Palamu is in Lohardaga, Chhota Nagpur.
76. *M.U.* text, Vol. I, pp. 180-82 and Beveridge Tr. Vol. I, pp. 714-15 also see: *Amal-i-Salih,* Vol. I, p. 494 and See: *Tuzuk,* Tr. by Rogers, Vol. I, p. 218, 319, 320, 373 and Vol. II, pp. 2, 7, 269.
77. *Z.kh.,* Vol. II, p. 209-210.
78. See: This text under his name and T. Auhadi, Fol. 972.
79. In *Tuzuk,* he received title of Khan in 10th year. See: *Tuzuk,* Tr. by Rogers, p. 310.
80. This seems to be incorrect, as in *Tuzuk-i-Jahangiri* (Rogers Translation), Vol. I, p. 301, he is mentioned in the 10th year as having been granted an increase of 300 *sawar* bringing his rank to 1,000 *zat* and *sawar.*
81. *M.U.,* text, Vol. II, pp. 729-30.
82. *Tuzuk,* Tr by Rogers, Vol. I, p. 425.
83. *M.U.,* Tr by Beveridge, Vol. II, pt. II, p. 657, cited from Lahori, Vol. I, part I, p. 181.
84. *M.U.,* text, Vol. II, pp. 730-31 and Beveridge Translation, Vol. II, p. II, p. 657 cited from Lahori, Vol. I, pt. I, p.186.
85. *Z.kh,* Vol.II, p. 209.
86. *M.U.* Beveridge Translation, Vol. II, pt. II, p. 657.
87. *M.U* Tr. by Beveridge, Vol. II, pt. II, p. 658 also see: *Z. Kh.,* Vol. II, p. 209. For details also see: *Jahangir Nama,* 1980, pp. 176, 438, 410 and *Amal-i-Salih,* Vol. I, pp. 616-17, Vol. III, p. 452.
88. *M.U.,* text, Vol. II, pp. 729-31.
89. *Ibid.,* pp.729-31.
90. S. Mustaid Khan; *Maasir-i-Alamgiri,* ed., Agha Ahmad Ali, Bib. Indica Calcutta, 1871, p. 103. For an account of Jafar Khan, See also: Sir Jadunath Sarkar, *History of Aurangzeb,* Vol. III, New Delhi, 1928, p. 65-67. He was appointed *Wazir A'zam* on 30th December 1663, and died on 6th May, 1970.
91. *M.U.* text, Vol. I, pp. 531-35 and Beveridge Translation, Vol. I, pp. 722-23.
92. Blochmann says: Mirza Zain-ul-Abidin was a commander of fifteen hundred, 500 horse, and died in the second year of Shahjahan's reign. See, Blochmann, Vol. I, p. 453.

93. *M.U.* text, Vol. I, pp. 113-114 and Tr. by Beveridge, Vol. I, p. 286.
94. T. Auhadi, Fol. 284.
95. M.T. Nasrabadi; 1938, p. 60.
96. Mir Yahya is the author of a historical compendium called *Lubabul-Tawarikh,* composed in 1514. His second son Ala-ud-daula wrote under the penname name of Kami, and is the author of the *Nafais-ul-Maasir*, a *tazkira,* or work on literature.
97. He was first to teach Akbar the principle of *Sulh-i-Kull* (peace with all), the Persian term which Abul-Fazl so often uses to describe Akbar's policy of toleration. Abul Fazl (*A.N.*, Vol. II, 23) says that Abdul Latif was accused in Persia of being a Sunni and in Hindustan of being a Shia.
98. The rider of the grey horse Mir Sayyid Husain is a saint who has a shrine at Ajmer.
99. About Mir Muhammad Sharif See: Badauni, Vol. II, p. 230.
100. *A.N.*, Vol. III, p. 357, Beveridge transl., Vol. III, p. 524. According to Kewal Ram the title was conferred on Naqib Khan in the 25th year for his gallant conduct in repelling a night attack made by Masum Khan-i-Kabuli on the Imperialists under Todar Mal and Sadiq Khan.See: *Ain-i-Akbari*, Blochmann Trans., Vol. III, p. 497 note 4 and see: Kewal Ram, *Tazkirat-ul-Umara,* Trans. by S.M. Azizuddin Husain, New Delhi, 1985, p. 178.
101. *Ain-i-Akbari,* Blochmann Trans., Vol. I, pp. 497-8.
102. Badauni, trans., by S.W. Haig, Vol. III, p. 444, note. 3.
103. Kewal Ram, trans., by S.M.A. Husain, p. 178.
104. *Jahangir Nama,* 1980, pp. 17, 150 and also see: Reges Trans., pp. 264-65.
105. *Ain-i-Akbari,* Blochmann Trans., Vol. I, p. 498 cited from, Badauni, III, p. 321.About Naqib Khan also see: *M.U.* text, Vol. III, pp. 812-17, B. Nihavandi, Vol. III, p. 41, T. Auhadi, Fol. 776.
106. See: *Ain*, Tr. by Blochmann, Vol. I, pp. 369-71.
107. *M.U.*, text, Vol. III, p. 817 and see: M.U., Tr. by Beveridge, Vol. II, p. 384.
108. About Qamar Khan See: *M.U.* text; Vol. III, pp. 53-54.
109. See; under Naqib Qazwini.
110. For details see.*Tuzuk*, Tr. by Rogers, Vol. I, p. 71.
111. *Tuzuk,* Tr. by Rogers, Vol. I, pp. 441-42.
112. *Ain-i-Akbari,* Tr. by Blochmann, Vol. I, p. 454.
113. See: A.G. Maani, 1948, Footnotes of pp. 117, 303, 917.
114. *Jahangir Nama,* Tehran Press, pp. 48, 207 and also see: *Tuzuk*, Tr. by Rogers, Vol. I, pp. 13, 16, 82, 190.

115. *Jahangir Nama,* 1980, pp. 209, 210 also see, *Tuzuk,* 1914, Vol. II, pp. 18, 24.
116. *M.U.,* text, Vol. III, p. 376.
117. See: *A.N.,* Vol. III, p. 784.
118. *M.U.* text, Vol. III, pp. 376-79 and also see : *M.U,* Tr by Beveridge, Vol. II, part I, pp 357-59, also see: *Z.kh,* Vol. I, pp. 206-7.
119. T. Auhadi, Fol. 494.
120. The author of *Maasir-i-Rahimi* mentions under the title: Salih Ardavani, Mirzai and Mirza Salih Beg. See: B. Nihavandi; Vol. III, p. 1643. The author of *Arafat-ul-Ashiqin* has written Shah Beg Hemati Azadani; see: T. Auhadi, Fol. 399.
121. *Ibid.*
122. M.T. Nasrabadi, p. 452.
123. M.S. Mina. *Subh-i-Sadiq*, pp. 42-43, 75-76 also see: B. Nihavandi, Vol. III, pp. 1643-47.
124. In *Tuzuk,* Tr. by Rogers, Vol. I, p. 418, it is stated that it the 12th year Nur-ud-din Quli was honoured with the *mansab,* original and increase of 300 *zat* and 600 *sawar.*
125. *M.U.* text, Vol. III, pp. 817-18 and *M.U.* Tr. by Beveridge, Vol. II, pt. I, p. 463 cited from Lahori, Vol. I, p. 82.
126. The author of *Zakhratul-Khawanin* says: A party of some foolish persons attacked him at night, cut him to pieces and disappeared. The killers could not be traced. He was simple-minded, loved company and a friendly person. It is said that Nur-ud-din Quli had sent money and got constructed a mosque in the *Bazar* (market) at Esfahan. See: *Z.Kh,* Vol. II, pp. 371-72.
127. *M.U.* Tr. by Beveridge, Vol. II, pt. I, p. 463 also see: *Jahangir Nama,* 1980, p. 79.
128. *Jahangir Nama,* 1980, pp. 34, 67 and also see; *Tuzuk,* Tr. by Rogers, Vol. I, pp. 117, 300, 372.
129. T. Auhadi, Fol. 728 and see: A.A. Razi, Haft Iqlim, Vol. III, ed. Dr. Ishaq, Calcutta, 1939, p. 176.
130. About Darsani see: *Ain-i-Akbari,* Lucknow Press, 1869, Vol. I, p. 185 and also see: Badauni, Vol. II, pp. 325, 391.
131. T. Auhadi, Fol. 576.
132. Saveh lies between Qom and Hamadan in Markazi province. The Burhan Qati says that Saveh had a small lake or stream (*daryacha*) which every year drowned a man, and that it dried up on the night of Muhammad's birth.
133. It is better to say Iraq-*Ajam* or Iran.

134. M.U. text, Vol. I, p. 174 and Tr. by Beveridge, Vol. I, p. 315 also see: *Z.kh.*, Vol. II, p. 200.
135. Lahori, Vol. I, p. 159.
136. *Ibid.*, p. 186, where the date given is 8 Rajab.
137. Khafi K., Vol. I, p. 424.
138. She died in the 7th year of the reign. See: Lahori, Vol. II, p. 137.
139. The author of *Zakiratul-Khawanin* says: Azam Khan died a natural death during his governorship of Patna. See: *Z.kh.*, Vol. II, p. 200.
140. *M.U.* text, Vol. I, pp. 174-180 and see *M.U.*, Tr. by Beveridge, Vol. I, pp. 317-318 also see: *Amal-i-Salih,* Vol. I, p. 508 and Vol. III, pp. 69, 450, M.S. Mina, *Subh-i-Sadiq*, p. 74.
141. T. Auhadi, Fol. III.
142. M.S. Mina, *Subh-i-Sadiq,* p. 49.
143. For Ganj Ali Khan See: M.I. Bastani Parizi, *Ganj Ali Khan*. Kerman, Farhang-i-Honar, 353/1979.
144. *A.A.A.*, Vol. II, p.1041. Zig is a Kurdish tribe who lived in the mountains of Giluyah. See: S. Abdur Rashid, *Farhang-i-Rashidi,* ed. Maulavi Zulfiqar Ali and Azizur Rahman, 2 Vols, Calcutta, 1875, Vol. I, p. 377.
145. *A.A.A.*, 1955 Vol. I, pp. 414, 559, 576.
146. *M.U.*, Tr. by Beveridge, Vol. I, p. 186.
147. *A.A.A.*, Vol. II, p. 1041, See also; H.I.S. Kanwar, Ali Mardan Khan in: *Islamic Culture,* Vol. XLVIII, No. 2, April, 1973, p.105.
148. *A.A.A.*, Vol. II, pp.1041, 1086.
149. H.I.S. Kanwari, Ali Mardan Khan; In; *Islamic Culture*, Vol. XLVII, 1973, p. 106.
150. Bernier says that Ali Mardan Khan was recalled from Qandahar to give an account of his governments, see.: F. Berneir, ed. by Constable, 1891, p. 184.' For details see: Ishwari Prasad, *A Short History of Muslim Rule in India,* Allahabad, 1939, Vol. II, pp. 497-98.
151. *Z.kh.*, Vol. III, p. 28, See also; Lahori, Vol. II, pp. 92, 123-26, 222-23.
152. Lahori, Vol. II, pp. 320-21, Waris, *op.cit.*, p. 135.
153. *M.U.*, Tr. by Beveridge, Vol. I, p. 188 see also, Lahori, Vol. II, pp. 401-404, 456-63.
154. *M.U.* text, pp. 188-90, see also; Lahori, Vol. II, pp. 482-92, 512-43 548-56.
155. For details, see; Lahori, Vol. II, p. 68.
156. *Ibid.*, pp.163, 128.
157. *M.U.*, text, Vol. II, p.799.
158. *Ibid.*, p. 806, See also; Ishwari Prasad, 1939, Vol. II, p. 526, note 57.
159. *M.U., op.cit*, Tr. by Beveridge, Vol. I, p. 191, See also; Lahori, p.633.

160. *M.U.* Tr. by Beveridge, Vol. I, pp. 191-92, Lahori, Vol. II, pp. 686- 709.
161. *M.U., Ibid.*, see also; Waris, *op.cit*, pp. 131, 138, 140.
162. *M.U.*, text, Vol. I, p. 192, See also; *Amal-i-Salih*, Vol. III, p. 246.
163. Pir Ghulam Husain Khuihami, *Tarikh-i-Hasan*, Srinagar, 1954, Vol. I, p. 299, See also; Lahori, Vol. II, p. 504.
164. Lahori, *op.cit,* Vol. II, pp. 169-70.
165. *Tarikh-i-Hasan,* 1954, Vol. I, p. 300.
166. H.I.S. Kanwar, 1973, pp. 108-12, See also; *Z.kh.*, Vol. III, p. 28, Lahori, Vol. II, pp. 168-69, 233-34, 311-12, 315. For more information about Ali Mardan Khan see: *Amal-i-Salih*, Vol. II, 296-297 and Vol. III, pp. 264, 448, *M.U.*, text, Vol. I, p. 44, and Aslah Kashmiri, *Tazkira Shuarai Kashmir*, ed. Sayyid Hasam-ud-Din Rashidi, Karachi, 1967, pp. 98-99.
167. Lahori, Vol. II, pp. 497-98.
168. *M.U.*, Tr. by Beveridge, Vol. I, pp. 193-94, *M.U.* text, Vol. II, p. 807, and Lahori, Vol. II, p. 246.
169. For Ali Mardan Khan see: *M.U.* text, Vol. II, pp. 795-807.
170. *M.U.* text, Vol. I, pp. 295-98 and Beveridge Translation, Vol. I, pp. 653-54.
171. *M.U.* text, Vol. I, pp. 295-98 and Beveridge Translation, Vol. I, pp. 653-54.
172. *M.U.* text, pp. 298-99 and Beveridge Translation, Vol, I, pp. 656-57 also see: Muhammad Kazim, *Alamgir Nama.* Ed. Maulavis Khadim Husain and Abdul Hai, 2 Vols, Bib. Indica, Calcutta, 1868-73, pp. 426-27
173. *M.U.* text, Vol. I, p. 300 and Beveridge Translation, Vol. I, p. 657. For details see: *Maasir-i-Alamgiri,* 1871, pp. 297, 496-97.
174. *M.U.* text, pp. 300-301.
175. The letter exists in four versions. Two of these, one mainly congratulatory and one condolatory, may have been actually sent. For details, see; R. Islam, 1979, pt. I, pp. 239-242.
176. While the Safavid sources make only casual references to the embassy of Muhammad Ali Afshar Esfahani, the Mughal chronicles describe it in profuse detail (see: *Amal-i-Salih,* Vol. I, pp. 425/427, 428, 455, 480, also see: Lahori, Vol. I, pt. I, pp. 304, 361-62, 365-67, 397, 422, 427, 429, 433.
177. See: *M.U.* text, Vol. II, pp. 283-85.
178. For Sati Khanam see: *M.U.* text, Vol.II, pp. 791-92.
179. The title granted was that of Rahmat Khan, See; Lahori, Vol. II, p. 223.
180. *M.U.* Tr. by Beveridge, Vol. II, pt. I, p. 561. Cited from *Amal-i-Salih*, Vol. III, p. 183.

181. For a detailed account see: Sir Jadunath Sarkar, *History of Aurangzib*, Vol. I, pp. 302-305.
182. *M.U., op. cit*, cited from *Alamgir Nama*, p. 139.
183. *M.U.* text, Vol. II, pp. 284-85 and Beveridge Translation, Vol. II, pt. I, pp. 561-62.
184. *Amal-i-Salih,* Vol. II, pp. 388-89.
185. *Ibid.*, p. 117.
186. *Ibid.*, pp. 210-11, see also; *M.U.*, Vol. I, Tr. by Beveridge, p. 447.
187. *Ibid.*, see also; *Amal-i-Salih,* Vol. III, p. 389.
188. *M.U.*, Vol. I, Tr. by Beveridge, p. 447, from Bernnier, Vol. I, p. 67. He resigned because he did not approve of Dara Shukoh.
189. *M.U.* Tr. by Beveridge, Vol. I, p. 447.
190. *Ibid.*, p. 448 see also; G.A. Azad Bilgrami, *Sarv-i-Azad* (*Maasir-ul-kiram*), Lohore, 1913, pp. 110-111, but the author of *Amal-i-Salih* mentions Mulla Shafia died in 1081/1669. See: *Amal-i-Salih,* Vol. III, p. 389. For more information about him also see; Waris, pp. 175,194, 206, 289, 306.
191. *M.U.* text, Vol. II, pp. 31-32, See also; *M.U.* Tr. by Beveridge, Vol. I, p. 448.
192. F. Bernier, Vol. I, p. 4.
193. *M.U.* text, Vol. III, pp. 385-409.
194. *Z.Kh,* Vol. II, pp. 116-173.
195. *Tuzuk,* 1863, p.10.
196. *Tuzuk,* 1863, p.10.
197. *Z.Kh.*, Vol. II, p. 17. Manucci believes that this was the main reason for the rise of Mahabat Khan (See: Niccolao Manucci, *Storia do Mogor*, ed. and Tr. William Irvine, London, 1970, Vol. I, pp.166-67).
198. According to Khafi Khan, I, p. 259, he received rank of 3000 *zat* with 2000 *sawar*. For detailed chart of Mahabat Khan's offices see: Banaresi Prasad, 1939, p. 195, note 25.
199. *Tuzuk,* 1863, p. 148, *Z.Kh.*, Vol. II, p. 117, but it does not mention about *du aspa*, *sih aspa* rank being given to him.
200. Shah Beg Khan, Khan Dauran was transferred as the governor of Thatta and Mahabat Khan appointed to Kabul and Bangash, *Tuzuk,* Tr. by Rogers, Vol. I, p. 397.
201. A. Husain, 'Mahabat Khan and Court Politics during Jahangir's Reign', in: *Proceedings of the Indian History Congress,* Mysore, 54th Session (1993), p. 2/111, Cited: From *Tuzuk*, 1863, pp. 267, 280, 320 and *Iqbal-Nama Jahangiri,* pp. 129-30, 189.
202. A. Husain, 'Mahabat Khan and Court Politics during Jahangir's Reign', in; *P.I.H.C*; 1993, p. 212 cited from *Tuzuk,* pp. 343-44.

203. *Ibid.*, cited from, *Iqbal Nama*, p. 195, *Tuzuk*, p. 348.
204. Lahori, *op. cit*, Vol.I, pp. 116-17.
205. *M.U.* Tr. by Beveridge, Vol.II, Pt. I, pp. 20-21, cited, from Lahori, Vol. I, p. 424.
206. *M.U.*, Tr. by Beveridge, Vol. II, pt. I, p. 27, See also, *Z.Kh.*, Vol. II, pp. 172-73.
207. *Z.Kh.*, Vol. II, pp. 164-65.
208. *Ibid.*, p. 162.
209. *M.U.*, Tr. by Beveridge, Vol. II, pt. I, p. 28, See also, *Z.Kh.*, Vol. II, p. 171.
210. For details see: I. Ahmad, Mahabat Khan, Khan-i-Khanan A Case Study of Iranian Cultural Influences on the Mughal Nobility in: *Islamic Culture*, Vol. LII, No. 2, 1978, pp. 160-62. For details and more information about Mahabat Khan see: *M.U.* text, Vol. III, pp. 385-409, see also Mirza Nathan, *Baharistan-i-Ghaibi*, transl. Borah, 2 Vols, Gauhati, 1939, pp. 755-56, N. Qazwini, 1961, pp. 762-63 and T. Auhadi, fol. 731.
211. Lahori, pp. 339-40 also see: Qazwini, Fol. 420b, *Amal-i-Salih;* Vol. III, pp. 385-86.
212. *M.U.* Tr by Beveridge, Vol. I, p. 149, Lahori, p. 339-40, *Tuzuk*, Tr. by Rogers, Vol. I, pp. 368, 387, 402 and Vol. II, p. 206, See also *Amal-i-Salih*, Vol. II, p. 385.
213. *M.U.* Tr. by Beveridge, Vol. I, pp. 152-53 also Qazwini, Fol. 420 and Lahori, pp. 339-40.
214. *M.U. op. cit.* For details and more information about his character see: *Amal-i-Salih,* Vol. III, pp. 385-86 Lahori, pp. 339-40, Qazwini, Fol. 420.
215. But Rogers say, Afzal Khan had son by the name of Mirza Muhammad who was killed in India. For details see; *Tuzuk*, Tr. by Rogers, Vol. II, pp. 289-90. It is not correct, because he adopted his brother's son Inayat Ullah Khan, who had the title of Aqil Khan, was brought up by him as a son. See: *M.U.* Tr. by Beveridge, Vol. I, p. 153.
216. Q.A. Mir Munshi Qomi, *Khulasatul Tawarikh*, Tehran, Malik Library, N. 4067, pp. 729, 741, 913, 915.
217. B. Nihavandi, Vol. III, pp. 1613-27.
218. T. Auhadi, Fol. 512.
219. M.S. Mina, *Subh-i-Sadiq*, p. 58.
220. *Tuzuk*, Tr. by Rogers, Vol. I, p. 167.
221. *Ibid.*, p. 256 but this was in the 8th year.
222. *Z.Kh.*, Vol. II, p. 305.

223. *Tuzuk*, Tr. by Rogers, p. 303, not in the 8th year as in the text, but in the 10th year.
224. *M.U.*, text, Vol. II, pp. 736-37 and Beveridge Translation, Vol. II, pt. II, p. 671 cited from *Iqbalnama-i-Jahangiri*, pp. 278-79, also see Beni Prasad, 1930, p. 419, this took place near Shahabad.
225. *Z.Kh.*, Vol. II, p. 306.
226. *M.U., op. cit,* quoted from Lahori, Vol. I, pt. I, p. 250.
227. *M.U., op. cit.*, quoted from Lahori, Vol. I, pt. I, p. 725.
228. *M.U.* text, Vol. II, pp. 736-38 and Beveridge Translation, Vol. II, pt. II, p. 672 also see; *Jahangir Nama*, 1980, pp. 146, 172.
229. *Z.Kh.*, Vol. II, p. 306.
230. *Tuzuk*, Tr. by Rogers, Vol. I, p. 79.
231. For details see: *M.U.* text; Vol. I, pp. 737-39 and Beveridge Translation Vol. I, pp. 128-130 also see; *Tuzuk*, Tr. by Rogers, Vol. I, pp. 103, 172, 192, 219, 221, and Vol. II, pp. 5, 82, 127, 193, 220, 251, 254 and see: M.G.A. *Azad-i-Bilgrami*, 1913, p. 95.
232. *M.U.* Tr. by Beveridge, *op. cit*, Vol. I, p. 694 also see: *Z.kh.*, Vol. III, p. 25.
233. That is, 1st *Bakhshi* (see; Lahori, Vol. I, p. 542.
234. See: *M.U.* text, Vol. I, p. 757.
235. *M.U.* Tr by Beveridge, *op. cit.*, Vol. I, pp. 694-95 for details see: *M.U.* text, Vol. I, pp. 162-67 also see: *Z.Kh.* Vol. II, pp. 26-27 and see: *M.G. A.Azad-i-Bilgrami*, 1913, p. 64.
236. Mir Abd-ur-Rahman was sent off in the 16th year of Aurangzeb as the chamberlain (*Hajabat*) of Haidarabad Suba, and for some time was *Bakhshi* and Reporter of Aurangabad and also for a time he was master of the horse and *Darogha-i-Arz Mukarrar* or superintendent of revision department. (See: *M.U.* text, Vol. I, p.167).
237. *M.U.* text, Vol. II, pp. 812-13 and Beveridge Translation, Vol. I, p. 65.
238. See: *M.U.* text, Vol. I, pp. 162-67.
239. *Amal-i-Salih*, Vol. II, pp. 433-34.
240. *Ibid.*, Vol. III, p. 9.
241. *Ibid.*, p. 105.
242. *Ibid.*, p. 151. *Ibid.*, p. 175.
243. *M.U.* Tr. By Beveridge, Vol. II, pt. II, pp. 667-68., also see: *Alamgir Nama*, 1868-73, p. 292.
244. See: *Massir-i-Alamgiri;* 1871, pp. 90, 132, 167, 181, 243.
245. *M.U.* Tr. by Beveridge, Vol. II, pt. II, p. 669 also Kafi Khan, Vol. II, p. 827, for details see: *M.U.* text; Vol. II, pp.740-42.
246. T. Auhadi, Fol. 167.

247. *Jahangir Nama,* 1980, p. 414.
248. M.S. Mina: *Subh-i-Sadiq,* p. 73.
249. *Jahangir Nama,* 1980, pp. 104, 224.
250. *M.U.* text, Vol. II, p. 427 and also *Jahangir Nama,* 1980, p. 260 and *Tuzuk,* Rogers Translation, Vol. II, p. 9.
251. *A.A.A;* Vol. I, 1350/1971, p. 478.
252. *A.A.A;* Vol. I, pp. 478-87, *A.N.* Calcutta, 1873-97, Vol. III, pp. 645-46, 670-71.
253. *A.N.* III, pp. 646, 671.
254. She died in 1675, vide see: T. Beale, *An Oriental Biographical Dictionary,* London, 1894, p. 309.
255. For details about Muzaffar Husain Mirza and his family see: *M.U.* text, Vol. III, pp. 296-302 and see also, *Ain-i-Akbari,* Blochmann Translation, Vol. I, pp. 327-28.
256. According to Lahori he died in 1052/1642-43 see; Lahori, Vol. II, p. 302. The author of *Zakhiratul Khawanin* says: Mirza Rustam died a natural death at Akbarabad in 1048/1638-39, see: *Z.Kh,* Vol. I, p. 100.
257. For details see: *M.U.* text; Vol. III, pp. 434-42; *Ain-i-Akbari*; Tr. by Blochmann, Vol. I, pp. 328-29, *A.N.* Vol. III, pp. 644-46; *Jahangir Nama,* 1980, pp. 148-49, *Amal-i-Salih,* Vol. I, p. 309, *A.A.A.*, 1955-56, pp. 485-86, see also; N. Qazwini, 1926, pp. 868-69 and T. Auhadi, fol. 266. See also: Yusuf Mirak; *Tarikh-i-Mazhari-i-Shah Jahani,* ed. Sayyid Hasam-ud-din Rashidi; Karachi, 1962, pp. 123, 298-300.
258. The author of *Arafatul Ashiqin* mentions, Mirza Murad was born in India (T. Auhadi, Fol. 712) which is not correct. See also; *A.N.*, Vol. III, pp. 644-46.
259. *Jahangir Nama,* 1980, pp. 169-70 also see; Lahori, Vol. II, p. 303.
260. *M.U.* text. Vol. III, pp. 477-79 and Beveridge Translation Vol. I, p. 622.
261. For Muzaffar Husain Safavi, see, Blochmann's translation of A in Vol. I, pp. 328-29 also See: *M.U.* text, Vol. III, pp. 296-302.
262. Lahori, Vol. I, p. 185
263. *M.U.,* text; Vol. III, pp. 555-57 also see; Beveridge translation Vol. II, p. 388.
264. *A.A.A.* 1314/1896, p. 552 also see : Khafi Khan, Calcutta, 1869, Vol. I, p. 262.
265. *Tuzuk*, Aligarh, 1281/1864, p. 93.
266. *Tuzuk,* pp. 93, 99,100,116, and see: *Iqbal Nama Jahangiri;* Bib. Indica, Calcutta, 1865, pp. 69, 71.
267. *Tuzuk;* 1864; p. 121.
268. This refers to the missions of Chalabi Beg from India and Uwaisi Beg from Persia.

269. *Tuzuk;* 1864, p.117 and *Tuzuk*, Tr. by Rogers and H. Beveridge, London, 1909-14, pp.158, 448.
270. *Tuzuk*, tr. by Rogers. Vol. II, p, 262, according to which Amanat Khan was the brother's son of Asaf Khan for whom see: *M. U.* Vol. I, pp.107-15. According to this account Malika Banu was the younger sister of Mumtaz Mahal.
271. For account of Safi Khan and of the defeat of Abdullah Khan See: *Tuzuk,* Vol. II, pp. 262-67.
272. *M.U.* Tr. by Beveridge, Vol. II, pt. II, p. 691 cited from Lahori, Vol. I, pp. 177, 228.
273. *Ibid.*, p. 426.
274. *Ibid.*, p. 102.
275. Lahori, Vol. II, p.198.
276. For details see: *M.U.* text, Vol. II, pp. 416-21 and Beveridges Translation, Vol. II, Pt. II, pp. 689-92.
277. For Saif Khan See: above and also see: *M.U.* Text, Vol. II, pp. 416-21.
278. *M.U.* text, Vol. II, p. 421 also see; Beveridge Translation, Vol. II, Pt. II, p. 692 also, Lahori, Vol. II, p. 736.
279. T. Auhadi. fol. 492.
280. *Tuzuk;* Tr. by Rogers, p. 59.
281. *Tuzuk;* 1864, p. 40 and also see, Roger's tr., pp. 68-69.
282. *Tuzuk;* 1864, p. 94, *Tuzuk,* Tr., by Roger, pp. 164-65.
283. T. Auhadi, Fol. 492.
284. M.S. Mina, *Subh-i-Sadiq,* p. 73.
285. Waris, pp. 18, 284, 313.
286. M.S. Mina, p. 73.
287. *Amal-i-Salih*, Vol. I, pp. 428-55.
288. For Afzal Khan See; *M.U.* text, Vol. I, pp.145-51.
289. For Sati Khanam see: *M.U.* text; Vol. II, pp. 290-92 and under her name in this text.
290. *M.U.* Tr by Beveridge, Vol. I, pp. 259-60 and see also; N. Qazwini, 1961, pp. 552-53.

3

Poets as Administrators

We have located in our sources 28 such Iranians who excelled in administration at various levels and were also known in their time as reasonably good versifiers and poets, 13 of them arrived in India in later day's of Akbar's reign; 11 during Jahangir's period and 5 persons in the reign of Shahjahan.

Among 28 people 2 persons came from North of Iran, 5 from West and North-West, 10 came from central plateau, 7 from regions in the East, and North-East. About the homelands of the remaining 4 our sources are unclear. They left Iran to India for various reasons and purposes. Sharif Amuli, a leader of Nuqtawi sect,[1] is also said to have migrated to India from Amul because of religious persecution in Iran. He received the office of *Sadr* of Kabul, Bihar, and Bengal during Akbar's reign. He also was poet-Laureate and was granted a *mansab* with 5200 *sawar* during jahangir's reign.

Another important factor which led to migration was the policy regarding the nobility pursued by the Safavid rulers in sixteenth and seventeenth centuries. Leading nobles of the Safavid empire were frequently executed and deprived of their posts.[2] A good number among them proceeded to India in search of security as much as wealth. Mirza *Qawam-ud-din* Jafar Beg, left Iran under such circumstances. He was son of *Badi-uz-zaman,* who was the *Wazir* of Kashan the reign of Shah Tahmasp Safavi. Jafar Beg received title of Asaf Khan by Akbar. He composed *Nur-nama*, named after *Nur-ud-din* Jahangir and dedicated to him.

The most important of these poets-cum-administrators was Hayati Gilani, who received a *jagir* and *mansab* by Akbar, and weighed in silver by jahangir. The others in this category were (1) Salih Tabrizi belonged to noble family of Tabriz. He came to India in search of employment. He joined the literary circle of *Khan-i-Khanan.* Prince

Parviz recommended him to be granted a *mansab*; (2) Lutfi Tabrizi came to the court of Akbar, later Jahangir bestowed upon him the title of *Mauzun-ul-mulk* and appointed him controller of the seaport of Lahri Sind. Later he hold several small posts in Gujarat;[3] (3) Mirza Muhammad Bazil was a poet. He was appointed governor of Gwalior and Bareily; (4) Ibrahim-i-husain *Bakhshi*, who earned from jahangir the title of Aqidat Khan, the office of *Bakhshi* of Deccan and a *mansab* of 1000 *zat* and *sawar;* (5) Girami Shamlu belonged to Shamul Turk of Iran, who was appointed by Shah Jahan *Bakhshi* of Gujarat and *Mir Bahr* of Bengal.

Still among others in this group belonged the following. Sameri Tabrizi migrated to India in order to trade. He was attached to Shah Nawaz Khan the son of Abdur-Rahim Khan-i-Khanan. Wajhi Heravi left Iran because of Uzbeks attacks on Khurasan. he was a brother of Haidar Khisali, who was in the service of the immigrant Safavid prince Muzaffar Husain Mirza. Later he joined the service of Mahabat Khan.[4] Mir Abdul Wahab Mamuri, left Iran to visit his relatives in India. He was made *divan* of the *Suba* of Sarhind, *Bakhshi* of Qandahar and Gujarat during Jahangir's reign.

Raqim *Sad-ud-din*, Hashim Khan and Qasim Khan Juwaini came to india in the company of their father. *Sad-ud-din* joined to noble's service in India. After his return to Iran shah Sulaiman Safavi appointed him governor of Herat and later to the *Wizarat* of Kashan. Hashim Khan was made *faujdar* of Fathpur Sikri. Qasim Khan got a *mansab* of 5000 *zat* and 5000 *sawar.* Later, he was appointed governor of Bengal.

Asad Beg Qazwini, Qazi Zada Kashani and Tabhi Kandu Sulqani arrived in India by a sheer tryst of Destiny. Asad Beg was a poet and inkstand holer (*davatdar*) of Khwaja Afzal Esfahani *wazir* of Heart. Later he was sent as an ambassador the by Mughal government to Bijapaur and Golkonda, and then he was appointed *Bakhshi* of Kabul. Qazi Zada Kashani was a poet and calligraphist, later he was made *Divan* of Mirza Isa Tarkhan.

Murshid Borujerdi came to India on Mirza Ghazi Beg Tarkhan's invitation. He was appointed *wakil* (agent) and keeper of the seal of Mirza Gazi Tarkhan. Later he joined the services of Mahabat Khan and prince Khurram. Shah Jahan invited Hasan Beg Rafi Mashhadi and conferred upon him a *mansab* of 500 *zat.* Mir Muhammad Amin

(Ruh -ul Amin-i-Sharestani) came to India tiwce. First he left Iran (1604) to Deccan in search of better opurtunities. Secondly he came to India (1617) because of Jahangir's invitiation. Mir Muhammad Amin was a member of a Sayyid family in Esfahan, one of whose members was nominated *Mostoufi-ul-Mamalek* at the beginning of the Safavid dynasty under Shah Ismail I.[5] Mir Muhammad Amin's nephew, Mirza Razi was a favorite of Shah Abbas I and had the honour of marrying one of his daughters.[6] In the description of Esfahan by the French traveller Jean Chardin, there appears a blind prince who was incredibly good at mathematics. He was a son of this Mirza Razi.[7] Mirza Razi succeeded his uncle to the post of *Sadr*, the most important office in religious administration under the Safavids. Mir Jalal-ut-din Husain Salai in 1016/1607-088 and remained in that position until his death in 1026/1617. His cousin, Mirza Rafi succeeded him. Thus Mir Muhammad Amin belonged to one of the most distinguished families in Safavid Iranian society at the time. Mir Muhammad Amin went to Golkonda in 1013/1604-5. No source tells us the real reason for this move. The king of Golkonda at that time recognized his talents and gave him an important position in his government. He finally became *wakil* (regent). According to Lahori, Mir Muhammad Amin, Mir Jumla Sharestani was *wazir* of Golkonda under Muhammad Quli Qutb Shah. After the death of the king, however, he was dismissed by the new monarch and subsequently moved to the kingdom of Bijapur seeking employment there. Unable to find an opening there, he returned to Iran in autumn 1614. His nephew being. *Sadr* at that time[8], he was received courteously by Shah Abbas. He expected a high post at the court, but the Shah despite his land welcome, did not offer him position to his satisfaction. He was only eager to cash on the fortune Mir Muhammad had accumulated in India. After four years, Mir Muhammad gave up his post at the Safavid court with the intention of going back to the Mughal court. Aware of Mir Muhammad's ability, the emperor Jahangir wrote him an invitation and Mir Muhammad left Esfahan for the Mughal court in 1027/1617-18.[9]' Jahangir rewarded him with 2500 *zats*[10] and 200 *sawars* for his painstaking journey and his precious gifts.[11] Later, he received important positions at court such as the ones of *Mir-Saman* and *Mir-Bakhshi* and was promoted to 5000 *zat* and 2000 *sawars*. He died in India in Rabi I 1047/September 1637.[12] An ardent Shiite, he donated according to the *Zakhirat-ul-Khawanin*, a great deal of money in charity for people starving as a result of a drought in the Deccan though certain Iranian people at the Mughal court insisted that it was not enough and claimed he sent two hundred thousand rupees every years to his sons and relatives in Iran to buy houses, gardens and property there.[13] The reasons of migration of the remaining five—Subhi Hamadani, Maliki Qazwini, Shakibi Esfahani as well as Jam-i-Esfahani and Jafar Heravi of these Iranian poets-cum-administrators in Mughal India are unclear.[14]

Table : 3.1
Poets as Administrators

Name of the migrants	Place of birth	Provinces	Regions	Period of migrations	Contexts and reasons of migration	Position in Iran	Position in India	Place of death
Sharif Amuli	Amul	Mazandaran	North	Akbar 1576	Nuqtawi sect	Poet	*Amin* and *Sadr* of Kabul; Bihar and Bengal during Akbar's reign. Poet laureate and rank of 2500 *sawar* in the reign of Jahangir.	India
Hayati Gilani	Rasht	Gilan	North	In the later days of Akbar's reign	In search of better opportunities	Poet	Akbar granted him a *Jagir* and *mansab*. Hayati was weighed in silver by Jahangir.	Agra
Sameri Tabrizi	Tabriz	Azarbaijan-i-Sharqi	West and North-West	Akbar 1594	Trade	Poet and merchant	*Mir Saman*, Service of Shah Nawaz Khan the son of Abdur-Rahim Khan-i-Khanan	Deccan
Salih Tabrizi	Tabriz	Azarbaijan-i-Sharqi	West and North-West	Jahangir	In search of better employment	Noble family, poet and gunsmithing	Literary circle of Khan-i-Khanan, Parviz granted him a *mansab*.	Unclear
Lutfi Tabrizi	Tabriz	Azarbaijan-i-Sharqi	West and North-West	Jahangir	In Search of better opportunities	Poet	Title of Mauzunul-Mulk by Jahangir controller of the seaport of Lahri Siad	Gujarat
Murshid Borujerdi	Borujerd	Lurestan	West and North-West	Jahangir	Invitation of Gazi Beg Tarkhan	Poet	*Wakil* (agent) and keeper seal of Mirza Gazi Tarkhan; Service of Mahabat Khan and Prince Khurram	India
Subhi Hamadani	Hamadan	Hamadan	West and North-West	Jahangir	Unclear	Poet	Mahabat Khan's service	India

Table Contd...

Jafar Qazwini	Qazwin	Qazwin	Central Plateau	Akbar 1577	In search of security as much as wealth	His father Mirza Badih-uz-Zaman was the *wazir* of Kashan in the reign of Shah Tahmasp	Title of Asaf Khan by Akbar Shah; Author of Nur-Nama which was dedicated to Jahangir	Burh-anpur 1912
Asad Beg Qazwini	Qazwin	Qazwin	Central Plateau	Later days of Akbar	By destiny	Poet and Inksland (*Davatdar*) of Khwaja Afzal of Esfahan, *Wazir* of Herat.	Ambassador of Mughal Government to Bijapur and Golkonda, Author of Halat-i-Asad Beg, Bakhshi of Kabul.	Unclear
Malaki Qazwini	Qazwin	Qazwin	Central Plateau	1605	Unclear	In the Service of Shah Abbas I	Soldier in military, he dedic-ated Saqi Nama to Parviz	Unclear
Shakibi Esfahani	Esfahan	Esfahan	Central Plateau	Akbar 1588	Unclear	Poet, Noble Family of Esfahan	Literary Circle of Khan-i-Khanan, *Sadr* of Delhi during Jahangir's Reign	Delhi 1614
Mir Abdul Wahab Mamuri (Inayat Esfahani)	Esfahan	Esfahan	Central Plateau	Akbar 1588		To Visit relatives	Poet *Divan* of the *Suba* of Sarhind *Bakhshi* of Qandahar and Gujarat during Jahangir's reign	Gujarat
Munhi Zavarehi	Zavareh	Esfahan	Central Plateau	Later days of Akbar	Unclear	Poet	Incharge of Lahari Port (a port in Bengal)	India
Ruh-ul-Amin-i-Sharh - estani	Esfahan	Esfahan	Central Plateau	Twice Deccan 1604 Mughal court 1617	In search of better opportunities. Jahangir's Invitation	Sayyid and distinguished Family of Esfahan	*Wakil* (regent) in Golkonda; *mansab* of 5000 *zat* and 2000 *sawar*, *Mir Saman* and *Mir Bakhshi* in Mughal court	India 1637

Table Contd...

Jam-i-Esfahani	Esfahan	Esfahan	Central Plateau	Jahangir	In search of better opportunities invitation	Poet	*mansabdar* of Jahangir	India 1637
Qazi Zada Kashani	Kashan	Esfahan	Central Plateau	Jahangir	By destiny	Poet	*Divan* of Mirza Isa Tarkhan, Poet and Calligraphist.	India 1637
Tabhi Kandu Sulqani	Kandu-sulqan	Tehran	Central Plateau	Jahangir	By destiny	Poet	One of nobles at the court of Jahangir	India 1637
Hashim Khan Juwaini	Juwain	Khorasan	East and North-West	Akbar	In the company of relatives	Poet, Sayyid family of Juwain	*Faujdar* of Fathehpursikri	Kashmir
Qasim Khan Juwaini	Juwain	Khorasan	East and North-West	Akbar	In the company of relatives	Poet, Sayyid family of Juwain	*mansab* of 5000 *zat* 5000 *sawar*, governor of Bengal	India
Wajhi Heravi	Herat	Khorasan	East and North-East	Akbar 1593	Uzbek Attacks	Service of Rustum Mirza and Muzaffar Husain Safavi	He received *jagir* by Khan-i-Khanan	Unclear
Jafar Heravi	Herat	Khorasan	East and North-East	Jahangir	Unclear	Poet	Chief Pay master of Ataga Khan	Unclear

Table Contd...

Raqim Sad-ud-Din	Mashhad	Khorasan	East and North-East	Shahjahan	In the company of relatives	Poet, when he came back to Iran from India, Shah Sulaiman Safavi appointed him to the governor of Her-at and then *Wazarat* of Kashan.	Poet, noble's Service	Iran
Hasan Beg Rafi Mashhadi	Mashhad	Khorasan	East and North-East	Shahjahan	Shahjahan invitation	Poet	*mansab* of 500 *zat*	Delhi 1672-82
Mirza Mahmud Bazil	Mashhad	Khorasan	East and North West	Shahjahan	In search of employment	Poet	Governor of Gwalior and Bareilly	India (1711)
Hazini	Unclear	Unclear	Iran	Akbar	In search of fortune	Poet	He received *mansab* and *Jagir* by Khan-i-Khanan Title of Aqidat Khan, *Bakhshi* of Deccan *mansab* of 1000 *zat* and 200 *sawar*	Unclear
Girami Shamlu	Unclear	Unclear	Iran	Shah jahan	In search of fortune	Poet, Shamlu Turk	*Bakhshi* of Gujarat and *Mir Bahr* of Bengal	Unclear
Muhammad Munem	Unclear	Unclear	Iran	Shah jahan	In search of employment	Poet	Service in the army	Unclear

NORTH OF IRAN

Sharif Amuli

Sharif Amuli was born at Amul, a small town in the south of the Caspian sea. His name was Muhammad and Talib was his penname. He was the cousin of Hakim Ruknuddin Masih, better known as Hakim Rukna Kashi. Talib's position as a literary genius of the age needs no comment. The reasons of his migration from Iran appear to be chiefly religious in nature. According to Badauni.[15] Sharif Amuli sought asylum in Hindustan in 984/1576 to escape accusation of heresy on account of his *Nuqtawi*[16] sympathies. Even according to Eskandar Beg Munshi 'Talib' escaped to India, to save himself from facing wrath of the *Ulama.*[17] This is further endorsed from the account of Khwaja Nizamuddin Ahmad Heravi who says: Mir Sharif belongs to the heretics of the age. He is well acquainted with *sufis* and is at present (1002/1593) in Bihar.[18]

The *Ain-i-Akbari*, contains the following note of him: In the 30th year (993/1584-5) prince Mirza Muhammad Hakim of Kabul died, and the country was annexed to India. Mir Sharif Amuli was appointed *Amin* and *Sadr* of the new province. In the following year, he served under Man Singh in Kabul. In the 36th year,[19] he was appointed in the same capacity, though with more extensive powers, to Bihar and Bengal. In the 43rd year, he received Ajmer in *Iqta*, and the *Pargana* of Mohan near Lucknow, as *tiyul.* During the siege of Asir, he joined the imperial camp with his contingent, and was well received by the emperor. He is said to have risen to the rank of a commander of three thousand. He was buried at Mohan. On his death, neither books nor official papers were found; his list of soldiers contained the names of his friends and clients, who had to refund him six months' wages per annum.[20] Sharif Amuli was poet-laureate at the court of Jahangir. Jahangir in his memoirs says: I promoted Sharif Amuli to the rank of 2,500. He is a pure-hearted, lively-spirited man. Though he has no tincture of current sciences, lofty words and exalted knowledge often manifested themselves in him. In the dress of a *faqir,* he made many journeys, and he has friendship with many saints and recites the maxims of those who profess mysticism.[21]

He died in 1035/1625[22] at Fatehpur.[23] Some of recent *Tazkira* writers often mistake between him and the other Sharif Amuli who was a contemporary of Shahjahan and Aurangzeb.[24]

Hayati Gilani

Kamal-ud-din Hayati Gilani belonged to Rasht, which he left in young age and stayed at Kashan. Taqi Kashi, the contemporary author of *Khulasat-ul-Ashar* attested that Hayati had already gained acknowledgement from the poets of his country before leaving for India. Having arrived in the reign of Akbar, he was offered hospitality by Hakim Abul Fath Gilani, the emperor's boon companion. As Abdur-Rahim Khan-i-Khanan was assigned the military command of the Deccan affairs, Hayati accompanied that nobleman and resided in Burhanpur. He constructed a house and a mosque and laid a garden in that city. Jahangir in his estimate placed him higher than other poets of his court. For, he chose Hayatai to compose the lost portions of Amir Khusrau's poem, *Tughluq-Nama*, the last literary exercise by the great poet's pen. After he completed the task, Hayati was weighed in silver by the emperor's order (1019/1610). Also, he was the author of another *masnavi* composed in *hazaj* metre.[25]

According to Badauni, he had not received much education, but had real genius for poetry.[26] But *Maasir-i-Rahimi* says, he had received a good education and was well versed in all sciences. After acquiring sufficient fame in his own native country he came to India in order to better his prospects.[27] Akbar liked him and granted him a *jagir* and *mansab*.[28] When he was shifted from Fatehpur to Burhanpur he died in Agra and was buried there.[29] Hayati possessed a very robust sense of humour. He would brighten the assembly by his wit. He was fond of wine and all that is sensational in life. His verses are fluent, fine and life giving. He was inferior to none of the poets of his age in maturity of thought and expression. He was very popular among the courtiers and noblemen of his time. *Rasmi Qalandar* in one of his *qasidas* in praise of which Khan-i-Khanan says that, Hayati had acquired fame and popularity due to the service of Abdur Rahim Khan-i-Khanan.

Hayati got new life by your bounty,
Yes, essence is the patron of accident.[30]

The author of *Tabaqat-i-Akbari* praises him to be a man of feeling and sympathy,[31] Badauni states that his poems equal those of great poets.[32]

In *Ain-i-Akbari* he has been praised in the following words: A stream from the ocean of thought passes by his house; correctness and equity are visible on his forehead. Serenity and truth are in him united. He is free from the bad qualities of poets.[33]

WEST AND NORTH-WEST

Sameri Tabrizi

He was the son of Maulana Haidari Tabrizi who lived as a merchant and poet. Maulana Haidari migrated to India during Akbar's period in order to trade. Afterwards he returned to Iran and died in 1002/159.[34]

After the death of Maulana Haidari, his son Sameri came to India in order to trade. He was appointed to the office of *Mir Samani* by Abdur Rahim Khan-i-Khanan. Sameri was killed during the Deccan wars, when he was in the service of Shah Nawaz Khan,[35] the son of Khan-i-Khanan.[36]

"My disgrace has made me famous, and my shame (love) has rendered me well known; perplexed, I ask myself why remain concealed.

The farmers have committed their seeds to the field, and now hope to receive aid from the flood of my tears.[37]

Sameri had two sons: Mirza Darab Beg Juya-i-Kashmiri and Mirza Kamran Beg Guya-i-Kashmiri.[38]

Salih Tabrizi

Muhammad Salih Beg was the son of Ustad Ghazanfar Tabrizi, who was a noble, famous for his skill in gunsmithing, which was superior than the skills of the Europeans. Salih's father was influential in the Safavid court. When the Ottoman army conquered Tabriz, Ghazanfar escaped to Gilan, and joined the literary circle of Khan Ahmad Karkiya who was governor of Gilan. The people of Iran called his court as a white India. When Shah Abbas occupied Gilan, Khan Ahmad escaped to Rome. Ghazanfar and his son, Salih, attached themselves to Shah Abbas Safavi. Ghazanfar died unexpectedly and Salih was engaged in his father's job of gunsmithing. Afterwards, Salih travelled to India in the reign of Jahangir in search of a better job, and entered in the literary circle of Khan-i-Khanan. He was introduced by Khan-i-Khanan to prince Parviz who extended his patronage to Salih. In 1024/1615 Salih was at Burhanpur, Khandesh, and Parviz recommended him a *mansab*.[39]

Lutfi Tabrizi

Lutfi was a native of Tabriz who came to India in search of better fortunes during the reign of Jahangir. Lutfi's father, Maulana Urfi Kamangar[40] was also a well known poet of Azarbaijan.

In the first instance of his arrival he received the patronage of Abdur Rahim Khan-i-Khanan. Lutfi flattered the attention of his patron by composing a chronogram, by way of congratulations, which records the year of birth of Mirza Darab Khan, second son of Khan-i-Khanan, as 994/1585. Thereafter, he had the good fortune to receive the attention of the Sultan.

According to Auhadi and Nihavandi, Jahangir conferred on him the title of *Mauzun-ul-Mulk* (acclaimed for composing quatrans in recognition of his poetic gifts.[41] Nihavandi records that the Sultan appointed him as controller of Lahri Sind and thereafter, posted him to Ahmadabad as chief of the unit of Gujarat. To this information "Auhadi adds that before his appointment in the unit, for a while he joined Zain Khan Kokultash,[42] the son of Khwaja Maghsud Ali Heravi, who was one of the great men of Akbar's time. Commenting on his character Auhadi notes that Lutfi was a soft spoken man with a mystic bent of mind. In fact, he calls him an *arif* (gnostic) who died in Gujarat in 1025/1616.10

CENTRAL PLATEAU

Murshid Borujerdi

He was born in Borujerd in Lurestan province and both his name and his penname was 'Murshid'.[44] He had acquired knowledge of all sciences while he was still young. He was apparently under the influence of Mir Hasti, one of the prominent poets of Borujerd. After a short time Murshid Khan left his native town and went to Hamadan. Here he met the great learned man Mirza Ibrahim Husni Hamadani. Under the latter's patronage Murshid Khan lived in very affluent circumstances, and made himself felt as a poet of some distinction to the poets of Hamadan like, Rashki, Helaki, Mir Aqil Bazmi, Zaki Jesmi, Shukohi, Mir Moghis Mahvi, Musa Reza, Mudriki and his son Baqi Nihavandi, Nasir Mehrabadi, Mir Razi Artimani and others. He composed *qasidas* of a very high order and *ghazals* full of pathos and abounding with temporal and spiritual love. At times he went from Hamadan to Borujerd and from there to Khurramabad which was the capital city of the sultans of Lurestan. But after a short time he left his native place and went to Shiraz. In a very short time, the poets and learned men of Shiraz recognised his merits and considered him among the great poets and invited him in assemblies and appreciated his poems. For seven or eight years he was the companion of Muhammad Quli Khan[45] the son of Murtaza Quli Khan Parnak Turkman, who was the ruler of Shabankareh. Murshid composed a *Saqi nama*[46] in the name of Muhammad Quli Khan, its title was *Masti-Avar*. The governor of Darabgerd, capital city of Shabankareh had appointed Murshid his *wakil* and entrusted the reins of administration to him, but Muhammad Quli died a sudden death and he was left without a patron. As his fame as a poet and administrator reached far and wide, he was invited by Ghazi Beg,[47] son of Mirza Jani Beg. Murshid Khan thought that his prospects lay in undertaking a journey, so he left Iran and arrived in Sind.[48] In a very short time he was given the rank of Khan and made the chief advisor of the *Amir*, who knowing his talent very soon raised his rank and made him his *Wakil* (agent) and the keeper of the seal. After the Mirza's sudden death he came under the patronage of Mahabat Khan, the general of Mughal armies, who employed Murshid as tutor to his son, Mirza Amanullah. Thereafter, he entered the imperial service and marched under prince Khurram to the Deccan, where he met his fellow-townsman, Abdul Baqi Nihavandi. The two friends lived together for two years. He was in the service of prince Khurram until he died in 1030/1620.[49] Murshid was a great poet and prose writer. He could compose verses both in the style of ancient and modern poets. He was also an expert in writing chronograms and *Insha*.[50] Murshid's *divan*[51] of verses has survived.

Subhi Hamadani

Although the reasons for his migration are not clear, Subhi Hamadani came to India during Jahangir's time.

Muhammad Sadiq Mina met him at Junnair in the Deccan in 1036/1626, when he was in the military encampment. For a long time Subhi wandered in the company of Mahabat Khan, and then left him and Joined Shahjahan's court. He was killed in a skirmish during the supression of Khan Jahan Lodi's revolt.[52] Subhi was poetically inclined and some verses are attributed to him.[53]

Jafar Qazwini

Mirza Qawam-ud-Din Jafar Beg was the son of Mirza Badi-uz-Zaman Qazwini.[54] Badi-uz-Zaman was the *wazir* of Kashan in the reign of Shah Tahmasp Safavi.

Jafar Beg had also been introduced to the Persian court. He combined in his charactor the qualities of a scholar and soldier and made himself prominent both as a man of sword and pen. He migrated to India from his native place, Qazwin, in the 22nd year of Akbar's reign (985/1577). He and his family members had been nobles of high position in Iran and India. Akbar conferred on him the title of Asaf Khan after his uncle's death who held the same title. He continued to be an officer of rank till his death in the reign of Jahangir. But the best period of his career passed under Akbar, who reposed great trust in his integrity and sound judgement. Asaf Khan subscribed to the emperor's religious views and was a declared follower of the so-called *Din-i-Ilahi*. Akbar included him in the bureau of writers for *Tarikh-i-Alfi* (993/1585). Next to Mulla Ahmad of Thatta, his contribution was the largest in having brought the work to completion. He picked up the thread from the point left by Mulla Ahmad and continued the narrative to the year 997/1589.[55] He died in the 7th year of Jahangir's reign in 1021/1612 at Burhanpur at the age of 63.23 The chronogram of his death is *Sad haif Asaf Khan* (a hundred regrets for Asaf Khan).[57]

He possessed a sharp intellect and was very quick witted. He was one of the unique personalities of his age. He had a thorough knowledge of the current sciences. He was an eloquent speaker and possessed great skill in financial matters. He had a passion for nature and a liking for planting flowers, especially rose beds and sometimes himself worked with spade in hand. A fluent poet Jafar Beg collected his wan and left a *masnavi* version of Shaikh Nizami's romantic tale *Khusrau-shireen*. As the poem was dedicated to the emperor, Nur-ud-din Jahangir its title proposed by the author was *Nur-Nama*.[58]

Asad Beg Qazwini (d.1041/1632)

Asad Beg was the son of Khwaja Muhammad Murad Qazwini who was a famous poet. According to Nabi Qazwini, Asad Beg shifted to Herat from Qazwin and Khwaja Afzal,[59] *wazir* of Ali Quli Khan Shamlu, appointed him as keeper of inkstand (*Davatdari*). Later, he migrated to India as fate would have it and served under Akbar and Jahangir. He was sent as ambassador of the Mughal government to Bijapur and Golkonda in the Deccan. Taqi Auhadi notes that, Asad Beg Qazwini joined Jafer Asaf Khan and Jahangir. He was received as a *Bakhshi* of Kabul.[60] His contmeporaries accepted him as a poet with a *divan* of verses to his credit. But more intersting than poetry was a volume of memoirs left by him. It disclosed the drama of events that occured during the last four years of Akbar's reign, particularly, giving details of the murder of his benefactor, Shaikh Abul Fazl. The memoir was entitled *Halat-i-Asad* Beg or simply, *Waqai*.[61]

Malaki Qazwini

Mir Malaki Qazwini[62] was son of Mir Zahir ud-Din Ilmi. Both father and son being scholars, served at the court of the Safavid monarch

Shah Abbas the great. Mir Malaki left Iran without any distinct reason and arrived in Agra at the juncture of Akbar's death in 1014/1605. His elegy, mourning the emperor's death made him familiar among the literary circles of the Mughal court. Jahangir dispatched him to a number of military campaigns, and Mir Malaki fighting under Mahabat Khan, Khan-i-Jahan Lodi and other high ranking generals, proved his efficiency as soldier. He approached the author of *Mai Khana* in Patna with a piece of *Saqi-nama* that was dedicated to prince Parwiz, son of Jahangir.[63]

Shakibi Esfahani

Muhammad Reza better known as Shakibi was born in 963/1555.[64] His father, Khwaja Zahir-ud-din Abdullah Imami of Esfahan, was a famous saint. Jami has given his life sketch in his famous book *Nafahat-ul-uns*.

His grandfather Amin-un-din Hasan was one of the patrons of the *Lisan-ul-Ghaib* of Shiraz who has imortalised him in the following verse.

Be rendi Shora Shod Hafez Pas az Chandin varah; Likan cha gham daram ke dar alam Amin-uid-din Hasan daram.[65]

Shakibi studied under Amir Taqi-ud-din Muhammad of Shiraz. In early years of his life he went from Esfahan to Khurasan. He passed a very long time in Mashhad, the capital city of Herat. It is there that he learnt most of the current sciences of his time acquired proficiency in music and became acquainted with poets like; Sanai, Mayeli, and Wali Dasht Bayazi. When he was well known as a poet, he returned for a short time to Shiraz. After this he came to India in 997/1588 at age of 34, in the later years of Akbar's reign. His patron was Abdur-Rahim Khan-i-khanan in whose circle he rose to the position of a leading poet. In Thatta, Sind, Khan-i-khanan rewarded him with eighteen thousand silver coins for his single poem, *Saqi nama* also.[66] Yar Quli Beg Anisi in a *masnavi* praises Shakibi thus:

Shakibi Kesh Reza nam ast-o-zib ast;
Bali har ja Reza amad Shakibi ast.

Shakibi whose name is Reza and who is the ornament.
It is true wherever there is agreement there is patience.

Rasmi Qalandar Yazdi also praises him in a *qasida* which he wrote in praise of Khan-i-khanan.

Sawad-i-Shar-i-Shakibi cho Kohl Esfahan;
Bar tohfa suiie Khurasan barand ahl-i-basar.

The ink of the verses of Shakibi like of Esfahan, men of sight carry to Khurasan by way of present."[67]

The *Mirat-ul-Alam* notes that Shakibi later fell out with his patron, and went from the Deccan to Agra, where Mahabat Khan introduced him to Jahangir.[68] After some time he asked for permission to return to Iran, but Jahangir did not allow him to go and appointed him *Sadr* of Delhi[69]. He died there at the age of sixtyseven in 1023/16143[70]. Jesmi Hamadani found the chronogram of his death in *Sadr Dehli raft* (the *sadr* of Delhi passed away). Another chronogram *Shakibi raft* gives only 1022/1613. According to the author of *Ain-i-Akbari*, Shakibi possessed a fine taste for writing poetry and wrote good poems. He was acquainted with chronology and other sciences and the purity of his nature led him to philosophical independence[71]. Badauni does not write much also about him but notes that he possessed good taste.[72]

Inayat Esfahani (Mir Abdul-Wahhab Mamuri)

He was a leading Sayyid from Mamur of Esfahan. His pen name was 'Inayat'. Abdul-Wahhab was a distinguished person of his time, noted for his learning, worthiness and magnanimity. He and his brother Mir Abdur-Razzaq migrated to India in the later days of Akbar's reign because his ancesters were in India. Abdul-Wahhab was one of the *mansabdars* of Jahangir's court. For a while he was *divan* of Sultan Parviz. In 1024/1615 he secured from Parviz the *divani* of the *Suba* of Sarhind.

Auhadi saw him at Agra and informs us[73] about his *divan* of *ghazals* and *qasida*. He also wrote a *masnavi* about *Farhad and Shireen.* According to *Maasir-ul-Umara* Mir Abdul Wahhab, a younger brother of Mir Abdur-Razzaq, was a poet and his name was Inayat.[74] Under Jahangir he was made *Bakhshi* of Qandahar and afterwards. when prince Dawar Bakhsh was appointed *subadar* of Gujarat, he was made *Bakhshi* of Gujarat where he died.[75]

Munhi Zavarehi

Mir Munhi[76] was from the Sayyid family of Zavara, a city near Ardestan in Esfahan province. He was witty and intelligent and had expertise in mathematics. Munhi emigrated to India in later days of

Akbar's reign and entered in the service of prince Jahangir. He promoted his position and was appointed incharge of Lahari port (a port in Sind). During his time in India he amassed a lot of money, but bandits attacked him at night and killed him at his house. Munhi composed six thousand verses. Auhadi saw him in Esfahan.[77]

Ruhul-Amin-i-Shahristani

His name was Mir Muhammad Amin and Ruh-ul-Amin was his penname. He was one of the noble Sayyids of Esfahan, who were Known as the Sayyids of Shahristan. His elder brother Mir Jalal-ul-Din Husain had the penname of Salai. He was very learned and a great favourite of Shah Abbas I. He was appointed the *Sadr* which showed his high position in the Iranian government.

Mir Muhammad came to India in 1013/1604-5 in search of better opportunities. He went to Deccan and entered the service of Muhammad Quli Qutb Shah[78], the ruler of Telang (Hyderabad and Golkonda) through the mediation of Mir Mumin of Astarabad. Mir Mumin was the sister's son of Mir Fakhr-ud-din Samaki, and had a high reputation for devotion and piety, and was the tutor of Sultan Haidar Mirza, son of Shah Tahmasp Safavi in Iran. After the Shah died and Mirza Haidar was killed, and Shah Ismail II succeeded to the throne, Mir Mumin's stay in Iran was not pleasant and he migrated to the Deccan. As he belonged to the same religious sect as the ruler of that area, he became a servant of Muhammad Quli Qutb Shah, and was appointed the *peshwa* and *wakil* and for a long time he was the *Sahib Saman* or factotum of the Qutb Shahi government. Mir Muhammad Amin by his good fortune gained such influence with Muhammad Quli, that he was granted the title of Mir Jumla (Prime Minister).[79]

Jahangir in his memoirs says: On Sunday, the 27th Rabi ul-Awwal, 1027/1618, Mir Jumla came from Persia and has the good fortune to pay his respects. The aforesaid is one of the respectable Sayyids of Esfahan and his family has always been held in honour in Persia, and now his brother's son, Mir Reza, is in the service of my brother Shah Abbas and has the rank of *sadr* and the Shah has married his own daughter to him. Mir Jumla had left Persia fourteen years before this, and gone to Golkonda to Muhammad Quli Qutbul-Mulk. His name is Muhammad Amin. Qutbul-Mulk gave him the title of *Mir Jumla.* For ten years he had been in the centre of affairs there his (*madar alaih*). He held the office of *sahib saman* (Factotum). After Qutbul-Mulk died and the rule came to his brother's son, the latter did not treat the Mir properly, and so he took leave and hastened to his native country. The Shah on account of his connection with Mir Reza, and the respect which he had for men of merit[80], showed much consideration for and kindness to him. He (the Mir) also presented fitting offerings, and passed three or four years in Persia and amassed properties (estates)[81]. As he represented several times that he wished to enter the service of this court, I sent a *farman* and invited him, immediately as the *farman* arrived he severed his connections there and shifted his loyalty towards this court. This day he attained the honour of kissing the carpet and produced as a offering twelve horses, nine (*Tuquz)*[82] of silk cloths and two rings. As he had come with devotion and sincerity, I conferred favours and kindness on him, and presented him with 20,000 *Darbs* (Rs.10,000) for his expenses and a dress of honour.[83]

He received the rank of 1,5001 *zat*[84] and 200 *sawar*,[85] and was appointed as the reviser of petitions (*arz-i-mukarrar*).[86]

When Shahjahan succeeded to the throne, he by virtue of his long service, retained the office of *Mir Saman* for some time.[87] In the 8th year he was appointed to the high office of *Mir Bakhshi* in succession to Islam Khan and by the fact of his promotion became a *mansabdar* of 5000 *zat* and 2000 *sawar*.[88] On the 10th Rabi II, 1047/1637, in the 10th year he died of paralysis and hemiplegia.[89] Though the Mir was of a high birth and a Sayyid, he was without good manners. He was not only hot tempered and arrogant in his conduct but was also a *Shia* bigot.[90]

He was a prolific writer and could write *ghazals* very well. He was an expert in coining technical terms and the art of letter writing. His literary compositions, influenced by Nizami's style', include a *divan*[91] and a few *masnavis* like; *Khusrau-Shireen*, *Laili-va Majnum*, *Asman-i-Hashtum* and *Gulistan-i-Naz*.[92]

Jam-i-Esfahani

Mir Abdul-Karim Jam was a *mansabdar* of Jahangir. He was son-in-law of Mir Abdul-Raazaq Bakhshi.[93] Jam-i-Esfahani served as an administrator and poet.[94]

Qazi Zada Kashani

Qatai Heravi says: I and Qazi Zada were at Thatta by destiny. For a while he was the *divan* of Mirza Isa Tarkhan[95] in Sind. He could write *Nastaliq* very well. Occasionally he composed lyrics and satirical poems. Qazi Zada also composed some verses in praise of Mirza Isa Tarkhan.[96]

Tabhi Kandu Sulqani

Ismail Tabhi belonged to Kandu Sulqan, a village between Tehran and Qazwin and received early education in Qazwin. As his destiny commanded he travelled to India in his early youth. His humour made him a welcome companion to men of every description, particularly, the upper classes; and he wandered freely in the cities of India streteching from Golkonda and Bijapur to Agra and from Ahmadabad, Gujarat, to the cities of Bengal in the east.[97] He was disciple of Iran's great satirist, and the court-poet of Shah Abbas, Hakim Shifai (d.1037/ 1627).[98] The author of *Mai-Khana* saw him in Patna around the year 1026/1617, and found in his possession a *divan* containing no less than three thousand verses.[99]

After acquiring a good reception he returned to Iran, and in the year 1037/1627 shifted to India for the third time. According to M.S. Sistani, Mir Tabhi Rabi was from Kandu-Sulqan but grew up in Ray. In Iran he was in attendance of Isa Khan Beg Qurchi Bashi[100] for some time, then he came to India and was one of the nobles at the court of Jahangir. Malik Husain Sistani saw him at Farah in 1036/1626 when he was on way to India.[101]

EAST AND NORTH-EAST

Hashim Khan

He was the son of Mir Murad Juwiani.[102] Hashim Khan came to India during Akbar's time in the company of his father and brother Qasim Khan.[103] The author of *Zakhiratul-Khawanin*[104] indudes the following observation of him:

Hashim Khan was brother of Qasim Khan, son of Mir Murad. He was a young man who was adorned with good qualities. He used to compose firm verses. He took most elaborate pains in the matter of clothes, carpets, canopies, food and perfumes and he enrolled many good men of excellence. He was for some time the *faujdar* of Fatehpur-Sikri in the neighbourhood of Akbarabad. Since the late Nawwab Islam Khan Chishti took great pains in promoting the interest these two brothers, Hashim Khan during the days of his *faujdari*, by way of recompense of the obligations of that departed soul, did whatever was necessary to (improve) the condition of his descendants. Afterwards he went to the Kashmir, and was afflicted by a disease which resulted in his prolonged illness. Physicians were helpless to treat his ailment and he died after a while in Kashmir.[105]

Qasim Khan Juwaini

He was son of Mir Murad Juwaini,[106] who belonged to the Sayyid family of Juwain.[107] As he had for long been in the Deccan, he was also called Deccani. He was an excellent shot, and Akbar appointed him as Rifle-Instructor to Prince Khurram. Mir Murad died in the 46th year, as Bakhshi of Lahore. He had two sons Qasim Khan and Hashim Khan.[108]

Qasim Khan came to India with his father during Akbar's reign. Qasim was an accomplished poet, and his verses were highly polished. Earlier on he was the treasurer of the province of Bengal during the governorship of Islam Khan Chishti Faruqi.[109] Islam Khan gave all possible attention to him and his brother Hasim Khan.[110] He was the son-in-law of Itimad-ud-daula, the Prime Minister of Jahangir and husband of Nur Jahan's younger sister, Manija Bagum,[111] and thus became a friend of Jahangir. An example of happy repartee is given. Once Jahangir asked for a cup of water. The cup was so thin that it could not bear the weight of the water, and when handed to the emperor it broke. Jahangir looked towards Qasim Khan and said:

Kasa Nazuk bood ab aram natavanest Kard.
The cup was lovely, so the water lost its rest.
When Qasim completing the verse, replied:
Did halam ra-o-chashmash zabt-i-ashk-i-Khod nakard.
It saw my love grieve, and could not suppress its tears.

In the end of Jahangir's reign, Qasim Khan was *subadar* of Agra, and was incharge of the treasures in the fort. When the emperor died, and Shahjahan left the Deccan, Qasim paid his respects in the *Bagh-i-Dahra* (Agra), which in honour of Jahangir had been called Nur Manzil.[112] In the Ist year, he was promoted to the rank of 5000 *zat* and 5000 *sawar*, and appointed governor of the province of Bengal[113] in succession to Fidai Khan.[114]. As a rebel prince Shahjahan had heard about the wicked practices of the Portuguese in Bengal who converted natives by force to Christianity, he ordered Qasim Khan to destroy their settlement at Hugli. In the 5th year in 1041/1631,[115] Qasim Khan sent a corpse under the change of his son Inayatullah and Allah Yar Khan to Hugli. The Portuguese lay in a dry ditch in front of the Church.' Qascin's men dug a mine and blew up the church. The fort was taken. Ten thousand Portuguese are said to have perished during the siege, and 4.400 were taken prisoners. About 10,000 natives whom they had in their power were liberated. One thousand Muslims died as martyrs for their religion.[116]

Three days after the conquest of Hugli Qasim Khan died natural death in 1042/1632.[117] The Jami Masjid in the *Atga Bazar* of Agra was built by him.[118]

Wajhi Heravi

Maulana Wajih-ud-din was the brother of Maulana Haidar Khisali Herati.[119] They spent most of their time in attendance of Rustam Mirza and Muzaffar Husain Mirza Safavi, the descendent of Shah Ismail Safavi. His (Wajhi) source of livelihood was soldiery and companionship with Maulana Haidar. They were honoured, and dearly esteemed by people and government. They came to India in 1002/1593 with Rustam Mirza and Muzaffar Husain Mirza Safavi subsequent to Uzbek raids and ruination of Khurasan. In India Maulana Wajhi joined the service of Khan-i-Khanan and received *jagir*. After some time he left the company of Khan-i-Khanan and enjoyed the patronage of Zafar Khan, son of Zain Khan Kuka,[120] who held important status both under Akbar and Jahangir. He composed a *masnavi* in praise of Zafar Khan.[121]

According to Auhadi Wajhi, Heravi was a traveller. He came to India and attached himself to Zafar Khan, son of Zain Khan. Auhadi met him in Gujarat. In 1024/1615 Wajhi was in Patna in the service of Zafar Khan.[122]

Jafar Heravi

He was a Sayyid of Herat and had good command in versification and was known for composing enigmas. He was the Chief Pay Master of Atga Khan[123] and had written an ode and composed an enigma dedicated to Mirza Aziz Kuka,[124] containing a list of his titles. Kuka had earned and prayers for his long life and prosperity. The following couplets have been selected from his poems:

Shana bar ham zada on silseleh meshkin ra;
Ah agar bad be gosh tu resanad in ra.

"Now that the comb has disturbed those musky locks, Ah, that the wind would bear this message to thine ear!"

Ghobar-i-moshk nakhaham bar on izzar neshinad,
Az in mabad ke bar khaterat ghobar neshinad.

"I would not that the dust even of musk should settle on that cheek, God forbid that dust should have a place near thy heart."

Sabze ra dar bagh bashad jay zire paye gol;
Bagh hosnat ra fitada sabze bar balaye gol.

"The place of her bage in the garden is beneath the foot of the rose; In the garden of thy beauty[125] her bage has settled on the rose.[126]

Raqim Sad-ud-din

Mirza Sad ud-Din[127] Muhammad belonged to Mashhad. His father Khwaja Ghiyas was one of the leading traders in India. Sad-ud-din accompanied his father to India during Shahjahan's reign.[128] Sadud-din's patron was the emperor's noble and prime minister, Islam Khan (d.1057/1647). Raqim impressed many poets by his style and left a *divan* of verses.[129]

After some time Raqim went back to Esfahan and Muhammad Beg Itimad-ud-daula introduced him to Shah Sulaiman Safavi. The king of the Safavid dynasty appointed him to the governorship of Herat and then granted him the *Wizarat* of Khurasan.[130]

Hasan Beg Rafi Mashhadi

Mirza Hasan Beg Rafi was originally an inhabitant of Qazwin,[131] But since he stayed at Mashhad for a long time he is better known as Mashhadi.[132] The author of *Majma un Nafais* relates that when Abdullah Khan Uzbek invaded Khurasan, (993/1585) he took away Mirza Rafi with him along with other prisoners. Rafi was very young at that time. Rafi's remarkable intelligence attracted the attention of Nazar Muhammad Khan, the governor of Balkh. According to Siraj-ud-din Ali Khan Arzu, when Shahjahan conquered Balkh and defeated Nazar Muhammad Khan in 1056/1646 Rafi came to India with the son of Nazar Muhammad.[138] The author of *Nataijul Afkar* states that Rafi came to India before Shahjahan's expedition to Balkh.[139] Rafi's contemporary biographer, Tahir Nasrabadi writes that the poet (Rafi Mashhadi) was the *kitabdar* (Librarian) of Nazar Muhammad Khan and that he was married to Nazar Muhammad Khan's wife's sister. Shahjahan had heard about his penmanship and wrote to him to came to India.

It is also stated in the same *Tazkira* that Haji Muhammad Jan Qudsi maliciously reported to Shahjahan that Rafi was only an ordinary poet. Hasan Beg was, therefore, deprived of the imperial favour for ever.[135] But according to the author of *Reyaz-ush-Shoara* and other later biographers the statement of Tahir Nasrabadi is to be accepted with a pinch of salt.[136]

In *Khazana-i-Amira* it is related that on the 14th Rajab 1054/1644 Hasan Beg Rafi, *Munshi* of Nazar Muhammad Khan came to pay respect to the imperial throne and received *Khilat* (robe of honour), was awarded three thousand rupees and was subsequently honoured with a *mansab* of five hundred *zat*. On 4th Rabi I 1063/1652, the poet also received an award of three thousand rupees for composing a poem in praise of the emperor.[137] The same author supported by several others relates that Rafi also received a reward of five hundred rupees from Shahjahan's daughter, Jahan Ara Begum for a verse in a poem which he composed in praise of the garden named *Bagh-i-Hayat Bakhsh*.[138]

During the time of Aurangzeb, Rafi was appointed *Divan* of Kashmir, but very soon he resigned his post and lived a life of retirement in Delhi.[139]

Nasrabadi writes that at the time of the composition of his *Tazkira* in 1083/1672 he heard that Rafi was then living in great distress in India.[140]

Mir Afzal Sarkhush, who completed his *Tazkira* in 1093/1681, speaks of the poet in the past tense. The author of *Mirat-ul-Alam*, which was compiled in 1078/1667, states that the poet had resigned from the imperial service and had been living a retired life.[141] In the light of these statements, one concludes that Rafi died in Delhi some time between 1083/1672+1093/1682. Rafi's *diwan* contains besides *ghazals* and *rubais* several *qasidas* mostly in praise of Shahjahan and Dara Shukoh. He possessed a graceful style. The following verses are by him:

Pay ta sar-i-Khish ra chon Sham-i-Mahfel Sokhtam;
Gar neshinad ashiq as pa in chonin khahad nishast.

"I burnt myself from head to foot like the candle in an assembly; if a lover loiters he would settle down like this."

Masnavi: *ba ab-i-zindagi shoyam dahan ra;*
Cho maddahi konam Shah Jahan ra.[142]

"I wash the mouth with the water of immortality, when I eulogise the king of the world (Shahjahan).

Mirza Mahmud Bazil

Mirza Mahmud belonged to Mashhad. He and his brother migrated from their native place to India in Shahjahan's reign in search of employment. Mirza Mahmud soon rose to high positions in the Mughal government.

Mirza Mahmad had a son (Muhammad Rafi), who was born in Shahahanabad (Delhi), and is mentioned among the noted poets of Aurangzeb's time. Muhammad Rafi Bazil himself was a trusted servant of Aurangzeb, and was appointed *faujdar* of Gwalior and then Bareilly. One of his noted contributions as a poet was a *masnavi* narrating the life and achievements of the Prophet. It covered the period between Revelation and the Prophet's death. He borrowed details from the *Maarijun-Nabu-wah* of Moin-ud-Din Farahani (d. 907/1501). His intended project was to bring the poem down to the days of Ali. His ambition however, remained incomplete. He had composed forty thousand verses. The topic being appealing, other poets picked up the theme subject and carried their own continuations under different titles. Bazil's proposed name for the poem was: *Hamlah-i-Haidrai*. He also left a collection of letter under the title of *Munshat-i-Bazil*. He died in 1123/1711.[143]

FROM UNKNOWN AREAS

Hazini

Mulla Hazini is so known as he was a sorrowful person. His birth place is not stated in our sources clearly. He came to India in the reign of Akbar on a pleasure trip. Hazini joined the service of Khan-i-Khanan in 992/1584. He was granted a *mansab* and *jagir* in Khan-i-Khanan's court. The author of *Ma'asir-i-Rahimi* mentions some of his verses.[144]

Ibrahim-i-Husain Bakhshi

His name was Khwaja Ibrahim Husain Bakhshi and his title was Aqidat Khan. He migrated to India from Iran in search of better opportunities. He spent some time as a prisoner in Daulatabad fort along with Lashkar Khan. His son Mirza Rashid, who was unequalled in soundness of intellect, correct judgement, witticism and in the science of music, was also with his father during this captivity.[145]

According to *Jahangir Nama*, Ibrahim Husain Bakhshi was made *Bakhshi* of Deccan in 1026/1616 and a *mansab* of 1000 *zat* and 200 *sawar* was awarded to him along with the title of Aqidat Khan in 1027/1617.[146]

After some time Aqidat Khan was perhaps retired, from his *mansab* on account of advanced age. Mahabat Khan granted him an annual allowance of 30,000 rupees. He became Said Khan's companion and his *Wakil.* He was sharp-tongued, but had no wickedness in him. His son Rashid became a companion of Nawwab Khan-Dauran. Since he also had no control over his tongue, he annoyed Said Khan and fell in trouble. His son Arshaḍ was also a man of merit.[147]

Girami Shamlu

It may be noted that our sources have described a number of poets with the *takhallus* of Girami. Naturally they have also thus confounded them with one another.

Hasan Beg Girami belonged to a Shamlu Turk tribe. He came to India after the accession of Shahjahan to the throne, in order to better his prospects. Hasan Beg entered in the service of Shah Jahan who made him *Bakhshi* of Gujarat and the *Mir Bahr* of Bengal.[148]

Besides several *qasidas* and *qita's* in praise of Shahjahan and Dara Shukoh, Girami Shamlu was also noted for composing chronography recording dates of some important contemporary events. One such chronogram expresses the birthday of his son as 1050/1640. Girmani's *divan* of contains *ghazals, qitas' rubais* and *tarji bands.*[149]

Muhammad Munem

Muhammad Munem migrated to India during Shahjahan's reign to seek employment. In 1041/1631 he was employed in the army of Bengal, through the intercession of one Muahmmad Sadiq Mina, who held *Bakhshigari* of *Sipah* (army) at that time, visited him at Jahangirnagar (Dacca). Muhammad Munem is reported to have been in the service of Aqa Zaman, one of the Bengal amirs, for quite some time. He has left some verses.[150]

Table 3.2
POETS AS ADMINISTRATORS

Rg	Pr	Nu	Reasons and Contexts of Migration																									
			X1	X2	X3	X4	X5	X6	X7	X8	X9	X10	X11	X12	X13	X14	X15	X16	X17	X18	X19	X20	X21	X22	X23	X24	X25	X26
NO	Ak	2	1													1												
2	Ja	0																										
	Sh	0																										
WNW	Ak	1																			1							
5	Ja	4														1	1			1								1
	Sh	0																										
SW	Ak	0																										
0	Ja	0																										
	Sh	0																										
CP	Ak	5									1		1	1														2
10	Ja	5									2							1										2
	Sh	0																										
SO	Ak	0																										
0	Ja	0																										
	Sh	0																										
ENE	Ak	3			1					2																		
7	Ja	1																										1
	Sh	3								1								1		1								
SE	Ak	0																										
0	Ja	0																										
	Sh	0																										
UA	Ak	1														1												
3	Ja	0																										
	Sh	2														1				1								
Total		27	1		1					3	3		1	1		4	1	2		3	1							6

Graph : 3.1

Number of Poets as Administrators according to the reasons and contexts of their migration

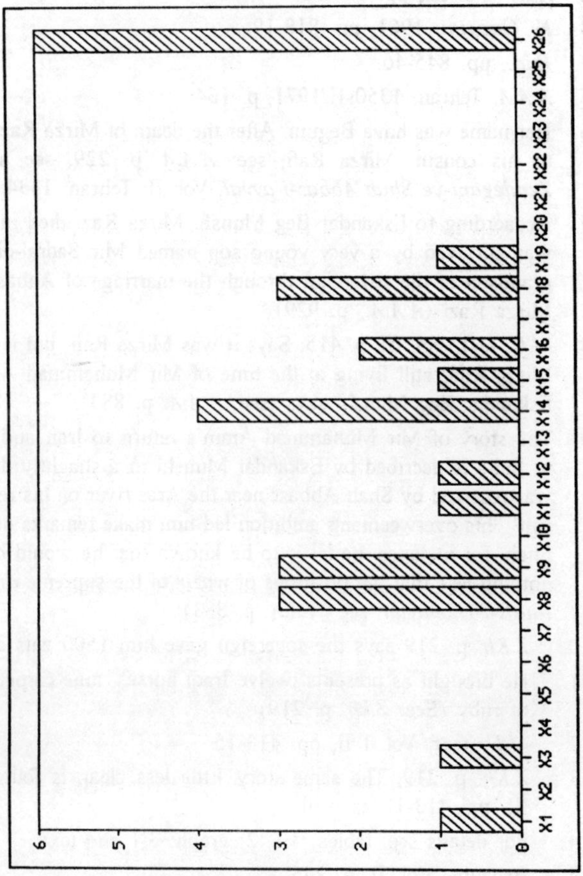

REFERENCES

1. *A.A.A.*, 1350/1971; Vol. II, p. 476.
2. *A,N.* V. I. III, pp. 590-92.
3. *N. Qazwini,* 1961, pp. 818-19.
4. *Ibid.*, pp. 845-46.
5. *A.A.A,* Tehran, 1350sH/1971, p. 164.
6. Her name was hava Begum. After the death of Mirza Razi, she was given to his cousin, Mirza Rafi, see; *A.A.A.* p. 229, see also; N. Falsafi, *Zendegani-ye Shah Abbas-i-avval*, Vol. II; Tehran, 1334/1955, p. 201.
7. Accaording to Eskandar Beg Munshi Mirza Razi died in 1026/1617. He was survived by a very young son named Mir Sadral-din Mushammad, grandson of the sovereign through the marriage of Abbas's daughter and Mirza Razi (*A.A.A.*, p. 929).
8. *M.U.* text, Vol. III, p. 415, Says it was Mirza Rafi, but it must have been Mirza Rafi, still living at the time of Mir Muhammad Amin's return, as Eskandar Beg Munshi says (see; *A.A.A.* p. 883).
9. The story of Mir Muhammad Amin's return to Iran and second journey to India is decribed by Eskandar Munshi in a sliaghtly different way. He was received by Shah Abbasr near the Aras river on his return from Tiflis. But "his overweeniang ambition led him make remarks displeasing to the Shah, for instance, he let it to be known that he would be satisfied with nothing less that the positions of *wazir* of the supreme *divan* and *wakil-i-nafs-i-Humayun*; see (*A.A.A,* p. 883).
10. *Z.Kh,* p. 219 says the sovereign gave him 1500 zats and 200 sawars.
11. He brought as presents twelve Iraqi horses, nine carpets and two rings of ruby (See: *Z.kh,* p. 219)
12. *M.U;* text, Vol. I II, pp. 413-15
13. *Z.Kh,* p. 219, The same story, little less clear, is found in: *M.U.* Vol. III. pp. 413-15 as well.
14. For details see: tables; 3.1, 2; graph; 3.1 and text.
15. Badauni, Vol. II, p. 245.
16. About Nuqtawis: see: S.Kiya, *Nuqtawian or Pasikhanian*, Tehran, 1320/1911.
17. For details see: *A.A.A.* 1971; p. 476.
18. *Tabaqat-i-Akbari*; 1931, Vol. II, p. 451.
19. The author of *Akbar Nama* (Lucknow Press, Vol. III, p. 629) says he was made at the same time a commander of four thousand. This must be a mistake, because Mir Sharif was at Jahangir's accession a commander of 2,500 (*Tuzuk*, Tehran Press, p. 22).

20. *Ain-i-Akbari*, Tr. By Blochmann, p. 502 and see: *Z.kh, Ibid,* Vol. I, p. 193 also for details see: *M.U.* text, Vol. II, pp. 285-90.
21. *Jahangir Nama*, 1980, pp. 28-29 and Tr. By Rogers, p. 478.
22. N. Qazwini, 1961, p. 388.
23. A. Eteh, *A History of Persian literature;* Translation to Persian by Reza Zada Shafaq, Tehran, 1337 A.s/1958, p. 195.
24. M.T. Nasarbadi, 1938, p. 223.
25. T. Kashi, op.cit., Ms and also see: *Tabaqat-i-Akbari*, Calcutta Press; p. 506; Also see : *Tuzuk*, Tehran, p. 92.
26. Badauni, Vol. III, pp. 219-21.
27. B.Nihavandi, Vol. III, pp. 738-39.
28. *Ain-i-Akbari*, Vol. I, pp. 307-308 and also see : tr. By Blochmann, Vol. I, p. 644.
29. T. Kashi, Ms, also see, N. Qazwni, 1961, pp. 809-10.
30. *Tabaqat-i-Akbari*, Calcutta Press, p. 506 also see: A.A. Razi, 1939, Vol. III, pp. 149-51.
31. *Tabaqat-i-Akbari*, p. 506.
32. Badauni, Vol. III, p. 219.
33. *Ain-i-Akbari*, Tr. by Blochmann, Vol., I, p. 644.
34. A.A. Razi, 1939, Vol. III, p. 245, see also : T. Auhadi, Fol. 317.
35. Malik Iraj entitled Shah Nawaz Khan was *subadar* of Berar and Ahmadnagar in Jahangir's reign. He died in 1028/1618. (See: *Jahangir Nama*, 1980, Tehran Press, pp. 305-306 also see: *M.U.* text, Vol. II, pp. 645-48.
36. B. Nihavandi, Vol. III, pp. 1477-87.
37. *Ain-i-Akbari*, Vol. I, p. 318 and see: *Ain-i-Akbari*, Tr. By Blochamann, vol. I, p. 673.
38. Aslah; *Tazkira Shuarai-Kashmir*, 1967; Vol. I, p. 181 and Vol. III, p. 1424.
39. B. Nihavandi, Vol. III, pp. 1683-87.
40. T. Auhadi, *op.cit.,* fol. 502, also see: A.A. Razi, 1939, Vol. III, pp. 247-48; and see: T. Kashi, MS.
41. B. Nihavandi, *op.cit.,* Vol. III, pp. 1252-55.
42. About Zain Khan see: A. N, Vol. I, p. 222 and Vol. III, pp. 796-7, *Tabaqat-i-Akbari*, Vol. II, p. 431, *M.U.* text, Vol. II, p. 369, A.A. Razi, Vol. I, p. 469.
43. T. Auhadi, Fol. 641 and for details See:N. Qazwini; 1926, pp. 537-39 the author of *Mai-Khana* mentions Lufti Tabrizi died in 1021/1612 see: *Ibid*.

44. Most of the Indian authors have written: Yazdjerdi, Sanjeri and Neishapuri, instead of Borujerdi, Sajzi and Neishabouri respectively.
45. Muhamamad Quli Khan Parnak behalf of Yaqub Khan Zulqadr the ruler of Fars appointed to governorship of Darabagerd. See: Mir Munshi Qomi, *Khulaasat-ul-Tawarikh*, Ms, Tehran, Malik Library, no. 4067, p. 888.
46. About his *Saqi-nama* see : N. Qazwini, 1926, pp. 414-20.
47. About Mirz Ghazi Tarkhan see; T. Auhadi, Fol. 519 *M.U.* text; vol. III, pp. 345-48, *Jahangir nama*, p. 76 and also see : H. Rashidi, *Mirza Ghazi Tarkhan and Bazme Adab*, Karachi, 1350/1931.
48. M.S. Sistani mentions, Murshid Borujerdi reached to Thatta in 1021/1612, see: M.S. Sistani, *Khairul Bayan* Fols. 361-63.
49. N. Qazwini, 1926, pp. 408-13 and also see: T. Auhadi, Fols. 711-12.
50. M.G. Azad Bilgrami, 1913, p. 41.
51. About his *Divan* see: A. Munzavi; *list of Persian Manuscript copies*, Vol. III, p.252 and also see: *Azzorrieh*, thirth section, Vol. IX,, pp. 1029-30.
52. M.S. Mina, *Subh-i-Sadiq*, p. 61.
53. S.A. Hasan Khan Bhpali, 1878, p. 247.
54. For his ancestors see: *A.A.A* 1955, Vol. I, p.165 also see: *M.U*, text; Vol. I, pp. 90-91.
55. For details see: *M.U*, text, Vol., pp.107-115, Tr. by Beveridge, Vol. I, pp. 282-86; *Ain-i-Akbari*, Lucknow, 1869, Vol. I, pp. 306; Badauni, Vol. II, pp. 138-39, 392-93, T. Kashi, MS; *A.N*; Vol. III, pp. 64, 834; *Tabaqat-i-Akbari*, Vol. II, p. 442.
56. *Tuzuk*, 1914, p. 109.
57. Mutamid Khan, *Iqbalnama-i-Jahangiri*, ed. Abdul Hai and Ahmad Ali, Bib. Ind. Calcutta, 1865, p. 67.
58. *Tuzuk*, 1914, p. 109 and also see : *Z.Kh*; Vol. I, pp. 186-190 also see; T. Auhadi, Fols 116-17.
59. For Khwaja Afzal Esfahani *Wazir* of Herat see: *A.A.A*, 1334/1955, pp. 285, 303, 305.
60. T. Auhadi, Fol. 112.
61. N. Qazwini, 1926, pp. 554-55 also see: A.A. Razi, Calcutta press, 1939, Vol. III, pp. 181-83.
62. Some of Indian recent *tazkira* authors made mistake him with Malaki Beg Sarkani, who was poet and his source of livelihood was agriculture in his native place. His death occurred in 1004/1593 at Najaf Ashraf.
63. For details about Malaki and his *Saqi-nama* see: N. Qazwini, 1926, pp. 456-67.

64. *Ibid.*, pp. 234-38, but Beale says: He was born in 964/1556, (See: Beale, Thomas, *An oriental Biographical Dictionary*, London, 1894, p. 381.
65. M.G.A. Azad-i-Bilgrami, 1913, p. 29.
66. B. Nihavandi, Vol. III, pp. 66-70 see also: M.Q. Fireshta; Lucknow Edition, 1863, Vol. I, p. 78.
67. B. Nihavandi, Vol. III, p. 67.
68. *Ain-i-Akbari*, Tr. By Bolchmann, I, 646, note 2.
69. N. Qazwini, 1926, pp.236-38, also see: T.Auhadi; Fols: 383-84.
70. N. Qazwini, 1926, pp. 236-38 also see: M.G.A, Azad Bilgrami, 1871, p. 59.
71. *Ain-i-Akbari*, Tr.by Blochmann, Vol. I, p. 646.
72. Badauni, Vol. III, p. 253, for details see: A.A. Razi, 1961, Vol. II, pp. 424-29, and *Tabaqat-i-Akbari*, Vol. II, p. 502, *Ain-i-Akbari*, Vol. I, P. 308, *M.U*, text, Vol. I, p. 698, S. Kitabdar, 1948; pp. 205-206 and A.G. Maani, 1348/1969, Vol. II, pp. 704-706.
73. T. Auhadi, fols, 492-93; M.M. Husain Lucknowi, *Rauz-i-Raushan*,1343/ 1964, pp. 441, 481; Sayyid Nurul-Hasan, *Nigarestan-i-Sukhan*, Bohpal, 1293/1876, pp. 60, 68.
74. *M.U* text. Vol. I, p. 140.
75. *Z.kh*; Vol. II, p. 304 and also; *M.U*, text, Vol. I, p.140.
76. The author of *shame-i-Ghariban* mentions his name Mir Muntahi, see; Lachmi Narayan Shafiq Aurangabadi; 1977; p. 221. The Indian recent *Tazkira* authors mixed his poets and his biodata with Mir Atai Munhi Tehrani, who was poet and contemporary of Shah suliman Safavi.
77. T. Auhadi, Fol. 828.
78. He was the 5th ruler of Golkonda from 1580-1612 see: *Cambridge History of India*, Vol. III, p. 706
79. *M.U.* text, Vol. III, pp. 413-16; *M.U.* Beveridge trnaslation, Vol. II, pt., pp. 117-18, see also; *Z.Kh*, Vol. II, pp. 217-18; *A.A.A.*, 1971, p. 883.
80. See; *Iqbal nama*, p. III. he is not the famous Mir Jumla who was Aurangzab's general, though possibly the latter was his son. According to the *Iqbal-nama*, he was the nephew and not the uncle of Mir Reza but Jahangir's statement agrees with the *Alam Ara*. (p. 623). Mir Jumla's patron, muhammad Quli Qutb-Shah died in 1612. He himself died in 1637 which Aurangzeb's general died in 1663.
81. The *Iqbal-nama* says that Abbas only gave Mir Jumla flattering words and did not give him any high appointment (see also : *A.A.A*, 1971, p. 623).
82. *Tuquz* means nine, hence present gifts such being offered to kings by nines as a sacred number.

83. *Jahangir nama*, 1980, p. 265 and *Tuzuk*, Tr.by Rogers, Vol. II. pp. 3-4 also see: *Z.kh,* Vol. II, pp. 218-19.
84. In *Massir-ul-Umara*. 2.500 see: *M.U.* Tr. by Beveridge, Vol. II, pt. I, p. 119.
85. *Jahangir nama*, 1980, p. 263.
86. *Ibid,* p.276 also see; *Z.kh,* Vol. II, p. 219.
87. Lahori; Vol. I, p. 258.
88. *Ibid* and also see: *Amal-i-salih*, Vol. II, p. 98.
89. Lahori; Vol. II, p. 279.
90. *Z.kh*, Vol. II, p. 219.
91. For his *Divan* see: *Nuskahi Khatti Farsi*, Vol. III-IV, Majlishi Library, Vol. III, pp. 289-93 and Fihrest Razavi, Vol.VII, pp.187-88.
92. M.T. Nasrabadi, 1938, pp. 56-57.
93. For Abdul Razzaq see:, *M.U,* Tr.by Beveridge,, Vol. II, pp. 54, 634.
94. T. Auhadi, Fol. 200.
95. For Isa Tarkhan see: *Aini-i-Akbari*, Tr, by Blochmann, Vol. I, pp. 392 463, 465.
96. For details and Qazi Zada's Verses see: Qatai Heravi, 1979, pp. 61-62.
97. N. Qazwini, 1926, pp. 851-53.
98. M.T. Nasrabadi, 1938, pp. 304-5.
99. N. Qazwini; *Ibid.*
100. He was descendant of Masum Beg and esteemed of Shah Abbas.
101. M.S. Sistani, *Khairul Bayan*, Fol. 407.
102. For Mir Murad Juwiani see: *Ain-i-Akbari*. Tr By Blochmann, Vol. I, p. 559.
103. For Qasim Khan see: this text under Qasim Khan.
104. Except Shaikh Farid Bakkari nobody have written his biography.
105. *Z.Kh.* Vol. II, pp. 293-94.
106. The author of *Akbar nama* mentions: Mir Murad Choli and Juni which are distortion of Juwain. see: *Akbar nama*, Vol. III, p. 798.
107. Juwain is small town in north west of Khurasan. It lies between Bastam and Sabsvar.
108. *Ain-i-Akbari*, Tr by Blochmann, Vol. I, p. 559.
109. For Islam Khan Chisti see: *Ibid,* pp. 552, 586-87 also see: Mirza Nathan, *Baharistan-i-Ghaibi*, Transt, by M.I. Borah. 2 Vols, Gauhati 1936, Vol. I, pp. 3-6, 28-77.
110. For Qasem Khan's administration of Bengal see: *Baharist-i-Ghaibi*, 1939; pp. 270-90 also see; *Jahangir nama*, 1980, p. 174.
111. See: *Ibid*, p. 174.

112. *Ain-i-Akbari*, tr. by Blochmann, Vol. I, pp. 559-60.
113. M.S. Mina, *Subh-i-Sadiq*, pp. 64-65 also see: M.Q. Gopamavi, 1957, pp. 560-62.
114. For Fidai Khan see: *M.U,* text; Vol. III, pp. 12-18.
115. Quoted from Lahori, Vol. I, pp. 435,. 437.
116. *Aini-i-Akbari*, tr. by Blochmann, Vol. I, p. 560 also see: M.G. Azad Bilgrami, 1913, pp. 48-49.
117. *Ibid,* p. 49 and M.Q. Gopamavi, 1957, p. 62.
118. *Z.Kh*, Vol. II, p. 252 for more information about him see: *Amal-i-Salih*, I, pp. 266, 507, M.T. Nasrabadi, pp. 63-64, M.A. Khafi; *Baharistan-i-Sukhan*, Madras, 1958, pp. 463-64 for his *Divan* see: Qasim Khan, *Divan* ed. by Muhammad Shamon Israeli, *in: Index Islamica*, June 1962, pp.100-46 and December, 1963, pp.114-42.
119. Mir Haidar Khisali was younger brother of Wajhi Heravi. He was born at Heart. In 1023/1614 Mir Haidar entered to service of Mahabat Khan and then he attached himself to court of Shahjahan and received *Divani* of Kashmir *Suba*.
120. About Sukrullah Zafar Khan see; *M.U,* text, Vol. II, p. 755 and also see: *Jahangir nama;* 1980, pp. 132, 174, 390.
121. B. Nihavandi, Vol. III, pp.1289-97.
122. T. Auhadi, Fol. 789.
123. Shams-ud-din Muhammad Ataga (Foster father) Khan was the foster-father of Akbar and was commander of five thousand. He was murdered by Adham Khan May 16,1562 vide *Ain-i-Akbari*, trans. Blochamann, I, pp. 274, 337-38.
124. Mirza Aziz Kuka Khan-i-Azam was the son of Ataga Khan and a commander of five thousand. See: *Akbar nama*, Vol. III, pp. 33, 308, 638, 654-55, 669, 806 *Tabaqat-i-Akbari*, Vol. II, p. 5428, Badauani, Vol. I, p. 675.
125. *Hosnat*, as in both Ms. The test has joined paradise which does not suit the meaning of the verse. The reference is to the down on the cheek of th beloved.
126. Badauni, Vol. III, pp. 215-16 and trans. by S. Haig Vol. III, pp. 298-99.
127. Nasrabadi has written about Mirza said-ud-din see; M.T. Nasrabadi, 1938, p. 85.
128. *Ibid.*
129. M.Q Gopamavi, 1957, pp. 268-69.
130. *Ibid* also see: M.T. Nasrabadi, 1938, pp. 85-86 also see: M.G.A. Azad Bilagrami, 1913, p. 119 and same author, 1871, pp. 238-44, S.M.S Hasan Khan Bahadur, 1876, p. 167, Lachmi Narayan, 1977, p. 92).

131. See: M.Q Gopamavi, 1957, p. 270; M.T Nasrabadi, 1938, p. 268; M.G.A. Azad Bilgrami, 1913, p. 107; M.G.A. Azad Bilgrami; 1871, p. 233 but the others says; Hasan Beg was originally from Mashhad see: M.S.Sistani; *Khairul Bayan* Fol. 389; *Amal-i-Salih,* Vol. III, p. 424; Waris, *op.cit.*, Fol. 501; M. Bakhtavar Khan, 1979, Vol. II, p. 583.
132. M.Q. Gopamavi, 1957; p. 270 see also; M.T. Nasarabadi; 1938 p. 268
133. S.A.K. Aruzu, *Majma un Nafais*, Bankipur, MS. No. 696, Vol. I, Fol. 162a.
134. M.Q. Gopamavi, 1957, p. 270.
135. M.T. Nasrabadi, 1938, p. 268.
136. M.A.M. Khan Saheb; *Catalogue of Arabic and Persian*; Ms in; Oriental Public Library/Bankipur, Vol. III, Persian Poetry, p. 143-44.
137. M.G.A. Azad Bilgrami, 1871, pp. 233-38 also see, Lahori Vol. III, p. 386.
138. M.G.A. Azadi Bilgrami, 1871, pp. 235-38 see also : M.G.A Azad Bilagrami, 1913, pp. 107-108; M.A. Sarkhush, 1951, pp. 68-69.
139. *Ibid* also see: M.Q Gopamavi, 1957 pp. 270-71.
140. M.T. Nasrabadi, 1938, p. 268.
141. M.Baktavar Khan, 1979, Vol. II, p. 583.
142. *Amal-i-Salih,* Vol. III, p. 425.
143. M.G.A Azad. Bilgrami, 1913, p. 141, also see: M.Q. Gopamavi, 1957, p. 111 and M.A. Sarkhush, 1951, pp. 19-20 also see: A.G. Maani, *Hamasehai Dini* (Religious epic) in: *Nameh (letter) Astan-i-Quds*, Vol. VI, pp. 193-203).
144. B. Nihavandi, Vol. III, pp. 1195-99.
145. *Z.kh.* 1970, pp. 296-97.
146. *Jahangir Nama*, 1980, pp. 229, 278, 292.
147. *Z.Kh.* 1970, pp. 296-97 also see T. Auhadi, Fol. 106.
148. See: M.T. Nasrabadi, 1938, pp. 289-90; M.S. Mina, *Subh-i-Sadiq*, p. 68; S.M.S Hasan K. Bahadur, 1876, pp. 407-408; A.Q.K. Wala Daghistani, *Riyaz-ush-Shuara*, Asafiyeh, MS. No. 120, Fol. 3446-Aa. H.Q.K. Ashiqi, *Nishtar-i-Ishq*, Bank. MS. No. 716, Fol. 189; M.G.A Azad Bilgrami, *Yad-i-Baiza*, Azad Library Aligarh, MS. No. 920/46, Fol. 1936=A.A.K. Hashimi Sendilvi, *Makhzanul-Gharaib*, photo MS. Tehran University, No. 1671, Fol. 722.
149. Bank, III, *op.cit.,* no. 354.
150. M.S. Mina, *Subh-i-Sadiq*, p. 73.

4

Scholars, Artists and Physicians in Administration

In the category of administrators who were scholars and artists, and earned from the Mughal emperors varied ranks, offices and other rewards, we have identified eleven (11) persons.[1] Among them four persons came from the central plateau, five from the east and north-east, while about the region of the remaining two we have no information in the sources we used. Baqir Khan Najm-i-sani and Ibrahim Khan Fath Jang migrated to India during Akbar's reign, the rest of the nine came in the reign of Jahangir.

The most important among these persons of scholarly merit were Baqir Khan Najm-i-Sani, Mir Abdul Karim Mamuri Esfahani and Khwaja Jahan Khafi.

According to *Massir-ul-Umara* Muhammad Baqir-i-Najm Sani belonged to the noble family of Yar Ahmad Najm-i-Sani, from Esfahan who was in the service of Shah Ismail (d.1524). Baqir Khan came to India during the last days of Akbar.[2] As he was facing dire financial problems back home, he entered the state service and rose rapidly in the reign of Jahangir and Shahjahan serving as governor of Bihar, Bengal, Orissa, Gujarat, Delhi, Jaunpur and Allahabad, until his death in 1637. He was linked to the Mughal family through his marriage to the niece of Nur Jahan, and Jahangir called him *Farzand.* A man both of pen and sword, he represented the best of the Indo-Persian cultural norms of the ruling elite. He was equally accomplished in political affairs as well as in literary and cultural pursuits such as poetry, music, philosophy, mathematics, religion and ethics.[3]

Mir Abdul Karim belonged to the Mamauri Sadat of Esfahan.[4] He was an architect.[5] He visited India during Jahangir's reign to meet his relatives. He was engaged in the Mughal service and in 1638 he was promoted to the rank of 1500 *zat* and 200 *sawar*.[6] He was employed in the construction of the Taj Mahal, along with mulla Murshid Shirazi, Makramat Khan.[7] In 1655 he is mentioned as holding four posts *Bakhshi, Waqai Navis; Darogha* of buildings and *Mir-i-Bahr* of Agra. On these posts he was succeeded by Muttalib, son of Mutamid Khan.[8]

Khwaja Jahan belonged to Khaf, a town of Khurasan province in eastern Persia. Commenting on Khaf and its people during the reign of Akbar, Amin Ahmad Razi, the author of Haft Iqlim says that Khaf had always been the mother-soil of just and religious Salatin, of historians, Shaikhs, Ulama and beneficent *wazirs*.[9] He adds that the Al-Muzaffar dynasty belonged to Khaf and seven of its rulers had ruled in Fars and Shiraz for 59 years.[10]

A fourteenth century chronicler, Hamdullah Mustaufi Qazwini, writes that the people of Khaf were of the Hanafite sect, law-abiding and very much attached to their faith. They were friendly to strangers, being given to charity; and they often went on pilgrimage (to Mecca).[11] In the seventeenth century, the author of *Zakhiratul-Khawanin* states that formerly the people of Khaf were bigoted Sunnis. When Shah Abbas Safavi, in the beginning of his reign, went to Khaf, he forced them to recite *Tabarra* as is customary with Shias but they refused, for which many them were punished. However, the Khafis later emerged as staunch Shias as they, formerly, were bigoted Sunnis.[12] As religious persecution was very common in Persia in those days, particularly in the Sunni dominated areas; and only option left with people was either to forsake the country to adopt Shiism. From the account of Zain-ud-din Wasfi, the author of *Badai-ul-Waqaai*, who was in Khurasan when Shah Ismail defeated Shibani Khan and annexed that region to Persian empire, it appears that it was difficult even for Tafzili Sunnis to live freely in Khurasan.[13] Therefore, Khwaja Jahan Khafi and, etc. finding their life difficult in Khaf, migrated to India and joined Mughal court.[14]

According to Muhammad Afzal Khan Khwaja Jahan Khafi was in India during Shahjahan and Aurangzeb's reign.[15] Whereas Taqi Auhadi says Khwaja Jan Khafi was *divan* and *Waqia Navis* of Ahmadabad from 1021/1612 till 1030/162.[16] Khwaja Jahan with the rank of 2000 *zat* and 600 *sawar* appears to be the highest *mansabdar* among all the Khafis in India. No other Khafi was given even the rank of 1000 *zat* and above during the entire reign of Shahjahan. It is quite significant that from Akbar to Shahjahan no Khafi was given the office of *Subedar*, where as under Aurangzeb not less than seven governorships of important provinces were held by the members of different Khafi families.[17]

Table : 4.1
SCHOLARS AND ARTISTS IN ADMINISTRATION

Name of migrants	Place of Birth	Provinces	Regions	Period of migration	Contexts and Reasons of migration	Position in Iran	Position in India	Place of Death
Baqir Khan Najm-i Sani	Esfahan	Esfahan	Central Plateau	Later days of Akbar's reign	In dire financial straits	His ancestor was powerful *wakil* of Shah Ismail I	*Mansab* of 2000 *zat* and governor of different states like: Multan, Patna, Bihar, Bengal, etc.	India (1637)
Ibrahim Khan Fath Jang s/o Itimad-ud-Daula Tehrani	Tehran	Tehran	Central Plateau	Akbar	In the company of relatives	His ancestors had high position in Safavid dynasty	*Mansab* of 5000 *zat* and 300 *sawar*, *Waqia Navis*, *Bakhshi* of Ahmadabad, governor of Bengel and Orissa	Akbarnagar
Nizam Qazwini	Qazwin	Qazwin	Central Plateau	Jahangir	Unclear	Relatives of Abdun-Nabi Qazwini	*Waqia* Navis, *Divan* and *Bakhshi* of Kashmir and *Diwan* of *Suba* Bihar	Unclear
Mir Abdul Karim Mamuri Esfahani	Esfahan	Esfahan	Central Plateau	Jahangir	To visit relatives	Architect	Architect, constructor of new building like: Taj Mahal; *mansab* of 1500 *zat* and 1200 *sawar*	Unclear
Khisali Heravi	Herat	Khurasan	East and North-East	Jahangir	Uzbek's pressure	Poet and calligraphist	Chief revenue officer of Kashmir	Unclear

Table Contd...

Table Contd...

Khawaja Jahan Khafi	Khaf	Khurasan	East and North-East	Jahangir	Probably because of religious persecution	---	*Divan* and *Waqia Navis* of Ahmadabad, *mansab* of 2000*zat* and 600 *sawar*	India 1643
Mir Muhammad Ghiyas	Mashhad	Khurasan	East and North-East	Jahangir	In the company of his father Islam Khan	---	*Bakhshi* and reporter of Burhanpur, *mansab* of 500*zat* and 100 *sawar*	India
Mir Muhammad Sharif	Mashhad	Khurasan	East and North-East	Jahangir	In the company of his father Islam Khan	---	*Bakhshi* and reporter of Delhi (capital) *mansab* of 6000 *zat* and 2000 *sawar*	India
Mir Muhammad Ashraf	Mashhad	Khurasan	East and North-East	Jahangir	In the company of his father Islam Khan	---	*Waqia Navis*, *Divan* and Bakhshi of the army, *mansab* of 2000 *zat* and 500 *sawar*	India
Asad Qissa Khan	Unknown	---	---	Jahangir	In order to better his prospects	Administrator and story-teller	Title of Mahzuz Khan, *mansab* of 200 *zat* and 20 *sawar*	In the way from Gujarat to Agra 1617
Eskandar Qissa Khan	Unknown	---	---	Jahangir	Unclear	Poet and story-teller	High position in Jahangir's court, story-teller and poet	Unclear

CENTRAL PLATEAU

Baqir Khan Najm Sani

Muhammad Baqir Najm-i-Sani was a descendant of Amir Yar Muhammad Khan Najm-i-Sani, Esfahani the powerful *wakil* of the founder of the Safavid dynasty, Shah Ismail Safavi (1524). Baqir, son of Mustafa Beg,[18] came to India in dire financial straits, either towards the end of Akbar's reign (1556-1605) or at the beginning of Jahangir's rule.[19] Baqir entered the imperial service at the rank of either one hundred or three hundred sawar and rose rapidly in the administration of Jahangir and Shahjahan. He was linked to the Mughal family through his marriage to the niece of queen Nur Jahan, Khadija Begum[20] and immediately the gates of power were thrown open for him. Jahangir affectionately called him son (*farzand*).[21] He obtained a *mansab* of 2000-and the government of Multan[22] with the *Faujdari* of the Alam Khan[23] river. Baqir Khan Najm-i-Sani after serving as the governor of Patna, Bihar, Bengal, Orissa, Gujarat, Delhi, Jaunpur, and Allahabad,[24] his political career ended with his death in 1637.[25]

A man of both the pen and the sword, Baqir symbolised the Indo-Persian social and cultural norms of the ruling elite. Among his extant works are the *Mauizah, Kulliyat* (collect poetry and prose works),[26] and *Siraj-al-Menhaj* (a work on Shia theology [Kalam] written in Persian).[27] Baqir's contemporaries remember him as extremely capable in political affairs[28] and highly versatile in his literary and cultural pursuits. Balkhi, in particular, highlights Baqir's literary skills, his mastery of epistolary writing (*Insha*), history, and calligraphy, and his love of music.[29] The extant of Baqir's works demonstrate his very sophisticated style of writing as well as his interest in philosophy, mathematics, religion and ethics.[30] Maintaining the tradition the Mughal nobility. Baqir extended his patronage to poets and literatures, and he actively contributed to the enrichment of Mughal culture.[31]

Written in concise and lucid prose, the *Mauizah* represents a pragmatic approach to political problems. Baqir covers a wide range of topics in the two chapters (*bab*). The first is divided into six sections (*Fasl*) and two sub-sections (*qism*) and includes the personal qualities of the ruler, such as generosity, valour, and sound judgment of people; the use of diplomacy in state-craft and in dealing with enemies and rivals; the significance of such state policies dispensation of justice, virtues of consultation, high standards in recruitment, and training of advisers and officials, and the merits of a patriarchal relationship between the ruler and high ranking officials that generates intense loyalty of subjects toward their patron. In the second chapter, Baqir addresses the subjects (*Zir Dastan*) and peers (*Akhwan-i-Zaman*).

He ends the *Mauizah* with praise for the ideal rule of his patron, Jahangir, and a conventional prayer for his long life and growth in might and grandeur. The *Mauizah* was written in 1612 to satisfy Baqir's intellectual interests and was named after his patron. There is, however, no indication that his work was ever presented to Jahangir.

The ideas on politics and society in the *Mauizah* refer particularly to such topics as the ruler, the state, the nobility, justice, the religious elite, the structure of society *(Tabaqat)*, and various skills required for running the state.[32]

Ibrahim Khan Fath Jang

He was the son of Mirza Ghiyas Itimad-ud-Daula. At first he was appointed, by Jahangir, as the *Bakhshi* and *Waqia Navis* of Ahmadabad. At that time Shaikh Farid Murtada Khan, was the *Subadar* and he had not allowed four *Bakhshis*, in succession who wanted to do their work according to the rules, to enter on their duties. Mirza *Ibrahim*, by tact and studying the circumstances, did not even use his designation, but everyday went to pay his respects. After a month the Shaikh said: "Why don't you take up your duties ?". The Mirza replied, "I do not want to any work, I only want to please the Nawwab". The Shaikh wrote to the (i.e. his) *Court-wakil* requesting him to write to him without suppression or addition whatever Ibrahim wrote to I'timad-ud-daula. As the Mirza had written nothing about the Shaikh, except what was favorable, the *wakil* reported accordingly. Murtada Khan was pleased with the quietness and discretion of the Mirza and left the affairs of the *mansabdars* to him and presented him a house, elephant and money.

When Itimad-ud-daula's family was promoted the Mirza came to the court, and, in the 9th year, obtained a *mansab* of 1,500 *zat* with 300 *sawar* and the title of Khan, and was made the court *Bakhshi*. By degrees he rose to the rank of 5,000, and received the title of Ibrahim Khan Fath Jang, and was appointed governor of Bengal and Orissa.

When in the 19th year, prince Shahjahan proceeded from Telengana towards Bengal, Ahmad Beg Khan, the brother's son of Ibrahim Khan, who was the naib (deputy) of Orissa, had gone to attack the *Zamindars* of Kokrah.[33]

The prince came to Orissa and sent a message to Ibrahim Khan through Jan Nisar Khan, and I'timad Khan Khwaja Idrak to the effect By destiny he had come to this country, and although in the eye of mainly courage the extent of this country was no more than a practising ground (Jaulangah), but as it was on his road he could not avoid a cursory view of the area. If Ibrahim Khan wishes to go to the presence (of Jahangir),[34] there would be no opposition and no injury to his honour property or, if he likes to stay in the country, he might choose any place he likes to reside in. Ibrahim Khan who, on hearing of Shahjahan's expedition, had come from Dacca to Rajmahal, replied that the orders of the prince were the interpretation of the commands of God, and that his life and property were at the prince's disposal, but that the laws of faithfulness to one's salt, and his having been nurtured by the king were obstacles in his way, and that he could not come to wait upon the prince. Nor could he resolve upon departing and showing the face of shame to his equals and contemporaries. As the king had entrusted this country to his old servant, he could not, for the sake[35] of his borrowed life of no value, for it is known what remains of life, show, slackness in the work of his benefactor. He was helpless and would give his head to be trodden by the hoofs of the prince's troops. He desires that after his death the country should be given to the servants of the king. As his men were scattered, and the fort of Akbarnagar (Rajmahal) was very large, Ibrahim Khan went to the tomb of his son, which was one was from the fort and on the bank of the Ganges. Ibrahim Khan sought protection in the tomb, which was unique in solidity and strength, and where the fleet could bring auxiliaries and supplies by way of the river.

Ibrahim Khan had (i.e. left) no children. His wife was Haji Hur Parwar (nourished by *houris*) Khanam who was the maternal aunt of Nur Jahan Begum. She had a long span of life and survived till the middle of Aurangzeb's reign; she had Aligarh (Kol-jalali) as her *Jagir* (*altamgha*). She lived there in repose and tranquillity till she died.[36]

Nizami Qazwini

Mirza Nizami belonged to Qazwin. He was related to Abdun-Nabi

Qazwini. Mir Nizami was *Waqia-Nawis* of Jahangir's court. Nabi Qazwini visited him at Agra and found skill in storytelling because of Nizami's encouragement.

Mirza Nizami Qazwini was *diwan* and *Bakhshi* of Kashmir 1025-1026/1616. In the latter part of 1026/1616 Mirza Nizami went to Mandu and after one month he appointed to the *diwani* of *Suba* Bihar.[37]

Mir Abdul Karim Mamuri Esfahani

He belonged to Mamuri Sadat of Esfahan.[38] He was a noted architect. In 1615 he was sent to Mandu with orders to construct new buildings for imperial use and to repair the buildings of the previous Sultans.[39] Accordingly, in about a year's time Mir Abdul Karim got some old buildings repaired and a few new ones constructed. Besides, he constructed in the city a whole new building on which Rs. 3 lakh were spent.[40] When the Emperor visited these buildings he granted to Mir Abdul Karim the rank of 800 *zat* and 400 *sawar* along with the title of Ma'mur Khan.[41] He is also said to have constructed buildings at Lahore at an expense of 7 lakh rupees in 1620 A.D.[42] The famous poet and historian Chandra Bhan Brahmin was in his service at Lahore.[47]

It seems that on the death of Jahangir Mir Abdul Karim was appointed *Diwan* of Punjab and was removed in 1631 by Hakim Jamala-i-Khan.[44] In 1633 he was appointed *Darogha-i-Imarat* (superintendent of buildings) an Agra.[45] In 1634 he was promoted to the rank of 1000 *zat* and 200 *sawar.*[46] In 1638 he was given a promotion to 1,500 *zat* 1200 *sawar.*[47] He was employed in the construction of the Taj Mahal, along with Mulla Murshid Shirazi, Makramat Khan.[48] In 1655 it is mentioned that he held four posts: *Bakhshi*, *Waqia Navis*, *Darogha* of buildings and *Mir-i-Bahr* of Agra. In these posts he was succeeded by Muttalib, son of Mutamad Khan.[49]

EAST AND NORTH-EAST

Khisali Heravi

He was a native of Herat and the younger brother of Wajhi Heravi. He was initially offered hospitality by Muzaffar Husain and Rustam Mirza Safavi. The poet imparted instruction to the children of noblemen. After the Uzbek invasion of Khurasan he accompanied Muzaffar Husain Safavi to India during the reign of Jahangir. Thereafter, he served under Mahabat Khan, the military general, for five years.[50] In the reign of Shahjahan, he was appointed chief revenue officer (*Diwan*), of Kashmir, where he stayed for a long time.[51] Khisali's merits were calligraphy and poetry.[52] His *diwan* was popular among the contemporaries.[53]

Khwaja Jahan Khawafi (Khafi)

His name was Khwaja Jan. According to Auhadi he came to India during Jahangir's reign from his native place Khaf, a city in Khurasan province, probably because of religious persecution. Khwaja Jahan entered in the service of prince Khurram. He was *Diwan* and *Waqia Navis* of Ahmadabad from 1021/1612 till 1030/1620. When Shahjahan ascended the throne, he made him *Khwaja Jahan* and appointed him as *Diwan* and *Waqia Navis* of Ahmadabad again.[54]

The author of *Maasir-ul-Umara* says: Khwaja Jahan was one of the old servants of Shahjahan. When after the receipt of the news of Jahangir's death, Shahjahan moved form Junair and arrived near Ahmadabad, he made the Khwaja, who was exalted to the rank of 2,000 *zat* and 600 *sawar*,[55] *Diwan* of Gujarat.[56] In the end of the 4th year he begged permission to go an a pilgrimage and this was granted. As the King had allocated five lacs of rupees to be sent to the needy in those blessed places, he ordered that the officers of Gujarat should hand over to the Khwaja, who was known for his honesty, 2 lacs and 40,000 rupees worth of such goods as would be saleable at the two holy places of Mecca and Medina. He was to sell these goods and distribute the money (i.e, the capital and the profit) to the poor there. In the 9th year he returned and presented nine Arab horses as a *Peshkash* to the Sustani. In the 12th year he was removed from the *Diwani* of Gujarat and died in the 17th year; 1053/1643.[57]

Mir Muhammad Ghiyas

He was the Fifth son of Islam Khan Mashhadi. After his father's death (1057/1647) he rose to the rank of 500 *zat* and 100 *sawar*. In the 28th reignal year of Shah Jahan he was appointed as *Bakhshi* and reporter of Burhanpur, and superintendent of the wardrobe (*Karkiraqkhana*) there. In the time of Aurangzeb he was appointed *Bakhshi* and reporter of Aurangzeb. He died[58] in the 22nd year of Aurangzeb's reign.

Mir Muhammad Sharif

Mir Muhammad Sharif was the son of Islam Khan Mashhadi[59] and accompanied his father to India. After the death of his father (1057/1647), he rose to the rank of 1000 *zat* and 200 *sawar*. In the 22nd year of Shah Jahan's reign he went on the Qandahar compaign with made superintendent (*darogha*) of the jewelled weapons. Afterwards he was made *Bakhshi* and reporter of the capital. During the last years of his service, Mir Muhammad Sharif apparently suffered a demotion in rank and was appointed as a clerk in the part of Surat. Finally he was imprisoned by the royal forces at the time when prince Murad Bakhsh, raised the banner of sovereignty in his name.[60]

Mir Muhammad Ashraf

He was the eldest son of Islam Khan Mashhadi.[61] Muhammad Ashraf possessed all spiritual qualities, and was noted for his possessing excellent human qualities. When his father was the Nazim of the Deccan he was appointed by him to take charge of Burhanpur. When his father died he got a promotion of 500 *zat* and 200 *sawar* and obtained the mansab of 1500 *sawar*. In the 26th year he was made superintendent of the branding. In the 27th year Ashraf attained another promotion of 500 *zat* with the title of Itimad Khan. After that he was made superintendent of the royal library at the end of the 31st year, when the reign of Shahjahan was nearing its end, he was made *Diwan* and *Bakhshi* of the army of Sulaiman Shukoh.

In early years of Aurangzeb's reign Ashraf was made governor of Kashmir. In the 13th year he obtained the rank of 3000 *zat* and was made Khan Saman. He served in this post for a long time and in the 21st year was made *Waqai nawis* (reporter). He died in 1097/1686. Ashraf had a taste for sufism, he made a selection from the *masnavi* of the Maulana Jalal-ud-Din and had much pleasure in studying the poem. He also wrote in Naskh, Shikasta, Taliq and Nastaliq[62] styles perfectly high and low[63] made his *Shikasta-writing* their exemplar of good penmanship. He had no son.[64]

FROM THE UNKNOWN AREAS

Asad Qissa Khan

According to Auhadi, Maulana Asad was the son of Maulana Haidar Qissa Khan. He had a mystic nature and a bent of mind powerful imagination like his father. Asad migrated to India in the reign of Jahangir in order to better his prospects. In the initial period, after his arrival in Thatta, he was attached to Mirza Ghazi.[65] After death of Mirza Ghazi in 1021/1612 he remained in Thatta. Afterwards he entered the service of Jahangir and received the title of Mahfuz Khan.[66] He died on the way from Gujarat to Agra in 1027/1617.[67] According to Jahangir, Mulla Asad, the story-teller, one of the servants of Mirza Ghazi, came from Thatta. As he was a reciter and story-teller full of sweetness and smartness, I liked his company, and I made him happy with the title of Mahzuz Khan, and gave him, 1000 rupees, a dress of honour, a horse, an elephant, and a palanquin. After some days I ordered him to be weighed against rupees, and granted him *mansab* of 200 *zat* and 20 *sawar*. I ordered him to be always present at the meetings for discussion (gap).[68]

Eskandar Qissa Khan

Eskandar came from Iraq (Iraq. Ajam). It is said that he was expert in the art of story telling. He used to narrate stories and fiction which have been recorded by writers from time to time in such a way that the hearer used to accept them as true. He had also written poems and introduced new ideas in poetry. He held a high rank among the courtiers of Jahangir. He had also written *qasidas* in praise of Abdur Rahim Khan Khanan for which he was lavishly rewarded.[69]

Table 4.2
POETS AS ADMINISTRATORS

Rg	Pr	Nu	Reasons and Contexts of Migration																									
			X1	X2	X3	X4	X5	X6	X7	X8	X9	X10	X11	X12	X13	X14	X15	X16	X17	X18	X19	X20	X21	X22	X23	X24	X25	X26
NO	Ak	0																										
0	Ja	0																										
	Sh	0																										
WNW	Ak	0																										
0	Ja	0																										
	Sh	0																										
SW	Ak	0																										
0	Ja	0																										
	Sh	0																										
CP	Ak	2								1			1															
4	Ja	2												1														
	Sh	0																										1
SO	Ak	0																										
0	Ja	0																										
	Sh	0																										
ENE	Ak	0																										
5	Ja	5	1		1					3																		
	Sh	0																										
SE	Ak	0																										
0	Ja	0																										
	Sh	0																										
UA	Ak	0																										
2	Ja	2														1												1
	Sh	0																										
Total		11	1		1					4			1	1		1												2

Graph : 4.1

Number of Scholars and Artists in Administration according to the reasons and contexts of their migration

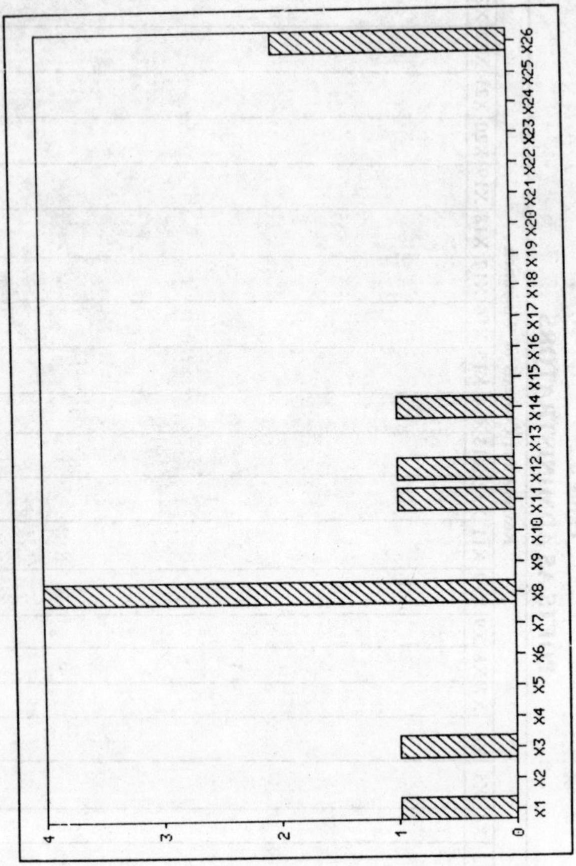

Physicians and *Qazis*

The accompanying table shows that among the seven physicians and two *Qazis* immigrating to India four of them came from central plateau such as Kashan, Qazwin and Esfahan.Some of them from the northern, southern and eastern (each I) regions like, Gilan; Shiraz and Mashhad.The remaining two (*Qazis*) came from south-west. Four of them departed Iran during Akbar's reign; one in the reign of Jahangir; two in Shahjahan's time. Qazi Nurullah and Qazi Najm-ud-Din Ali came to India during Akbar's reign.

Among them Fayez Gilani, Hakim Sadra (Ilai Shirazi) and Hakim Mashhadi migrated to India as adventurers in search of better opportunities. The purpose of Qasim Deylami, Qazi Nurullah and Qazi Najm-ud-din Ali *shushtari* are unclear. A further three (Masih Kashani, Hakim Dawud Taqarrob Khan and his son) came to India because of losing royal favour. Hakim Dawud's father and mother were both physicians at Shah Abbas' court and *harem* respectively. After the death of his father in 1029/1619-20,[70] Dawud succeeded him and entered the royal service as a physician. He stayed at the Safavid court throughout the reign of Shah Safi (1629-42), but received no special attention. After the enthronement of Abass II, Dawud realizing that he had little chance of promotion, decided to change masters and came to India in 1053/1643-44. He was successful in gaining favour from one of Shahjahan's daughters and so received royal patronage. He became an Amir with the name of Taqarrob Khan in 1957/1647-48 and was given 5000 *zats* and 3000 *sawars* in 1068/1657. He died on 1073/1662-63. His high influence at the Mughal court is reflected in the fact that his name appears several times in European travel accounts, including those of Manucci, Bernier and Chardin.[71] Dawud's son, Muhammad Ali Khan, who had gone to India with his father, was, unlike his father, a recipient of the favour of Aurangzeb and served him throughout his life.[72]

Having acquired a fortune in India, Hakim Dawud ordered a large mosque to be built in his home town of Esfahan and named after him. The construction of the Masjed-i-Hakim was begun in 1067/1656-57, and completed in 1073/1662-63, the year of Dawud's death.[73] Hakim Dawud never returned to Iran after his visit to India, but he kept contact with his relatives and friends in Esfahan and seems to have identified with Esfahan until the end of his life.

Table : 4.3
PHYSICIANS AND QAZIS

Name of migrants	Place of Birth	Province	Regions	Period of migration	Contexts and Reasons of migration	Position in Iran	Position in India	Place of Death
Feyez-i-Gilani	Gilan	North	Gilan	Jahangir 1616 ca	In Search of better opportunities	Physician	Physician	Unclear
Masih Kashani	Kashan	Esfahan	Central Plateau	Akbar 1602	Losing royal favour	Physician and Poet	Physician and Poet	Kashan 1655
Qasim Deylami	Qazwin	Qazwin	Central Plateau	Jahangir	Unclear	Physician	Physician	//
Hakim Dawud Taqarrub Khan	Esfahan	Esfahan	Central Plateau	Shahjahan 1643	No special attention by Safavid Kings	Physician and Administrator	Physician, *mansab* of 500 *zat* and 3000 *sawar*	India 1662
Muhammad Ali Khan; Khan-i-Saman	Esfahan	Esfahan	Central Plateau	//	With his father Hakim Dawud	//	Physician, *mansab* of 1000 *zat* during Shahjahan's reign	India 1687

Table Contd...

Table Contd...

Hakim Sadra (llai Shirazi)	Shiraz	Fars	South	Akbar 1602	In Search of better opportunities	Physician poet and Administrator	Physician' *mansab* of 3000 *zat* and 5000 *sawar* Title of Masih-uz-Zaman	Kashmir 1651
Hakim Mashhadi	Mashhad	Mashhad	East and North-East	Akbar	In search of better opportunities	Physician	Physician, *mansab* of 3000 *zat*	Unclear
Qazi Nurullah Shushtari	Shushtar	Khuzestan	South-West	Akbar 1584	Unclear	Theologian	Scholar and *Qazi* of Lahore	Agra 1610
Qazi Najm-ud-Din Ali Shushtari	Shushtar	Khuzestan	South-West	Twice Akbar and Jahangir	//	//	Scholar and *Qazi* of Agra	Iran

NORTH OF IRAN

Fayez Gilani

Mir Fayez Gilani was a learned man in theory and practice. He was well known for his skills in medicine. He came to India in search of better opportunities and settled in Lahore in 1025/1616. Mir Fayez wrote some verses in praise of Aqa Tahir (Wasli Tehrani) elder brother of Iitimad-ud-Daula Tehrani, and sent them to Ajmer.[74]

CENTRAL PLATEAU

Masih Kashani

Hakim Rukn-ud-Din Masud was the son of Hakim Nizam-ud-Din Ali Kashan. He was also known as Hakim Rukna. He had adopted the poetic surname of Masih. He belonged to a noble family of physicians, who commanded influence and respect in Iran. In fact, he was an expert physician and a skillful poet. Shah Abbas the Great accommodated him among his courtiers.[75] Incidentally he incurred the displeasure[76] of the Shah and Masih came to India during the last days of Akbar.[77]

Gar Falak Yek Subhadam ba man garan bashad sarash;
Sham biroon miravam chon Aftab az Kishvarash.[78]

"If the sky feels offended with me early in the morning like the sun I shall quit his dominion in the evening".

Hakim Rukna received the title of Masih-uz-Zaman from Akbar after the death of Akbar. Jahangir enlisted him in the circle of his boon companions. Earlier, fearing the unpredictable consequences of prince Salim's revolt against his father, Masih trotted away from Allahabad towards the Deccan, where Muhammad Quli Qutb Shah, King of Golkonda, and Mir Muhammad Mumin Astarabadi, *Pishwa* (leader) and *wakil* of Golkonda, received him with Kindness. One day the Mir Mumin Astarabadi came to see Masih at his residence.In excitement and haste Masih welcomed his guest by spraying alcohol instead of rose water, which was usual custom among the nobles. The mistake created odious scene and Masih was so much ashamed that he instantly fled from the Deccan. He witnessed the heydays of the Mughal empire; on the occasion of Shahjahan's coronation, he presented a *qasida* congratulating the young sovereign.

Badashah Zamaneh Shah Jahan; Khurram-i-Shad-i-Kamaran bashad.
Ba har sal Jolos O-goftam; Dar Jahan bad ta Jahan bashad =(1037/ 1627)

"The King of the time Shahjahan, May be he happy and prosperous.

For the year of his accession I said.

May he remain in the world as long as the world exists."

Masih had enjoyed warm favours of Shahjahan. Masih wished to retire from imperial service in his old age, therefore, on the 8th of Rabi Sani 1042/1632[79] on the occasion of the lunar weighing of the King Shahjahan, he sought leave from the King to pass his old age in peaceful sojourn in Mashhad. He was given a robe of honour and five thousand rupees as reward and was sent away to Mashhad.[80]

After pilgrimage to Mecca and Mashhad Masih returned to his native city of Kashan and passed his last days in peace and plenty.[81] Hakim Rukna died at Kashan at a very advanced age in 1066/ 1655.[82]

Qasim Deylami

He was born in Qazwin and acquired knowledge of sciences there on attaining the age of discernment he adopted the course of acquiring worldly knowledge, and in a short time he gained great skill in medicine.He came to India, for reasons which are not specified and joined Mirza Rustam Safavi, who was a *mansabdar* during Akbar and Jahangir's reigns. Later he entered in the service of Jahangir. "Auhadi visited him at Ajmer. He was among the distinguished persons of his time, and he has said some verses in praise of Jahangir.[83]

Taqarrub Khan

His name was Hakim Dawud, and he was the son of Hakim Inayat Ullah. He was a favourite student of Hakim Mirza Muhammad, father of Hakim Masih-al-Zaman who was skilled in the science of medicine. After the death of his father, he became the chief of the physicians of Iran. But got fed up with the fatal intrigues of his enemies and perpetual ill-treatment from Shah Safi and his successor Shah Abbas II. For a time he remained in seclusion and then went on a pilgrimage to the two holy cities Mecca and Medina. After the visit to those two venerable places, he returned and went to Baghdad and from Baghdad he came to Basra and from there to Bandar Lahiri. In the 17th year 1053/ 1643, Hakim Dawud presented himself at the court, and due to the abundant experience in diagnosis he attained the high status of a *mansabdar* of 1500 *zat* and 200 *sawar*. Several times he applied remedies commended by physicians.[84] In the 20th year he received the high title of Taqarrub Khan and in the 23rd year his rank was advanced to 3,000 *zat* and 800 *sawar*. In the 27th year his *mansab* was increased to 4000 *zat* with 3000 *sawar*. In the 31st year when the emperor was afflicted with strangury his condition worsened due to use of cooling medicines. This ended in diabetes and great weakness of the body; no prescriptions of the ablest physicians proved of any use. But for the relief of strangury much benefit was derived from the use of manna (Shir-Khisht) which was ably prescribed by Taqarrub Khan. In accordance with a presage, the emperor changed his residence, and in 1068/1657, he came from the capital to Agra, and by taking Ma-ul-labm (essence of meat) and strong sopus recovered his health. Taqarrub Khan was promoted to the exalted rank of 5,000 *zat* and beat loudly the drum of his high office. After the accession of Aurangzeb, Taqarrub Khan was appointed to complete the cure, and to restore Shahjahan to health. After this he, for some reason, became the object of censure by Aurangzeb, and for a time lived in retirement. In the beginning of the 5th year of his reign, Aurangzeb suffered from a severe attack of fever, and became extremely weak. On this occasion, Taqarrub Khan was again restored to favour. He died in 1073/1662.[85]

Muhammad Ali Khan Khan-i-Saman

He was the son of Taqarrub Khan, Hakim Dawud.[86] Muhammad Ali came to India in 1053/1643 with his father. He followed in the footsteps of his father. Towards the end of Shahjahan's reign, Muhammad Ali was granted a *mansabs* of 1,000 *zat*. After Aurangzeb's accession when the victorious army returned to the capital from Punjab, Muhammad Ali was granted the title of Khan. In the 17th year, he was appointed superintendent of the Furring[87] (*Karkiraqkhana*) and his *mansab* was increased to 2,000 *zat* and 1,000 *sawar*. Later he was made superintendent of the chinaware department (*Chini Khana*).

Muhammad Ali Khan died in 1098/1687.[88] He was distinguished for his skill in physiognomy, wisdom, magnanimity and high-mindedness. He was scrupulously honest, and exercised great care in looking after the royal property. He was very affable, and whoever approached him was gratified. He was also very pious and observed abstinence.[89]

SOUTH

Hakim Sadra (Ilahi Shirazi)

Hakim Sadra[90] was the son of Hakim Fakhr-ud-Din Muhammad Shirazi, who was given the title of Mirza Muhammad Hakim.[91] Many of his relations, and people of his tribe were physicians. His genealogy traced to Haris Tabib (the physician Haris), the son of Kaladah,[92] who was in the service, of "The seal of the Prophets (Muhammad)"[93] who chose him for his favours. It is well known that the Prophet had prayed for the science of medicine to be professed in his household. This is proved to be a true augury, for proficient physician have taken birth in his family by the grace of the Prophet's prayer.[94]

Hakim Fakhr-ud-din was an expert physician and a man of good words. He was very skilled in the diagnosis and cure of diseases. The learned of the age regarded his dictat as authoritative, and his treatment as trustworthy. The physicians of the day prided themselves on being his disciples, and discussed medical books on the basis of his opinions. But as he was a free thinker (*ba tawassu mashrab mashhur bud*), the Shah did not pay much regard to him.[95] Hakim Sadra, after acquiring knowledge of medicine, arithmetic, and all the skills of medicine came to India in the 46th year of Akbar's accession, corresponding to 1011/1602[96] search for better prospects. In the time of Jahangir he was appointed head of the physicians, received the title of *Masih uz-Zaman*[97] (Messiah of the age) and the *mansab* of 3,000 *zat* and 5000[98] *sawar*.

After the accession of Emperor Shahjahan he continued to rise in Sultan's favour, and was appointed reviser of petitions (*Arz-i-Mukarrar*), an appointment given to a really trusted persons only. In the 4th year he obtained leave to go to Mecca, and through divine guidance successfully performed the pilgrimage.[99] After his return in accordance to his request, he entrusted with the administration of the port of Surat.[100] Apart from medicine, Hakim Sadra Shirazi was also proficient in other sciences as well. Having studied many of the customary subjects under Shaikh Bahad-ud-din Muhammad Jabal-Amili, and the science of medicine under Hakim Muhammad Baqir, son of Hakim Imad ud-Din Mahmud in Iran, he had come to Hindustan. Here also, he became a pupil of Hakim Ali Gilani, who was the leading physician of the auspicious regime of His Majesty *Arsh-Ashyani*.[101]

As the Hakim was a confirmed believer in the Imamiya sect and possessed perfect piety and purity, he resigned his service at court and with a tranquil mind lived in retirement at Lahore. He spent most of the time in Lahore, but used to go to Kashmir during summer. He died in Kashmir in 1061/1651.

He had a poetical van and his nom-dé-plume was *Masih-i-Ilahi.* The following verse is attributed to him:

'My flavour is limited, but my price is beyond count. One would say it is an early fruit from the garden of my life.'[102]

The author of *Zakhiratul-Khawanin* says: He was a follower of the Imamiya sect. He had complete expertise in the science of medicine. He was honoured and respected in reigns of Jahangir and Shahjahan. Hakim went on a visit to the holy Mecca and spent much money there, then he returned to serve at the court and received a *mansab* and fief (literally *Jagir*).[103]

EAST AND NORTH-EAST

Hakim Mashhadi

He hailed from the holy city of Mashhad and was well informed about medicine. He was one of the greatest physicians of India. In the beginning of his career, he had come in extremely destitute state from Persia to India and His Majesty *'Arsh-i-Ashyani,* having recognised his talent patronised him. He rose to the *mansab* of 3,000, became a favourite, a boon-companion and a close associate of Akbar and Khan-i-Khanan. He constantly attended upon them in private and public. Once, it so happened that Akbar fell ill but Hakim Ali could not cure him. When Jahangir acceeded to the throne he reproached Hakim Ali for his failure. Hakim Ali passed away during Jahangir's reign.[104]

QAZIS

SOUTH-WEST

Qazi Nurullah Shushtari

According to Arif Shirazi he was born at Shushtar, a city in Khuzestan province, in 956/1549. He moved from his native place to Mashhad in 979/1571, and received religious education there. Nurullah migrated to India in 993/1584 though reasons of his departure are unspecified.[105]

The contemporary historian, 'Badauni' visited him and *mentioned* his account in detail, when Nurullah served as Qazi of Lahore. Badauni says: Although he was by religion a Shia,[106] he was distinguished for his impartiality, justice, virtue, modesty, piety, continence, and such qualities as are possessed by noble men, and was well known of his learning, clemency, quickness of understanding, singleness of heart, clearness of perception, and acumen. He is the author of several able works, and he has written a monograph on the 'undotted commentary'[107] of Shaikh Faizi which is beyond all praise. He also possesses poetic faculty and writes impressive poetry. He was introduced to the emperor by the instrumentality of the physician Abul-Fath [Gilani] when the victorious imperial army reached Lahore Shaikh Muin the Qazi of Lahore, when he was paying his respects to the emperor, was afflicted suddenly in the presence chamber with the falling sickness, which came upon him in consequence of the feebleness of old age and the failure of his natural powers, the emperor took pity on his weakness, and said, the Shaikh is past his work, and we have therefore appointed Qazi Nurullah to the post which he held. In truth he has reduced the insolent Muftis and the crafty and subtle Muhtasibs of Lahore, who venture to give lessons to the teacher of the angels, to order, and has closed to them the avenues of bribery, and restrained them within due bounds as closely as a nut is enclosed in its shell, and to such a degree that stricter discipline could not be imagined. One might almost say that the author of the following verses had the Qazi in his mind when he wrote them:

Toyi on kas ka nakardi hama omor qabul;
Dar qaza hish ze kas joz ka shadat ze guvah.[108]

"Thou art he who has never in all his life admitted any statement by anybody in a law-suit, except the sworn testimony of a witness."

After Akbar's death, there was a swing of pendulum in opposite direction and the religious reaction that followed led to the decline and death of a number of innocent souls. The orthodox fanatics discovered in the writings of Qazi Nurullah had many objectionable ideas which smacked of heresy. In deed, he was an outspoken Shia. Jahangir, on receiving the complaint, summoned him to his own presence and demanded clarification of the charges of unsound faith levelled against him. The defence put forth by the Qazi did not satisfy the emperor, nor were the rival *Ulama* silenced by his arguments. In the state of drunkenness, perhaps, Jahangir ordered him to be put to death by flogging, the customary, sentence for a confirmed heretic. He was a prodigious author of around hundred books. Most remarkable among them is the anthology of celebrated Shias, *Majalis-ul-Muminin.* Also, mention may be made of *Ihqaq ul-Haq* etc.[109] Qazi Nurullah Shushtari was put to death in 1019/1610, and was buried at Agra.[110]

Najm-e-Shushtari

Qazi Najm-ud-din Ali was the son of paternal uncle of Maulana Abdul-wahab who was great scholar of Shushtar.Najam Shushtari received education in his native place. He moved to India, during Akbar's reign. For a while he was Qazi of *Dar-ul-sultan,* i.e. the capital city of Agra. Afterwards he returned to Iran. He however, came to India for a second time in the reign of Jahangir with reasons for his migration remain obscure. Najam Shushtari had some poetic talent which to evident from the few verses which are attributed to him. He died after a few years in India.[111]

Table 4.4

PHYSICIANS AND QAZIS

Rg	Pr	Nu	Reasons and Contexts of Migration																									
			X1	X2	X3	X4	X5	X6	X7	X8	X9	X10	X11	X12	X13	X14	X15	X16	X17	X18	X19	X20	X21	X22	X23	X24	X25	X26
NO	Ak	0																										
1	Ja	1														1												
	Sh	0																										
WNW	Ak	0																										
0	Ja	0																										
	Sh	0																										
SW	Ak	2																										2
2	Ja	0																										
	Sh	0																										
CP	Ak	1		1																								
4	Ja	1																										1
	Sh	2	1							1																		
SO	Ak	1														1												
1	Ja	0																										
	Sh	0																										
ENE	Ak	1														1												
1	Ja	0																										
	Sh	0																										
SE	Ak	0																										
0	Ja	0																										
	Sh	0																										
UA	Ak	0																										
0	Ja	0																										
	Sh	0																										
Total		9	1	1						1						3												3

Graph: 4.2

Number of Physicians and Qazis according to the reasons and contexts of their migration

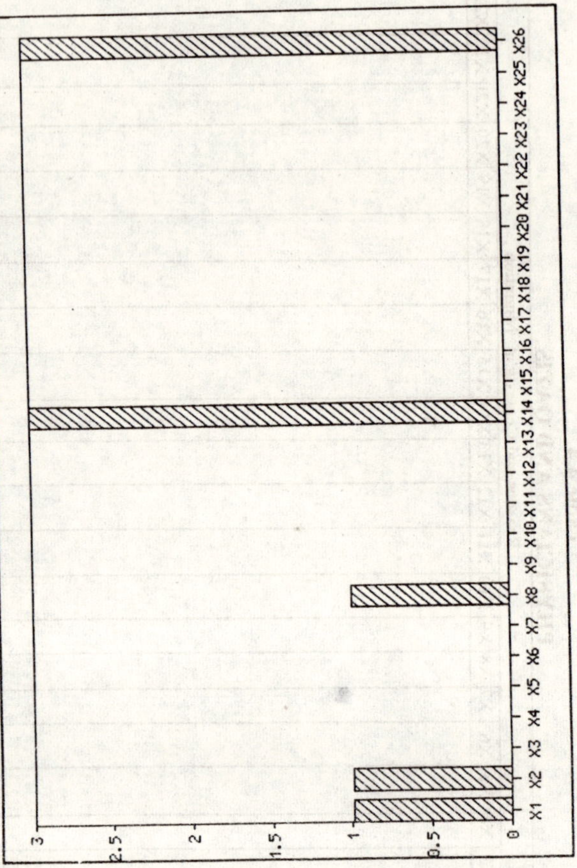

REFERENCES

1. See; Tables: 4.1.2 and graph; 4.1 for reasons of their migration see; *Ibid.*
2. M.U. text. Vol. I. pp. 385-88.
3. Sajida Sultana Alvi (ed), *Advice on the Art of Governance: Mauiza-i-Jahangiri of Muhammad Baquir Najm-i-Sani,* New York, 1980 pp. 12-13, 39 for Baqir Khan's Insha See: Momin Mohiuddin, *The chancellery and Persian Epistolography under the Mughals,* Calcutta, 1971, pp. 201-210.
4. A.G. Manni Vol. I, 1369/1948, p. 244.
5. *Tuzuk-i-Jahangiri,* 1863, p. 137.
6. Lahori, Vol. II, p. 137.
7. *Ibid.*, 330.
8. *Ibid.*, p. 49.
9. Amin Ahamad Razi, 1961, Vol. II, p. 169.
10. For details see; *M. U.*, text, Vol. I, p. 669 also see; A. A. Razi, 1961, Vol. III, 171.
11. Hamdullah Mustaufi, *Nuzhat-Ul-Qulub;* tr, G. Le strange, London, 1919, p. 152.
12. *Z.Kh.*, Vol. I, pp. 195-96 also see; *M.U.* text, Vol. I, pp. 664-69.
13. Afzal Husain, 1975, p. 168.
14. For details see; Mohd. Afzal Khan; *`Iranis in the Mughal Nobility: A case study of the Khafis,* in: *proc IHC,* 1980, pp. 250-51.
15. M.A. Khan, 1980, p. 251.
16. T. Auhadi, fol. 229.
17. M.A. Khan, 1980, pp. 251-52.
18. S.S. Alvi, 1980, pp. 11-12, Muhammad Bin Amir Wali Balkhi's travelogue is the only primary source in which the name of Baqir's father is recorded (*Bahr-al-Asrar Fi Manaqib-al-Akhyar*), ed. by Riazul Islam, Karachi. 1980, p. 66. Shaikh Farid Bhakkari, Baqir's hear contemporary, noted that Baqir's father was employed for some time by the chancery (*Diwan*) in Farah, Khurasan. See: *Z.Kh.* Vol. II, p. 254 Baqir wrote the name of the place, Farah in a poem that he composed for his father and sent it with his poet friend, Itabi, who was returning to Iran. (Farah is the name of a mountain and a river in sistan, mid way between Herat and Jalalabad, see: Sayyid Hasan, Askari, *Mirza Muhammad Baqir Najm-i-Sani*, Arshi presentation volume, eds. Malik Ram and M.D. Ahmad (New Delhi: Majlis-i-Nazr-i-Arshi) 1965, p. 104.
19. Shah Nawaz Khan speculates taht Baqir came to India either during the reign of Akbar (being given the rank of 300 *sawar*) or during the reign of Jahangir (being given the rank of 250 *sawar*). See; *M.U.* Tr. by Beveridge, Vol. I, p. 386 Farid Bhakkari states that he received an initial appointment of 100 *sawar* in Jahangir's service. After serving the emperor in various

capacities during which he displayed great brilliance in subduing various tribes between Multan and Qandahar, he rose rapidly into the upper echelons of the Mughal *mansabdari* system. See; *Z.Kh*, Vol. II, p. 254-55.

20. She was wife of Hakim Beg, (see; *M.U.*, text, Vol. I, p. 574).
21. *M.U.* Tr. by Beveridge, Vol. I, p. 386.
22. *Tuzuk*, Tr. by Rogers, Vol. II, pp. 4, 82.
23. Text *Ab-i-Alam* Khan. Apparently this is the Shah Alam river. It is the Southern branch of the Kabul river. (see, *M.U.* Vol., by Beveridge, Vol. I, p. 387.
26. *Ibid.*, p. 388.
27. In two volumes: pers Kalam, 1409, 1409-11, Sajida Alvi says: during my library research trip to India in 1986, I located it in the Oriental Manuscripts Library, Research Institute, Hyderabad, see: S.S. Alvi, 1980, p. III, note. 74.
28. For details of his political appointments and distinctions, see, S.H. Askari, 1965, pp. 106-14.
29. *M.U.* Tr. by Beveridge, Vol. I, p. 388, *Z.Kh*, Vol. II, p. 254. One of Baqir's works, *Siraj-al-Menhaj* written by the author himself in beautiful *Nastaliq* bears testimony to Baqir's skills in calligraphy.
30. S.S. Alvi, 1980, p.12; As an example of Baqir's interest in prosody, philosophy, mathematics, and astronomy, see one of his published *Qita* composed as a riddle (S.S. Alvi, *'Shiism in India during Jahangir's Reign, some reflections'*, *Journal of the Pakistan Historical Society*, 27, no. 1; 1979, pp. 50-65.
31. A.S. Alvi, *op.cit.*, 1980, p. 12 for details and more information in this connection: see; M. Mohiuddin, 1971, pp. 207-210.
32. S.S. Alvi, 198, pp. 12-13.
33. In *Iqbalnama-i-Jahangiri*, p. 217, Jkaroh. In *Tuzuk-i-Jahangiri* (Rogers and Beveridge's translation) II, p. 298, it is transcribed as Khurda.
34. Vide; *Iqbalnama-i-Jahangiri*, p. 218.
35. The passage is somewhat obscure in the text. In *Iqbalnama-i-Jahangiri*, p. 219. From where the passage is taken, it is quite clear, for Ibrahim Khan states that he knows from the good things of past life, what there is in store for the future.
36. See; *M.U.* text. I, pp. 135 and *M.U.* Tr. by Beveridge, Vol. I, pp. 657-59, *Ain-i-Akbari*, Tr. by Blochmann, Vol., p. 575, and *Jahangir Nama*, Tehran Press, pp. 438, 463, *Tuzuk*, Tr. by Rogers and Beveridge. Vol. II, pp. 90, 167, 161, 298-99.
37. N. Qazwini, 1926; pp. 502-03, 509.
38. A.G. Maani, 1369/1948, Vol. I, p. 244.

39. *Tuzuk*, Tr. by Rogers, Vol. I, p. 368.
40. *Tuzuk*, ed. Sir Sayyid; Ghazipur, 1863, pp. 179-180.
41. *Tuzuk*, Tr. by Rogers, Vol. p. 368.
42. *Tuzuk*, 1863, p. 318.
43. *Amal-i-Salih,* Lahore, 1960, vol. III, pp. 423-32.
44. Lahori; 1867, Vol. I (a), p. 407.
45. *Ibid,* p. 474; I (b) p. 76.
46. Lahori I (a); pp. 2-3, 311.
47. *Ibid,* II, pp. 103, 732.
48. *Ibid,* p. 330.
49. *Ibid,* p. 491.
50. B. Nihavandi, Vol. III, pp. 1289-91 also see: N. Qazwini, 1926, pp. 550-52.
51. *Amal-i-Salih*, Vol. I, p. 493 also see: Lahori Vol. I, p. 432.
52. T. Auhadi, Fol. 226.
53. N. Qazwini, 1926, p. 552.
54. T. Auhadi, fol. 229 also see: *Amal-i-Salih*, Vol. I p. 272.
55. *M.U.* text, Vol. I, pp. 748-49 also see: *Amal-i-Salih*, Vol. I, pp. 268-69.
56. *Z.Kh.*, Vol. III, p. 128.
57. Should be the 11th year quoted from Lahori, Vol. II, p. 105.
58. *M.U.* Tr. by Beveridge, Vol. I, p. 696.
59. For Islam Khan see: *M.U.* text; Vol. I, pp. 162-67.
60. *M.U.* Tr. by Beveridge, Vol. I, p. 696.
61. For Islam Khan see: *M.U.* text: Vol. I. pp. 162-67.
62. There is in the British Museum an album presented by him. (see: Rieu's Catalogue II, pp. 778. There is also a reference to Ashraf in Khafi K. Vol. II, p. 381.
63. Perhap's young and old.
64. *M.U.* Tr. by Beveridge, Vol. I, pp. 303-304 and *M.U.* text, Vol. I, pp. 272-74.
65. For Mirza Ghazi see: *Ain-i-Akbari*, Tr. by Blochmann, Vol. I, p. 392 also see: *M.U.* text; Vol. III, pp. 857-62 and *M.U.* Tr. by Beveridge, Vol. I, pp. 582-83.
66. Mahfuz Khan is mistake. Correct name is Mahzuz Khan.
67. T. Auhadi, Fol. 112 vide see: N. Qazwini, 1926 pp. 229, 333, 411-12.
68. *Jahangir Nama*, Tehran Press, p. 215 also see: *Tuzuk*, Tr. by A. Rogers and H. Beveridge, London, 1909, Vol. I, pp. 376-77.
69. B. Nihavandi, Calcutta, 1931, Vol. III, pp. 1242-43.
70. *A.A.A*, 1971, p. 955.

71. M. Handeda, *Emigration of Iranian Elites to India during the 16-18th centuries* in: *L.'heritaage timouride,* ed. Maria szuppe, Paris, 1997, pp. 136-37 cited: N. Manucci, *Stonade Mogoror Moghul India*, 1653-1708, tr. W. Irvine, London, 1907-08, vol. II, p. 65, According to Manucci, Hakim Dawud died after taking in place of Shahjahan, the poison sent by Aurangzeb to assassinate the emperor, (see: *Ibid.*, p. 65).
72. *M.U.* text; Vol. I, pp. 490-93, Vol. III, pp. 625-27.
73. Lotf Ullah Honarfar; *Ganjina-ye-Athar-e-Tarikhi-ye-Esfahan*, Esfahan, 1344/1965, pp. 612-20.
74. T. Auhadi; Fols: 562-63.
75. Qazwini, Fol. 425; Lohoari, p. 349; *Amal-i-Salih,* p. 394, also see: Q.A. Mir Munshi; 1910, pp. 122-23.
76. M.T: Nasrabadi; pp. 214-17 but the author of *Khirul-Bayan* says: Hakim Rukna went to India because he could not treat somebody who was one of Shah Abbas's esteemed. See: M. Sistani; *Khirul Bayan,* Fols. 299-301; Qazwini and Lahori say: Hakim Rukna could not stay in Iran due to his own harsh nature and improper behaviour see: Qazwini, Fol. 425 and Lahori, p. 349.
77. He came to India in 1011/1602 in companion of Hakim Ilahi Shirazi and joined to Akbar's court. See: *A.N,* Vol. III, p. 816.
78. M.T. Nasrabadi, 1938, p. 215, see also: M.Q. Gopamoy, *Nataij-ul-Afkar*, Bombay, 136/1957, pp. 640-41, see also: M.S. Mina; *Subh-i-Sadiq*, p. 52.
79. The author of *Amal-i-Salih* mentions: 1043/1633 see: *Amal-i-Salih*, Vol. I, p. 504
80. Lahori, Vol. I, p. 441.
81. M.S. Mina, pp. 52-53 also see: Nasrabadi, p. 215.
82. M.Q Gopamavi, 1957, p. 642 also see: Nasrabadi, p. 215 for details about Hakim Rukna see: N. Qazwini, 1926, pp. 359-375 and A. Munzavi, *Fihret-e-Nuskhai Khatti Farsi*, 1972, Vol. III, pp. 2527-28.
83. T. Auhadi, Fol. 595.
84. For details see: Lahori, Vol. II, pp. 367, 368, 399, 505, 627, 679, 756; Waris, pp. 6, 126-27, 257; *Amal-i-Salih*, Vol. II, pp. 402-418, Vol. III, pp. 395-96.
85. For details see: *M.U.* text, Vol. I, pp. 490-93 and see also. *M.U.* Tr. by Beveridge, Vol. II, pt. II, pp. 924-25; *Alamgir Nama*; 1868-73, pp. 749-757; *Maasir-i-Alamgiri*; 1871, p. 42 See also, F. Bernier; pp. 100-101.
86. See: *M.U.* text, Vol. I, pp. 490-93.
87. These appointments are mentioned in *Maasir-i-Alamgiri,* 1871, pp. 131, 165.
88. *Ibid.*, p. 297.

89. *M.U.* Tr. by Beveridge, Vol. II, pt. I, pp. III-112 also see : *M.U.* text, Vol. III, pp. 625-27.
90. T. Auhadi says: Hakim Ilahi's birthplace is Qom. (For details see: T. Auhadi; Fols. 123-24).
91. Qazwini, Muhammad Amin, *Padshah Nama*, Ms. Br. M.Or, 173, Rotograph and transcript of the Riza Library Ms (Rampur) in the Dept. of History Aligarh, Fol. 424.
92. I have followed *Amal-i-Salih*, Vol. III, p. 347, Kalawab in the text of *M.U.*, Vol. I, p. 577 is apparently incorrect.
93. M.U. text; Vol. I, p. 577 and Tr. by Beveridge, Vol. II.
94. Qazwini, Fol. 4246.
95. *M.U.* text, Vol. I, pp. 577-78 and see: Beveridge Tr. Vol. II, p. 663.
96. *Amal-i-Salih*, Vol. III, pp. 393-94 Lahori, p. 348 but Qazweini says: He came to India in 1015/1606. Qazweini, Fol. 424b.
97. *Jahangir Nama*, 1980, pp. 89,151, *Tuzuk*, Tr. by Rogers, Vol. I, p. 155.
98. *M.U.* text, Vol. I, pp. 577-78.
99. *Ibid.*
100. Lahori, pp. 347-48.
101. *Ibid;* also see Qazwini, Fol. 4246.
102. *M.U.* text; Vol. I, pp. 578-79 and Beveridge translation, Vol. II, part II, p. 664.
103. *Z.Kh.* Vol. II, pp. 341-42. For details about Hakim Sadra see: *Jahangir Nama*, 1980, pp. 173, 261, 380, 383, *Tuzuk*, Tr by Rogers, Vol. I, pp. 155, 267, 374 and Vol. II, p. 217 also see: M.M.H. Lucknowi; *Tazkira Rauz-e-Raushan*, Tehran, 1343/1964, pp. 12, 388.
104. *Z.Kh.* Vol. I; pp. 243-5 also see: B. Nihavandi, Vol. III, 1243-52.
105. M.A. Shirazi, *Latiful-Khayal*, MS. In addition of Mir Sayyid Sharif, who had accompanied Nurullah on journey to India, he had three more sons who were born in India. All of them were scholaars and learned men of that time. (See: *Diwan of Sayyid Hasan Chazhavi*, ed. By Ustad Modarres Razavi, Tehran University, 1328/1921, pp. 111-117) also for details see: Sayyid Abdullah Jazayeri, *Tazkira Shushtar*, ed. By Khan Bahadur Mulla Bakhsh and Muhammad Hadayat Husain, Calcutta, 1343, A.H./1924, p. 251 also see: A Khayampur, *Farhang-i-Sukhanvaran*, Tabriz; 1961, p. 620, and A. G. Maani, 1348. AS/1961, Vol. II, pp. 759-66 and S.A. Hasan Khan Bohpali, *Subh-i-Gulshan* Bohpal; 1295 A.H./ 1878, p. 56.
106. According to "Auhadi" Qazi Nurullah practiced *Taqiya*, or concealment of his religious views, among Sunnis, and was well acquainted with the system of jurisprudence of Abu Hanifah. After Jahangir's accession he was recalled from Lahore, once he offended the emperor by a hasty word, and was executed. See: T. Auhadi, Fol. 777.

107. The *Sawati-ul-Ilhani*, vide *Ain-i-Akbari*, I, p. 549.
108. Badauni, Vol. III, pp. 137-7 also see, Badauni, Tr. by S.W. Haig, Vol. III, pp. 193-94.
109. For details see: T. Auhadi, Fol. 777, and also see: S.A. Jazayari, Ahwaz Press, p. 251.
110. M. Arif Shirazi, *Tazkira Lataiful Khayal*, Manuscript, Tehran, Malik Library, No. 42325.
111. M.A. Shushtari, *Risaleh Firdous* ed. Muhaddth Armavi, Tehran, Anjuman Athar Melli 1325 A.s/1973 also see: A.A Jazayari, Calcutta Press, 1924, under Najm-e-Shushtari.

5

Iranian Poets in Mughal Culture

During the seventeenth century there was a large influx of poets from Safavid Iran to Mughal India and the Deccan. Persian poetry blossomed in India rather than in its birthplace in Iran and Central Asia. The explanation of this so far held is best summed up in Mirza Muhammad Qazwini's communication to the noted modern historian of Persian literature E.G. Browne, which runs as follows:

> The chief reason for this (i.e. lack of patronage by the Safavids to the poets) seems to have been that these kings, by reason of their political aims and strong antagonism to the Ottoman empire, devoted the greater part of their energies to the propagation of the Shia doctrine and the encouragement of divine learning in its principles and laws.

Browne subscribed to this theory fully, as have many others, including Jan Rypka more recently, who asserts that the cultural interest of the Safavids was confined to the consolidation of Shiism. He does concede some development of, and interest in, non-religious poetry in the Safavid Iran as exemplified by Ismail I's Turki *divan* and Sam Mirza's *Tazkira*.[1] Another noted Iranologist, Minorsky advanced the view that the decline of poetry under the Safavids might be explained in terms of the decline of mysticism in Iran.[2] But it is not easy to accept this, because there was also a decline of Sufism in poetry in Mughal India, where non-religious poetry flourished. Yet there were some of Sufi poets in Mughal India, but, it must be admitted, they were really very few, such as Dara Shukoh, Sarmad and Bidil.

Rypka also gives another explanation where she is closer to the truth. She suggests that the comparative decline of interest in poetry in early Safavid Iran could have been due to economic decline in the

Middle East. The facts of the matter seem to be that the India of Akbar, Jahangir and Shahjahan was richer than was Iran from Tahmasp to Abbas II, and that the Safavid resources of patronage of poets were inadequate compared to the resources of the Mughals. A sojourn in India, whether permanent or temporary, appeared to offer better opportunities of economic gain to the Persian poets, as also to a considerable cross-section of the Persian elite. Browne has also noted and rightly so that a considerable number of Persian poets returned to Iran after making their fortunes in India where they had enjoyed more affluence and, therefore more generous, patronage. But he is wrong when he talks about "lack of patronage" to poetry in Iran.[3]

The fact however remains that a large number of Persian poets migrated to India either permanently or temporarily. Our table would show that 201 Iranian poets came to India in later days of Akbar and during Jahangir and Shahjahan's period. In the accompanying table the places of origin of 15 people from North of Iran such as Gilan and Mazandaran are described. One of them came in later days of Akbar's reign, 9 during Jahangir's time and the other 5 in the reign of Shahjahan taking into account that 32 people came from West and North-west (One in later day's Akbar's reign, 21 in Jahangir's and 10 during Shah Jahan's period) like: Hamadan, Ardabil and Tabriz. Most of the Iranian immigrants (75) came from central part (14 during later days of Akbar, 36 in the reign of Jahangir and 25 in Shahjahan's period) from places such as Esfahan, Kashan, Tehran, Yazd and Qom. A very limited number came from the south-west and south-east as are shown by the fact that there were only 2 immigrants from Shushtar and one from Sistan. Some of them migrated from south too; among 21 people from south 3 of them came in later days of Akbar 6 persons migrated during Jahangir's period and the other 12 in the reign of Shahjahan. From east and north-east 32 people came to Mughal India; of them 7 arrived in later days of Akbar, 18 in Jahangir's period and further 7 came in the reign of Shahjahan. The places of origin of the remaining 23 are unknown.

One of the important factors of the migration from Iran was, yet again, the unfavourable religious atmosphere in Safavid Persia during the sixteenth and seventeenth centuries. Badauni states that Saifi Sayyids were all orthodox Sunnis and Shah Tahmasp deprived them of their estates[4] in Iran, thus compelling Ghiyas Beg (Itimad-ud–daula Tehrani) and his brother Wasli Tehrani and his son Sharif to come to

India. Sharif Amuli, a leader of Nuqtavi sect, is also said to have migrated to India from Amul under similar circumstances of persecution[5]. Further, Muhammad said Sarmad Kashani, belonged to Jewish family of Kashan. He was a *qalandar* poet, who went about naked in ecstasy and wrote moving quatrains, was held in esteem by Dara Shukoh and was executed by Aurangzeb.[6] Tashbihi Kashi, Ebadullah Kashani, Ghani Yazdi, Adai Yazdi, Dakhli Esfahani and Amini Darsani escaped Iran for fear of religious persecution. There were some poets (4) who for one reason or the other incurred the displeasure of a Safavid monarch and then escaped to India. Thus Ghururi Kashi incurred the displeasure of Abbas I for having plagiarised a *qasida* of Anwari, came to India and attached himself to Abdur-Rahim Khan-i-Khanan[7]. Mir Ilahi Hamadani and Tasalli Lurestani also constrained to come to India under similar conditions. Mir Ilahi, who had gained access successively to the courts of Jahangir and Shahjahan, chose finally to attach himself to Zafar Khan whom he accompanied to Kashmir in 1041/1631-32[8], he is the author of a *divan* and a *tazkira* of poets, the *Khazina-i-Ganj-i-Ilahi.*[9] Again, in an another case there are two accounts of Abbas I's displeasure with Hasan Beg Takallu Itabi. The more convincing is that the poet claimed to be a *Qutb*, the less convincing is that he refused to drink a cup of wine offered by the monarch. In any case, he was forgiven and did not visit India until later, he decided to accompany Akbar's envoy Mir Masum Bakkari on his return journey in 1602. Later, he went back to Iran and again visited India during the reign of Jahangir and attached himself first to the entourage of Mirza Ghazi Beg Tarkhan at Qandahar, and then to that of Nur Jahan's father, Itimad-ud-daula. He died in India, probably in 1025/1616.[10]

There are a few cases of the poets who fell into disfavour, not of the Safavid monarchs, but of their *wazirs* and governors, and therefore left for India. Salim Tehrani, a disciple of Khalifa Sultan rose to be *Shaik-ul-Islam* of Tehran, but fell from favour when Mirza Mahdi became *wazir*, and felt that he could find peace only in India.[11] Muhammad Jan Qudsi Mashhadi, who came to India under Uzbek Pressure, and because of this was unhappy (*dilgir*) in Iran.[12] He migrated through Hijaz in 1042/1632-33. He soon gained the favour of Shah Jahan and composed for him a *Padshah Nama* in verse, but he was not appointed his. *Malikal-Shuara*[13] (poet laureate), a position which went to Kalim. The statements of several *Tazkira*-writers that he was appointed to that position have to be discounted.[14] Nevertheless he enjoyed Shahjahan's bounty, was weighed in gold, and once even accompanied the emperor to Kashmir. He died in 1056/1646.[15]

Poetry appreciation was one of the pre-eminent cultural occupations of Mughal nobles. A large number of the nobles and higher *mansabdars* had poets in their entourage. Patronage of poets was a status symbol, and the expense incurred was well-justified in a noble's view. Since his *mansab* and estate was not hereditary, he tried to spend his wealth as lavishly and as elegantly as possible during his lifetime. Some of the higher nobles of the Mughal court stand out here as patrons of poets. Most outstanding of the patrons of poets among the Mughal nobility, was Abdur–Rahim Khan-i-Khanan, himself a poet in three languages. His generosity was princely. He had Mulla Nawai weighed in gold, gave a thousand gold coins to Shakibi; and took Hayati and Shawqi to his treasury to carry away as many gold coins as they could.[16] His protégé Abdul–Baqi Nihavandi has left in his *Maasir–i-Rahimi* accounts and specimens of verses of scores of poets, most of them of Persian origin, who enjoyed his patronage.

The principal luminary of Khan-i-Khanan's entourage was Naziri (d.1021/1612). Naziri Neishabouri travelled as a merchant in Iran and lived for some time at Kashan, and had already gained fame as a poet when reports of Abdur-Rahim Khan-i-Khanan's generous patronage attracted him to India. He gained access to Akbar's court and wrote panegryics in his honour. He continued to remain in the entourage of Khan-i-Khanan, until Jahangir called him to the imperial court in 1019/1610, two years before his death, impressed by his reputation[17]. It is quite possible that Naziri was a Sunni. Though the hagiological report that he spent the last twelve years of his life as a pious recluse has to be discounted in view of the historical evidence, he did perform the Hajj and he studied *tafsir* (explanation) and *hadis* (tradition) under Maulana Husain Jawahari and Ghausi Mandawi[18]. Another distinguished poet of his circle was Shakibi Esfahani (D. 1023/1614), who was later appointed to the religious office of Sadr by Jahangir and who may have been a Sunni.[19] Other poets worth mentioning, from among the multitude of them in his service, were Mahvi Hamadani, Hamzeh Bowanati, Maulana Nizam, Wafai Heravi, Abu-Turab Razavi Mashhadi, who was earlier in the service of the Nizam Shahs at Ahmadnagar and had been entrusted to carry the bones of Chand Bibi to Mashhad, and for that reason had temporarily incurred the displeasure of Jahangir; Baqi

Damavandi, who was in Khan-i-Khanan's service, but later settled down at Golkonda in the Deccan;[20] Baqi Esfarayeni, a friend of Naziri and Shakibi, Qasim Asiri, who left Akbar's service to join that of Khan-i-Khanan; Sharari Hamadani, who finally returned to the life of a darvish;[21] Baqai Khurasani, who wrote in the style of Urfi; Fahimi, who returned to Iran enriched by his patron's bounty; and Siraj Esfahani, who was also a good poet and the compiler of Urfi's *divan*.[22]

Nizam-ud-din Bakhshi, the famous author of the *Tabaqat-i-Akbari*, also had some poets in his entourage. These included Baqai, who later changed his penname to Mashghuli, and Ahdi Shirazi.[23]

Next only to Khan-i-Khanan, the most eminent patron of poets in Jahangir's India was Ghazi Beg Tarkhan.[24] During his governorship of Qandahar several Persian poets who came to India tried their fortune first in his service, several remained with him permanently and sought other patrons only after his death. Murshid Burujerdi received from him a *jagir* in Sind, and he was the cause of arrival from Iran of other poets to seek the patronage of Ghazi Beg, including Mahwi Ardabili and Wasli Shirazi, who later received from Jahangir the title of Rashid Khan.[25] One of his proteges, Soruri Yazdi, had earlier been in the service of Abbas I. Ahsani Gilani returned to Iran after Ghazi Beg's death.[26]

Mahabat Khan Zaman Beg, a Shirazi Sayyid, Shia and a rough soldier, who had for a time held the person of the emperor Jahangir in detention, was also a patron of poets, probably more for prestige rather than for any genuine appreciation of poetry.[27]

Zafar Khan, the generous patron of Saib, attracted several Persian poets to his entourage.[28] Mir Ilahi Hamadani, who was in the service of Jahangir and Shah Jahan, finally chose to attach himself to Zafar Khan whom he accompanied to Kashmir in 1041/1631-32.[29] Other poets in Zafar Khan's service were Farigh, Subhi Burjerdi and Mulla Ashub Mazandarani.[30] Also some nobles encouraged poets in their service to enliven their cultural life. Thus Sattar Tabrizi was in the service of Munim Khan in Bengal during the reign of Shah Jahan, and Ibrahim Farsi was in the entourage of Ibrahim Khan Fath Jang, the governor of Bengal.[31]

There were further more Persian nobles in the Mughal court who were poets themselves and patronised and helped other poets of their land of origin. Among them we can mention, Nur Jahan, Asaf Khan Mirza Jafar of Qazwin, Baqir Khan Najm-i-Sani, and Mir Jumla Muhammad Amin Shahrestani.

Muhammad Quli Salim (D. 1057/1647) a poet of some distinction who later found the patronage of Shah Jahan's *wazir* Islam Khan found help initially from Mir Abdul-Salam, a nobleman of Persian origin.[32] Salik Yazdi, an eloquent poet, came through Golkonda to Mughal India and attached himself to an Irani Amir, Danishmand Khan.[33] Ishrati Gilani joined the service of Mir Jumla's son Amin Khan. Mirza Muhammad Sakit came to India after the death of his father Mirza Mumin, who had held a minor *mansab* under Shah Jahan and took service under Aurangzeb[34]. Naui Khabushani wrote a moving poem *Suz-u-Gudaz* on the *sati* of a Hindu woman[35]. Shaukati Esfahani came to India twice. Mirza Ibrahim Adham was a *qalandar* and somewhat insane, living in India a life of tactlessness and licentiousness, as a result of which he was imprisoned.[36]

The court of Bijapur was proud to have in its circle the great Zuhuri (d. 1025/1616) who preferred the patronage of Ibrahim Adil Shah II (1580-1627) to that of Akbar, despite his contact with Faizi who admired him and wanted to take him to the Mughal emperor.[37] More significantly, the fact also remains that with the exception of Muhtasham Kashi and Wahshi Bafqi, all the great poets of Safavid Iran migrated to India.

Kalim Hamadani was one of great poet, who tried his fortune first in the Deccan, like Ufri before him, and joined there the service of Shah Nawaz Khan Shirazi (d.1020/1611) *wazir* of Ibrahim Adil ShahII and later of Mir Jumla Shahrestani.[38] In 1028/1619 he returned to Iran with a group of Hajjis for two years. There is definite evidence in his divan that he was happier in India, and unhappy for having undertaken a journey back to his homeland. He returned to India, this time to Shah Jahan's court, and was appointed *Malik-ul-Shuara.* He versified the *Padshah-Nama* under the title *Zafar-Nama-i Shahjahani*, he also wrote poems on the occasions of imperial festivities and on the rare objects in possession of the emperor such as the Peacock throne, the emperor's sword shield and pen-box. On the throne as elsewhere his verses were inscribed in gold letters. Of all the Persian immigrant poets, he had the most successful career in India and though the *Malik-ul-Shuara* of the court, he was granted the emperor's permission to live in Kashmir on grounds of ill-health. Also, compared to other eminent poets of Persian origin, he was more responsive to Indian culture. He uses Hindi words frequently, such as *Tanbuli*, *Dhobi*, *Pathani*, *Gadhal* and *Nim*.[39]

Most eminent of the Persian immigrant poets returning to Iran was Saib, who may have been a Sunni, though he wrote an eloquent *qasida* in honour of Imam Ali Reza.[40] Saib, well-educated and from a rich merchant family, had travelled through the Hijaz and the Ottoman empire in his youth, came to India in 1036/1627, frustrated with his life in Esfahan either in the fashion of the poets of the age or for the purpose of trade.[41] In India he joined the service of Zafar Khan Turbati at Kabul, and later at Burhanpur and Kashmir. He was presented to the Imperial court and received from Shahjahan the title of Mustaid Khan, but preferred to continue in the service of Zafar Khan. His old father came to fetch him whom he accompanied back to Iran in 1042/1632-33 where, as we have seen, he became Abbas II's *Malik-ul-Shuara* and lived in honour and comfort during the reign of Sulaiman, until his death in 1081/1670. He had lived in India for only six years.[42] Other Safavid poets who returned to Abbas II's Iran though not necessarily to his court, were Yahya Kashi, who benefited greatly from the bounty of Shah Jahan for versifying the chronicle of his reign, which was left incomplete. Also Mulla Ali Reza Tajalli, who had served in India as a tutor to the son of Ali Mardan Khan who had defected to the Mughals, had surrendered Qandahar to them in 1638 and was consequently a traitor in Safauid eyes, returned to Iran. He received a land grant from Abbas II and later became a favourite court poet of Shah Sulaiman.[43]

There is considerable evidence that most of the Safavid Monarchs from Ismail I to Abbas II continued to write poetry and to patronize religious as well as non-religious verse. It would be wrong to assume, as is generally held, that compared to other arts they were indifferent to poetry in general and hostile to non-devotional panegyric poetry. If their patronage made lesser impact on Persian poets, and the latter migrated to India, the probable reason is the greater wealth and richer economic resources of India at that stage in history. Therefore, most of the 123 Persian poets came to India in search of better job opportunities. Service, along with opportunities to join the Mughal service, hospitality of Iranians in India, liberal atmosphere and invitation of nobles etc attracted them. The attitudes of the Safavid immigrant poets to India range from enthusiastic nostalgia to bitter dislike. Usually they came full of hope and expectation. Many of them, like Abdun-Nabi, the author of the *Mai Khana*, had heard the praise of

India from merchants and other Iranians who had been there. Abdun-Nabi's first impression was that it was an extraordinary country where every thing was cheap and plentiful. Everyone had the freedom to live as he pleased without any interference or persecution. The same author reports the impression of another immigrant, Hakim Arif who found India populous and plentiful, providing all the comfort of living one could desire.[44] Munim Hakkak Shirazi wrote a *masnavi* in praise of Agra.[45] Several *ghazals* of Murshid Burujerdi praise India and denounce Iran. As we have seen, Kalim expressed his unhappiness on having to return to Iran temporarily. Muhammad Quli Salim both praised and blamed India. His verse is famous as stating that there is no chance of acquiring perfection in Iran. Henna acquires colour only in India. He also wrote that old age brings no sorrow In India.[46]

Table : 5.1
IRANIAN POETS IN MUGHAL CULTURE

Name of migrants	Place of Birth	Provinces	Regions	Period of migrations	Contexts and reasons of migrations	Position in Iran	Position in India	Place of death
Ahmad Ali Mazandarani	-	Mazandaran	North	Later days of Akbar	In company of Shah Abbas 'I ambassador	Poet	Poet	Iran
Muqim Astarabadi	Astarabad (Gorgan)	Mazandaran	North	Later days of Akbar	For attending (service)	Scientist and poet	Service of nobles	Unclear
Humai Astarabadi	Astarabad (Gorgan)	Mazandaran	North	Jahangir	Betterment of his prospects	Poet	Poet	Unclear
Zamani Astarabadi	Astarabad (Gorgan)	,,	North	,,	,,	,,	,,	Unclear
Qaili Gilani	—	Gilan	North	Akbar	Travelling	,,	,,	Unclear
Faghfur Lahiji	Lahijan	Gilan	North	Jahangir 1605	To visit India	Seientist and poet and Sayyid family	Hakim (Physician) Poet, Calligraphist	Allahabad
Nadim Gilani	—	Gilan	North	Jahangir	To visit India	Poet	Poet	Iran
Sikandar Mazandarani	—	Mazandaran	North	,,	Unclear	,,	,,	Unclear
Ruhi Mazandarani	-	,,	North	,,	,,	,,	,,	Unclear

Table Contd...

Table Contd...

Makhfi Rashti	Rasht	Gilan	North	,,	,,	Imam Quli's Khan Service governor of Fars	,,	Unclear
Sharif Amuli	Amul	Mazandaran	North	Shahjahan	Displeasure of his position in Iran and Religious persecution	Poet and relative's of Talib Amuli	Service of Ibrahim Khan son of Ali Mardan Khan	Unclear
Ashub Mazandarani	Sourk of sari	,,	North	,,	For employment	Poet and Calligraphist	Poet and calligraphist	Agra 1656
Husain Mazandarani	-	Mazandaran	North	Shahjahan	In order to better his prospects	Poet	Poet and service of Ibrahim Khan S/o of Ali Mardan Khan	Unclear
Ishrati Gilan	-	Gilan	North	Shahjahan	In order to better his prospects	Poet	Poet and service of Muhammad Amin S/o Mir Jumla	India
Tahir Mazandarani	-	Mazandaran	North	Later days of Shah-jahan's period	Unclear	Poet	Poet	Unclear
Sharari Hamadan-i	Hamadan	Hamadan	West and North-West	Akbar and Jahangir	Pecuniary purpose and travelling	Poet	Poet	Iran

Table Contd...

Table Contd...

Mir *Ilahi* Hamadani	Asadabad	Hamadan	West and North-west	Jahangir	Displeasure from Abbas I	Sayyid family of Asadabad, poet	Poet & author of *Tazkira Khazinah-i-Ganj-i-Ilahi*	Kashmir 1652
Kalim Hamadani	Hamadan	Hamadan	West and North-West	Jahangir	In search of fame	Poet	Malik-ush-Shoara of Shah-jahan's court	Kashmir 1651
Wazhi Dargazini	Dargazin of Hamadan	Hamadan	West and North-West	Jahangir	By destiny	Poet	Poet	India
Asdaq-i-Hamadani	Hamadan	Hamadan	West and North-West	Jahangir	To get better position	Poet	Poet	Unclear
Said Hamadani	Sadabad	Hamadan	West and North-West	Jahangir twice	In search of fortune	Poet	Poet	India (1613)
Taqi Hamadani	Hamadan	Hamadan	West and North-West	Jahangir	In search of fortune	Poet	Poet	Unclear
Seyani Hamadani	Seyan	Hamadan	West and North-West	Jahangir	In search of fortune	Poet	Poet and in service of Abdur-Rahim Khan-i-Khanan	Unclear service of
Haidar Beg Hamadani	Hamadan	Hamadan	West and North-West	Jahangir	In search of fortune	Poet	Poet	Unclear

Table Contd...

Table Contd.

Ami Nihavandi	Nihavand	Hamadan	West and North-West	Jahangir	In search of fortune	Poet and Gnostic	Poet	Unclear
Girami Tabrizi	Tabriz	Azarbaij-an-i-Sharqi	West and North-West	Jahangir (1609)	In company of Yadgar Ali Sultan ambassador of Shah Abbas I	Poet	Poet	Iran
Sattar-i-Tabrizi	Tabriz	Azarbaij-an-i-Sharqi	West and North-West	Jahangir	In order to better his prospects	Poet	Poet and service of nobles	India
Nami Urduabadi	Urduabad of Tabriz	Azarbaij-an-i-Sharqi	West and North-West	Jahangir	In order to better his prospects	Poet	Poet	India
Iishi Ardabili	Ardabil	Ardabil	West and North-West	Jahangir	In order to better his prospects	Poet	Poet	Unclear
Addul Ali Mahwi Ardabil	Ardabil	Ardabil	West and North-West	Jahangir	Travelling	Poet	Poet	Burhanpur
Tasalli Lurestani		Lurestan	West and North-West	Jahangir (1616)	Fear of Shah Abbas	Poet	Literary circle of Khan-i-Khanan	-
Subhi Borujerdi	Borujerd	Lurestan	West and North-West	Jahangir (1611)	Service of nobles	Poet	Noble's service	Unclear

Table Contd.

Table Contd.

Monim Chekini	Chekini	Lurestan	West and North-West	Jahangir	Unclear	Poet	Poet	Unclear
Hobabi Hamadani	Hamadan	Hamadan	West and North-West	Jahangir	Unclear	Poet	Poet	Unclear
Bahrami Hamadani	Hamadan	Hamadan	West and North-West	Jahangir	Unclear	Poet	Poet	Unclear
Saib Tabrizi	Tabriz	Azarbaij-an-i-Sharqi	West and North-West	Jahangir (1624)	Unclear	Poet Malik-ush-Shuara (poet laureate) by Shah Abbas II, after return to Iran	Title of Mustaid Khan by Shahjahan and command of one thousand	Esfahan
Edham-i-Turkman	-	Azarbaij-an-i-Sharqi	West and North-West	Jahangir (1622)	Unclear	Attending of nobles	Poet	Unclear
Ziyai Tabrizi	Tabriz	Azarbaijan Sharqi	West and North-West	Shahjahan	In company of relatives	Poet	Poet	Unclear
Sakit-i-Tabrizi	Tabriz	Azarbaijan Sharqi	West and North-West	Shahjahan	Betterment of his position	Poet	Poet and service of nobles	Unclear
Muzaffar Tabrizi	Tabriz	Azarbaijan Sharqi	West and North-West	ShahJahan	Travelling	Poet	Poet	Esfahan

Table Contd...

Table Contd...

Munshi Khalkhali	Khalkhal	Ardabil	West and North-West	Shahjahan	In order to better his prospects	Poet	Poet	Unclear
Edham-i-Artimani	-	Kordestan	West and North-West	Shahjahan	Travelling	Poet	Poet and service of nobles	India (1649)
Dawud Tuysarkan	Tuysarkan	Hamadan	West and North-West	Shahjahan	Unclear	Poet	Poet	Unclear
Sharaf Tabrizi	Tabriz	Azarbaijan Sharqi	West and North-West	Shahjahan	Unclear	Poet	Poet	Unclear
Qasim Khan	Tabriz	Azarbaijan Sharqi	West and North-West	Shahjahan	Unclear	His ancestor was imperial treasurer of Shah Tahmasp	Poet	Unclear
Mashhour Tabrizi	Tabriz	Azarbaijan Sharqi	West and North-West	Shahjahan	Unclear	Poet	Poet	In the way of Heart
Humai Azarbaijani	-	Azarbaijan Sharqi	West and North-West	Shahjahan	Unclear	Poet	Poet	Unclear
Muhaqqaqi Shushtari	Shushtar	Khusestan	South-West	Jahangir	In company of relatives	Poet	Poet	Unclear

Table Contd...

Table Contd...

Ozlati Shushtari	Shushtar	Khusestan	South-West	Shahjahan	In search of better opportunity	Poet	Poet	Unclear
Tashbihi Kashi	Kashan	Esfahan	Central Plateau	Akbar	Nuqtawi Sect	Poet, Sayyid family	Poet	Unclear
Rafii Kashani	Kashan	Esfahan	Central Plateau	Akbar (1591) and Jahangir	Suffering from Safavid Kings, possibility Nuztawi Sect	Poet, Tabatabai Sayyid of Kashan	Poet	Kashan (1623)
Ebadullah Kashani	Kashan	Esfahan	Central Plateau	Jahangir	Nuqtawi Sect	Poet	Poet, service of Jahangir	Unclear
Ghani Yazdi	Yazd	Yazd	Central Plateau	Jahangir	Nuqtawi Sect	Poet	Poet, service of Jahangir	Unclear
Dakhli Esfahani	Esfahan	Esfahan	Central Plateau	Akbar (1589)	Nuqtawi Sect	His ancestors were in Safavids service	Poet, service of Khan-i-Khanan	Unclear
Wasli Razi Tehrani	Tehran	Tehran	Central Plateau	Akbar	In company of relatives because of religious persecution	Brother of Itimud-ud-daulla	Poet	Unclear
Sharif Tehrani	Tehran	Tehran	Central Plateau	Akbar	In company of relatives because of religious persecution	Son of Itimud-ud-daulla	Poet	Kabul (1607)
Qasim Razi	Ray	Tehran	Cental Plateau	Twice Akbar and Jahangir	In order to better his prospects	Poet	Poet, noble's service	Unclear

Table Contd...

Table Contd...

Khalqi Yazdi	Yazd	Yazd	Central Plateau	Akbar (1602)	Pleasure-seeking	Poet	Poet	India
Bahari Qomi	Qom	Qom	Central Plateau	Later day's of Akbar	In search of fortune	Poet	Poet	Lahore (1616)
Munsif Esfahani	Esfahan	Esfahan	Central Plateau	Akbar twice	In search of furtune	Poet	Poet and noble's service	Burhanpur (1610)
Taqi Esfahani	Esfahan	Esfahan	Central Plateau	Akbar (1604)	In search of furtune	Poet	Poet, librarian, author of *Ruzatul-Ahbab*	Burhanpur (1612)
Majlisi Esfahani	Esfahan	Esfahan	Central Plateau	Akbar	Travelling	Poet and weave manufacturing	Noble's service	Subrub of Ahmadabad
Shams Dada Iraqi	Esfahan	Esfahan	Central Plateau	Twice Akbar and Jahangir	In order to Luxurious	Poet weave manufacturing	Poet, noble's service	India
Muizz-i-Esfahani	Esfahan	Esfahan	Central Plateau	Jahangir	In seach of better opportunities	Poet weave manufa-cturing	Poet, noble's service	Parlonat (1615)
Mirza Ali Asghar-Wazih Esfahani	Esfahan	Esfahan	Central Plateau	Jahangir	In seach of better opportunities	Gold embroiderer and poet	Poet	Deccan (1620)
Rouzbahan-i-Esfahani	Esfahan	Esfahan	Central Plateau	Jahangir	Financial purpose	Poet	Poet	Iran
Tasalli Esfahani	Esfahan	Esfahan	Central Plateau	Jahangir	In order to better his prospects	Poet	Poet	Kashan

Table Contd...

Table Contd...

Fareghi Esfahani	Esfahan	Esfahan	Central Plateau	Jahangir	In order to better his prospects	Poet	Poet	Lahore
Ghiyas Nasrabadi	Nasrabad of Esfahan	Esfahan	Central Plateau	Jahangir	In order to better his prospects	Poet	Poet and service of Prince Shahjahan	Unclear
Mumin Esfahani	Esfahan	Esfahan	Central Plateau	Jahangir	For employment	Poet	Poet	Esfahan
Waqari Esfahani	Izhneh of Esfahan	Esfahan	Central Plateau	Jahangir	For employment	Poet	Poet	Unclear
Akbar Esfahani	Esfahan	Esfahan	Central Plateau	Jahangir	Travelling	Poet	Poet	Unclear
Shuguni Golpayagani	Golpaya-gan	Esfahan	Central Plateau	Jahangir	To betterment of his prospects	Poet	Poet	Unclear
Taqi Kashi	Kashan	Esfahan	Central Plateau	Jahangir	To betterment of his prospects	Poet	Noble's service	Unclear
Rashid Kashani	Kashan	Esfahan	Central Plateau	Jahangir	In search fortune	Poet	Poet	Unclear
Ghururi Kashi	Kashan	Esfahan	Central Plateau	Jahangir	Travelling	Poet	Poet	Unclear
Ibrahim Shireen Ojaq	Qazwin	Qazwin	Central Plateau	Jahangir	In company of Yadgar Ali Sultan ambassador of Shah Abbas	Poet	Service of Jahangir	Unclear
Yunes Abhari	Abhar	Zanjan	Central Plateau	Jahangir	In order to job	Poet	Poet	Kabul (1614)

Table Contd...

Table Contd.

Ahank-i-Yazdi	Yazd	Yazd	Central Plateau	Jahangir	Displeasure and his son's death	Poet	Poet	Unclear
Qutrati Yazdi	Yazd	Yazd	Central Plateau	Jahangir	Travelling	Poet	Poet	Agra (1615)
Muhammad Razi	Ray	Tehran	Central Plateau	Jahangir	Travelling	Poet	Poet	Unclear
Warastah chimini Razi	Ray	Tehran	Central Plateau	Jahangir	By destiny	Poet, Chikini tribe	Poet	Zirabad Esfa-han (1664)
Shoqi Savoji	Saveh	Markazi	Central Plateau	Jahangir	In search of better opportunities	Poet, Sadat family	Poet, service of Itimad-ud-dauala	Saveh
Anwar Esfahani	Esfahan	Esfahan	Central Plateau	Akbar	Unclear	Mamuri Sadat of Esfahan; poet	Poet	Unclear
Fauqi Yazdi	Yazd	Yazd	Central Plateau	Twice Jahangir	Unclear	Poet	Poet	Surat
Ghafuri Taleqani	Teleqan	Tehran	Central Plateau	Jahangir	Unclear	Poet	Poet	Unclear
Baqi Damawandi	Damawand	Tehran	Central Plateau	Jahangir	Unclear	Poet	Poet	Unclear
Khatmi Razi	Ray	Tehran	Central Plateau	Jahangir	Unclear	Poet	Poet	Unclear
Rahai Razi	Ray	Tehran	Central Plateau	Jahangir	Unclear	Sayyid family	Poet	Unclear
Tahzim-i-Qomi	Qom	Qom	Central Plateau	Jahangir	Unclear	Poet	Poet	Iran

Table Contd...

Table Contd.

Munsif Qupayehi	Qupayeh	Esfahan	Central Plateau	Jahangir	Unclear	Poet	Poet	Unclear
Monai Esfahani	Esfahan	Esfahan	Central Plateau	Jahangir	Unclear	Poet	Poet	Unclear
Mir Husain Tajalli Kashi	Kashan	Esfahan	Central Plateau	Jahangir	Unclear	Poet	Poet	India (1610)
Mansur Kashi	Kashan	Esfahan	Central Plateau	Jahangir	Unclear	Poet	Poet	Unclear
Muhammad Masum Kashani	Kashan	Eafahan	Central Plateau	Jahangir	Unclear	Poet	Noble's service	India (1642)
Razmi Qazwini	Qazwin	Qazwin	Central Plateau	Jahangir	Unclear	Poet	Poet	Unclear
Moin Yazdi	Yazd	Yazd	Central Plateau	Jahangir	Unclear	Poet	Poet	India (1617)
Sarvari Yazdi	Yazd	Yazd	Central Plateau	Jahangir	Unclear	Poet	Noble's service	Unclear
Shuhudi Yazdi	Yazd	Yazd	Central Plateau	Jahangir	Unclear	Poet	Poet	Unclear
Adai Yazdi	Yazd	Yazd	Central Plateau	Shahjahan	Accusation to heresy	Poet	Poet	Surat Yazdi (1651)

Table Contd...

Table Contd.

Salik Yazdi	Yazd	Yazd	Central Plateau	Shahjahan	Invitation of his friends	Poet	Poet	India
Ibrahim Orduabadi	Orduabad	Yazd	Central Plateau	Shahjahan	Financial purpose	Poet	Poet	Esfahan
Nazim Yazdi	Firuzabad	Yazd	Central Plateau	Shahjahan	Financial purpose	Poet	Poet	Firuzabad of Yazd
Hasan Ali Yazdi	Yazd	Yazd	Central Plateau	Shahjahan	Travelling	Poet and mathematician	Poet	Esfahan
Husain Wahdat	Kohbandan	Kerman	Central Plateau	Shahjahan (1648)	In search of fortune	Poet	Poet	Delhi (1659)
Amani Kermani	Kerman	Kerman	Central Plateau	Shahjahan	Financial purpose	Poet	Poet, service of Mir Muhammad Said Mir Jumla	Esfahan
Salim Tehrani	Taresht	Tehran	Central Plateau	Shahjahan	Dissatisfaction with position in Iran	Poet, service of lahijan governor	Noble's service	Kashmir (1647)
Sayyidi Tehrani	Tehran	Tehran	Central Plateau	Shahjahan (1653)	In search of better opportunities	Poet	Shahjahan's service	Delhi (1658)
Monsif Tehrani	Tehran	Tehran	Central Plateau	Shahjahan	Trade	Poet	Poet	Tehran
Sharif Taleqani	Taleqan	Tehran	Central Plateau	Shahjahan	In search of fortune	Poet	Poet	India (1639)
Salik Qazwini	Qazwin	Qazwin	Central Plateau	Shahjahan	In search of fortune	Poet	Poet	Qazwin

Table Contd...

Table Contd.

Ishrati Forushani	Esfahan	Esfahan	Central Plateau	Shahjahan	In company of Muhammad Ali ambassador of Shah Safi	Poet	Poet	Mashhad
Mast Ali Esfahani	Esfahan	Esfahan	Central Plateau	Shahjahan	In search of fortune	Poet	Poet	Esfahan
Mashud Esfahani	Esfahan	Esfahan	Central Plateau	Shahjahan	In search of fortune	Praiser of Shah Abbas Sani	Poet	Esfahan
Ilham-i-Esf:hani	Esfahan	Esfahan	Central Plateau	Shahjahan	In search of fortune	Poet	Poet	Esfahan
Abbasi Esfahani	Esfahan	Esfahan	Central Plateau	Shahjahan	In search of fortune	Poet	Noble's Service	Bengal
Rizwan-i-Esfahan	Esfahan	Esfahan	Central Plateau	Shahjahan	For better position	Poet	Poet	Unclear
Shukati Estahani	Estahan	Estahan	Central Plateau	Shahjahan	Financial purpose	Poet	Poet	India
Shakip Esfahani	Esfahan	Esfahan	Central Plateau	Shahjahan	Travelling	Poet, Sayyid family	Poet	Iran
Mir Yahya Kashi	Kashan	Esfahan	Central Plateau	Shahjahan	For employment	Poet	Poet, Librarian, he versified a part of Padshah-Nama	1064 Unclear
Sarmad Kashani	Kashan	Esfahan	Central Plateau	Shahjahan	Trade and possibly because of religious persecution	Poet, Sufi, Jewish family	Poet, noble's service	Delhi (1662)

Table Contd...

Table Contd.

Ahmad Esfahani	Esfahan	Esfahan	Central Plateau	Shahjahan	Unclear	Poet	Poet	Unclear
Nasib Razi	Ray	Tehran	Central Plateau	Shahjahan	Unclear	Poet	Poet	Unclear
Type Tafreshi	Tafresh	Markazi	Central Plateau	Shahjahan	Unclear	Poet	Poet	India
Fahimi Hormuzi	Hormuz	Hormuzgan	South	Akbar	Service of Abdur-Rahim-Khan-i-Khanan	Poet	Poet	Unclear
Lutfi Shirazi	Shiraz	Fars	South	Jahangir twice	Poets persecution	Poet	Poet	India
Bazmi Quz	Shiraz, origin from Gorjestan	Fars	South	Jahangir	Noble's attending	Poet	Poet	India (1614)
Ebadi Shirazi	Shiraz	Fars	South	Jahangir	Noble's service	Poet	Poet	Unclear
Sayyidi Bowanati	Bowanat	Fars	South	Jahangir	Pleasure seeking	Poet	Poet in literacy circle of Khan-i-Khanan	Unclear
Hamzeh Bowanati	Bowanat	Fars	South	Jahangir	Khan-i-Khanan's service	Poet	Literary circle of Khan-i-Khanan	Shiraz
Muhibb-i-Shirazi	Shiraz	Fars	South	Akbar	Unclear	Poet	Poet	Unclear

Table Contd...

Table Contd.

Wujudi Shirazi	Shiraz	Fars	South	Akbar	Unclear	Poet	Khan-i-Khanan's service	Unclear
Abu Muhammad Dasqib Shirazi	Shiraz	Fars	South	Jahangir (1615)	Unclear	Poet	Poet	Shiraz (1620)
Mumtaz Shirazi	Shiraz	Fars	South	Shahjahan	In search of fortune	Poet	Poet	Azimabad of Patna (1635)
Wahidi Shirazi	Shiraz	Fars	South	Shahjahan	In search of fortune	Poet	Poet	Unclear
Qaisar Shirazi	Shiraz	Fars	South	Shahjahan	In search of fortune	Poet	Poet	Unclear
Hakkak Shirazi	Shiraz	Fars	South	Shahjahan	In search of fortune	Poet	Poet	India
Nasir Shirazi	Shiraz	Fars	South	Shahjahan	In search of better opportunities	Poet	Poet	Unclear
Ummi Shirazi	Shiraz	Fars	South	Shahjahan (1644)	For service	Poet	Poet	Unclear
Tajalli Shirazi	Shiraz	Fars	South	Shahjahan	In search of fame	Poet	Poet and tutor of Mirza Ibrahim son of Ali Mardan Khan	Esfahan

Table Contd...

Table Contd.

Hokmi Shirazi	Shiraz	Fars	South	Shahjahan	Unclear	Poet	Service of Qasim Khan Juwaini governor of Bengal	Unclear
Nisbat Neyrizi	Neyriz	Fars	South	Shahjahan	Financial purpose	Poet	Poet	Esfahan
Safi Kazeruni	Kazerun	Fars	South	Shahjahan	In search of fortune	Poet	Noble's service	Unclear
Burhan Abarqui	Abarqu	Fars	South	Shahjahan	By destiny	Poet	Poet	India (1654)
Muhammad Farsi	Deh Ali	Fars	South	Shahjahan	By chance	Poet	Poet	Esfahan
Naui Khabushani	Quchan	Khurasan	East and North-East	Akbar twice (1579) and (1582)	Financial purpose and to visit relatives	Poet	Poet, noble's service	(1610)
Zuhuri Turshizi	Jumand of Turshiz	Khurasan	East and North-East	Akbar (1580)	In order to better his prospectus	Poet	Poet Laureate of Deccan	Deccan (1616)
Naziri Neihshabouri	Neihshab-our	Khurasan	East and North-East	Akbar (1584)	For service of Khan-i-Khanan	Poet	In service of nobles and Jahangir's court Rs. 1000, a horse robe of honour	Ahmadabad (1614)
Hairan Qaini	Qain	Khurasan	East and North-East	Twice Akbar and Jahangir	Death of his relatives in India	Poet, Sayyid family	Poet	Unclear

Table Contd...

Table Contd.

Amini Darsani	-	Khurasan	East and North-East	Akbar	Religious persecution	Poet	Poet	Unclear
Jam Mashhadi	Mashhad	Khurasan	East and North-East	Jahangir	For service	Poet	Poet	India (1623)
Mohazzam Mashhadi	Mashhad	Khurasan	East and North-East	1606	In order to better opportunities	Poet	Poet	Unclear
Nazir Mashhadi	Mashhad	Khurasan	East and North-East	1612 C.A.	In order to better opportunities	Poet	Poet	Unclear
Turabi Mashhadi	Mashhad	Khurasan	East and North-East	Jahangir twice	Travelling	Poet, Sayyid family	Poet	Mushhad
Itabi Taklu	Herat but originally from Ray	Khurasan	East and North-East	Akbar (1604) and Jahangir twice	Travelling	Taklu tribe, Poet	Noble's service	Near Qandahar (1612)
Wafai Heravi	Herat	Khurasan	East and North-East	Jahangir (1018)	Travelling	Poet	Khan-i-Khanan's service	Herat
Arifi Sarakhsi	Sarakhs	Khurasan	East and North-East	Jahangir	Financial purpose	Poet, Sadat family	Poet	Unclear

Table Contd...

Table Contd.

Muzaffar Gonabadi	Gonabad	Khurasan	East and North-East	Jahangir	In search of fortune	Poet	Noble's service	Iran
Shitabi Gonabadi	Gonabad	Khurasan	East and North-East	Jahangir	In order to better his prospectus	Poet	Poet	Deccan
Burhan Neishabouri	Neishabour	Khurasan	East and North-East	Jahangir	For employment	Poet, Sayyid family	Service of Prince-Parviz and Itimad-ud-daula	Unclear
Unsi Jami	Jam	Khurasan	East and North-East	Jahangir	In order to better his prospectus	Poet	Poet	India
Waresi Sabzevari	Sebzevar	Khurasan	East and North-East	Jahangir	In order to better his prospectas	Poet	Poet	Unclear
Jalal Neishabouri	Neishabour	Khurasan	East and North-East	Akbar	Unclear	Poet	Poet literary circle of Khan-i-Khanan	Unclear
Taqi Neishabouri	Neishabour	Khurasan	East and North-East	Jahangir	Unclear	Poet	Poet	Unclear
Baqir Mashhadi	Mashhad	Khurasan	East and North-East	Jahangir (1607)	Unclear	Poet	Poet	Unclear

Table Contd...

Table Contd.

Mumin Turshizi	Jumand of Turshiz	Khurasan	East and North-East	Jahangir	Unclear	Poet	Poet	Unclear
Amni Khafi	Khaf	Khurasan	East and North-East	Jahangir	Unclear	Poet	Poet	Unclear
Shahab Sabzvari	Sabzvar	Khurasan	East and North-East	Jahangir	Unclear	Poet	Poet	Unclear
Amini Heravi	Herat	Khurasan	East and North-East	Jahangir	Unclear	Poet	Poet	Unclear
Walih Heravi	Heat	Khaurasan	East and North-East	Jahangir	Unclear	Poet	Poet	Unclear
Qudsi Mashhadi	Mashhad	Khurasan	East and North-East	Shahjahan	Uzbek pressure, invitation of his friends, dissatisfaction of his job	Poet, treasurer of Imam Reza Tomb, Chief crocer of Mashhad	Versification of Padshah nama Rs. 2000 robe of honour, weighed against gold and silver	Lahore 1646 buried in Kashmir
Hasan Mashhadi	Mashhad	Khurasan	East and North-East	Shahjahan	Dissatisfaction with his position in Iran	Poet	Poet	India
Husain Mashhadi	Mashhad	Khurasan	East and North-East	Shahjahan	In search of fortune	Poet, Sayyid and noble's family	Poet	Unclear

Table Contd...

Table Contd.

Qasim Mashhadi	Mashhad	Khurasan	East and North-East	Shahjahan	Pleasure seeking	Poet	Poet	Shah Jahanabad (Delhi) 1674
Danish Mir Razi	Mashhad	Khurasan	East and North-East	Shahjahan	Travelling	Poet, Sayyid family	Poet	Iran 1665
Ulfati Khurasani	-	Khurasan	East and North-East	Shahjahan	For employment	Poet	Poet	Unclear
Muqim Fauji	Neishabo-ur	Khurasan	East and North-East	Shahjahan	In order to better his prospectus	Poet	Poet and noble's service	Neishabour
Ahvali Sistani	Sistan	Sistan Va Baluchestan	South-East	Jahangir	In order to better his prospectus	Poet	Poet	Iran
Unsi Seyadani	Iran	-	Unclear	Akbar	In order to better opportunities	Poet	Poet	Agra 1616
Khazri	Iran	-	Unclear	Jahangir	In order to better opportunities	Poet	Poet, Khan-i-Khanan's service	Unclear
Muhammad Zaman	Iran	-	Unclear	Jahangir	In order to better opportunities	Poet	Poet	Unclear
Munes	Iran	-	Unclear	Jahangir	In order to better opportunities	Poet	Poet	Unclear
Sayyid Ashraf Muhiid	Iran	-	Unclear	Jahangir	Financial purpose	Poet	Poet	Iran

Table Contd...

Table Contd.

Kalbi Baharlu	Iran	-	Unclear	Jahangir	To visit relatives like; Khan-i-Khanan	Poet	Poet, Khan-i-Khanan's service	Unclear
Maulana Nizam	Iran	-	Unclear	Jahangir	In order to service of Khan-i-Khanan	Poet	Poet, Khan-i-Khanan's service	Unclear
Baqai	Iran	-	Unclear	Akbar	Unclear	Poet	Poet, noble's service	Unclear
Navidi	Iran	-	Unclear	Akbar	Unclear	Poet	Poet	Unclear
Maulana Ali Mani	Iran	-	Unclear	Jahangir	Unclear	Poet	Poet	Unclear
Nizam Tabatabai	Iran	-	Unclear	Jahangir	Unclear	Poet	Poet	Unclear
Tarzi	Iran	-	Unclear	Jahangir	Unclear	Poet	Noble's service	India
Muhibbi Shamlu	Iran	-	Unclear	Jahangir	Unclear	Poet	Poet	Mecca
Malik Muhammad Muzaqi	Iran	-	Unclear	Jahangir	Unclear	Poet	Poet	Unclear
Natiq	Iran	-	Unclear	Jahangir	Unclear	Poet	Poet	Unclear
Salih	Iran	-	Unclear	Jahangir	Unclear	Poet	Poet	Unclear
Muhammad Mahdi	Iran	-	Unclear	Jahangir	Unclear	Poet	Poet	Unclear

Table Contd...

Table Contd.

Khamoshi	Iran	-	Unclear	Jahangir	Unclear	Poet	Poet	Unclear
Siraji	Iran	-	Unclear	Shahjahan	In search of better opportunities	Poet	Poet and noble's service	Akbarabad
Ghani Frahani	Iran	-	Unclear	Shahjahan	In search of fortune	Poet; Sayyid family	Poet and noble's service	Jahangirn -agar (Dacca)
Abu Said	Iran	-	Unclear	Shahjahan	In search of fortune	Poet	Poet	Unclear
Abu Asafi	Iran	-	Unclear	Shahjahan	Unclear	Poet	Poet	Unclear
Sani Takllu	Iran	-	Unclear	Shahjahan	Unclear	Poet, Takllu tribe	Poet	Unclear 1656

Table 5.2

IRANIAN POETS

Rg	Pr	Nu	Reasons and Contexts of Migration																									
			X1	X2	X3	X4	X5	X6	X7	X8	X9	X10	X11	X12	X13	X14	X15	X16	X17	X18	X19	X20	X21	X22	X23	X24	X25	X26
NO	Ak	3							1								1					1						
15	Ja	7														2						2						3
	Sh	5	1													2				1								1
WNW	Ak	1											1															
32	Ja	21		2					1		1					9	1					1	1					5
	Sh	10								1						3						2						4
SW	Ak	0																										
2	Ja	1								1																		
	Sh	1														1												
CP	Ak	13	5													5						1				1		1
75	Ja	37	2			1			1		1		1			9				3		4						
	Sh	25	2			1			1				4			9				1	1	2		1				3
SO	Ak	3															1											2
21	Ja	6					1									1	3											1
	Sh	12									2		1			6	1						1					1
ENE	Ak	6	1										1	1		1	1					1						
32	Ja	19											1			6	1			1		2						8
	Sh	7			1	1										3				1		1						
SE	Ak	0																										
1	Ja	1														1												
	Sh	0																										
UA	Ak	3														1												2
23	Ja	15											1			3	2											9
	Sh	5														3												2
Total		201	11	2	1	3	1		4	2	4		10	1		65	11			7	1	17	2	1		1		57

Graph : 5.1

Number of Poets according to the reasons and contexts of their migration

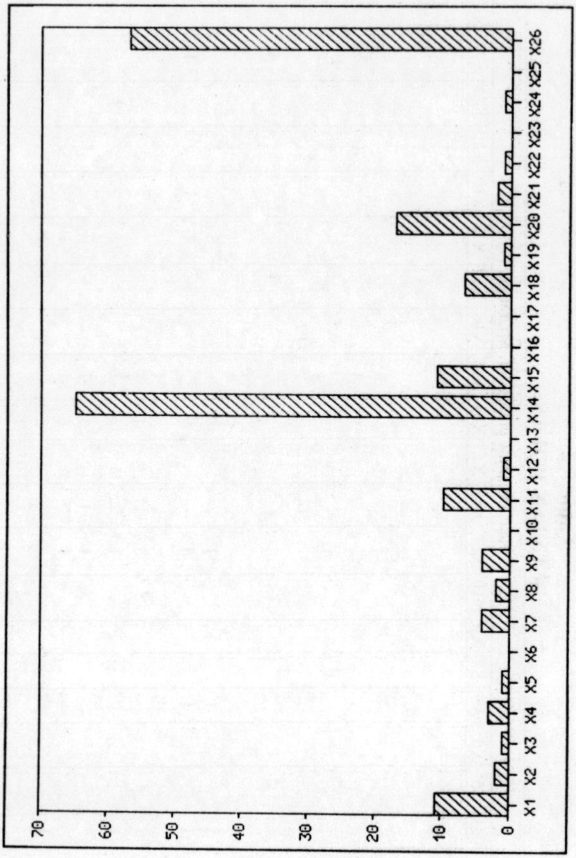

REFERENCES

1. Qazwini to Browne, in E.G.Browne: *A Literary History of Persia*; Vol. IV, (Cambridge; 1956-59), p. 26 see also Jan Rypka, *History of Iranian Literature*, ed. Karl. Jahn, Dordrecht, 1968, pp. 292-93.
2. V. Minorsky, *Iran' opposition, Martydom and Revolt, in E.G. Von Grunebaum(ed) Unity and Variety in Muslim Civilisation, Chicago,* 1955, p. 196.
3. J. Rypka, 1968, p. 293. See also: E.G. Browne, 1956-59 Vol. IV, p. 25.
4. Badauni. 1868-69, Vol. III, pp. 97-99.
5. *A.A.A.* 1350/1971, Vol. II, p. 476.
6. S.M.S Hasan Khan Bahador, 1293/1876, p. 361, see also; M.Q. Gopamavi, 1336/1957, pp. 334-36.
7. B. Nihavandi, Vol. III, pp. 1133-34, M.T. Nasrabadi, 1317/1938, p. 291 N. Qazwini, 1340/1961, pp. 692-93.
8. M.Q. Gopamavi, 1957: pp. 17-18, M.A. Sarkhush, 1942, p. 4 Mahdi Darakhsh; *Buzurgan–i-Sukhan Sarayan-i-Hamadan*, Tehran, 1341/1962 Vol. I, pp. 241-44; storey ½ pp. 815-16.
9. Rieu, II, p. 6876.
10. S.M.S. Hasan Khan Bahador, 1876, p. 292; M.Q. Gopamavi' 1957, p. 474; N. Qazwini, 1961, pp. 437-43, *A.N.* 1881-83, Vol. III, p. 836. On Mir Masum Bakkari's embassy see: L Riyazul Islam, *Indo-Persian relations*, Tehran, 1970, pp. 65-67.
11. M.T. Nasrabadi, 1938, p. 182; N. Qazwini, 1961. p. 617.
12. M.T. Nasrabadi, 1938, p. 225.
13. *Amal-i-Salih,* 1923-39, Vol. III, p. 402.
14. Sher Khan Lodi, *Mirat-ul-Khayal*, Bombay, 1906, p. 86; M.Q. Gopamavi, 1957; p. 563.
15. *Amal-i-Salih*, Vol. I, p. 508, II, pp. 87, 161, 472; N. Qazwini, 1961, pp. 821-22, Lahori, 1867, I, pp. 444-46, 530; II, pp. 19-21-22, 5051 M.G.A. Azad Bilgrami, 1931, pp. 61-62; M.Q. Gopamavi, 1957 p. 563, which gives Kalim's Chronogram on his death.
16. *M.U.* text, Vol. I, pp. 693-712 see also: *Z.Kh,* 1970, Vol. I, p. 61.
17. B. Nihavandi, Vol. III, p. 115; Badauni, III, p. 375, N. Qazwini, 1961, pp. 785-93; Sadiqi Kitabdar, 1948, pp. 219-20.
18. S.M.S. Hasan Khan Bahadur, 1876, p. 453; G.A. Azad Bilgraimi, 1913, pp. 24-25.
19. Badauni, III, p. 253; M.Q. Gopamavi, 1957; p. 371.
20. B. Nihavandi, III, pp. 560, 1224-25, 1237-38, 1408-9.
21. N. Qazwini, 1961, p. 801; *Suhuf-i-Ibrahim*, FF. 97a-b.

22. *Ibid.*, F. 105a; B. Nihavandi, III, pp. 887-89, 1354-56, 1427, G.A. Azad Bilgrami, 1913, p. 21; S.M.S. Hasan Khan Bahadur, 1876; p. 25.
23. Badauni, III, pp. 196-97, 282.
24. A comprehensive study of his literary circle is Hasamud-din Rashid's *Mirza Gazi Beg Tarkhan awr Uski Bazm-i-Adab*, Karachi, 1970. For his official career, see; *ZKh*, II, pp. 18-31 and *M.U.*, III, pp. 345-48.
25. B. Nihavandi, III, p. 784; N. Qazwini, 1961, pp. 669-70, G.A. Azad-i-Bilgrami, 1913, pp. 39-41, H. Rashidi, 1970, p. 469.
26. B. Nihavandi, III, p. 785, H. Rashidi, 1970, pp. 254-55; Muhammad Muzaffar Husain Saba Lucknowi, *Ruz-i-Raushan*, Bhopal, 1297/1879, p. 291.
27. *Z.Kh,* II, pp. 116, 173, M.U. text III, pp. 385-409.
28. M.T. Nasrabadi, 1938, p. 382, Lutf Ali Beg Azar, *Atashkada*, ed. Hasan Sadat Nasiri, Tehran, 1336/1957; Vol. III, pp. 116-70; S.M.S. Hasan Khan Bahadur, 1293/1876, p. 205; G.A. Azad Bilgrami, 1913, p. 109.
29. M.A. Sarkhush, 1951, p. 4, M.Q. Gopamavi, 1957, pp. 17-18, M. Darakhsh, 1962, pp. 241-44.
30. M.T. Nasrabadi, pp. 309, 339.
31. S.M.S. Hasan Khan Bahudor, 1876, p. 195, N. Qazwini, 1961, pp. 898-99.
32. M.T Nasrabadi, 1938, p. 227; M.Q. Gopamavi, 1957, p. 332; S.M.S. Hasan Khan Bahador, 1876. p. 201; Lutf Ali Beg Azar, 1957, Vol. I, p. 64.
33. M.T. Nasrabadi, 1938, p. 329, S.M.S. Hasan Khan Bahador, 1293, p. 207; G.A. Azad Bilgrami, 1913, p. 110.
34. M.Q. Gopamavi, 1957, p. 268.
35. *Suhuf-i-Ibrahim*, f.97a, *Amal-i-Salih*, II, p. 229, G.A. Azad Bilgram, 1871, p. 150.
36. M.A. Sarkhush, 1951, p. 5; S.M.S. Hasan Khan Bahadur, 1876, p. 41, M.T. Nasrabadi, pp. 244, 336, 359.
37. Badauni, III, pp. 269, 332; G.A. Azad Bilgrami, 1913, pp. 31-32.
38 M.T. Nasrabadi, 1938, p. 220; Sharif-un-Nisa Ansari, *Hayat Va Tasnifat-I-Mirza Abu Talib Kalim Hamadani*, Hyderabad Deccan, 1961 pp. 22-40.
39. M.A. Sarkhush, 1951, p. 155; S.K. Lodi, 1906, p. 90; *Suhuf-i-Ibrahim*, F.2959; M.T. Nasrabadi, 1938, pp. 220.
40. G.A. Azad Bilgrami, 1871, pp. 287-88, Muhammad Ali Tarbiat, *Danishmandan-i-Azarbaijan*, Tehran, 1314 A.H/1935, pp. 217-36.
41. L.A. Beg Azar, 1336/1957, Vol. I, p. 120.
42. S.K. Lodi, 1906, pp. 88-90; M.A. Sarkhush, 1951, p. 110; R.Q.K.

Hadayat, *Majma-ul-Fusaha*, Tehrani, 1284-95/1905-1916, II, pp. 23-24, M.Q. Gopamavi, 1957; p. 408, M.A Modarres, 1326-33/1947-1954, pp. 408-10.

43. *Ibid*, pp. 115-16, M.A. Sarkhush, 1951, p. 38, M.H. Saba Lucknowi, 1297/1879, p. 127.

44. N. Qazwini, 1340/1961, pp. 1129-30.

45. M.A. Sarkhush, 1951, p. 176; E.G. Browne, 1956, Vol. IV, p. 255.

46. M.A. Sarkhush, 1951, p. 76; G.A. Azad Bilgrami, 1913, p. 66; S.N. Ansari, 1961, pp. 41-42.

6

Scholars, *Sufis* and *Darvishes*

The Mughal court generously patronized the Persian scholars from Iran. According to our major sources in the 17th century 37 people came to India from Iran as scholars. Among them 5 persons came from regions in the North such as Mazandaran and Gilan, 6 came from regions in the west and north-west such as Tabriz, Hamadan and Nihavand, 3 came from south-west region like Shushtar, while eleven belonged to central regions such as Tehran, Qom, Damghan, Qazwin, Esfahan, Yazd, and Kashan. It would appear that most of the scholar immigrants hailed from the central plateau, and 7 persons came from southern part of Safavid territory. There were 5 immigrants from East, and north-east such as Mashhad, Herat and Sabsvar. Among the 37 people 7 person came to India in later days of Akbar's period, 25 migrated during Jahangir's reign, 4 in the reign of Shahjahan. There was only one immigrant from Herat who came during Humayun's period, and is mentioned as his court scholar. Further, one Qatai Heravi lived in India during Akbar and Jahangir's reign. He dedicated his book to Jahangir under the title of *Majma-Ush-Shuara-i-Jahangir Shahi*.

Among those who came during Akbar's reign we can mention Muhammad Sufi Mazandarani, who came had to leave Amul because of his *Nuqtawi* beliefs. He lived long to enjoy the favours from Jahangir and was employed to write books like *Tazkira* of the poets and *But Khaneh*. Nasira-i-Hamadani, Fusuni Tabrizi 'astronomer and author of Persian dictionary under the title *Meftahul-Maani*, Mumin Taleqani, Fusuni Qomi, Mali Shirazi, author of a *Tazkira*, and Ahadi Khurasani, also arrived in India during Akbar's reign.They continued to stay in India thereafter in the reign of Jahangir.

Among the 25 scholars who migrated to India during Jahangir's reign, we can mention in the first place Mir Abul-Qasim Findarski (D.1640-41. He was rebuked by Abbas I for his association with the vagabonds and *qalandars*; he travelled to India to study asceticism, and became a recluse for seven years.[1] He absorbed Zoroastrian and Hindu influences, but returned to Iran as a *Sufi*.[2] Among others was Mir Findarski[3] who has written many books on diverse themes. Still another was Fani Glani belonged to Kochian in Gilan. He heard from his friend, Mirza Sharaf Salmani the illustrious officer at Esfahan the fame of the munificent patronage of the Abdur-Rahim Khan-i-Khanan and at once left Iran for India. Khan-i-Khanan gave him presents and awarded him a *jagir* in addition to a regular stipend.[4] Another scholar was Baqi Nihavandi who was originally from Julak. His ancestors left that place and went to reside at Nihavand, they held the lands of Julak in rent free tenure from Shah Ismail. His brother was made deputy governor of Hamadan in the time of Shah Abbas (1587-1629).[5] Abdul-Baqi was also exalted with high ranks and favours by Shah Abbas.[6] He appears, for some reason or the other, to have given dissatisfaction to Shah Abbas on account of which he determined upon quitting his native country and arrived at Burhanpur in 1023/1614[7] at the invitation of the Khan-i-Khanan. He was received with kindness and was offered as a gift a *Jagir*.[8] He died about the year 1042/1632 in the reign of Shahjahan.[9] Abdul-Baqi composed his work in 1025/1616 under the encouragement of Khan-i-Khanan and called it *Maasir-i-Rahimi*. The other scholar was Taqiyai Shushtari. He composed *qasidas* in his praise and received rich rewards. Taqiyai was appointed Sadr in the reign of emperor Jahangir during the period about 1024/1615.[10] He was skilled in those sciences which call for the exercise of the reasoning faculty as the practitioner of the traditional language.[11] He was an exquisite poet and was well-versed in various species of poetic composition. He has made use of Ghayuri as his pen-name in some of his odes.[12] Usually Iranian immigrants came to India full of hope and expectation. Many of them like Abdun-Nabi, the author of *Mai-khana* had heard the praise of India from merchants and other Iranians who had been there. Abdun-Nabi's first impression was that it was an extraordinary country where everything was cheap and plentiful. Everyone had the freedom to live as he pleased without any interference or persecution.[13] Taqi Auhadi who has praised Shah Abbas I by highly eulogistic verses[14] came to India, in 1015/1606, because of legendary fame of the Mughal court. He compiled many book likes *Firdos-i-Khayal* and *Arafat-ul-Ashiqin*. Amongst other scholarly people, Aktari

Yazdi was basically an astrologer as his penname shows. Taqi Kashi, the author of *Khulasat-ul-Ashar,* known as Murwarid-Raqam was a scholar and calligraphist. The purpose of 5 scholars who came to India during Jahangir's period are unclear and the other 13 people came for better job and better future prospects.[15]

During Shahjahan's reign 4 scholars migrated to India, such as Mirza Jalala Tabatabai Sayyid was an expert at *Insha* and was held in esteem in the court of Shahjahan. He is the author of various books like a part of *Padashah nama*, *Tauqiat-i-Kisrawiya,* etc. Arif Darabi Shirazi, who came to India for financial reasons has written some books such as *Latifah-i-Ghaibiya*, *Maqamat-ul-Salikin* and a *Tazkira.* Baqir Shiraz was scholar, poet and gilder. He served his time in noble service. Hasil Mashhadi was another scholar. He belonged to a Sayyid family of Mashhad. He passed his time as a scholar and poet.

Table : 6.1
SCHOLARS

Name of migrants	Place of Birth	Provinces	Regions	Period of migration	Contexts and Reasons of migration	Position in Iran	Position in India	Place of Death
Muhammad Sufi Mazandarani	Amul	Mazandaran	North	Akbar (1591)	Accusation of Nuqtawi heresy	Scholar	Author of *Tazkira* and writer of *But-Khaneh*	In the way of Gujarat to Lahore (1642)
Mir Abul-Qasim Findarski	Astarabad	Mazandaran	North	Jahangir (1606)	Displeasurre of Shah Abbas I and to study asceticism	Philisopher and author of many books	Asaf Khan's service, author of *Farhang -i-Juk, kashf-ul-Loghat-i-Juk bashast*	Esfahan (1640)
Fuzuni Astarabadi	Astarabad	Mazandaran	North	Jahangir (1616)	Trade	Scholar, writer of *Saqi Nama*	Author of *Futuhat-i-Adil Shahi*	Unclear
Fani Gilani	-	Gilan	North	Jahangir	Service of Khan-i-Khanan	Theologist	Khan-i-Khanan's service	Unclear
Qudsi Gilani	-	Gilan	North	Jahangir	Unclear	Theologist	Scholar	Unclear
Nasira-i-Hamadani	Hamadan	Hamadan	West and North-West	Akbar	In search of better opportunities	Scholar	Service of Mughal emperors	India

Table Contd.

Table.Contd.

Fusuni Tabrizi	Tabriz	Azabaijan Sharqi	West and North-West	1592	Unclear	Astronomer, Calligraphist	Astronomer and author of Persian dictionary under the title *Meftah-ul-Maani*	India
Nazim Tabrizi	Tabriz	Azabaijan Sharqi	West and North-West	Jahangir	Unclear	*Tazkira* of Poets in order of Shah Abbas I	Author of *Nazm-i-Guzidah*	In the way of India to Iran
Baqi Nihavandi	Julak of Nihavand	Hamadan	West and North-West	Jahangir	Losing royal favour	His father was Wazir of Hamadan	Writer of *Maasir-i-Rahimi* *Amir* of the Deccan and Berar, *Diwan* of Bihar and Patna	India 1632
Fars-i-Hamadani	Hamadan	Hamadan	West and North-West	Jahangir	Dissatisfaction with position in Iran	Scholar story-teller	Scholar	India
Reza Hamadani	Hamadan	Hamadan	West and North-West	Jahangir	Service of Khan-i-Khanan	Expert in army and astronomy	Khan-i-Khanan's service	Unclear
Taqi Shushtari	Shushtar	Khuzestan	South-West	Jahangir 1017	Service of Khan-i-Khanan	Scholar	Service of Khan-i-Khanan, Akbar and Jahangir; post of *Sadr*, author of *Tazkira Arafat-i-Sulaimani*; title of Muwarikh Khan from Jahangir	Ajmer 1616

Table Contd.

Table Contd.

Nikhati Shushtari	Shushtar	Khuzestan	South-West	Jahangir 1031	In order to better his prospects	Scholar	Scholar	Unclear
Khalqi Shushtari	Shushtar	Khuzestan	South-West	Jahangir twice	Unclear	Skill in mathematics	Teacher of School	Golkonda
Mumin Taleqani	Taleqan	Tehran	Central Plateau	Akbar	In company of his father	Scholar	Scholar, his father was *Mir Adil* of Khan-i-Khanan at Burhanpur	Unclear
Fusuni Qomi	Qom	Qom	Central Plateau	Jahangir	For service	Scholar	Service in Akbar and Jahangir's court	Bengal 1618
Asri Damghani	Damghan	Semnan	Central Plateau	Jahangir	In order to better his prospects	Scholar	Noble's service Librarian of Mirza Safdar Khan	Unclear
Nabi Qazwini	Qazwin	Qazwin	Central Plateau	Jahangir 1608	Merchant's encourage-ment	Writer's story teller and poet	Librarian of various nobles, writer of *Mai -Khana* (1619), *Dastur-ul-Fushan, Terazul Akbar, Nawa Dirul-Hikayat/Gharibul Revayat*	Unclear
Dastour Qazwini	Qazwin	Qazwin	Central Plateau	Jahangir 1606	Asaf Khan's service	Scholar	Scholar	India
Taqi Auhadi	Esfahan	Esfahan	Central Plateau	Jahangir	Legendary fame of the Mughal court	Scholar of Shah Abbas I	Author of *Firdos-i-Khayal*-(1611) *Arafat-ul-Ashiqin* (1615) *Kabah-i-Irfan* (1626)	India

Table Contd.

Table Contd.

Akhtari Yazdi	Yazd	Yazd	Central Plateau	Jahangir	Unclear	Scholar in astronomy	Service's of Mir Jumla	India
Taqi Murwarid Kashi	Kashan	Esfahan	Central Plateau	Jahangir	Financial purpose	Author of *Khulasatul Ashar* and Calligraphis	Scholar, Literary circle of poets	Unclear
Sururi Kashani	Kashan	Esfahan	Central Plateau	Jahangir 1620	Unclear	Dictionary of *Majma-ul-furs, Farhang-i-sururi,*	Author of Khula-Satul - Majameh	India 1632
Atai Ardestani	Ardestan	Esfahan	Central Plateau	1622	Unclear	Scholar, Tabat-abai Sadat of Ardestan	Scholar and Poet	Iran
Jalalud-ud-din Tabatabai	Yazd	Yazd	Central Plateau	Shah-jahan 1634	Financial purpose	Tabatabai Sayyid of Ardestan in company of his friends	Authors of one part of *Padashah Nama, Tauqiat-i-Kisravaya, Shah Fahth Kangra* and etc.	Unclear
Mali Shirazi	Shiraz	Fars	South	Akbar 1591	To visit friends	Scholar	Author of *Tazkira* of poets	Unclear
Wasli Shirazi	Shiraz	Fars	South	Jahangir	For service	Scholar	Literary circle of Mirza Ghazi Tarkhan, title of Rashid Khan by Jahangir; writer of *Majma-ul-Lughat-i-Khani*	Unclear
Kamil Jahromi	Jahrom	Fars	South	Jahangir	For service	Scholar	Service of Deccan Kings and Khan-i-Khanan	Unclear
Muqim Darabi	Darab	Fars	South	Jahangir	For service	Scholar and Calligraphist	Noble's service	Unclear

Table Contd.

Table Contd.

Naji Servani	Servan near Kazerun	Fars	South	Jahangir	Unclear	Scholar	Scholar	Agra (1615)
Arif Darabi	Darab	Fars	South	Shah-jahan	Financial purpose	Scholar	Author of *Latifah-i-Ghaibi-yeh; Maqamat-ul Salikin, Tazkira* of poets	Shiraz
Baqir Shirazi	Shiraz	Fars	South	Shah-jahan	Unclear	Scholar, Poet and gilder	Noble's Service	Unclear
Qatii .Heravi	Harat	-	East and North-East	Humayun	Unclear	Belonged to educated family	Scholar of Humayun's court, author of *Majmaush-Shuara-i-Jahangir Shahi*	Agra 1615
Ahadi Kurasani	-	Khurasan	East and North-East	Akbar	Unclear	Scholar	Scholar	Iran
Kaifi Sabsvari	Sabsvar	Khurasan	East and North-East	Jahangir	For travelling	Jewis family of Sabsvar	Author of a *masnavi* under the title of *Agahnama*	Unclear
Mulla Tughra	Mashhad	Khurasan	East and North-East	Twice Jahangir and Shahjahan	In search of Fame	Poet	Author of *Ruqaat Maj, maul-Gharaib, Tazkiratul Akhyar* and etc.	Kashmir 1667
Hasil Mashhadi	Mashhad	Khurasan	East and North-East	Shahjahan	Unclear	Sadat family of Mashhad, Scholar in prose and poet	Service of Prince Murad Bakhash	Mashhad 1659

NORTH OF IRAN

Muhammad Sufi Mazadarani

He was a poet and scholar and combined in his character a *Sufi's* piety and austerity with the spontaneous wit of a poet. He was born at Amul, a city in Mazandarn province, and grew up at Shiraz. He came to India (1000/1591)[16] in the reign of Akbar, following a charge of being Nuqtawi.[17] In his homeland he had experienced harsh treatment. His association with Nuqtawi sect, then prevalent in Iran made him a controversial figure. On the other hand the India of Akbar welcomed all sort of intellectual adventurers. Mulla Muhammad lived in India free from molestation and enjoyed considerable honour in Gujarat where he passed many years. In Ahmadabad, his relations with the poet, Naziri, were not cordial as the latter had ridiculed his beliefs. He did not go to see the poet, when he was ill, but attended his funeral. At Ajmer when Jahangir had ascended the throne Mulla Muhammad was interviewed by the author of *Mai-Khana* whom he disclosed many interesting facts of his life (1024/1615): "I stayed for fifteen year in the holy cities of Mecca and Medina. And there must be few places situated along the caravan routes, which I have not seen." Indeed travelling was an irresistible passion with every member of his class.[18] He died in the course of a journey from Gujarat to Lahore in 1034/1624,[19] where the emperor Jahangir had invited him for a meeting. Among the literary works of Mulla Muhammad were,(I), a *Tazkira* containing notices of one hundred and twenty-six poets, but *Khaneh*[20] completed in 1010/1601 and (2) *diwan* of verses.[21]

The author of *Haft Iqlim*[22] praises his verses and the *Ain-i-Akbari*, contains the following notice of him:

"He is in affluent circumstances, but due to virtuous motives he mixes little with the world. He seeks retirement by travelling about.

Look upon me, when standing below the revolving roof of the heavens, as a lamp concealed under a cover.

1. O heart, thy road is not without thorns and caltrops, nor dost thou walk on the wheel of good fortune.

2. If it be possible pull the skin from the body, and see whether thy burden will be a little lighter."[23]

Mir Abdul-Qasim Findarski Astarabadi

Hakim Amir Abol-Qasim Astarabadi was the son of Mirza Beg Ibin Sadr-ud-din Musavi Astarbadi Findarski.[24] He was one of the great theologians and gnostics of Imamiya sect. He was skilled in mathematics, physics theology and philosophy.[25]

According to *Dahkhuda* Findarski was one of the noted gnostics and the logicians of Shah Abbas I period.[26]

Mir Findarski entered Esfahan in 1038/1628, when Shah Safi was king.[27] But Sayyid Jalal-ud-Din-Ashtiyani has written in introduction of *Tufatul-Murad*.[28] He came to Esfahan in 1038/1628 in the time of Shah Ismail.[29] Probably Ashtiyani was mistaken about the name of the king because Shah Ismail governed during 907-930/1501-1523. Most of authors believe that Mir Findarski died in 1090/1640 at the age of 80 in Esfahan. So he was born in 970/1562, when Shah Tahmasp was the Safavid king.

Auhadi says: Mir Findarski came to India in 1015/1606 in my company then he joined Mirza Jafar Asaf Khan. After some time he went to Iran, and again he came back to India.[30] M.A. Qazwini pens the following notice of him:

"Mir Abol-Qasim Findarski enjoys preference and eminence at present over the Iranian especially among the scholars of the age. Coming several times to India he enjoyed favours and patronage from this royal dynasty. He visited India twice after the accession of Shahjahan. Once he came to India during the 1st regnal year, and for the second time in the 10th regnal year.[31] As he was well-acquainted with Yamin-ud-daula Asaf Khan-i-Khanan, the commander-in-chief, he obtained the felicity of paying his respects to the emperor through his good offices. On both the occasions he was awarded a gift of 5,000 rupees from the benevolent royal exchequer."[32]

Mir Findarski's writings and works are as follows:

1. *Tarikh-i-Safaviya*
2. *Tahqiqul-Mozlleh*
3. Description of *Almehareh,* one of Indian wise men book famous to *Sharh-i-Jouk.* Shaikh Aqa Bozork-i-Tehrani has mentioned in his book under following titles:

(a) *Kashf-ul-Loghat-i-Juk ba Shast.*[33]
(b) *Loght-i-Juk ba Shast*[34]
(c) *Farhang-i-Juk*[35]

4. *Risala-i-Sanaiya*: About industries and its benefit.[36]
5. *Maqulatul-Harakat-va-Tahqiq Fiha*[37]
6. *Takhmiriya*[38]
7. His poems: Mir Findarski was famous in philosophy. But sometimes he also composed gnostic poems.[39]

Fuzuni Astarabadi

Mir Muhammad Hashim was the son of Jalal-ud-din Nakhash. In early youth he moved from his native place Astarabad, a city in Mazandaran province, in order to trade. He travelled in many parts of Iran and India, and spent his money in journey, and wore poors clothes, he had wandered across the cities of the Mughal empire; as paying several visits to India was a fashion among his countrymen. Abdun-Nabi saw him in Kashmir in 1025/1616, where his patron was a local nobleman, Safadar Khan. As noted by the author of Mai-Khanan, he was engaged in writing a general history on a large scale and intended to integrate his observations of contemporary life into it. Finally, the work appeared under the title: *Buhairah.*[40] Fuzuni's *Diwan* contained verses of all varieties. He dedicated his *Saqi-nama* to Shah Abbas the Great of Iran. He also entered the service of Muhammad Adil Shahi, the sixth ruler of the line. At his master's request, he wrote a history of the dynasty naming it: *Futuhat-i-Adil Shahi*, 1954/1644.[41]

Fani Gilani

He was born and brought up at Gilan. Mustafa Fani was a student of theological school. He migrated to India from Esfahan to join the services Khan-i-Khanan. Fani enjoyed the patronage of Abdur-Rahim Khan-i-Khanan and composed some verses in his praise.[42]

Qudsi Gilani

Maulana Mustafa was a scholar of practical and theoretical wisdom. Qudsi lived at Esfahan for a long time and was a student of Allama Chalabi Tabrizi, who was a great man from Tabriz's *Darul-Saltanah.* Auhadi mentions: I visited him at Esfahan. He was not a poet, but in India Qudsi composed poems. For a while he stayed in Bengal, and then he went to Agra (1022-1024/1613-1615).[43]

WEST AND NORTH-WEST

Nasira-i-Hamadani

Khwaja Nasir-ud-din Mahmud Hamadani was son of Khwaja Mashud and grandchild of Khwaja Hasan Beg Yazjerdi (Borujerdi).Khwaja Nasir came to India because of his difficulties in Iran. First he travelled in Mughal territory and then went to the Deccan.[44]

According to Auhadi, Nasira, was a scholar of many disciplines, particularly of mathematics, music and poetry. Having arrived from Iran, he entered the service of the Mughal emperors, Akbar and Jahangir at Agra. In the Deccan, Muhammad Qutb Shah, king of Golkonda, extended him patronage. Nasira left a *diwan* of verses and wrote a tract on prosody, which he dedicated to the above-named patron naming it *Lal-i-Qutbi*. Also his collection of official letters found entry in *madrasah* education: *Munshaat-i-Nasira/Ruqqat-i-Nasira*.[45]

Fusuni Tabrizi

Abul-Fazl and Amin Razi say: That Fusuni was from Shiraz[46]; Badauni call him Yazdi; and Daghistani and the author of *Atashkada* says that he came from Tabriz. Badauni says that Fusuni came over Thatta and entered the service of the emperor, and Daghistani adds that he also served under Jahangir and Shahjahan as *Mustaufi*. The *Miratul Alam* mentions: Fusuni who was an Amir under Jahangir and had the title of Afzal Khan.[47] Mahmud Beg was a learned and affable person. He was well versed in learning and accomplishments and expert in different sciences. Mahmud Beg shifted to India in 1001/1592, and was appointed as a writer and astronomer in Akbar's court. During Jahangir's time he received *mansab* of prince Khurram's *Mustaufi*. In the meantime he wrote some articles/about mathematics and a Persian dictionary under the title: *Meftah-ul-Maani*.

According to Amin Razi, Fusuni had skill in calligraphy, poetry and astronomy.[48] T. Auhadi says: He was able in many sciences, and it is near to 25 years when he came to India. Auhadi visited him many times at Shiraz and Esfahan.[49]

Nazim Tabrizi

According to M.T. Nasrabadi his name was Muhammad Sadiq and his resident place was Abbas Abad, a city near Esfahan. His brother was Muhammad Reza Beg *Murvarid foursh* (pearl seller) who was an educated person. Nazim shifted to holy city of Mecca and settled there for some time. He has written *Tazkira* of poets. His death occurred before 1083/1672.[50] Nazim has written in introduction of his *Tazkira*: I completed *Tazkira* on the order of Shah Abbas the Great. He composed masnavi of *Firuz-i-Shanaz* which was attached to this *Tazkira*.[51]

Muhammad Arif Shirazi says: Nazim went to India during Shah Abbas I's reign. He lived there for some time. On the way of return to Iran he was drowned in the sea.[52]

Nabi Hadi has mentioned Nazim came as free wanderer from Tabriz who stayed for some time at the court of Bijapur. Ibrahim Adilshah II and his *Wazir*, Shanawaz Khan Shirazi, welcomed him to the new city Nauraspur. And he sang his *qasida* in praise of the king and the minister in the glittering audience hall of the palace, *Nauras-i- bihisht*.[53] In India, Nazim found the leisure to complete major portion of his work, a *Tazkira* of poets on which he laboured for many year. Its title was *Nazm-i-Guzida*, 1036/1626.[54]

Baqi Nihavandi

Abdul Baqi Nihavandi was the son of Aqa Baba Julaki. He was born in Julak' a village near Nihavand in Hamadan province, in 978/ 1570. His ancestors hailed from Kurd tribe of Julak who numbered about 30,000 souls and lived in the vicinity of Baghdad and Iraq-Arab, near Qasr-i-Shireen. In the beginning of the reign of Shah Ismail Safavi, his ancestors, due to strife with other tribes of Kurdestan were obliged to leave their native country and enter his service. His father became the *wazir* and *Nazir* of Hamadan during the reign of Shah Abbas Safavi. He was poet and composed poems under the pen-name of Mudriki. He was very well acquainted with accounts, book keeping, logic and mathematics. Mudriki died in 1000/1591. His brother Aqa Khizra was the minister of Lahijan in Gilan and afterwards became the *divan* of the capital city of Hamadan and then wazir of Kashan. He was very well known for his administration, justice and public works. He was holding this post for twenty years. During this period the author was either with his father or brother and had visited Semnan, Bastam, Dilaman, Lahijan and Fars. After he had helped his father and brother in the accomplishment of their duties for a long time, he was appointed the revenue collector of Kashan. While he was holding the office of revenue collector he came in contact with large number of poets and learned men like Hakim Rukn-ud-din, Masud Masihi, Mirza Abu Turab Turkman, Maulana Hatim Fahimi, Shauri, Kisra, Rafi-ud-din Haidar and Amir Taqi-ud-din Muhammad, the *Tazkira* writer.

It so happened that the author's spiritual guide Amir Moghis-ud-din Mahvi Astarbadi, who was a *mozahheb* of Abdur Rahim Khan-i-khanan retuned to Kashan in 1006/1597-98; and told Abdul Baqi about the munificence and learning of Khan-i-Khanan. In the meantime events had taken a very sharp and swift turn in Iran.[55] His brother Aqa Khizra due to some court intrigue was assassinated by Shah Abbas I and the rank of the brother was transferred to Abdul Baqi, but the intrigue was so deep-rooted and grave that it became impossible for him to stay any longer in Iran.[56] He therefore left Iran and came to India, in 1023/1614 by way of port Dabail (Dabhol) and went to Burhanpur in Khandesh and joined the service of Khan-i-Khanan.[57] The latter conferred upon him a *Jagir* and fixed his salary and allowance and requested him to write *Maasir-i-Rahimi.* He started the work in 1023/1614 and finished it in 1025/1616.[58] The *Maasir-i-Rahimi* began with a fleeting description of ruling dynasties since the Turks entered India, and made extensive survey of contemporary life. The book contained a *Mugaddima*, four *fasl* and a *Khatima*, its interesting feature being detailed notices of contemporary poet, philosophers, physicians, men of letters calligraphists, military officers under the command of Khan-i-Khanan. In the estimate of literary critics an outstanding contribution made by Mughal India was the *Massir-i-Rahimi.* It is written in an ornate style which was the customary style of the age.[59] Baqi Nihavandi was also made the Amir of the Deccan and Berar, in which capacity he served till 1029/1619. After serving the Khan-i-Khanan for a long time Abdul Baqi was attached to Mahabat Khan,[60] after his patron's fall and on the recommendation of the latter, he obtained the favour of prince Parviz(the second son of Jahangir) who made him the *diwan* of Bihar and Patna.[61] According to the *Tarikh-i-Muhammadi*, Abdul Baqi died in 1042/ 1632.[62]

Baqi Nihavandi was not a professional poet. He was an administrator. Before coming to India he used to write *rubai's* in the style of his spiritual guide. When he came to India he wrote *ghazals* and *qasidas* in praise of Abdur Rahim Khan-i-Khanan. His rubai's have sufistic touch in them. Abdul-Baqi Nihavandi and Abdul-Qadir Terani in *Rauz-i-Rushan* is the same person.[63]

Fars-i-Hamadani

Mirza Muhammad well known to Fars, was the son of Hasan Beg Hamadani. He came to India during Jahangir's reign in search of better opportunities. In Iran he was famous as a soft spokenman. His poems number more than two thousand.[64]

Nasrabadi says: Mirza Muhammad, Fars *takhallus* originally is from Bowanat in Fars province. They were three brothers, among them Mirza Malik Mashriqi[65] was skilled in prose and poetry. After death of Mirza Malik Mirza Muhammad became a story teller of *Qawah khaneh* (tea-shop). Later his nature was offended by somebody and then he shifted to India. After some time he retuned to his native place but again he migrated to India and died here.[66]

Reza Hamadani

His origin and birthplace was Hamadan. Muhammad Reza was the son of Maulana Ismail Mufti. In the early age he came to India in order to join the services of Khan-i-Khanan, and attached to his literary circle. Reza had good knowledge about astronomy and was expert in military practices. He was living in an easy manner in India. He spent his time as a poet and scholar.[67] Nizam-ud-din Ahmad Bakhshi mentions some of his verses and his biographies.[68]

SOUTH-WEST

Taqi Shushtari

Maulana Taqi Shushtari had adopted the penname of Ghayuri. There is some controversy among the biographers regarding his name. Nizam-ud-din[69] calls him Taqi-ud-din Muhammad, whereas Badauni [70] mentions Taqi-ud-din only.

Taqi came from his native place to Shiraz in order to receive education and learnt theology and philosophy from the great professor

Shah Taqi-ud-din Muhammad, better known as Nasiba. He excelled all the pupils of his great teacher in accomplishment and learning. After receiving education he migrated to India and entered in the service of Abdur-Rahim Khan-i-Khanan, who patronised and rewarded him lavishly. In Khan-i-Khanan's court he met the great poet Shakibi, who was also a very distinguished scholar. Both these poets spent their whole life in the service of Khan-i-Khanan, but Shakibi was much more popular as a poet and Ghayuri as a companion. It is said that Ghayuri was primarily a scholar and at times composed verses, so he can be reckoned as a poet too. He had not adopted poetry as a profession. He was a disciple of Akbar's Divine faith and was employed by Akbar to write prose version of *Shah nama.*[71] He has composed verses in praise of Khan-i-Khanan which are of no mean order. It is said that at one time he told Khan-i-Khanan in the open court, that he has not seen twelve thousand rupees at one place in his whole life. He subsequently joined the service of Jahangir, who conferred the title of *Muwarikh* Khan, (biographer),[72] upon him in the third year of his reign 1017/1608.

He was occupying the post of *Sadra* in 1024/1616. Taqi should not be confused with Taqiya of Balban who according to *Mirat-ul-Alam* came to India in the beginning of Jahangir's reign. He is the author of a rare *Tazkira* of poets, entitled *Arafat-i-sulaimani*, which the lexicographer Muhammad Husain used for his *Burhan-i-Qateh.*[73] According to T. Auhadi he was in Jahangir's camp, and died in 1025/1616.[74] Mir Ala-ul-mulk says: Taqi died in Ajmer and was buried adjacent side to Khwaja Moinuddin Chishti's tomb.[75]

Nikhati Shushtari

He belonged to Shushtar, a city near Ahwaz in province of Khusestan. Nikhati was grandchild of Maulana Shakibi Shushtari, who was famous in mathematics, philosophy and poetry in the time of Shah Tahmasp Safavi. Nikhati was a scholar in current sciences of that time, he emigrated to Sistan in 1030/1620, and then came to India during the Jahangir's reign in order to better his prospects and for making money. He had poetic nature, and left some verses.[76]

Khalqi Shushtari

Maulana Khalqi Shushtari lived as a poet. He was intelligent, judicious, virtuous and of exquisite taste. Khalqi followed Anwari and

Abul Faraj in poetic field. Before coming to India he settled at Shiraz. Khalqi came to India two times. At first time he came to Lahore in 1015/1606 and after some time he came back to Shiraz.[77] Second time he migrated to Deccan and stayed there for 25 years. He was skilled in mathematics, rational and traditional sciences and was teacher in a school. His death occurred in 1047/1637 in Golconda and was buried there[78].

CENTRAL PLATEAU

Mumin Taleqani

He belonged to Taleqan, a town situated in Tehran province. Muhammad Mumin was son of Muhammad Amin Taleqani, who was Mir Adil of Khan-i-Khanan at Burhanpur. Muhammad Mumin migrated to India in company of his father in Akbar's reign. He was an accomplished and learned scholar. Occasionally he versed poems.[79]

Fusuni Qomi

Mirza Ali entitled as Afzal Khan came from Qom, the city of learned men in Iran, and stayed for many years in the service of Burhan Nizam Shah, the king of Ahmadnagar. Failing to resist the military pressure of the Mughals, its ruler, Chand Bibi, surrendered her sovereignty and Afzal Khan accepted Akbar's offer of service, whom the emperor posted to Bengal, the far-flung province. He was a scholar and poet and left a *diwan* containing more than four thousand verses. He died in 1028/1618 in Bengal.[80]

The author of *Mai-Khana*, Auhadi mentions Afzal Khan Fusuni, who was settled in India for a long time. and joined and attended Akbar and Jahangir's courts. For a while Fusuni was in Sind.[81]

Asri Damghani

He was born at Damghan, a city in Semnan province, the birthplace of one of the great poets of Iran, like Manuchiri. Asri was a great scholar of his native place, and he also had good knowledge about fortunetelling. He came to India during Jahangir's reign in order to better his prospects, whose *qasidas* vibrated with the diction of the pagan Arab poets. Asri stayed for some time in Lahore, where the author of *Mai-Khana* saw him, and came to Agra and served under Mirza Yadgar, noble of Jahangir. Thereafter, he moved to Kashmir and enjoyed the patronage of Mirza Safdar Khan, a scion of Chak rulers, whom Jahangir appointed governor of the province for a term of three years. 'Asri' took care of Mirza Safdar's personal library, and found ample time for creative work. He possessed a *diwan* of verses.[82]

Nabi Qazwini

Abdun-Nabi Fakhr-Uz-Zamani Qazwini known as Nabi was a writer, story-teller and poet. He was born at Qazwin in 998/1589. His father's name was Khalaf Beg, who was a merchant and a *Sufi*. Khalaf Beg died because of plague in 1001/1592. Fakhr-Uz-Zamani received literary training in his native place.In the beginning he used to write under the pen-name of Izati and then changed to Nabi. The author of *Farang-i-Sukhanvaran* has written Nabi's penname Zulali. He died in 1031/1621.[83] He was an adolescent youth of nineteen when the romantic tales of India, related by travellers and merchants, excited him to leave Iran. Soon, he took the road from Mashhad to Qandahar, reached Lahore in 1017/1608, and moved to Agra, the imperial capital of the Mughals in 1018/1609. He chosed Mirza Nizami his relative and news writer of Jahangir's court. Nabi found himself more skilled as story-teller because of Mirz Nizami's encouragement. In 1022/1613 Nabi went to Ajmer accompanying Mirza Nizami in Jahangir's camp. There he was introduced to Mirza Aman-Ullah Amani (Mirza Aman-ullah known as Amani was the son of Zamana Beg Mahabat Khan. He received to title of *Khaneh zad Khani* and *mansab* of 5000 in Jahangir's reign. In Shah-jahan time he attained title of Khan Zaman Bahadur. His death occurred in 1047/1637 at Doulatabad-i-Deccan and entered his service Fakhr-Uz-Zamani was a gifted story-teller; and his art, resembling more or less, that of a modern stage-actor, had bright prospects in Mughal India. Abdun-Nabi found employment, first, in that capacity, and then, as librarian, in the libraries of various nobles of Jahangir's reign. And, he lived at many places, chiefly, Ajmer, Kashmir, and Patna. His innovative nature is revealed in his work, *Mai-Khana*, the anthology of poets, who exclusively composed *Saqi-nama*, a special variety of poems praising the cup-bearer. He interviewed a large number of poets in order to obtain first-hand information about their lives. In fact, Abdun-Nabi's *Mai-Khana* may be placed among the extremely interesting books in the whole range of Mughal literature. His narrative style has a unique charm, which none of his contemporaries could surpass. The work was completed at

Azimabad, Patna in 1028/1619. While staying in Kashmir, he wrote a book for the guidance of story-tellers: *Dastur ul-Fusaha*. Also, he compiled an encyclopaedia of earlier and recents poets, its title was *Terazul Akhbar*, one uncompleted copy of this book is in central library of Tehran University. (Number 3295). He also compiled a collection of anecdotes *Nawadirul-Hikayat/Gharibul-Revayat*, the work was completed in 1041/1631. One copy of this work was introduced in the list of the library of law faculty (Tehran University), p. 222, number 55.[84]

Dastour Qazwini

Mir Rafi Dastour belonged to Qazwin. He spent his time in education of metaphysics and quatrain verses. He migrated to India in the company of Shiakh Khatan in order to join the services of Asaf Khan. Mirza Qawam-ud-din Jafar Qazwini (Asaf Khan) was one of nobleman of Akbar and Jahangir's reigns. Afterwards Dastour died in India.[85] According to Sarkhush, Mirza Rafi Dastour died in India during Jahangir's reign. He left some verses.[86]

Taqi Auhadi

His ancestors were from Kazerun, a city in Fars province, but he was born at Esfahan in 973/1565. Auhadi was the son of Muin Baliyani, who was very close to Shah Tahmasp's court. Muin's arrival to India was circumstantial and died here in the last days of 972/1565. Taqi was student of Shiakh-ul-Islam Shiakh Ali Mushar and Maulana Mir Qari in Esfahan and Shiraz respectively. He received education in mathematics, logic and theology. Auhadi was patronized as a young scholar by Shah Abbas the Great, but the legendary fame of the Mughals brought him to India in 1015/1606 along with Mir Abulqasim Findarski, Mir Abu Turb-i-Turabi, Aqa Taqi ibn Aqa Malik Esfahani, Mumin Aqa Haji Esfahani, Tajlli Gilani, Quli Khan Beg Mujrim Shamlu, Haidar Beg Hamadani and many others. He stayed at Lahore for one and a half year's and then shifted to Agra in Jahangir's camp. After one year he migrated to Gujarat and settled in Ahamdabad for three years. He compiled the *Firdos-i-Khayal* in 1020/1611. After the death of Naziri (1021/1612) he came back to Agra from Gujarat, and started writing the *Arafat-ul-Ashiqin* in 1022/1613 and completed in 1024/1615. It contains a wide variety of verses selected from the works of about three thousand poets placed in alphabetical order. There are 28 chapters according to the letters of the alphabet, each chapter is named *Arshah*, which has three sub-divisions, *Arafah*. The latter bears the account of ancient, medieval, and modern poets respectively.

Taqi Auhadi himself made an abridgment of the colossal *Arafat-ul-Ashiqin* and named it *Kabah-i-Irfan* in 1036/1626 at Gujarat. Further, Jahangir desired that an abridgment of the abridgment should be prepared. It came out as: *Intikhab-i-Kabah-i-Irfan.*

Auhadi got settled in Gujarat during the last days of his life. Some authors have written, Auhadi died between years of 1030,1031 and 1036/1620,1621 and 1626, but the Khwaja Jan Khafi is the last person thet Auhadi has mentioned. Auhadi gave following information about him: In 1037/1627 during the Shahjahan period Khwaja Jahan, who was *divan* and *Waqia Navis* of Ahmadabad was engaged in this job till 1040/1630.Therefore, Auhadi was alive during this time.[87]

Akhtari Yazdi

According to Auhadi, Mulla Akhtari Yazdi is a young poet in the prime of his youth. He was prudent in speech and cavalier.[88]

The author of *Khairul Bayan* says: Akhtari Yazdi came to India during Jahangir's period without definite reason. In the initial period after his arrival in India he was attached to Mir Jumla. Akhtari was in the service of Mir Jumla for a long time. When Mir Jumla went to Iran, Akhtari also was accompanying him. After some time they came back to India (1027/1617).[89] Nasrabadi says: Akhtari migrated to India and entered the service of Mir Jumla Sharistani for a long time. Akthar returned to Iran after death of Mir Jumla in 1047/1637. At Yazd he received the *mansab* of *Kadkhuda* (Head man of a village). He came to India and again died here.[90]

Taqi Murwarid Kashi

Taqi passed early life in Kashan and was the disciple of his fellow town man, Muhtasham-i-Kashi. In poetry Muhtasham was the only celebrated poet of Safavid era who unlike his contemporaries resisted the temptation of shifting to India and stayed in Iran. Taqi Kashi, however' availed himself a chance of an India visit in Jahangir's reign. He journeyed in the emperor's retinue from Fatehpur Sikri and Agra, where his main occupation was spending time with men of learning and culture. He interviewed poets and held literary discussions with them. From North India, he passed on to the Deccan and enriched himself with many interesting observations. His contribution was a *Tazkira* of poets, *Khulasatul Ashar* it *Zubdatul-Afkar*. "In completing it he devoted almost all his life seeming, the portion related to contemporary poets was added by him during the course of his travels in India. The book contained the biographies of over three hundred poets and a selection of not less than three hundred fifty thousand verses. He first dedicated it to Shah Abbas the Great, and a second time, to Ibrahim Adil Shah of Bijapur, ca.1006/1597. In addition he was calligraphist of *Nastaliq*.[91]

Sururi Kashani

Muhammad Qasim Sururi was the son of Mulla Haji Muhammad *Kafshduz* (Shoemaker). Earlier Sururi was engaged in shoemaking along with his father. After some time he left that job and then he took to verification. He also acquired good knowledge about Persian and Arabic vocabulary.[92] Sururi was the author of a comprehensive dictionary *Majmaul-Furs*.[93] Also many lexicographers mentioned it as *Lughat-i-Sururi/Farhang-i-Sururi*. He complied this in 1008/1599 at Kashan and Esfahan for Shah Abbas I. Sururi made an abridgment of the *Majmaul-Furs* and named it *Khulasat-ul-Majma* for Itimad-ud-duala Hatim Beg Urduabadi. Sururi also made some changes in *Farhang-i Jahangiri* in 1028/1618[94].

Auhadi says: Sururi came to India after the 1030/1620.[95] He passed many years in Lahore and Akbarabad (Agra), and died in 1042/1632.[96]

Atai Ardestani

Mir Atai belonged to Tabatabai Sayyid of Ardestan. He was scholar and accomplished person and was skilled in mathematics. Mir Atai moved to Herat in 1032/1622 and stayed there for five months and then he shifted to India via Balkh. He was settled in India for two years. Afterwards he retuned to Esfahan. He passed his time as a scholar and poet.[97]

Jalal-ud-din Tabatabai

There is a difference of opinion about the correct place of his origin. The author of *Amal-i-Salih* says: He was from Yazd,[98] whereas others believe that he was from Zavareh of Ardestan[99] in Esfahan province. He came to India in 1044/1634[100] to seek employment at the court of Shahjahan. The emperor appointed him official historiographer and Mirza Jalal prepared an account of the first five years. He was master of artificial and florid style, which has been in fashion in those days. He coined new words and thereby paved the way for the expression of new ideas. His stock of words was inexhaustible. His style is ornate, thought-provoking and interesting. It is beautiful and flawless. It is very difficult to find fault with his style even for person who possesses the most critical mind.[101] Tabatabai is the author of the following works:

1. *Padashah nama*: A history of five years of Shah Jahan's reign but owing to envy of his rivals he had to discontinue the work.[102] He died in 1090/1679.[103]

2. *Tauqiat-i-Kisrawiya:* The so-called institutes of Khusrau Anushirwan, Translated from Arabic into Persian by Tabatabai. The book is in the form of questions and answer and talks of cosmogony, philosophy, etc. according to the doctrines of the Mobeds or Magian priests. and was printed in Calcutta, 1824 and repeatedly lithographed in Lucknow and Cawnpore.[104]

3. *Shah Fath Kangra*[105] : It comprises six stylistic accounts of the one expedition which Shah Jahan, then governor of Gujarat, sent under command of Raja Bikramajit against the rebel Surajmal, son of Raja Basu, in the 13th year of Jahangir's reign, 1027/1618, and of the capture of the fort of Kangra in the Punjab below the Himalayas. In order to display the inexhaustible wealth of his rhetorical resources, the author relates the same events in six separate pieces, written in as many different styles of composition.[106]

4. *Muntakhab az Bayaz*[107] : A collection of letters, congratulatory pieces and other occasional compositions. The following letters are of special interest. Letter of Afzal Khan (Mulla Shukrullah Shirazi, *Wazir* of Shah Jahan, who died in 1048/1638.Letter written in the name of Shah Abbas to Abdullah Khan the Uzbek. Several congratulatory pieces were addressed to Shahjahan.

5. Prose preface to the *diwans* of:
   (a) Abdu Talib Kalim (died 1061 or 1062/1650-51)[108]
   (b) Qudsi (died 1055 or 1056/1645-46)[109]
   (c) Shifai (died 1037 or 1038/1627-28)[110]
   (d) *Saqi nama* of Zuhuri (died 1025/1616)[111]

(e) Munir Lahori (Abul Barakat, died 1054/1644) see; *Rieu, cat. Vol. III, p. 933.*[112]

SOUTH IRAN

Mali Shirazi

Shaikh Abu Haiyyan known as Mali was from Shiraz.Mali[113] was expert in medicine and other sciences. He composed some verses. He died before 1083/1672.[114]

Reza Quli Khan Hadayat has mentioned Abu Haiyan's *Tazkira* in his sources and added, Abu Haiyan Tabib came to India accompanying Mulla Hasan Ali Yazdi and Mulla Muhammad Sufi Mazandarani during Akbar's reign through holy city of Mecca. Besides the Tazkira, he has written introduction to *diwan* of Nizam Dasghib-i-Shirazi.[115]

Wasli Shirazi

Mir Nimat Ullah was student, disciple and adopted son of Murshid Borujerdi. (Borujerdi was in the service of Mirza Ghazi' Jahangir' Mahabat Khan and prince Shahjahan. He died in 1030/1620). Wasli came to India to visit Murshid Borujerdi. As the latter joined the literary circle of Mirza Tarkhan,[116] the Mughal governor at Qandahar, he invited Wasli also and arranged a government job for him. After Mirza Ghazi's death (1021/1612) the scholars dispersed and Wasli turned to Ajmer, for the emperor, Jahangir was camping there. The author of *Mai-Khana* and Wasli travelled together from Ajmer to Lahore and passed a few months in each other's company. Wasli moved onward to frontier area inhabited by the Bangash tribe and found service under Allah-dad Khan,[117] son of Jalal Khan Afghan, whose rebellion a few years ago had been a source of worry to the Mughal government. Later on, Jahangir conferred the title of Rashid Khan[118] on Wasli, as he assisted in negotiating the terms of treaty between his master, Allah-dad Khan, and the Mughal governor, Mahabat Khan. Wasli had shown his collection to Abdun-Nabi, the author of *Mai-Khana*, who found the volume containing about four thousand miscellaneous verses. The *diwan* has survived. Also, a dictionary compiled to the sixteenth year of Shahjahan's reign and dedicated to a nobleman, Makramat Khan was attributed to him. Its title was *Majmaul-Lughat-i-Khani.*[119]

Kamil Jahromi

Qiwam-ud-din Abdullah was the son of Nizam-ud-din Ali Tabbakh.

His birthplace was Jahrom a town near Shiraz, where he received early education. In the early youth he moved to Shiraz and greatly enjoyed in Maulana Malik said Shirazi's[120] (Khalkhali)[121] company. At the age of 25 Kamil migrated to India in order to join to literary circle and enjoyed the patronage of the kings of Bijapur and Golkonda, Mirz Abdur Rahim Khan-i-Khanan at Burhanpur and prince Khurram, at Agra. Abdun-Nabi who saw him in Patna, was struck by his wanderlust. He visited different parts of India from south of the subcontinent to the valley of Kashmir. And he had halted in Azimabad on way to Bengal. Nothing of the five thousand verses contained in his *diwan* have survived save the interesting *Saqi-nama*, which he passed on to the author of *Mai-Khana.* He had collected verses of eminent *Sufis* in a personal hand book naming it: *Murshid-i-Kamil.*[122]

Auhadi saw him at Agra in 1022/1613. He composed *masnavi*, it was named as Mahmud and *Ayaz*. Auhadi heard about his death in 1028/1618.[123]

Muqim Darabi

Khwaja Muhammad Muqim was the son of Muhammad Husian Beg Zul-Qadr well known to Muqim. His origin and birth place was Darabgard, a city in Fars province, but he grew up and received education at Karbala.According to Baqi Nihvandi, he was devoted and attractive, and he had proficiency in mathematics, *Insha* (writing letter), calligraphy (*Shikasta*), and system of notation and accounting. Some time he versed lovely poems. Afterwards he emigrated to India from Karbala for job purpose. He joined the services of Darab Khan,[124] son of Abdur Rahim Khan-i-Khanan and acoompanied him during the campaigns Deccan.[125]

Naji Servani

Baba Naji belonged to Servan, a village near Kazerun in Fars province. He had valuable knowledge in many kind of sciences, specially medicine, mysticism and geomancy. He moved from his native place to India and lived at Agra for a long time. Naji died at Agra in 1024/1615.[126]

Arif Darabi Shirazi

Muhammad b. Muhammad Arif Darabi Shirazi belonged to the town of Darab in Fars in south Iran. In the early youth he was student of Shiakh Bahai. He visited India three times. (Arif Darabi came to India three times for making money during 1062/1651, 1066/1655, 1068/1657. Later he retuned to Iran in 1083/1672 permanently).[127] In his life he roamed through the cities of Ahmadabad, Surat, and Daulatabad. As a young man, he met the great poets of his age, Hakim Rukna of Kashi, Mirza Saib and others. He is the author of the following works:

1. A book, in which he explored the literary merits of Khwaja Hafiz of Shiraz, its title is *Latifah-i-Ghaibiyeh,* completed ca.1076/1665.

2. *Maqamat-ul-Salikin*, a book containing music terms and opinion of Islamic scientists about singing (music).[128]

3. *A Tazkira* of poets, four hundred and fifty-four in number mostly contemporaneous, arranged in twentyeight sections according to regions and cities, known as *Lataif-ul-Khayal.*

He passed his life as a scholar and poet. Arif was his poetic name. He died at Shiraz.[129]

Baqir Shirazi

Mulla Muhammad Baqir Mozahheb belonged to Shiraz. He was student of Mirza Ibrahim son of Mulla Sadra in mathematics and theology. He served his time as a scholar, poet and gilder (Mozahheb). Muhammad Baqir emigrated to India during Shahjahan's reign and joined Ibrahim Khan who was the son of Ali Mardan Khan and great Amir of Shahjahan's period. After some time Baqir went to Mecca in 1083/1672. He composed some verses.[130]

EAST AND NORTH-EAST

Qatii Heravi

He belonged to an educated family of Herat. His ancestor was Shaikh Abu Nasr Frahi, the author of *Nisabus-Subiyan*, the famous book, rather the first in Persian language, related to the category of, so to say children's literature; Qatii-Heravi was a scholar at the court of Humayan when the emperor lived as an exile in Kabul. He was expert in binding, gilting and colouration. Having survived till the age of one hundred and three years he witnessed the days of Akbar and the early years of Jahangir. The author of *Arafat-ul-Ashiqin*, found Mull Qatii a healthy old man living at Agra, where later on, his death (1024/ 1615) seemed to have taken place. He wrote a *Tazkira* of poets most of them his contemporaries, and dedicated it to Jahangir. The book was planned in three parts, of which only the third and last part has survived. Before closing every entry, he repeated words of blessing and prayer for the emperor. The title of the work was *Majma ush-Shuara-i-Jahangir Shahi.*[131]

Ahadi Khurasani

He belonged to Khurasan, and came to India without definite proof. Qazi Abdur-Razzaq Ahadi was settled to India during Akbar and Jahangir's resign. He was classmate of Qazi Nurullah Shushtari, and was one of the great scholars of his time. Abdur-Razzaq was a *Qazi* of Kanbite for a some time then he moved to Kashmir and stayed there for a long time. According to Auhadi he came back to Iran and left *a diwan* of verses[132].

Kaifi Sabzvari

He belonged to a Jewish family of Sabzvar, in Khurasan, and embraced Islam in young age. He wandered freely in the garb of a *darvish* for twenty years and visited, among other places, many parts of India. Taqi Auhadi[133] saw him in Agra and Ajmer (1042/1615); and a year later, he was interviewed by the author of *Mai-Khana* at Lahore. In mature age he accepted the service under prince Khurram (Shahjahan). He was the author of a *masnavi* on the pattern of Rumi's master piece and named his work: *Agah nama.*[134]

The author of *Makhzanul-Gharayeb* says: Origin of Kaifi was Jewish and he came to Sabzvar from Sajestan in Sistan via Baluchistan province. He embraced Islam then migrated to India during Jahangir's reign.[135]

Mulla Tughara

Tughra's native place is a point of controversy. Some of the *Tazkira* writers call him Tabrizi;[136] which is not correct. The author of *Sarv-i-Azad* prefers to call him as Mashhadi.[137]

Mulla Tughra was a renowned poet of this period. He is one of those poets of Iran who came to India in search of fame and recognition and felt that skill will remain unidentified in Iran.

Mulla Tughra migrated to India two times. First time he came during the reign of Jahangir and after staying for some time with Mir Muhammad Said Mir Jumla, he returned to Iran and got married there. Suddenly his wife died and Tughra come to India again during the reign of Shahjahan[138] and served in various capacities under prince Murad, a son of Shahjahan. He stayed in the Deccan and accompanied the Mughal armies on their expedition to Balkh.[139] Finally, he got settled in Kashmir. His span of life coincided with the reign of Shah Jahan and the early decades of his successor. He was a nature poet, but his reputation has survived chiefly as a collector of prose specimens: *Ruqaat* or letters, documents, and rhetorical essays, familiar as *Resalah-Tughra, Miyar-ul-Idrak,* or the preface to the standard of perception in praise of *Hafiz's diwan, Firdauseyya* or Paradisical—a description of the beautiful city of Kashmir, *Taj-ul-Madaih* or the crown of eulogies—in praise of prince Murad Bakhsh, *Kenzul-Maani* the treasure of thought in praise of Shah Shuja, *Mujma-ul-Gharaib* or the collection of wonders, *Samar-i-Tibbi* or the medical fruit metaphors drawn from the medical art, *Tazkirat-ul-Akhyar* or memorial of the good. Mostly they were written on the known pattern of *Maqamat.* The work found entry into the curriculum of *Madrasah* education during the days of the later Mughals. Also he composed a *Saqi-nama* on Zuhuri's pattern which contained about five thousand verses. His *divan* is available.[140]

Tughra had introduced a large number of Indian words into Persian poems and written a *qasida* in Hindi in praise of Raja Jaswant Singh,[141] who was 6000 Amir of Shah Jahan and governor of Ahmadabad in 1068/1657. The poet used Tughra as his poetic surname but the poems which do not scan with that word contain Shifta[142] as penname. Tahir Nasrabdi says that in spite of the fact that he lives in comfort, he adopts Wahshat[143] as his penname. He died in Kashmir in 1078/ 1667.[144]

Hasil Mashhadi

Mirza Shah Baqir Husaini known as Hasil belonged to the Sadat family of Mashhad.[145] He was judicious and educated person.[146] He passed his time as scholar (prose) and poet.[147] Hasil migrated to India in Shah Jahan's reign without certain reason. Muhammad Sadiq Mina visited him at Jahangir Nagar (Dacca) in 1038/1628.[148] Muhammad Arif Darabi Shirazi says: I saw him at Surat. After some time he returned to Iran and died at Mashhad in 1070/1659.[149] According to Nasrabadi, for a while he was in the service of prince Murad Bakhsh.[150]

Table : 6.2
SCHOLARS

Rg	Pr	Nu	Reasons and Contexts of Migration																									
			X1	X2	X3	X4	X5	X6	X7	X8	X9	X10	X11	X12	X13	X14	X15	X16	X17	X18	X19	X20	X21	X22	X23	X24	X25	X26
NO	Ak	1	1																									
5	Ja	4		1													1				1							1
	Sh	0																										
WNW	Ak	2														1												1
6	Ja	4		1		1											1											1
	Sh	0																										
SW	Ak	0																										
3	Ja	3														1	1											1
	Sh	0																										
CP	Ak	1								1																		
11	Ja	9										1	1			1	2		1									3
	Sh	1											1															
SO	Ak	1													1													
7	Ja	4															3											1
	Sh	2											1															1
ENE	Ak	2																										2
5	Ja	2																				1	1					
	Sh	1																										1
SE	Ak	0																										
0	Ja	0																										
	Sh	0																										
UA	Ak	0																										
0	Ja	0																										
	Sh	0																										
	Total	37	1	2		1				1		1	3		1	3	8		1		1	1	1					12

Graph : 6.1

Number of Scholars according to the reasons and contexts of their migration

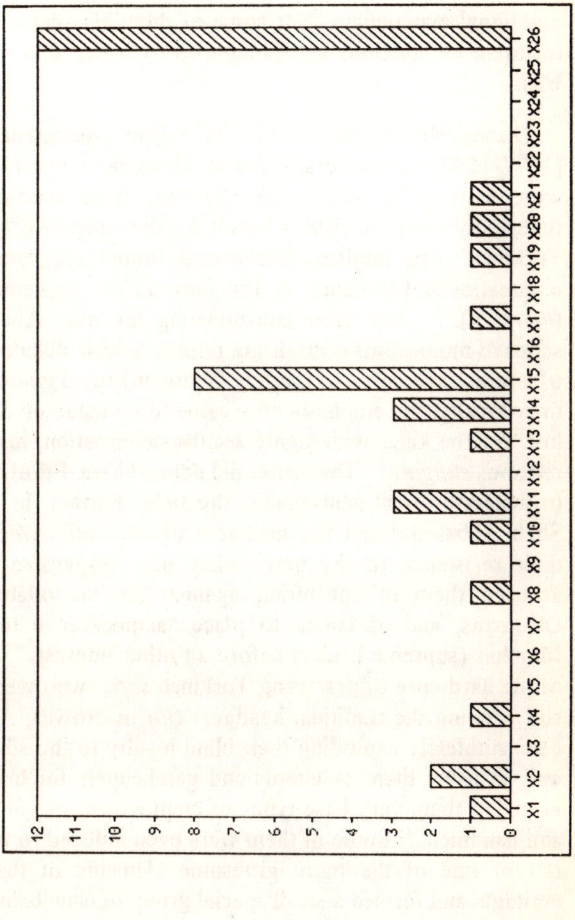

Sufi*, *Darvishes* and *Qalandars

A very significant group of Persian immigrants during our period included *sufis*, *darvishes* and *qalandars*. Most of them were motivated by a lust to wander and the quest of new spiritual or emotional experiences. But some of them also came running from the tortures, humiliations and indignities to which they were subjected in Iran.

During the unstable reign of Sultan Muhammad Khuda Banda (1577-1587) and the first years of Abbas the Great (1587-1629) which were marked by internecine Qizilbash tribal warfare, appeals were repeatedly made on Shah's behalf for the *sufigari* (*Sufi* probity) of the Turkmen. This implied *ikhalas* and *itiqad*, e.g., sincere loyalty and unqueationed obedience to the king as the supreme spititual leader (*murshid*).[151] But after consolidating his rule, Abbas carried out a series of momentous centralizing reforms which included the introduction of a new slave corps of (largely Georgian) royal *ghulams*.[152] To assure their loyalty, the emphasis now came to be made on *Shah-Sevani*, e.g., love for the king, with highly secular connotation, insead of the quasi-religious *sufigari*.[153] The matter did not end here. Efforts were encouraged to generate resentment against the *sufis*. Further, in 1614-15/1023-24 Shah Abbas ordered the massacre of the *Sufis*, when he feared that their resistance to the new policy may jeopardize his position. He accused them of conspiring against him in collaboration with the Ottomans, and of failing to place "acquiescence to the will of the Murshid (supreme leader) before all other interests".[154] As for the rest of the hard core of practising Turkmen *sufis*, who were distinguised by still wearing the traditinal headgear (*taj* or crown), Abbas had already been ruthlessly exploiting their blind loyalty to the supreme leader, not only in using them as guards and gatekeepers for his palace, but also in giving them very base types of employment as jailors, executioners, and hangmen.[155] Some of them were even induced to make a profession out of one of the more gruesome elements of their central Asian heritage, and formed a small special group of cannibalistic executationers whose function was the "live-eating" (*zindeh-khwari*) of the disgraced upon Abbas' order.[156] The Iranian *sufis'* migration in India is thus to be seen also in this context.

According to our major sources 19 Iranian *Shaiks*, *Sufis* and *qalandars* migrated to India. These sources mention different factors as reasons of their migration.[157] *Sharif-i-Shushtari* left Iran in 1585. He came to India in the company of his father Qazi Nurullah Shushtari. Sharif-i-Kashi and Talib Esfahani escaped to India in later days of

Akbar's reign because of persecution at the hands of the people of Kashan and Esfahan. Talib Esfahani a *darvish* and *Sufi*, was friendly with the luminaries of Akbar's court, and was appointed to the religious administrative post in the province of Gujarat during Jahangir's reign. Later he was given a diplomatic assignment in Kashmir. Safi Esfahani moved to India in search of safety and security as much as wealth. He was a *qalandar*, a calligraphist and also a poet. Amani and Wafai Esfahani, Rezai Farsi, Husain-i-Jami, Zamani Khurasani and Hozni Alavi migrated to India for ascetic, spiritual and *qalandari* reasons. Amani wandered alone, clad in skins, in several parts of India and was held in respect. Wafai Esfahani, a tramp, attached himself for some time to noble service.

There were also some *sufi*, *shaikhs*, who had been convicted in Iran as heretics, following which they escaped to India where Akbar's and to a certain extent Jahangir's liberal religious policy offered them refuge and freedom of belief. Javid-i-Qazwini, a believer in metempsychosis and possibly inclined towards Ismailism, gained access to Jahangir's service.

Nazri Qomshahi and Kalbi Zul-Qadr came to India for travelling. Nazri was attached to the military headquarter of Khan-i-Khanan.

Rasmi Qalandar and Golshan-i-Shirazi came to India in search of better opportunities. Rasmi was initially a *qalandar* and a *Sufi*, but later in India gave up the path of *qalandari* and joined service as a soldier under Khan-i-Khanan. Golshan was a *qalandar* and a poet. He belonged to Kurdish tribe of Shiraz. The reasons of migration of the remaining four, namely Makki, Fani Shirazi, Fathi Ardestani and Safi Turkman are unknown.

Among these 19 mentioned above, 5 persons came in later days of Akbar and 14 came during Jahangir's reign. None of them migrated to India during Shah Jahan's period, who was a contemporary of Shah Abbas II in Iran. The reign of Abbas-II (1642-1666) marked in certain respects the revival and reinstatement of the earlier status of the *sufis*, period of high *Sufism* and gnostic philosphy (*irfan*). The *sufi* virtuosity was once again respected and favoured by the Safavid Shah. Indeed Shah Abbas II is often described by his official historians as *Shah-e-Darvish dust* (the *darvish* loving Shah).[158] He used to frequent the *sufi* hospices to pay homage. In 1070/1661, he visited the Mulla Rajab Ali Tabrizi and Muhammmad Salih Lunbani.[159] In 1073/1663, he paid another visit to the convent of Darvish Muhammad Salih.[160]

Table : 6.3
IRANIAN SHAIKHS, SUFIS, QALANDARS AND *DARVISHES*

Name of migrants	Place of Birth	Provinces	Regions	Period of migration	Contexts and Reasons of migration	Position in Iran	Position in India	Place of Death
Sharif-i-Shushtari	Shushtar	Khusestan	South-West	Akbar 1585	In company of his father	Shaikh	Shaikh and *Qalandar*	Agra 1611
Sharif-i-Kashi	Kashan	Esfahan	Central Plateau	1587	Because of hostility and envy of the greatmen	Tailor and *darvish*	*Darvish*, service of Abdur-Rahim Khan-i-Khanan	Golkonda
Safi Esfahani	Esfahan	Esfahan	Gentral Plateau	In later days of Akbar	In search of security as much as wealth	*Qalandar, Sufi*	*Qalandar*, services of nobles, calligraphist and poet	Kabul 1618
Talib Esfahani	Esfahan	Esfahan	Central Plateau	In later days of Akbar	To escape the hands of the people of Esfahan	*Qalandar*	*Qalandar*, official Job, envoy of Akber' Court to the ruler of little Tibet; *sadr* of Gujarat during Jahangir's reign	India
Wafai Esfahani	Esfahan	Esfahan	Central Plateau	Jahangir	For ascetic and qaladari reasons	*Qalandar* and poet he belonged to Imamiya Turk	Nobles service, for a while he was wander in the desert.	Unclear
Amani Esfahani	Esfahan	Esfahan	Central Plateau	Jahangir	For ascetic and qalandari reasons	*Darvish* and poet	*Darvish* and poet	Unclear
Nazri Qomshehi	Qomsheh	Esfahan	Central Plateau	1614	To visit India	Afshar tribe, Sufi poet, soldier	Military head quarters of Khan-i-Khanan	Qomsheh 1645

Table Contd.

Fathi Ardestani	Ardestan	Esfahan Plateau	Central	1614	Unclear	*Sufi, darvish*	*Sufi, Darvish*	Unclear
Javid-i-Qazwini	Kharaqan	Qazwin	Central Plateau	1618	To escape the accusation of metempsychosis and heresy	*Sufi*	*Sufi* and poet regular salary from Ahmadabad mint by royal order	Unclear
Rasmi Qalandar	Yazd	Yazd	Central Plateau	Jahangir	In search of better opportunities	*Darvish* and poet	Job in Mughal army, service of Abdur-Rahim Khan-i-Khanan	Kashmir
Fani Shirazi	Shiraz	Fars	South	Akbar	Unclear	*Sufi*, scholar	Service of Khan-i-Khanan, poet, *darvish*, author of Ijaz Mafatihul-Eajaz	India
Golshani Shirazi	Shiraz	Fars	South	Jahangir	In search of better prospects	*Qalandar*, poet, he belonged to Kurdish tribe	*Qalandar* and poet	Iran
Rezai Farsi	Stehban	Fars	South	Jahangir	for ascetic and darvishi reasons	*Qalandar* and *darvish*	*Qalandar* and *Darvish*	Kashmir
Makki Shirazi	Shiraz	Fars	South	Jahangir	Unclear	*Sufi*	*Sufi*	India 1627
Husain-i-Jam	Jam	Khurasan	East and North-East	Jahangir	For ascetic and darvishi reasons	*Darvish*	*Darvish*, salary and gift by Jahangir	India 1614
Zamani Khurasani	-	Khurasan	East and North-East	Jahangir	for ascetic and darvishi reasons	*Sufi*	*Sufi*	Iran
Kalbi-zul-Qadr	-	-	Iran	Jahangir	To visit India	*Sufi*	*Sufi* and traveller	India
Hozni Alavi	-	-	Iran	Jahangir	For *qalandari* reasons	*Qalandar* and poet	*Qalandar* and poet	Iran
Saifi Turkman	-	-	Iran	Jahangir	Unclear	*Sufi*	*Sufi*	In the way of Gujarat to Agra

SOUTH-WEST OF IRAN

Sharif-i-Shushtari

Mir Sayyid Sharif was the son of Qazi Nur-ullah Shushtari. He migrated to India from Shushtar, a small town in the south west of Iran along with his father in 993/1584-85.He was among the great and meritorious men of his time. He died at Agra in 1020/1611.This verse is by him:

Yek chand sair-e-Agra-o-Lahoram arzu ast;
Boodan be majmah-i-pari-o-huram arzu ast.

He also composed some elegies about martyrdom of his father.[161]

CENTRAL PLATEAU

Sharif Kashi

Maulana Sharif belonged to the commoners of Badaqan, a village near Kashan. He had *sufic* temprament and inclinations, wore a patched garment and sought the company of *darvishes.* According to Nihavandi Sharif left Kashan for Khurasan. Later he came to India following the Uzbek invasions of Khurasan province in 996/1587.[162] Taqi Kashi says: Sharif migrated from his home to India in 994/1585, due to the hostility and envy of his contemporary poets and greatmen. He adds: Sharif served his time in Iran as a tailor and he was keen to associate himself with *darvishes.*[163] In India he joined the company of Khan-i-Khanan, and he died at Golkonda.[164]

Safi Esfahani

Aqa Safi was the son of Khwaja Qasim Mustaufi Esfahani. In early youth he travelled to many parts of Iran. Afterwards he migrated for safety to India (*Darul-Aman Hend*) in the later days of Akbar and found employment under Mirza Jafar Asaf Khan, who sent him on official duties to Kashmir and Sind.

Being a man of care-free disposition, he joined the company of the qalandars, filled with exalted ideas: possessing nothing and possessed by nothing, and thus, Safi roamed for years from one end to the other of Indian subcontinent.[165] The author of *Mai-Khana* once met him in Mandu, Malwa and obtained his verses for his book. Mahabat Khan, an important noble of Jahangir's time, was impressed by his intelligence and persuaded him to change his mode of living. At his insistence he gave up the *qalandar's* robe and returned to normal mundane life. The rest of his years were passed in Mahabat Khan's service, controlling the management of his land grants. When his master was posted as governor of Kabul he accompanied him there. He died in Kabul in 1028/1618. He was well versed in calligraphy and could write *Shikasta* very well.He also was a brilliant and witty poet. His contemporaries mentioned with admiration his verses, the following one in particular:

Khodavanda be eshgam rahbari Kon;
Khodai Karda Pighmbari Kon.[166]

"O God, guide me toward love, To be God must be enough; show, how to be a prophet."

Talib Esfahani

Baba Talib Esfahani shifted to India in his early youth to escape persecution at the hands of the people of Esfahan.[167] He went to Kashmir clothed in the garb of *qalandars* with antinomian tendencies.The beauty of the place and the pleasantness of its climate made him set his heart on the country and he settled there. After the Mughals conquered Kashmir he joined the service of Akbar, and became enrolled among the servants of the court. He lived long nearly 100 years, and he was with his sons and dependants in Kashmir, engaged in praying for the everlasting state.[168]

Badauni says: From Kashmir he was sent as envoy to the ruler of little Tibet (*Tibet-i-Khurd*) on his return presented to Shaikh Abul Fazl a treatise, which he had written on the wonders of that land, which Abul Fazl incorporated in the *Akbar Nama.*[169]

When Jahangir became king he was sent by him to summon Mirza Ghazi Beg Tarkhan, the Governor of Thatta (Sind) and afterwards appointed as the *sadr* of Gujarat. At that time he was working on the compitagin of the *Ma'asir i-Rahimi* in 1025/1616.[170]

Baba Talib died at the end of Jahangir's reign at the age of hundred years.[171] According to *Ain-i-Akbari* he was a thoughtful man and experienced in political matters.[172]

Wafai Esfahani

According to Badauni Wafai was in Kashmir for some time and then he shifted to Lahore and joined Zain Khan Kuka.[173] Badauni then cites the following verses attributed to Wafai:

Dar del-e-nim shaban koob ke chon rouz shavad;
Hama darha bekshainid-o-darash bar bandand.
Qaht-i-vafaast in ke nekooyan-i-roouzegar;
Khani nahand-o-khoon-i-del-i-mihman khorand.[174]

"Knock at the door of the heart in the middle of the night, For when the day appears, All other doors are opened, but this door is shut";

"The real death of fidelity is this, that the lovely ones of this age. Set out the well-spread table and then drink the heart's blood of the guest."

According to *Ain-i-Akbari*,[175] Wafai possesses sparkle of taste. He had been for some time wandering in the desert at retirement but has now put the mantle of worldliness on his shoulders.[176]

The author of *Atashkada* says: Wafai belonged to the *Imgadiya* Kurds, and was brought up at Esfahan, his *Rubai's* are good. Daghistani calls him a Turk, and states that Wafai at first was an *Uttukash* (Ironer). From a fault in his eye, he was called *Wafai-ye-koor*, "The blind Wafai".[177]

S. Kitabdar[178] says: Wafai Esfahani was an impolite man and he was not a poet, but considered himself so.

According to Auhadi Maulana Wafai was from Esfahan. He was a traveller for a long time and came travelling to India. He joined Zafar Khan, the son of Zain Khan in 1024/1615. He was in *sufi* garb when Auhadi saw him in Gujarat. Wafai had good knowledge about army and administration.[179]

Amani Esfahani

Mir Sharif Amani Esfahani came to India from Esfahan. He lived as a *darvish* for nearly 20 years.[180] Amin Razi says: for 50 years or so he was addicted to opium.[181] According to Molhemi Shirazi, Amani stayed at Lahore, and the people of that city confined and revered him. He lived as a gnostic (*arif*) and a poet.[182]

Nazri Qomshehi

Shaikh Shah Nazr better known as Nazri belonged to a noted family of Qomsheh, a city near Esfahan, inhabited by the Afshar tribe. He was a *sufi* and a poet. In addition to these merits, he had the inherited aptitude of a soldier. At the age of 20 he moved from his native place to Shiraz as a traveller, and then he sailed from the seaport of Hormuz and arrived in Burhanpur[183], the military headquarters of Khan-i-khanan. Shortly after his joining service in the army, a confrontation occurred (1018/11609) between the Mughals and Malik Ambar (d.1055/1625), the Abyssinian general of Bijapur king. Shah Nazar fought under the command of Khan-i-khanan's son, Mirza Iraj,[184] was seriously wounded, and carried away, almost half-dead, from the field. So bitter was his experience of battle that he at once announced his future determination in a quatrain: "If India were to be paradise, I shall prefer going to hell". The desire to visit Imam Reza's sacred shrine at Mashhad was a graceful way to go home.

Khan-i-khanan granted him permission to leave and paid lavish amount for the expenses of journey. Legends of his Indian visit were long remembered by his fellow-villagers and *Tazkira* writers who collected them from the later generations.[185] A gallant *sufi* full of tender feelings towards less fortunate people, he picked up from the streets of Esfahan a fallen woman, Khush-Nafis, as his wife.[186] In the realm of literature, he adhered to the path shown by great men of his category, and invariably composed quatrains.

According to Wali Quli Shamlu Heravi, Shaikh Shah Nazr died at Qomsheh in 1055/1645.[187]

Fathi Ardestani

Mulla Fathi was from Malikabad, a village in the suburb of Ardestan in Esfahan province. After receiving primary education in his native place he migrated to Esfahan. Later he came to Deccan. Auhadi saw him at Ajmer in 1025/1616. He had propensities of a *darvish* and a *Sufi*. Fathi composed some verses.[188] According to Azad-i-Bilgrami, Fathi died in 1045/1635.[189]

Javid Qazwini

According to *Khairul-Bayan*, his origin was from Kharaqan-i-Qazwin. He travelled to many cities of Iran and visited ascetics and renouncers. In his early life he chose the sufi path of piety. It is also said that he had fascination for metempsychosis. Javid shifted to Sistan in 1017/1608, and then he migrated to Hindustan, after he was accused of metempsychosis heresy which made stay in Iran difficult.[190] Javid was a youth of thirty, immersed in spiritual routines, when Abdun-Nabi, his fellow-townsman and author of *Tazkira*, saw him in India arriving fresh, from his homeland, Iran (1018/1609). A constant wanderer, he soon left for the holy cities of Mecca and Madina and again appeared in India after many years, presenting himself before the Itimad-ud-Daula, at the time of Jahangir's visit to Gujarat (1027/1617). On Itimad-ud-Daula's recommendation, the emperor summoned him to a private audience and was pleased by his manners. A royal order was issued for a regular grant of maintenance allowance for him payable from the Ahmadabad mint. The *darvish* Javid thus passed the rest of his life peacefully in that city. He was also authored a *masnavi* in Rumi's style, which both Abdun-Nabi and Taqi Auhadi have mentioned in their *Tazkiras*.[191]

Rasmi Qalandar

His name was Mir Abdur-Razzaq,[192] and belonged to Yazd. After receiving traditional education he became a *sufi* and wore a patched garment and sought the company of *darvishes*. In the course of his travels he came to India and stayed in Kashmir. There he cast off his ascetic garments and accepted a job in the Mughal army. He shifted to Lahore from there and entered the service of Abdur-Rahim Khan-i-Khanan.

Abdul-Baqi Nihavandi saw Rasmi in Golkonda in 1024/1615, and was impressed by his literary accomplishments. In a *qasida*, in praise of Khan-i-khanan, Rasmi mentioned all the important poets who received gifts from and benefitted from the patronage of that nobleman. Initially, a lover of freedom, he resigned from service and wandered towards Kashmir, where the rest of his life was spent in religious and intellectual pursuits.[193]

SOUTH OF IRAN

Fani Shirazi

Khwaja Muhammad Dehdar Shirazi better known as Fani was the son of Dehdar Mahmud Ayani. Khwaja Muhammad was a great Sufi, a scholar and a noted student of Mir Fathullah Shirazi[194] in traditional and rational sciences. He came to India in the reign of Akbar and enjoyed the patronage of Abdur-Rahman Khan-i-Khanan. Burhan Nizam Shah of Ahmadnagar conferred upon him a high position in his government. In his later life, Fani developed interest in sufism and retired to Surat, Gujarat, where he lived as a *darvish.* He died there at the age of 69 in 1016/1607. He composed several lucid verses and left a collection of *qasidas* and some books such as: Ijaz *Mafatih-ul-Eajaz*, comment in *Nafatul-Uns* and *Faslul-Khetab*.[195]

Golshani Shirazi

His origin was from Kurdish tribe, but he was born and brought up in Shiraz. Auhadi visited him at Jahangir's camp on his way from Ajmer to Mandu in 1025/1616. Golshani had earlier been in the Deccan. From Jahangir he received grant in cash and good. He lived at the Mughal camp for some time, then went back to Iran. He lived as a *qalandar* and as a poet, and had also some knowledge about music.[196]

Rezai Farsi[197]

Hakim Shah Reza was the son of Mir Jalal Jafar Stahbani. He was noted for his achievement in esoteric sciences, which eventually led him to the trajectory of a *qalandar* and *darvish.* He migrated to India from Stahban in Jahangir's reign. Later he moved to Kashmir and died there.[198]

Makki Shirazi

He was from Shiraz, but, he was brought up at Basra. Sayyid Omar Makki migrated to Mecca from Basra. He was Juris consult of Mecca people. Makki Shirazi came to India from Mecca in the reign of Jahangir. He was well-known for his *sufi* knowledge and *sufi* practices. He had profound knowledge of exoteric and esoteric sciences, and so many learned men of the time used to refer to him for solving their difficulties. He died in 1037/1627 in India.[199]

EAST AND NORTH—EAST

Husain Jami

His birthplace was Jam, a district of Khurasan, but he grew up in Shiraz. Having keen interest in *Sufism* he entered the circle of *darvish* Sabzez and was his disciple. In India he settled in Lahore, where he died in 1023/1614.[200]

Jahangir writes about Shaikh Husain Jami in his *Tuzak.* According to him he was one of the disciples of the *darvish* of Shiraz, had written to him from Lahore six months before his accession, mentioning about a dream that he had seen according to which saints and pious men delivered over the affair of the kingdom to him (Jahangir) and that, rejoicing in this good news, should await the event, and that he hoped that when it would occur, the faults of Khwaja Zakairiyya, who was one of the *Ahrariyas,*[201] would be pardoned. Jahangir adds saying that he sent 500 rupees to the *darvishes* though Shaikh Muhammad Husain Jami, and gave directions that each day one of the security officers[202] should give 50,000 *dams* to the *faqirs* Jahangir also says. As Shaikh Husain Jami had dreams about me which had come true, I gave him twenty lakhs of *dams* equivalent to 30,000 or 40,000 rupees, for his personal expenses and for his monastery and the *darvishes* who were with him.[203]

Zamani Khurasani

He belonged to Khurasan, but he spent most of his time in Shiraz. He acquired profound knowledge of exoteric and esoteric sciences and was extremely cognizant of all the head of traditional learning. Zamani was a follower of Khwaja Dahdar Mahmud Ayani Shirazi.[204] In old age he came to India and stayed here for some time, then he returned to Iran and died there. He passed his time as a *Sufi.* Auhadi says: I have seen him many times and I spoke to him.[205]

FROM UNCLEAR AREAS

Kalbi Zul-Qadr

Kalbi Beg was the son of Jani Beg. He was a *Sufi* and a poet. He travelled through many cities of Iran, then settled in Shiraz. Kalbi migrated to India from there. He travelled covering many parts of India until he died in India. His elder brother Ali Beg also spent most of his life as a *Sufi* and a poet. He died in Qazwin in the early years of Shah Abbas I.[206]

Hozni Alavi[207]

Mir Saif Ullah belonged to Alavi Sadat. He came to India during Jahangir's reign as a *qalandar.* Later he returned to Iran. He was witty and prudent in speech.Hozni left some verses.[208]

Saifi Turkman

His origin is traced from Oimaq Mosulo tribe. In his early youth, he was influenced by *Sufi* discipline and seemed to have wandered freely for many years. He migrated to India from Iran in the reign of Jahangir. For a while he was settled in Gujarat, and then he moved towards Agra in the company of Maulana Naziri,[209] but he died on the way in 1019/1610.[210]

Table : 6.4

SHAIKHS, SUFIS, QALANDARS AND *DARVISHES*,

Rg	Pr	Nu	Reasons and Contexts of Migration																									
			X1	X2	X3	X4	X5	X6	X7	X8	X9	X10	X11	X12	X13	X14	X15	X16	X17	X18	X19	X20	X21	X22	X23	X24	X25	X26
NO	Ak	0																										
0	Ja	0																										
	Sh	0																										
WNW	Ak	0																										
0	Ja	0																										
	Sh	0																										
SW	Ak	1								1																		
1	Ja	0																										
	Sh	0																										
CP	Ak	3						2					1															
9	Ja	6	1													1						1			2			1
	Sh	0																										
SO	Ak	1																										1
4	Ja	3														1									1			1
	Sh	0																										
ENE	Ak	0																										
2	Ja	2																							2			
	Sh	0																										
SE	Ak	0																										
0	Ja	0																										
	Sh	0																										
UA	Ak	0																										
3	Ja	3																				1			1			1
	Sh	0																										
Total		19	1					2		1			1			2						2			6			4

Graph : 6.2

Number of Sufis, *Darvishes*, and Qalandars according to the reasons and contexts of their migration

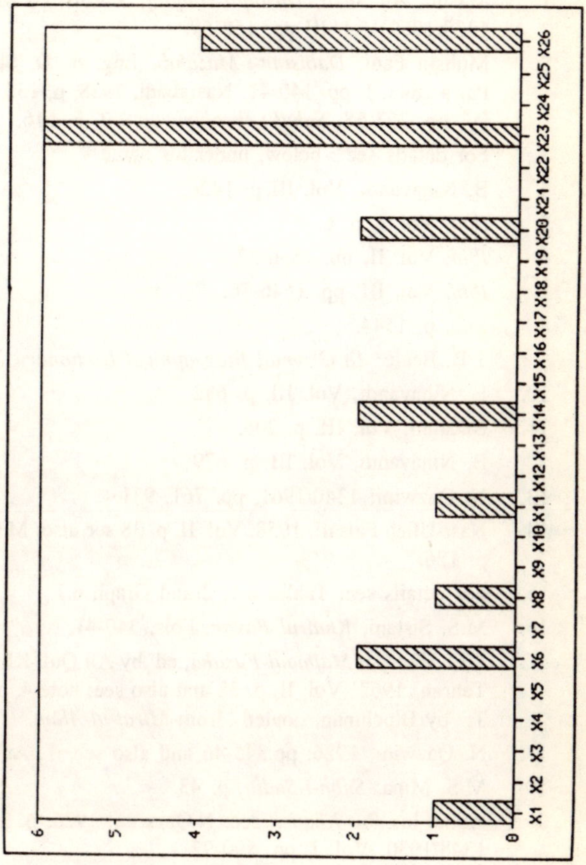

REFERENCES

1. Masum Ali Shah, *Taraiqal-Haqaiq*, 3 Vols, ed M.J. Mahjub, Tehran 1339/1960 Vol. III pp. 158-59.
2. Muhsin Fani, *Dabistan-i-Mazahib*, Eng. tr. D. Shea and A. Troyer, Paris 1843, I, pp. 140-41; Nasrabadi, 1938, p, 153, E. J. Browne, Vol. IV, pp. 257-58, *Suhuf-i-Ibrahim*, *op. cit,* F. 516.
3. For details see : below, under his name.
4. B. Nihavandi, Vol. III p. 1426.
5. *Ibid*, Vol. I, p. 6.
6. *Ibid*, Vol. II, pp. 1536-37.
7. *Ibid*, Vol. III, pp. 1546-76.
8. *Ibid*, p. 1544.
9. T.B. Beale, *An Oriental Biographical Dictionary,* London, 1894, p. 3.
10. B. Nihavandi, Vol. III, p. 682.
11. Badauni, Vol. III, p. 206.
12. B. Nihavandi, Vol. III, p. 679.
13. N. Qazwini; 1340/1961, pp. 761, 931.
14. Nasr Ullah Falsafi, 1958, Vol. II, p. 38 see also: M.Q. Gopamavi. 1957, p. 126.
15. For details see: Tables 6.1, 2 and Graph 6.1.
16. M.S. Sistani, *Khairul Bayan*, Fols. 340-41.
17. R.Q. Hadayat *Majmaul-Fusaha*, ed .by Ali Quli Khan 'Mukhbrut Daula Tehran' 1962' Vol. II, p. 38 and also see: note 4. p. 659, *Ain-i-Akbari*, Tr. by Blochman, qouted from *Mirat-ul-Alam*.
18. N. Qazwini, 1926; pp.345-46 and also see. T. Auhadi Fols: 702-3.
19. M.S. Mina, *Subh-i-Sadiq*, p. 43.
20. About his *But-Khaneh* see: N.Qazwini, 1926, p. 347 and A.G. Maani 1348/1930, Vol. I, pp. 590-97.
21. About his *Saqi nama* see: N. Qazwini, 1926, pp. 345-60.
22. A.A. Razi, 1939, Vol. III, pp. 128-32.
23. *Ain-i-Akbari*, *Ibid.*, 1869, Lucknow Press, Vol. I, p. 313 and also his Transls by Blochmann, Vol. I, pp. 659-60.
24. Findarski is village in Ramyan district in Gorgan. See: *Farhang-i-Moin*, *Ahlam*, Vol. VI, Findarsk.
25. See: *Ibid*, Vol. VI, Findarsk.
26. *Loghat-i-nama Dahkhuda* (lexicon) word of Abolqasim, p. 764.
27. Nasrabadi, p. 153.
28. Description about Yahya quatrain of Mir Findarski.

29. M.H. Akbari Savi, *Tufatul Murad* (Description of Findarski *qasida*)' Tehran' 1372 AS/1993, see: Preface.
30. T. Auhadi, Fol. 107.
31. Date of writing by Qazwini.
32. Qazwini, Fol. 421b.
33. *Azzorrieh*, Vol. XVIII, p. 57 for *Kashful-loghat-i-Juk ba Shast* see: Tehran Majlis Library; N. 4757. About description of 460 Indian *Loghat.* (word).
34. *Azzorrieh*, Vol. XVIII, p. 328.
35. *Ibid*, Vol. XVII, p. 197.
36. *Ibid*, Vol. XV, p. 89 and also: The list of manuscript copy, Qom, Marhashi Library, Vol. III, p. 162 this has been published in Bombay in 1267/1850 under the title, *Haqaya Qul Snayeh.*
37. *Azzorrieh*, Vol. II, p. 395 and also see: *Fihrest-i-Nuskhai* Khatti, *Ibid*, Vol. II, p. 203 for copy of this book see: Shushtari Library, Najafabad.
38. Azzorrieh, Vol. XVII, p.196 also see: *Fihrasti-Nuskhai Khatti Ibid*, Vol. II, p. 203.
39. *Azzorrieh*, Vol. XVII, p. 133, *Farhang-i-Moin*, Vol. VI, *Ahlam*, Findarski and also see: *loght-nama-Dahkhuda*, Word of Abulqasim, p. 764.
40. *Buhairah* has published in lithography, Tehran, 1328 A.H./1910.
41. N. Qazwini, 1926, pp. 443-49 and also see: T. Auhadi, Fol. 566.
42. B. Nihavandi, Vol. III, pp. 1423-26.
43. T. Auhadi, Fol. 597.
44. S.A. Hasan Khan Bhopali, 1878, pp. 522-23.
45. T. Auhadi, Fols: 767-68 and also see: S. Kitabdar, 1948, pp. 289-90.
46. See: *Ain-i-Akbari*, 1896, Lucknow Press, Vol. I, p. 318 and A.A. Razi, 1939, Vol. III, pp. 240-41.
47. See. Badauni, Tr. by Haig, Vol. III, pp. 408-9 also see: *Ain-i-Akbari*, Tr. by Blochmann, Vol. III, p. 474. The author of *Miratul Alam* got mistake between Fusuni Tabrizi, and Qomi. see: next.
48. A.A. Razi, Vol III, 1939, pp. 240-41.
49. T. Auhadi, Fols. 566-7 for details see: A.G. Maani, *Maktab-e-Wuqu*, Tehran, 1348 A.S./1969, 237-38.
50. M.T. Nasrabadi, 1938, pp. 411-12.
51. N. Tabrizi, Tazkira, Tehran, Malik library, N. 6456.
52. M. Arif Shirazi, *Latif-ul-khayal*, manuscript, 2 Vols in one, Tehran, Malik library N-4325.
53. I don't find this explanation in any book or *Tazkira*. Kalim Kashani had accompanied him in his voyage to the Deccan. (This is not correct because when Kalim Hamadami (Kashani) came to India in 1030/1620,

Nazim went to Mecca. see: A.G Maani, Tehran, 1969, Vol. I pp. 381-88.

54. N. Hadi, *Dictionary of Indo-Persian literature,* New Delhi, 1995, p. 457.
55. B. Nihavand; Vol. III, pp. 1535-44.
56. *Ibid*, p. 1545 also see: T. Auhadi, Fols: 491-92.
57. T. Auhadi, *Ibid.*
58. B. Nihavandi, Vol. III, p. 1546.
59. For details see: B. Nihavandi, *Maasir-i-Rahimi*, *Ibid* 3 Vols.
60. *Catalogue of Arabic and Persian;* MS in; Oriental Public Library Bankipur, Vol. III, p. 164.
61. M.S. Mina, *Subh-i-Sadiq*, p. 51.
62. Oriental Public Library, Cat. VII, 164 also see; A.G. Manni, 1969, Vol. II. pp. 746-47.
63. M.M.H. Lucknow, *Ibid*, 1964, pp. 432, 436.
64. W. Q. Shamlu Heravi, *Qasasul-Khaqani*, M.S. also see: W. Q. Shamlu Heravi, ed by Hasan Sadat Nasiri, 1995, Vol. II, p. 123.
65. For him see; N. Qazwini, 1926, pp. 401-403.
66. M.T. Nasrabadi; 1938 p. 401 also see: M.M.H Lucknowi, pp. 449-500.
67. B. Nihavandi, Vol. III, pp. 1674-75.
68. *Tabaqat-i-Akbari*, 1931, Vol. II, p. 514.
69. *Tabaqat-i-Akbari*, 1931, Calcutta Press, Vol. II, p. 513.
70. Badauni, Vol. II, p. 204 and Vol. III, p. 206.
71. *Ain-i-Akbari*, Tr. by Blochmann, Vol. I, p. 584.
72. *Tuzuk-i-Jahangiri*, Lucknow, Nawal Kishore Press, 1914, p. 70 and Tehran Press, 1359/1980, p. 83.
73. *Ain-i-Akbari*, Tr. by Blochmann, Vol. I, p. 584 also see : B. Nihavandi, *Ibid,* Vol. III, pp. 679-86.
74. T. Auhadi, Fols: 165-6 and see : *Khulasat-ul-Ashar*, MS.
75. M.A. Shushtari, *Risalih Ferdus*, Tehran, Anjum Athar-i-Melli, 1973; pp. 65-66 also see: A.A. Razi, 1961, Vol. I, p. 263.
76. M.S. Sistani, *Khairul-Bayan*, Fol. 407.
77. T. Auhadi, Fol. 227.
78. N.A. Shirazi, 1961, pp. 210-11.
79. B. Nihavandi, Vol. III, pp. 1406-08.
80. N. Qazwini, 1961, pp. 472-73.
81. T. Auhadi, Fol. 568.
82. N. Qazwini, 1961, p. 913.
83. See: A.R.Khaiyampur, 1961, p. 593.

84. A.G. Maani, *The Caravan of India,* 2 Vols, Mashhad, 1369 A.S/1990, Vol. II, p. 1421.
85. M.T. Nasrabadi, 1938, pp. 270-71.
86. M.A. Sarkhush, 1951, p. 59.
87. T. Auhadi, preface and Fols; 167-73.
88. T. Auhadi, Fol.11
89. M.S. Sistani, *Khairul Bayan*, Fol. 386.
90. M.T. Nasrabadi, 1938, p. 285.
91. A.A. Razi, 1961, Tehran Press, Vol. II, pp. 463-64 also see: T. Auhadi, Fol. 166.
92. T. Kashi, *Khulasatul-Ashar*; MS, Tehran, Malik Library, No. 4078.
93. M.Q.Sururi Kashani, *Majmaul-Furs*, ed. by Mahmud Dabir Siaqi, 3 Vols,Tehran, 1342 As/1963.
94. A.G. Maani, *Majmaul-Furs* (Forth writing) in: *Majalleh Danishkadeh Adabiyat va Hlum-i-Ensani*, Mashhad, No.I year.10 pp.105-125 for original copy of *Majmaul Furs* see: Mashhad; Astan-Qads-i-Razavi, No 10411.
95. T. Auhadi, Fol. 321.
96. A.G. Manni, *Ibid*, pp. 124-25. He survived *Saqi nama* (For his *Saqi nama*) see: A.G. Maani, 1980, pp. 242-48.
97. (M.S. Sistani, *Khairul-Bayan*, Fol. 395.
98. *Amal-i-Salih*, Vol. III, p. 435.
99. *Majmueh Munshat of Jalal*, Central library of Tehran University No. 2944, Firest, 10:1819 see also : M. M. H. Lucknow, 1964, pp. 148, 151 Lachmi Narayan, 1977, p. 55, Nurul-Hasan Khan, 1876, p. 121.
100. *Amal-i-Salih*, Vol. III, p. 435 see also; H. M. Elliot and John Dowson, *The History of India,* Vol. VI, p. 517.
101. *Amal-i-Salih*, Vol. III, pp. 435-36.
102. *Ibid* also see: B.P. Saksena, 1931, p. IV-V for copy of *Padashah nama* see; Hydarabad, cat. Vol. I, p. 244.
103. Aftab Asghar, *Tarikh Navisi dar Hend va Pakistan*, Lahore, 1364/1985, pp. 327-28.
104. see: Contemporary Historians during the reign of the Emperor Shah-jahan, in. *Islamic Culture*, Jan 1941, p. 65.
105. For copies see: *Asiatic society* (Curzon collection) No. 29, story, *Persian literature,* section II.
106. *Islamic Culture*, Jan, 1941, p. 65.
107. For copy see: Rieu, cat, Vol. II, p. 933.
108. see: Ethe, India office, Cat. No. 1771.
109. see: *Ibid*, No. 1552, I

110. see: *Ibid*, No. 1763. 21.
111. see: *Bankipore, Suppt. cat.* Vol. II, No. 2200 .
112. *Islamic Culture*, Jan, 1941, pp. 65-66.
113. Mali in; *Tazkira Nasrabadi* (p. 383) and *Farhang-i-Sukhanvaran* (p. 505) has mentioned Mani.
114. M.T. Nasrabadi, 1938, p. 383.
115. R.Q. Hadayat, 1878, Vol. I, p. 8 and Vol. II, p. 38 and also see: Maani, *The list of manuscript books of Astain-Quds-Razavi*, Vol. VII, No. 932 pp. 743-45 and see; A.G. Maani, 1969 Vol. I. p. 172-74.
116. About Mirza Ghazi Tarkhan and Wasli and Borujerdi'verses in praise of Mirza Ghazi Tarkhan, see: *M.U,* text Vol. III, pp. 345-48, *Maasir-ul-Umara* has mentioned Mir Niamatullah Asili instead of Wasli see: *Ibid*;
117. see: *M.U*, Text Vol. I, p. 106, 109.
118. For details see: *Tuzuk*, Tr. by Rogers, Vol, II. p. 402.
119. N. Qazwini, 1926, pp. 439-43.
120. *Ibid*, p. 468.
121. N. Qazwini, 1961, pp. 704-06.
122. N. Qazwini, 1926, pp. 468-74.
123. T. Auhadi, *Ibid*, Fols: 626-27.
124. Darab Khan was the son of Khan-i-Khanan, Darab Khan got *mansab* of 5000 in 1028/1618 and in place of his brother Shah Nawaz Khan (who was died because of drinking wine received the post of governor of Berar and Ahmadnagar.In rebe of Shah Jahan in 1033/1623, Darab Khan disobeyed from Jahangir's commands. Later he was killed by Mahabat Khan.See: *Jahangir nama*, 1980, pp. 306, 475 and also See: *Tuzuk*, Trby Rogers, Vol. II, pp. 49, 88, 158, 176, 127).
125. B.Nihavandi, Vol. III, pp. 1419-23 Campaigns of Deccan was in 1026/1616-17 and due to prince Khurram received to title of Shah Jahan, see; *Jahangir nama*, Tehran Press, pp. 217-25.
126. T. Auhadi, fol. 764
127. A.G Manni, 1669, Vol. II, pp. 87-105 also see: M.T. Nasrabadi, 1938, p. 185.
128. Danish Paju continuity in foundation of Iranian music, in: *First-i-Kitabai Chapi,* by Khan Baba Mushar; Tehran, Wazarat-i-Farhang, p. 167.
129 A. R. Khaiyampur, 1961, pp. 289, 367 also, see: H. Lahiji, *Tazkirat-ul-Measirin*, Esfahan, 1334/1955, pp. 19-20.
130. M.T. Nasrbadi, 1938, p. 202.
131. Q. Heravi, *Majma-ush-shuara-i-Jahangir Shahi*, ed Muhammad Salim Akbar, Karachi University, 1979 see also: T Auhadi, Fol. 594.

132. T.Auhadi, Fols, 513-14.
133. T. Auhadi, *Ibid*, fol.632.
134. N. Qazwini, 1926, pp. 560-62.
135. *Ibid*, p. 561 and also about Kaifi see: S.A. Hasan Khan Bohpali, 1878, p. 345 under the Kaifi Sistani.
136. M.T. Nasrabadi, 1938; p. 340.
137. M.G.A. Azadi-i-Bilgrami, 1913, p. 124.
138. M.T. Nasrabadi, 1938, pp. 339-40.
139. Prince Murad Bakhsh dispatched to conquer of Balkh in 1057/1647. Tughra has written *Mirat-ul-Futuh* or mirror of victories about conquest of Balkh and Badakhshan by prince Murad Bakhsh. see: *Amal-i-Salih,* Vol. II, p. 473 and A. Kashmiri, 1967, Vol. II, p. 745.
140. M.G.A.Azad-i-Bilgrami, 1913, pp.124-25, see also: K.M.A. Shah Kashmiri, 1855, pp. 151-52, A Kashmiri, ed, by Reshidi, 1967, Vol. II, pp.730-69, M.A Sarkhush, 1951, Madras Press, p. 121.
141. For Raja Jaswant Singh see: *Amal-i-Salih*, Vol. III, pp. 329-31, 449.
142. A. Kashmiri, 1967, Vol. II, pp. 735-36 qouted from *Majma-un-Nafais*, MS.
143. M.T. Nasrabadi, 1038, p .340.
144. Rieu, Vol. II, p. 742.
145. M.S. Mina, *Subh-i-Sadiq*, p. 66.
146. M.T. Nasrabadi, 1938, p. 140.
147. M.A. Darabi Shirzi, *Lataif-ul-Khayal*, MS.
148. M.S. Mina. *op.cit*, p. 66.
149. M.A. Darabi Shirazi, *Lataif-ul-Khayal*, MS.
150. M.T. Nasrabadi, 1938, P.140 see also, A.R. Khaiyampur, 1961, pp. 76, 146.
151. A.H. Navai,ed. *Asnad va Mukatibat-e-Tarikhi;Shah Abbas-e Avval*, Tehran, 1352/1973, vol. I, p. 125 and vol. II, p. 17; N. Falsafi, 1961, vol. I, pp. 184-85.
152. *The Cambridge History of Islam,* vol. I, pp. 418-19.
153. *Nq.A.* 1971, pp. 288-89; *A.A.A.* 1971, vol. I, p. 431 and Vol. II, pp. 617, 655, 734, 1000.
154. *Ibid*, Vol. II, p. 882.
155. N. Falsafi, 1961, Vol. I, pp. 184-86 and Vol. II, pp. 123-27, 407.
156. *Ibid*, Vol. II, pp.125-27.
157. For details see: Below, table 6.3 and graph 6.2, see also text.
158. M.M.T. Wahid Qazwini, 1950, p. 321.
159. *Ibid*, pp. 254-55.

160. *Ibid.*, p. 321.
161. M.A.M. Shushtari, 1973, pp. 37-39 also see: A.Darabi Shirazi, *Tazkira Latiful-Khayal*, Tehran, Malik Library, 4325, MS.
162. B. Nihavandi, Vol. III, pp. 811-815 also see: M.S. Sistani, *Khairul-Bayan*, fols, 275-76.
163. T. Kashi, *op.cit*, MS.
164. M.S. Sistani, *Khairul-Bayan,* fol. 276 also see: T. Auhadi, fols: 376-77.
165. T. Auhadi,fol.405 also see: A.A. Razi,Tehran Press, Vol. II, pp. 232-33.
166. N. Qazwini, Lahore Press, pp. 548-50 also see: N. Qazwini, Tehran Press pp. 429-31 For details see: B. Nihavandi, Vol. III, pp. 1653-55 and also see: M.T. Nasrabadi, 1938 p. 305.
167. T. Kashi, *op.cit*. MS also see: B. Nihavandi, Vol. III, p. 1259, but the author of *Khairul-Bayan* says: He came to India in old age in garb of a *Darvish* (see:M.S. Sistani, *op.cit*, fols:373-74.
168. *Jahangir Nama*, Tehran Press, p. 325 also see:*Tuzuk* Tr. by Rogers, Vol. p. 119.
169. Badauni, Vol. III, p. 265 also see : Badauni, TR. by S.W. Haig Vol. III, p. 367 and see, *A.N.* No. III, pp. 523, 552.
170. B. Nihavandi, Vol. III, pp. 11259-66 also see : T. Auhadi, Fol. 422, For details about Talib Esfahan, see : A. Kashmiri, 1967, Vol. II, pp. 266-73 also see : K.M.A. Shah Kashmiri, *Tarikh-i-Azami;* Lahore, 1303 A.H/1885, pp. 114-15 Calcutta, 1865, p. 133.
171. M. Sharif, *Iqbal Nama Jahangiri*, Calcutta, 1865, p. 133.
172. *Ain-i-Akbari*, Vol. I, p. 607.
173. For Zain Khan Kuka see; *Akbar nama*, Vol. I, p. 222 and Vol. III, pp. 796-97, see also, *Tabaqat-i-Akbari*, Vol. II, p. 431, and A.A. Razi 1961, Vol. I, p. 469, and *M.U* text, Vol. II, p. 369.
174. Badauni, Vol. III, p. 385 and *Ibid.*, Tr. by S.W. Haig, p. 520 also see; *Tabaqat-i-Akbari*, Vol. II, p. 516.
175. *Ain-i-Akbari*, Lucknow press, 1869, Vol. I, p. 314.
176. His impudent flattery was proverbial (Daghistani).
177. *Ain-i-Akbari*, Tr. by, Blochmann, Vol. I, note I, p. 662.
178. S. Kitabdar, 1948, p. 289.
179. T. Auhadi, Fol. 793-94.
180. Badauni, Vol. III, p. 184.
181. A.A. Razi, 1961, Vol. II, pp. 346-47.
182. B. Nihavandi, Vol. III, pp. 1400-1406.
183. T. Auhadi says; Nazri was Tourist and came to India for travelling in garb of *darvish*. For details see : T. Auhadi, Fol.375 The author of

Maasir-i-Rahimi has mentioned something mistake; he says Narzi arrived to Inida in 1023/161114 and visited *Khan-i-khanan* at Gujarat see: B. Nihavandi, Vol. III, pp. 14471-73.

184. About Mirza Iraj, son of khan-i-khanan see; *Jahangir Nama*, pp. 305-6 and M.U, text, Vol. II, pp. 645-48.

185. See: Qazwini, 1926, pp. 543-46 and also see: B. Nihavandi, Vol. III, pp. 1471-73.

186. M.T. Nasrabadi, 1938, pp. 277-78.

187. W.Q. Shamlu, Heravi, *Qasasul-khaqani*, manuscript, Tehran Majlis Library, numbers 2155 and 2156 also see : W.Q. Shamlu Heravi, 1995, Vol. II, pp. 110-111.

188. T. Auhadi, fol. 563 also see : M.T. Nasrabadi, 1938, p. 276.

189. M.G. Azad Bilgrami, 1913, pp. 49-50.

190. M.S. Sistani, *Khairul-Bayan*. fol. 370.

191. N. Qazwini, Lahore Press, pp. 575-77 also see: T. Auhadi, Fol. 193.

192. M.M.H. Luknowi, 1964, p. 241.

193. B. Nihavandi, Vol. III, pp. 1297-98.

194. Mir Fathullah was learned man of Fars, he entered to Akbar's court in 990/1582,and received title of Izzit-ud-daula and *mansab* of *Amin-ul-Mulk*, he died at Kashmir in 997/1588 because of Diarrhoa.

195. T. Auhadi, Fols: 705, 707 also see: R.L.M. Shafiq Aurangabadi, 1977, pp. 186-87, S.A. Hasan Khan Bhopali, 1878, p. 307 also see : A.J. Malika Puri, 1950, p. 578.

196. T. Auhadi, *Ibid*, 629-30.

197. About Reza Shirazi and Reza Farsi (See: S.Nafisi, *History of prose* and *verse in Iran*, Tehran, 1344/1965, pp.676, 709 also see: M.M.H. Lucknowi, 1964, p. 245, R.Q. Hadayat, *Reyazul-Arifin*, Tehran, 1305 A.M/1887, p. 195 and A.R. Khaiyampur, 1961, p. 231.

198. T. Auhadi, Fol. 269.

199. M.S. Dehlavi Hamadani, *Tabaqat-i-Shah Jahani*, Fols. 299b-300A.

200. M.S. Dehlavi Hamadani, *Tabaqat-i-Shah jahani*, Fols. 296-98.

201. That was descended from the famous Central Asian saint Khwaja Ahrar.

202. The word Yatish is omitted in text but occurs in the MS.

203. See; *Tuzuk*, Tr. by Rogers, pp. 30, 46, 72.

204. Khwaja Muhammad Dahdar Shirazi well known to Fani was one of Great *Sufis* of his time.He came to Deccan and entered in the service of Ali Adil Shah, Murteza Nizam Shah and Burhan Nizam Shah Sani.Later he went to Burhanpur and joined to Khan-i-Khanan. Afterwards he moved to Surat and settled there. He died in the age of 69 in 1016/1607 at Surat.

205. T. Auhadi, fol. 282-83.
206. T. Auhadi, fols:630-31 also see: M.S.Sistani, *Khairul-Bayan* p. 121.
207. Hozni Akbarabadi in *Rauz-i-Raushan* is same person, see: M.M.H Lucknow, 1879, p. 169.
208. For details about Hozni and his verses see:T. Auhadi, M.S, under the name of Hozni.
209. Naziri visited Jahangir in 1019/1610. See: *Jahangir Nama*, Tehran Press, p. 108.
210. T. Auhadi, Fol. 325.

7

Artists, Craftsmen and People With Diverse Skills

Mughal empire was a place where the wishes of aspiring artists were fulfilled with unmatched generosity. Large number of people of excellence and quality, men of pen, artists, calligraphers, skilled artisans, and other skilful persons from various cities of Iran, like from other parts of the world visited he imperial court as well as the nobles establishments with expectations and anticipations. They entered into the service of the Mughals, which served as a kind of asylum for the people of the entire world.

In this part we will try to identify those Iranian artists and craftsmen who came temporarily or permanently to India in the period under our review. There were 47 Iranians immigrants during this period who were principally known as artists (*hunarmants*), even as they were also poets. Among these 47, 3 persons came from the north, 7 from the regions in the west and north-west, 21 from the central plateau, 10 from the south, 3 from regions in the east and north-east, and about the remaining 3 our sources are unclear.

Out of these 47 people, 6 of them came to India in the later days of Akbar's reign, 30 persons in the reign of Jahangir and 11 during Shahjahan's reign.[1]

Among these artists-cum-poets, Tajalli Gilani, Jesmi Hamadani, Yusuf Aziz Esfahani, Siraja and Ali Esfahani migrated to India for joining the services of Abdur-Rahim Khan-i-Khanan and Jahangir.

Most of them, eighteen, came as adventurers in search of better opportunities, knowing that the Mughal court was open to talented people, where by merit they might be able to achieve distinct positions and *mansabs* in the Mughal government. The most important of these were Said-i-Gilani, who received the title of Bibadal Khan and a *mansab* of 1000 *zat* from Jahangir and was also weighed in gold by Shahjahan. Others were: Fayeq-i-Lahijani, who was in the service of the governors of Gilan and Mazandaran in Iran, and was sent to Sistan and Herat as an ambassador by Mirza Gazi Tarkhan and Abul-Bi-Uzbek, the governors of Qandahar; Wasfi Kermani a famous calligraphist and powerful poet, who was granted the title of Meshkin Qalam by Akbar. He composed verses and left a *divan;* Bahri Kashani who migrated to India during Jahangir's reign in order to better his prospects, and served as the binder in Dar-ul-Saltant of Lahore; Suti Yazdi, who was a musician and a poet, and received gift from Shah Jahan; Iksir Esfahani who was a *katib* (*insha navis*) of Shah Jahan's court.

Among still others Mir Sayyid Ali Tabriz came to India on Shah Jahan's invitation. He received the title of Jawahar Raqami by Shah Jahan. Muhammad Baqir Khurdah Kashani was accused to heresy because he followed the path of Mahmud Pasikhani, the founder of Nuqtawi sect. Muhammad Baqir suffered hardship in prison for two years. After release he escaped to India in 1597 and joined Nizam Shah's court. After some time he was attached to Adil Shahi's government and then he went to Bengal. Mir Muhammad Mumin and Mir Muhammad Salih came to India during Akbar's reign in the company of their father.

Ali Esfahani, architect and Ibrahim Farsi, calligraphist and secretary of Ibrahim Khan Fath Jang, migrated to India with an objective of visiting. Amini Mashhadi who had come to India to escape the disaster in the wake of Uzbek attacks on Khurasan. He was gilter of Imam Reza Library at Mashhad, and designer and decorator of Khan-i-Khanan's library in India. Muhammad Naii Neyrizi, who was a musician and a poet, left Iran when he lost royal favour there. He joined Khan-i-Khanan's service and later he received the title of Ishrat Khani by Jahangir.

Ismail Nasrabadi and Samandar Shamlu came to India to visit their relatives. The reasons of the migrations of the remaining 14 are unclear.[2]

Table : 7.1
Artists and Craftsmen

Name of migrants	Place of Birth	Provinces	Regions	Period of migration	Contexts and Reasons of migration	Position in Iran	Position in India	Place of Death
Tajalli Gilani	Rudsar	Gilan	North	Jahangir	Service of Khan-i-Khanan	Calligraphist	Calligraphist, poet	Unclear
Saida-i-Gilani		Gilan	North	Jahangir	Betterment his prospects	Poet, Calligraphist, engraver and goldsmith	He received title of Bibadal Khan from Jahanger, *Dargha* of goldsmith and *mansab* of 1000 *zat*	Unclear
Fayeq-i-lahijani	Lahijan	Gilan	North	Jahangir	betterment his prospects	Service of Gilan and Mazandaran's governors	Calligraphist, Musician, Mirza Ghazi Khan and Abul Bis's ambassador to Sistan and Herat respectively	Unclear
Jesmi Hamadani	Hamadan	Hamadan	West and North- West	Jahangir	Service of Khan-i-Khanan	Calligraphist, Musician and poet	Service of Khan-i-Khanan	Unclear
Raunaqi Hamadani	Hamadan	Hamadan	West and North-West	Twice 1616, 1619	In search of better opportunities	Musician and poet	Musician and poet	India 1628
Chalabi Tabrizi	Tabriz	Azarbaijan Sharqi	West and North-West	Jahangir	In search of better opportunities	He was esteemed to Itizad-Daula Farhad Khan governor of Tabriz	Calligraphist, poet service of Jahangir	Iran

Table Contd...

Table Contd...

Rafati Tabrizi	Tabriz	Azarbaijan Sharqi	West and North-West	Jahangir	In search of better opportunities	Calligraphist	Calligraphist	Iran
Wesali Tabrizi	Tabriz	Azarbaijan Sharqi	West and North-West	Jahangir	Unclaear	Calligraphist and poet	Calligraphist and poet	India
Jawahar Raqam Tabrizi	Tabriz	Azarbaijan Sharqi	West and North-West	Shahjahan	Shahjahan's invitation	Calligraphist	Jawahar Raqami by Shah Jahan	Delhi 1682
Muqim Tabrizi	Tabriz	Azarbaijan Sharqi	West and North-West	Shahjahan	In search of better opportunities	Calligraphist	Calligraphist	India
Baqir Kashani	Kashan	Esfahan	Central Plateau	Akbar 1597	Naqtawi sect	Calligraphist and poet	Poet, calligraphist	Burhanpur 1628
Wasfi Kermani	Kerman	Kerman	-do-	Akbar	In search of better opportunities	Calligraphist and poet	Title of Meshkin Qalami by Akbar	Ajmer 1616
Mir Muhammad Mumin Akbarabadi	-do-	-do-	-do-	-do-	In company of his father	Calligraphist and poet	Calligraphist and poet	India 1680
Mır Muhammad Salih	-do-	-do-	-do-	-do-	-do-	-do-	-do-	India 1650
Yusuf Aziz Esfahani	Esfahan	Esfahan	-do-	Jahangir	Service of Jahangir	Goldsmith, poet	Goldsmith, poet	Agra

Table Contd...

Table Contd...

Siraja Esfahani	-do-	-do-	-do-	Jahangir 1615	Service of Khan-i-Khanan	Musician; astronomer and poet	Khan-i-Khanan's service	Unclear
Ali Esfahani (Musannef)	-do-	-do-	-do-	Jahangir	Service of Khan-i-Khanan	Musician and poet	Musician, poet	Unclear
Zamani Esfahani	Esfahan	Esfahan	Central Plateau	Jahangir	Unclear	Calligraphist and poet	Calligraphist and poet	Unclear
Zaman Esfahani	-do-	-do-	-do-	-do-	-do-	Goldsmith and poet	Goldsmith, poet	Lahore 1644
Ali Esfahani	-do-	-do-	-do-	1608	Travelling	Architect and	-	Unclear
Bahari Kashani	Kashan	-do-	-do-	Jahangir	In order to better his prospects	Poet, Binder	Binder of Dar-ul-Saltant of Lahore	-do-
Baqiyai Naini	Nain	Esfahan	Central Plateau	1614	Unclear	Musician and poet	Service of Itimad-ud-daula, musician, weighed in silver by Shahjahan	Benares
Sirati Qazwini	Qazwin	Qazwin	-do-	Jahangir	-do-	Great family of Qazwin, calligraphist, poet	Calligraphist and poet	Unclear
Muizz Yazdi	Yazd	Yzad	-do-	-do-	-do-	Calligraphist	Calligraphist	India 1625
Shamimi Yazdi	-do-	-do-	-do-	1618	-do-	Calligraphist, musician and pot	Noble's service	Karnataka

Table Contd...

Table Contd...

Suti Yazdi	Yazdi	-do-	Shahjahan	-do-	in order to be better his prospects	Musicion and poet	He received gift from Shahjahan	Iran 1669
Ismail Nasrabadi	Nasrabad	Esfahan	-do-	-do-	To visit his uncle Mirza Ghiyas	Calligraphist and poet	Service of Mahabat Khan	India
Iksir Esfahani	Esfahan	Esfahen	Central Plateau	-do-	In search of better opportunities	*Katib* (*Insha nawis*) poet	*Katib* of court	Unclear
Wahshat Ardestani	Zavareh	-do-	-do-	-do-	-do-	Tabatabai Sayyid of Ardestan	Calligraphist and poet	-do-
Rashida Abbasi	Abbas Abad of Esfahan	-do-	-do-	-do-	-do-	Goldsmith, enamelist and poet	Goldsmith, enamelist and poet	Esfahan
Asaf Qomi	Qom	Qom	-do-	-do-	-do-	He belonged to Baharlu tribe, *Katib*	Poet	Unclear 1682
Forsi Shidani	Shidan of Fars	Fars	South	Akbar	Unclear	Calligraphist	Librarian of Akbar and Jahangir, title of Maktub Khan from Jahangir	Unclear
Muhammad Naii Neyrizi	Neyriz	-do-	-do-	Jahangir	Losing royal favour	Musician and poet	Khan-i-Khanan's service, title of Ishrat Khani from Jahangir	-do-
Walih Shirazi	Shiraz	-do-	-do-	-do-	In search of employment	Calligraphist	Noble's service	India

Table Contd...

Table Contd...

Moshin Shirazi	Shiraz	Fars	South	1623	In order to better his prospects	Shah Abbas's service	Calligraphist and poet	Unclear
Ibrahim-i-Farsi	-do-	-do-	-do-	Jahangir	For travelling	Calligraphist and travelling	Secretary of Ibrahim Khan Fath Jang	-do-
Asiri Shirazi	Shiraz	Fars	South	Jahangir	Unclear	Calligraplhist and pet	Calligraphist and poet	-do-
Muhammad Tanburah	-do-	-do-	-do-	1014	Musician,	Jahangir's painter, poet	-do- painter, title of Maktub Khan from Jahangir	
Ruzbeh Shirazi	Shiraz	-do-	-do-	Jahangir	-do-	Calligraphist, gilder and poet	Calligraphist gilder and poet	-do-
Atai Cherudi Shirazi	-do-	-do-	-do-	-do-	-do-	Calligraphist	Khan-i-Khanan's service	-do-
Abul -Baqa Abarquii	Abarqu	-do-	-do-	Shahjahan	In search of better opportunities	Sadat family of Abarqu, calligraphist and poet	Noble's service	Iran
Amini Mashhadi	Mashhad	Khurasan	East and North-East	Akbar 1587	Uzbek pressure	Great gilter of Imam Reza Library, expert in dyeing and colouration	Designer and decoration of Khan-i-Kahana's library and poet	Mashhad

Table Contd...

Table Contd...

Mumin Gonabadi	Gonabad	-do-	-do-	Jahangir	In search of better opportunities	Calligraphist and poet	Calligraphist and poet	Unclear
Khadim Heravi	Heart	-do-	-do-	-do-	Unclear	Bow-maker, calligraphist, poet	Poet and calligraphist	-do-
Mujrim Shamlu	Iran	-	Unclear	Jahangir 1606	Unclear	His ancestors were in the service of Safavid kings	Calligraphist, musician and poet	Ahmadabad 1611
Abdul-Haq	Iran	-	Unclear	Shah-jahan	For employment	Calligraphist	Rank of 1000 *zat*, 200 *sawar*, title of Amant Khan from Shahjahan	India
Samandar Shamlu	-do-	-	Unclear	-do-	His relatives were in India	Shamlu tribe	Musician and poet	Junnar

NORTH IRAN

Tajalli Gilani

Maulana Tajalli belonged to Rudsar of Gilan. He was the son of Mulla Sulaiman, who was one of the most learned men of Gilan. Tajalli had also acquired proficiency in all branches of learning under the care of his father and was expert in the art of writing *Khat-i-shikasta*. In the beginning he entered the service of Mulkash Sultan Istajllu of Qizilbash tribe. He composed poems under the surname of Jamali. The Sultan was a man of fine taste and appreciated poetry and patronised poets. From there he shifted to Mashhad to pay homage to the holy shrine of Imam Musa Reza and later he migrated to India and joined the retinue of Khan-i-khanan. Here he changed his poetic name from Jamali to Khawari.

At the time of the composition of *Maasir-i-Rahimi*, he was in Golkonda and Hyderabad, wrote poetry under the pen name of Tajalli. For a long time he was attached to literary circle of Khan-i-Khanan and was staying with him at Burhanpur. His poems show his mature taste and acquaintance with old and new masters in Persian poetry. He had a ready pen and could compose with ease and quickness. In 1012/1613, he took leave from Khan-i-Khanan to go on a pilgrimage to the holy cities of Mecca and Karbala-i-Mualla. Nothing further is known about him. He has written many poems describing the buildings of Khan-i-Khanan.[3]

According to T.Auhadi he changed his title from Khavari to Tajalli. Katib, the author of *Arafat,* has mentioned him as Khavari Semnani instead of Khavari Gilani. Auhadi saw him in Qandahar. He says that Tajalli came to India accompanying us in 1015/1606 and that his title was Tajalli in India.[4]

M.T.Nasrabadi has mentioned him under the surname of Lahiji, but he adds that in the beginning his title was Khavari which was later changed to Tajalli.[5]

Saida-i-Gilani

Saida-i-Gilani as the name suggests hailed from Gilan. He came to India during the reign of Jahangir in search of fortune. He had received a good education and was well versed in the art of trade and commerce. He was expert in calligraphy. He was also adept in the art of cutting and polishing stones (engraving) and in appreciation of this quality of his that he was made *Darogha-i-Zargar-Khana* (superintendent of goldsmithy) by Jahangir. This post he retained till the time of Shah Jahan. In recognition of his merits Jahangir had also conferred upon him the title of Bibadal Khan.[6] It was under his personal supervision that the famous Peacock Throne of Shah Jahan was made, and Shah Jahan was so much please by his workmanship that he had him weighed in gold.[7] He was expert in composing chronograms. After the conquest of Kangra, Bebadal Khan presented a chronogram to Jahangir. He recorded it in his memoirs as according to him Bibadal Khan composed it well.

"World-gripper word-giver, world-holder, world-king,
with the sword of Ghazi-ship he conquered this fort.
Wisdom spoke the date the Jahangir fortune opened this fort.
He also composed the chronogram of the building of the mosque".[8]

According to Qazwini, Saida had a wonderful fluent nature and powerful imagination. He was matchless in most of the arts of his age.

He was honoured during the reign of Jahangir with the title of Bibadal Khan, and the office of the *Darogha* of Goldsmithry. As a result of his majesty's patronisation his status was enhanced and he was promoted to a *mansab* of 1000. He was a very kind, gently, jolly and soft-spoken person. These are some of his verses:

"That moon is coming mounted on a horse with golden stirrup.
He is coming with a face which causes jealousy for thousand suns.
Today the diamond is water and the flag flower a sword, tomorrow the ruby-coloured lily will become the fire of armour."[9]

Fayeq-i-Lahijani

Shamsai Zarrin Qalam was born in Lahijan. In the beginning he had received education under Mosayyeb Khan Takllu.[10] who was the governor of Tehran. For a long time he was in the service of Gilan and Mazandaran's kings and governors. After that he moved to Qandahar and was attached to Mirza Ghazi Khan,[11] and stayed there for one year, then he went to Sistan as an ambassador. In 1021/1612 Mirza Ghazi died and Abul Bi[12] was appointed as the governor of Qandahar. Abul Bi also dispatched Fayeq to Heart as a ambassador. According to Sistani: Presently Fayeq (1023/1614) is esteemed of Jahangir Badashah. He was very well versed in calligraphy and could write *Naskh* and

Nastaliq very well. He was also a skilled musician.[13] According to Auhadi, Shamsai Fayeq was eloquent and prudent in speech. He came to Qandahar and entered the service of Mirza Ghazi Khan.[14]

WEST AND NORTH-WEST

Jesmi Hamadani

Maulana Kamalud-Din Jesmi belonged to Hamadan. His ancestors had always enjoyed wealth, honour, and position in their country. Jesmi due to his natural inclination took to poetry, after finishing his education.

He was one of the pupils of Mirza Ibrahim Hamadani. He was a versatile genius and knew calligraphy, music and mathematics. His poems are even and free from all the defects that are found in the poems of the other common poets of the age. In the heyday of Safavid kings he enjoyed favour in the court of kings their ministers and noble men of Iran. For some time he even acted as a *divan* and in that capacity laid down certain rules and principles, that were conducive to the well-being and prosperity of the people. He never cared for money and was never accused of any crime. Before coming to India, he went to Shiraz and passed some time there; from Shiraz he came to Surat by way of port of Jarun (Bandar Abbas). He stayed there for some time and then came to Muhammadabad Gujarat. At that time Naziri Nieshahbouri was staying there. He held poetical contests with him and then repaired to the court of Abdur Rahim Khan-i-Khanan via Ahmadabad, and got a job in army with him at Burhanpur. He composed chronograms of buildings of Khan-I-Khanan at Burhanpur and wrote *qasidas* in his praise.

One of the *qasidas* that he composed in praise of Khan-i-Khanan contains the following lines:

Jaz ba shoq keshanid be shiraz mara,
Ta khod in jazba resanad be koja bare mara
Qatreim-o-dar dast-i-sahab oftada,
Mibard ta be che darya fekanad baz mara.

"The force of love drove me to Shiraz;
I do not know where will this force carry me.
I am a drop of water and have fallen in the hands of cloud;
I do not know in which ocean it will drop me again."[15]

Raunaqi Hamadani

Maulana Raunaqi Hamadani lived as a poet, and musician.[16] He was a student of Maulana Sharari Hamadani and was well versed in his style. Raunaqi migrated to India in 1025/1616 for security reasons and attached himself to Khwaja Darya Dle Raushan Zamir and Khwaja Abul Hasan Turbati.[17] According to Auhadi, Raunaqi composed a chronogram (1027/1617) when *darvish* Sabri Esfahani carried away the bones of Urfi (d. 999/1590) for burial to Najaf in compliance of the great poet's will that his mortal remains be mingled with the dust of that city ennobled due to its association with the name of his spiritual master and Imam Ali ibn Abi Talib. Raunaqi collected his verses in a *diwan.*[18]

M.S. Sistani contains the following notice of him:"

''His birth place was Hamadan. He shifted to paradise like-India from his native place in 1023/1614. He was in the service of Khwaja Abul Hasan Turbati for five years.[19] Afterwards he returned to Iran. After one year again he migrated to India in 1029/1619.[20] Raunaqi died in India in 1038/1628''[21]

Chalabi Tabrizi

According to Malik Shah Sistani, Muhammad Husain Chalabi was originally from Tabriz. When Itizad-Daula Farhad Khan[22] had independent government at Tabriz; Chalabi was honoured by him. After utter indigence of Farhad Khan (1007/1598) Chalabi migrated to Rume and then he travelled to Egypt and stayed there for some time. Later on he left Egypt to holy city of Mecca. Afterwards he came to India as a servant of Jahangir Padashah. He served his time as a calligraphist.[23]

According to *Tuzuk-i-Jahangiri* Jahangir sent him to purchase jewels and collect curios. He got money and was asked to go by way of Iraq to Constantinople and buy and bring curios and rarities for the *Sarkar*. For this purpose, it was necessary that he paid his respects to the ruler of Iran. Jahangir had given him a letter and memorandum (of what he was to procure).[24]

Nasrabadi mentions: Husain Chalabi was one of the great men of Tabriz. He settled in Esfahan for a long time. Chalabi developed all perfections and attainments, specially in prose and verse. His assembly was crowded by poets, cultured and learned men. He left some poems.[25]

Rafati Tabrizi

Mirza Ibrahim Rafati Tabrizi was the small son of Maulana Sahvi Khushnavis. He came to India in Jahangir's period with his father and elder brother. They had come in order to better their prospects. They travelled in many parts of India. After earning money they came back to Iran. Thereafter Auhadi added: I heard the news of his death in 1027/1617.[26]

According to Nasrabadi, Mulla Rafati belonged to Tabriz. He could write shikasta very well. He earned a lot of money in India. For a while he was in the service of Arab Khan, the governor of Shirvan probably he also died there.[27]

Wesali Tabrizi

Sultan Muhammad Wesali belonged to Tabriz. According to Taqi Kashi he was a poet and calligraphist, he could write Nastaliq very well. Wesali moved from his native place to Kashan. Taqi Kashi saw him at Kashan. Wesali was seeker of knowledge and he had good nature. He came to India with unknown reasons, and died here. Taqi Kashi has recorded a couple of his verses.[28]

Jawahar Raqam Tabrizi

Mir Sayyid Ali was the son of Mir Muqim and grand child of Mir Shahmir, who was originally from Tabriz, but he grew up in Abbasabad of Esfahan. Mir Sayyid Ali and his father were famous in *Nastaliq*. They migrated to India during the reign of Shah Jahan in search of fortune. Mir Muqim died in early years, but Mir Sayyid Ali entered the court of Shah Jahan and received title of *Jawahar Raqami*. He worked as a tutor of Prince Aurangzeb. After succession of Aurangzeb Mir Ali was appointed to *Darugha* of Aurangzeb's library. He died in 1094/ 1682[29] and was buried at Delhi.

The Author of *Tazkirat-ul-Khattatin* says: when Shah Jahan heard the fame of Mir Sayyid Ali he wrote him letter in order to invite him to India, then Mir Sayyid Ali migrated to India.[30]

Muqim Tabrizi

Mir Muqim was the son of Mir Shah Mir, who was originally from Tabriz, but he was brought up and settled in Abbasabad of Esfahan. Mir Muqim was very famed in calligraphy and could write *Nastaliq* very well. He migrated to India during Shah Jahan's reign as an adventurer in search of better opportunities.[31]

CENTRAL PLATEAU

Baqir Kashani

Muhammad Baqir Khurdah known as Baqir belonged to Kashan and passed his early life in Esfahan. He was a poet and calligraphist. In poetry he was a student of Muhtasham Kashani and in calligraphy he was a student of Mir Muizud-din Muhammad Kashani, who was famous in *Nastaliq.*[32] Baqir's involvement in the heresy of Mahmud Pasikhani, the founder of Nuqtawi Sect, brought him to the brink of death as Shah Abbas ordered execution of the Nuqtawis. His life was saved, but he suffered hardship in prison for two years on being released, his first worry was to leave Iran and try to find safety in India. So he came to India in 1006/1597, and Burhan Nizam Shah treated him with kindness and Baqir enjoyed comfortable life in Ahmadnagar, the seat of Nizam Shah's government. Then he moved to Ibrahim Adil Shah's capital, Bijapur, where Zuhuri and Malik Qomi offered him hospitality of the surviving verses of Baqir Khurdah, there is an interesting poem: *Saqi-nama.*[33]

According to *Subh-i-Sadiq,* Baqir[34] went to Bengal and settled there for some time, then he moved for pilgrimage to Mecca, afterwards returned to India, and chose Burhanpur for his stay. He died in 1038/1628 at Burhanpur.

Wasfi Kermani

Mir Abdullah Wasfi[35] was the son of Mir Muzaffar, descendant of Shah Nimatullah. He was a famous calligraphist and powerful poet. Wasfi migrated from his native place to India during Akbar's reign in order to better his prospects. He received title of Meshkin Qalami. He lived at the court of Akbar and was one of the celebrated calligraphists having left his mark in the cultural history of Mughal India. The emperor conferred on him the title mentioned above in old age, he renounced the world and passed his life in prayers and contemplation of God. He composed verses and left a divan. One of Wasfi's disciples prepared an account of his saintly habits, naming the work Fathul-Qulub. Wasfi composed a masnavi on the pattern of Shaikh Nizami and named it *Gulshan-i-Asrar*. Among his surviving specimens of calligraphy there are:

1. Inscriptions in Khusrau Bagh and the fort of Allahabad, and
2. A copy of Hasan Dihlavi's *divan* of verses. His death occurred in 1025/1616 at Ajmer.[36]

The *Muntakhabu-t-Tawarikh* contains the following notice of him:

His name is Mir Abdullah[37] and he is an excellent penman. He is the pupil of Shah Ghiyas and Maulana Raqimi, and writes seven scripts. He is enrolled among the Ahadis. Through his mother he is related to Mirza Nizamud-din Ahmad. He sometimes turns his attention to poetry.[38] He had two sons:1. Mir Mubammad Mumin Akbarabadi known as Arshi and Mir Muhammad Salih known as Kashfi.[39] The following verses are his:

"Now that I have experienced the sweetness of love's sorrow,
I enjoy a thousand bursts of weeping for every laugh of mine"
A quatrain :
"Where is love, for my inner self is dark as the darkest night.
The secrets of god are hidden from my understanding
It may be that love will lead me to them, but, if not,
Then is the end of my journey for indeed from my lame efforts."[40]

Mir Muhammad Mumin Akbarabadi and his brother Mir Muhammad Salih

Mir Muhammad Mumin known as Arshi and Muhammad Salih known as Kashfi were the son of Mir Abdullah Wasfi[41] entitled *Meshkin-Qalam*; the greatest calligraphist of Akbar and Jahangir's reigns. Mir Muhammad Mumin and Mir Muhammad Salih migrated to India accompanying their father in Akbar's reign. Sulaiman Shukoh, son of Dara Shukoh, and other princes of the royal family were Mir Muhammad Mumin's pupils in the art of calligraphy. They lived like a Sufis and passed their time as a calligraphist and poet. Mir Muhammad Salih died in 1061/1650, but Mir Muhammad Mumin died in 1091/1680[42]. The author of *Amal-i-Salih* says: Mir Muhammad Mumin and Mir Muhammad Salih, sons of Mir Abdullah, Meshkin-Raqam are men of literary disposition, having blooming script and magical pen. Every piece of their writing has the property of ambergris like the downs of the houri faced ones; and a segment of their poem also is an object of envy for a quarter of paradise. The curves of their letters are ornaments for the circle of sky; and the point of their writing is the pupil of the eye of sun.[43]

Yusuf Aziz Esfahani

Mulla Yusuf Aziz Esfahani was very capable and expert goldsmith. He was engaged in the work in the gold factory of the Safavid court under Yaqub Zargar Bashi. Yusuf Aziz came to India from Esfahan in order to join the service of Jahangir *Padashah,* and for a while he was here and then in 1023/1614 he planned to return to Iran, but his death occurred at Agra. He also composed some verses.[44]

Siraja Esfahani

Muhammad Qasim Siraja was the son of Muhammad Ali Esfahani. He came from a family of the commoners (*Ami*) of Esfahan, who were known for wealth and plenty. He had received good education, according to the tradition of the family and was held in great esteem in Iran. He was very well versed in the art of music and astronomy, had inclination for the company of poets and himself composed some good poems. From Esfahan he came to India and entered the service of Abdur Rahim Khan-i-Khanan in 1015/1606, through the agency of Aqa Muhammad Bakhshi. In 1024/1615 Khan-i-Khanan entrusted him the work of the compilation of the divan of Urfi Shirazi from his original papers sent to his library by the author at the time of his death. Siraja worked hard for a year and collected 14,000 verses from the *ghazals, qasidas, rubais* and *masnavis* of the poet. When the work was presented to Khan-i-Khanan, he was amply rewarded for his labour. The author of *Maasir-i-Rahimi* wrote an introduction to it and Qasim Siraja composed a chronogram. But the chronogram gives the date of the compilation as 1026/1616-17, whereas the work was already finished in 1025/1616. Siraja had a ready pen and could write fluent verses, though he did not make it his profession. The very fact that Khan-i-Khanan entrusted the work of compilation of Urfi's *divan* to him shows his worth and speaks of his poetic talent.[45]

Some of Indian Tazkira writers have mistaken him for Muhammad Qasim Siraja Naqqash Esfahani,[46] a painter of Shah Sulaiman Safavi's reign (1077-1055/1666-1693) who never visited India.

Ali Esfahani Musannef

His name was Ali Beg and he belonged to Esfahan. He was a musician and player of violin (*Kamancheh*). Musannef was unique in his technique. Like many others of his compatriots he joined the services of Khan-i-Khanan at his arrival in India. He also composed some verses which include a quatrain in praise of Khan-i-Khanan.[47]

Zamani Esfahani

Muhammad Zaman Esfahani, known as, Zamani was the son of Ostatd Ali Ajri Tabbakh. He migrated to India in the company of Majlesi Esfahani. After arrival in India Zamani together with Majlesi chose to be with Khwaja Beg Mirza[48] son of Masum Beg at Doulatabad and Ahmadabad. After Majlesi's death the Deccan, Zamani moved to Gujarat and then to Agra. Zamani is noted as a calligraphist and poet.[49]

Zaman Esfahani

Aqa Zaman entitled *Zarkash* was an associate of Hakim Shafai, Mirza Fasihi and Mirza Malik Mashriqi. His birth place is Esfahan, and his job was that of a gold-wire drawer (gold embroiderer). He came to India several times. In the beginning he preferred a pen name of Faribi and then he changed to Zaman. His death occurred at Lahore in 1054/ 1644.[50]

Ali Reza Esfahani

Maulana Ali Reza Sufi Mahmur was the great Architect of Esfahan. He was very clever and intelligent, learnt most of the current sciences of his time and was also known for his proficiency in architecture. He migrated to India in 1017/1608. For travelling Ali Esfahani travelled to many parts of India. Auhadi met him at Agra in 1024/1615 and testifies that he also wrote several poems with Simgol as his *takhallus*.[51]

Bahari Kashani

According to Nihavandi he belonged to Kashan. Bahari migrated to India in the reign of Jahangir in order to better his prospects. After arrival in India he was attached to Khan-i-Khanan, and composed satirical poems in praise of him. For a while he served him as a book-seller and binder of *Dar-ul-Saltant* of Lahore.[52]

Baqiyai Naini

He was born at Nain, a city near Kashan. Baqiya came to India in 1023/1614. After his arrival he joined the service Mirza Ghiyas Beg Itimad-ud-daula through the intercession of Talib Amuli. After some time Baqiya shifted from Ajmer and then to the Deccan where he was attached to Prince Khurram. He remained in the retinue of Khurram for two years, then having resigned his *mansab* and *jagir* engaged and in trade and travelling.[53]

Baqiya rose to fame under Shah Jahan, who ordered him to be weighed in silver for one of his poems (1016/1636).[54] More significant aspect of his career is the fact that while in India, he acquired extraordinary skill in Indian music. In old age, he travelled back to Esfahan, where the Safavid monarch, Shah Sulaiman, accommodated him in the circle of his court-poets and artists. According to some writers, he visited India for second time and died in Benares. Popular among his many poems is the Sufistic masnavi, *zat*-o-*sifat*.[55]

Sirati Qazwini

Mirza Muhammad Husain Sirati Ghaffari belonged to a noted family of Qazwin. He lived as a poet and a calligraphist. Sirati came to India during Jahangir's reign. He entered the service of Prince Parviz and received *mansab*. After the death of Parviz (1035/1625) he went to Bengal and then he settled in Patna, Bihar. In 1041/1631 Sirati shifted to Lahore with the intention to visit Mecca. The author of *Subh-i-Sadiq* mentions some of his verses.[56]

Muizz Yazdi:

His origin and birth place was Yazd. He belonged to the great Sadat family of Yazd. Mirza Muhammad Sadiq Mina, author of *Subh-i-Sadiq* had friendship with him. In India he enjoyed the company of Prince Parviz for a long time, and was killed by one of the rogues in 1035/1625. There is considerable confusion in the accounts of his tryst in India in some of the *Tazkiras*. The authors of *Rouz-e-Raushan*[58] and *Tazkira Nasrabadi*[59] say: Mir Muizz Khushnavis Kashani went to India and died there. This is not correct.[60] The author of Farhang-i-Sukhanvaran[61] mentions: Mir Muizz-ud-Din Muhammad Kashani was one of the famous calligraphist of Shah Tahmasp's period. He died in 995/1586 at Kashan. The author of *Golestan-i-Honar*[62] says that it was the merchants who carried the specimens of his calligraphy to India and this was only after his death.

Mir Muhammad Mumin Shamimi Yazdi

Mir Muhammad Mumin who belonged to Yazd, came to India in the reign of Jahangir, ca, 1028/1618. He found employment under Mirza Ahsan son of Khwaja Abul Hasan, the *Mir Bakhshi,* or the chief paymaster of the Emperor. Mirza Ahsan later on obtained the title of Zafar Khan from Shah Jahan and his reputation was next only to Abdur-Rahim Khan-i-Khanan for the lavish patronage he offered to the men of learning, art and culture. Shamimi was an expert of calligraphy, music and poetry. He was killed in Karnataka.[63]

Suti Yazdi

Mir Sayyid Ali Suti Yazdi was a skilled musician and expert in current sciences. Suti migrated to India in the reign of Shah Jahan in order to better his prospects. He received valuable gifts from the Emperor. Then he returned to his native place where he entered in the service of Shah Abbas II in 1067/1656 and after him Shah Sulaiman Safavi in 1078/1667. To him are attributed many poems.[64] He died in 1080/1669.[65]

Ismail Nasrabadi

Mirza Ismail was the son of Mirza Muhammad Nasrabadi. He was a calligraphist. Ismail migrated to India to visit his uncle Mirza Ghiyas, who was in the service of Prince Shah Jahan. In India he joined the retinue of Mahabat Khan. He died when he was still quite young. He was like almost all other Iranians a poet also, composed some verses in praise of Shah Jahan.[66]

Iksir Esfahani

Mirza Iwaz Beg Iksir Esfahani came to India during Shah Jahan's reign in search of better opportunities. He was employed in Delhi in the Emperor's Dar-ul-Insha. His interest was also reportedly in poetry and the literary men of the capital acknowledged his views about poetic taste and style.[67]

Wahshat Ardestani

Born at Zavareh[68] in 1034/1624.[69] Mulla Jamal-ud-Din Wahshat was the son of Mir Ziya, who belonged to the Tabatabai Sayyids of Ardestan.[70] He came to India twice, first in the later days of Shah Jahan's reign. He returned to Esfahan in 1973/1662, and revisited India after the death of his wife in 1082/1671.[71] Jamal-ud-din lived as a poet and as a calligraphist.[72]

Rashida Abbasi

Rashida belonged to Abbasabad of Esfahan. He passed his career as a goldsmith, enamelist and poet. Rashida emigrated to India in the reign of Shah Jahan to better his prospects. After some time he returned to his native place. He died before 1083/1672.[73]

Asaf Qomi

Muhammad Quli Asaf or Asifa of Qom came to India during the reign of Shahjahan in order to better his prospects. He belonged to Baharlu tribe. He was earlier in Esfahan for some time as a writer (*munshi*) of Mirza Habibullah Sadr.[74] Asaf, then came to India and undertook a pilgrimage to Mecca. From there he returned to India.[75]

Asaf died in 1093/1682. His incomplete divan consists of a number of *qasidas* and *ghazals*.[76] Sarkhush writes: That Asaf had a small *divan*,[77] he could not attain fame as a poet.[78]

SOUTH OF IRAN

Forsi Shidani

Khwaja Inayatullah known as Forsi was from Shidan a district of Fars. Our sources give his with more than suffixes, like, Inayatullah *Kitabdar*, Inyatullah *Katib Shirazi* and Inyatullah *Shirazi*. From Auhadi, the author of *Arafatul-Ashiqin* we get, however, his real name. Auhadi[79] writes that *Khwajagi* Inayatullah Forsi known as Shirazi *Kitabdar* was one of the great calligraphists of Shiraz. He migrated to India during Akbar's reign and entered his service and was there for a long time. After Akbar's death he joined the services of Jahangir padashah, and served as his Librarian with a title of *Maktub Khan*.[80] Forsi is thus described in the *Muntakhabu-t-Tawarikh*: Inyatullah[81] the scribe is from Shiraz, and is now employed in the imperial library as a librarian. He has a merry and nimble wit and occasionally writes poetry. The following verses are his

"I am trapped, like a helpless bird, into the cage
My broken heart is like a soundless bell
Though I am contemptible than an ant or a fly
I am suffocated by the straitness of the two worlds."[82]

A.A. Razi says: Inayatullah had good nature, and he wrote excellent *Nastaliq*. He was librarian of Akbar.[83]

Besides, Forsi was a poet at the court of Muhammad Quli Qutb Shah, the fourth king of Golkonda. He composed a versified chronicle of the dynasty and brought the account to the early years of Muhammad Quli Qutb Shah's reign (988/1580-1020/1611). Its double title was: Nasab-nama-Shahr Yari and *Nasab nama-i-Qutb Shahi*. This chronicle was completed in 1016/1607.[84]

Muhammad Naii Neyrizi (entitled Ishrat Khan)

Ustatd Muhammad Naii was son of Haji Ismail Neyrizi, who was in the service of Shah Ismail II Safavi. Naii was born at Neyriz a town in Fars province. He was a poet and musician, living at the court of Shah Abbas I.

Baqi Nihavandi says: Naii was very brave and heedless, so he talked out of his condition, authority and capability. Thereafter Shah Abbas thus ordered to banish him from Safavid territory. He then left for India where he was attached to Khan-i-Khanan's *sarkar*.

In 1023/1614 he moved to Mecca and settled there for sometime. Afterwards he returned to India and joined Prince Khurram, and was respected by him. Prince Khurram introduced Naii to Jahangir, from who he received title of Ishrat Khani.[85] Jahangir in the events of 1026/ 1616-17 writes: Some time ago my son Khurram sent Ustatd Muhammad Naii for attendance he played some new tune and recited a ghazal (lyric poem) about me. I ordered Rs. 6,300 and an elephant to be given to him for road expenses, and allowed him to go. The next day he travelled the road of non-existence.[86]

Walih Shirazi

Jamalaya Walih, known as Shirazi, was brother of Shamsa better known as Bini, who was student of Mir Imad. Walih was well versed in calligraphy and was also a poet. He migrated to India in search of employment and joined there the services of several nobles. Nasrabadi has recorded some of his verses.[87]

Mohsin Shirazi

He was born and grew up in Shiraz. He began versification while he was still young. He was associated with Mirza Nizam[88] and Ghiyasai Halvai[89] in his native place. Mohsin is first spotted in Shah Abbas's camp with some position in 1031/1621. For a while he passed his time at Mazandaran, then he migrated to Qandahar, from where later he shifted to India in 1033/1623, in order to better his prospects.[90]

Mirza Muhammad Sadiq Mina says: I met him at Jahangirnagar (Dacca) in 1041/1631. He was in the service of Muhammad Zaman.[91] Mohsinai Shirazi was famed for his calligraphy.[92] Nasrabadi mentions him as a poet, with some significant verses.[93]

Ibrahim-i-Farsi

He came to India from Shiraz during Jahangir's reign initially as a traveller, but then he also passed his time as a secretary of Ibrahim Khan Fath Jang,[94] son of Jahangir's Prime Minister Itimad-ud-Daula. Ibrahim had considerable command over juristic sciences; he also attained fame as a calligraphist and poet.[95]

Asiri Shirazi (Bu Ali)

He was born in Shiraz. His father Sahifi Zolqadr, was also a poet and calligraphist in 1022/1613. The author of *Arafatul Ashiqin* says: Maulana Sahifi had good disposition, but after the death of his son Bu Ali in India, his nature changed.[96]

Muhammad Tanbureh

He was born at Fars province and was brought up in Qazwin. Tanbureh was a guitar-player, poet, painter and story-teller, who arrived from Iran in 1014/1605. He acquired fame as a reciter of Firdausi's great classic, the *Shah-nama*, which was then regarded as a highly specialized and appealing art possessing all the merits of stage-play. The combination of so many qualities in a single character sufficiently proved his genius. A true artist having merged his existence in guitar, hence called Tanbureh, he exhibited total disregard for dress and manners. On the other hand, Mughal society being extremely polished, no breach of public etiquette could be imagined. One day, Tanbureh appeared before Khwaja Wais Hamadani, a noble man in his vagabond style. The Khwaja, deeply offended, slapped him out of the assembly. The artist avenged the insult by composing a satire against his enemy; it has survived in Mughal literature. Finally, Tanbureh was enlisted among the Jahangir's painters by Khwaja Inayatullah Forsi Shidani,[97] who was scriber of Akbar library and after Akbar's death had migrated to Golkonda in 1014/1605. In 1020/1611 he reentered the Mughal service and received from Jahangir the title of *Maktub Khan*.

Ruzbeh Shirazi

According to *Sham-e-Ghariban*, Mulla Ruzbeh Shirazi was matchless in calligraphy. His migration to India from Shiraz is unknown. He served his time as a calligraphist. He lived in India for a long time and died here. He left some verses.[98]

The *Arafatul-Ashiqin* contains the following notice of him: Maulana Ruzbeh Khushnavis Shirazi was talented and intelligent. He was well versed in calligraphy and could write *Naskh* and *Taliq* very well. He also had expertise in gilding and in many other things. *Arafat* also notices a brother of his who was an equally accomplished calligraphist. Until 1022/1613-1024/1615 both these brothers were alive.[99]

Atai Cherudi Shirazi

According to Baqi Nihavandi, Atai served most of his time in India in the army. He cut his right hand in one of the Deccan's battles. Still he could write *Nastaliq* very well. Atai was engaged in scribing for a long time. Later he went to Burhanpur and entered the service of Khan-i-Khanan. He also had inclination of poet and wrote verses in praise of Khan-i-Khanan.[100]

Abul Baqa Abar Quii

Mirza Abul-Baqa was the son of Abul-Wali and a grand son of Shah Abul Fath. They belonged to the Sadat family of Abarqu, a city in Fars province. His ancestors were *Kalantar* (headman) and *Pishwa* (leader) of that city. Abul-Baqa was an accomplished and a highly learned man. He could write *Naskh* and *Taliq* very well. Abul-Baqa migrated to India during Shah Jahan's reign in search of better opportunities. Taqarrup Khan[101] welcomed with great honour in India. After his death around 1083/1671 Abul-Baqa returned to Esfahan.[102]

Amini Mashhadi

Mulla Muhammad Amin *Jadvel Kesh* Mashhadi was a great gilter of Khurasan. He worked in the Library of Imam Reza. According to Qazi Ahmad Mir Munshi: Amini Mashhadi was expert in dyeing and coloration. He coloured (duped) paper in 70 colours. For some time he had no rival in this technique. Amini died at Mashhad.[103]

Baqi Nihavandi says: Amini came to India in the company of his family during the Uzbek raids on Khurasan. In India he joined the company of Khan-i-Khanan and decorated most of his library books. Amini also had poetic inclination and left some verses.[104]

Mumin Gonabadi

Mumin belonged to Gonabad, a town situated in Khurasan province. He shifted to India from his native place in the reign of Jahangir in search of better opportunities. He passed his time as a calligraphist and a poet.[105]

Khadim Heravi

His origin is from Herat. His job and his skill was bow-making. He also was noted for his calligraphy. In versification Heravi was a student of Mirza Fasihi.[106] He came to India in 1034/1624. The author of Khairul Bayan mentions some of his verses.[107]

FROM UNKNOWN AREAS

Mujrim Shamlu

Quli Khan Beg Shamlu[108] was the son of Hasan Sultan, who was one of great and notable men of Shamlu tribe. His ancestors had served the Safavid Kings in various capacities. After his father's death he inherited huge money. Subsequently he resigned from the service of Shah Abbas I and left for India in 1015/1606. Auhadi had close relations with him and they came to India together. He was very intelligent, warm hearted and was skilled in calligraphy and music. He stayed during the reign of Jahangir and established his position as a poet. On his way to the holy city of Mecca, his death occurred in Ahmadabad in 1020/1611 Besides a *divan*, he left a *masnavi* on the pattern of the old Munazara-strife-poem. Its name was Mubahasa-i-Kuknar va tanbaku (Disputation between opium and tobacco.[109] The author of *Khairul-Bayan* says: Oulu Khan Beg was the son of Hasan Sultan, he had proficiency in calligraphy, music and mathematics. He migrated to India in 1013/1604[110] and received suitable *mansab* there.[111]

Abdul-Haq

Abdul-Haq came to India during Shah Jahan's reign to seek employment. He attained the rank of 1000 *zat* with 200 *sawar* and was called Amanat Khan. He wrote *Naskh* exceedingly well, and in the 15th year of the Emperor's reign, as a reward for the inscription which he had written on the Cupola (The Taj) of Mumtaz-i-Zamani, he received an elephant as a gift. He died in the 16th year of Shah Jahan's reign.[112]

Samandar-i-Sahmlu

He was the son of Imam Quli Beg Shamlu, one of the great Amirs of Jahangir and died at Bengal. His name was Chiragh Beg Shamlu and migrated to India in the reign of Shah Jahan to join his father.

According to Muhammad Sadiq Mina, Chiragh Beg reached Jahangir nagar in 1041/1631, then he shifted to Orissa. Again he went to Bengal in the time of Islam Khan (1048/1638). Afterwards Samandar settled at Jounnar and died there. Sadiq Mina says: Samandar was my teacher and he was a skilled musician, with significant poetic sensibilities.[113]

Table : 7.2
ARTISTS AND CRAFTSMEN

Rg	Pr	Nu	Reasons and Contexts of Migration																								
			X1	X2	X3	X4	X5	X6	X7	X8	X9	X10	X11	X12	X13	X14	X15	X16	X17	X18	X19	X20	X21	X22	X23	X24	X25	X26
NO	Ak	0																										
3	Ja	3														2	1											
	Sh	0																										
WNW	Ak	0																										
7	Ja	5														3	1											1
	Sh	2														1		1										
SW	Ak	0																										
0	Ja	0																										
	Sh	0																										
CP	Ak	4	1							2						1												
21	Ja	11														1	2	1				1						6
	Sh	6												1		5												
SO	Ak	1																										1
10	Ja	8		1												1				1		1						4
	Sh	1														1												
ENE	Ak	1			1																							
3	Ja	2														1												1
	Sh	0																										
SE	Ak	0																										
0	Ja	0																										
	Sh	0																										
UA	Ak	0												1														1
3	Ja	1																										
	Sh	2																		1								
Total		47	1	1	1					2				2		16	4	2		2		2						14

Graph : 7.1

Number of Artists and Craftsmen according to the reasons and contexts of their migration

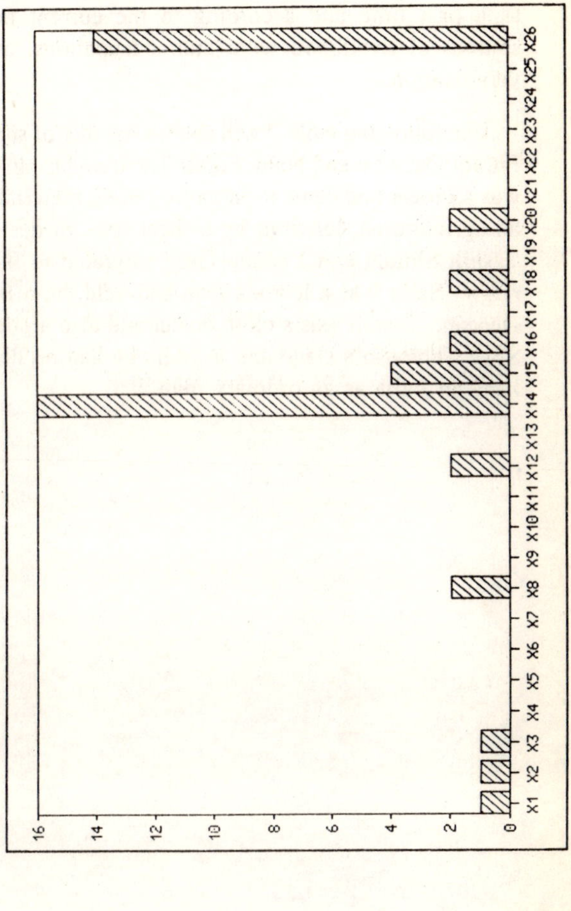

People with Diverse Skills

There were Iranians with diverse skills and occupations. Persians, belonging to diverse classes who arrived in Mughal India in search of better opportunities. Some of them were also engaged in versification as a past time and according to the current fashion, but the main sources of livelihood were their occupations, other than poetry and versification.

The following table[114] will show a number of such Iranian immigrants. Furuqi Qazwini and Nami Forahi left Iran during Akbar's reign. Furuqi was a grocer and came to India for purely material purposes. Nami was an agriculturist, left Iran by a sheer tryst of destiny. Sabir-i-Esfahani, Tasalli Shirazi and Yamani Gurji migrated to India during Jahangir's reign. Sabir was a learned man and held the office of *Waqia Navis* in Deccan. Tasalli was a cloth dealer and also a poet. Yamani Gurji was Shah Tahmasp's slave and in India he had no definite profession. He lived in India as an ordinary man.[115]

Table : 7.3
PEOPLE WITH DIVERSE SKILLS

Name of migrants	Place of Birth	Provinces	Regions	Period of migration	Contexts and Reasons of migration	Position in Iran	Position in India	Place of Death
Furouqi Qazwini	Qazwin	Qazwin	Central Plateau	Akbar	Financial purpose	Grocer, poet	Trader	Iran
Sabir-i-Esfahani	Esfahan	Esfahan	-do-	Jahangir	Unclear	Learnedman	Waqia-Navis of Deccan State, in the service of Jahangir's court	Burhanpur 1653
Tasalli Shirazi	Shiraz	Fars	South	Jahangir	In order to better his prospects	Cloth dealer	Poet in the court of Jahangir	India
Nami Forahi	Iran	-	Unclear	Later days' of Akbar	By destiny		Nobles' service, agriculture and poet	Unclear
Yamani Gurji	-do-	-	Unclear	Jahangir	In order to better his prospects	Shah Tahmasp's slave	Ordinary man	India

CENTRAL PLATEAU

Furuqi Qazwini

His origin was from Qazwin. He passed most of his time as a grocer (dealing in tea, sugar, spices etc.), but he is also mentioned as a cavalier and eloquent.[116]

According to the author of *Majma ul Khawas*, Maulana Furuqi was a wonderful and proud man. He came to India for making money, and after some time he returned to Iran. Later Furuqi had a jeweller shop.[117]

The author of the *Arafatul-Ashiqin* says: Mulla Furuqi Attar Qazwini was a famous poet of his time. Auhadi met him at Qazwin in the period of Shah Abbas I. He then had a grocery shop there. According to Alam *Ara-i-Abbasi* Furuqi was prudent in speech, and his grocery shop was the place of poets and great-men.[118]

Sabir-i-Esfahani

Mir Sabir Esfahani, a learned and accomplished person, migrated to India during Jahangir's reign. He entered the court on the recommendation by Itimad-ud-Daula Jahangiri. The author of *Zakhiratul-Khavanin* reports: He is the *Waqia-navis* of all the provinces of Deccan. He is not greedy and he is not married. Mir Sabir died in 1064/1653 at Burhanpur.[119]

SOUTH OF IRAN

Tasalli Shirazi

Mirza Ibrahim Shirazi was engaged to weave horse whip (*Tazi Yaneh Bafi*) in his native place. He migrated to India in the reign of Jahangir in order to better his prospects. He lived as a poet in the court of Jahangir. For a while he was in the service of, Ilahi Shirazi, (Masih-uz-Zaman) and then he went with him to Mecca in 1034/1624. Afterwards he came to India from Mecca and died here.[120]

FROM UNKNOWN AREAS

Nami Forahi

He was a student of Qazi Abul-Barekeh.[121] He migrated to India accompanying his son during the later days of Akbar. For a while he passed his time in the assembly of greatmen and nobles. Finally Nami engaged in cultivation. He was alive until the early years of Jahangir's reign. Auhadi has not mentioned the date of his death. Nami also composed some verses.[122]

Yamani Gurji (Georgia)

He was a Georgian, but he was born and brought up in Iran. Yamani was one of the slaves of Shah Tahmasp Safavi. He migrated to India in order to attain good position. He stayed in India between 1022/1613 till 1024/1615, and then died here.[123]

Table 7.4
People with diverse skills

Rg	Pr	Nu	Reasons and Contexts of Migration																									
			X1	X2	X3	X4	X5	X6	X7	X8	X9	X10	X11	X12	X13	X14	X15	X16	X17	X18	X19	X20	X21	X22	X23	X24	X25	X26
NO	Ak	0																										
0	Ja	0																										
	Sh	0																										
WNW	Ak																											
0	Ja	0																										
	Sh	0																										
SW	Ak	0																										
0	Ja	0																										
	Sh	0																										
CP	Ak	1											1															
2	Ja	1																										1
	Sh	0																										
SO	Ak	0																										
1	Ja	1														1												
	Sh	0																										
ENE	Ak	0																										
0	Ja	0																										
	Sh	0																										
SE	Ak	0																										
0	Ja	0																										
	Sh	0																										
UA	Ak	1									1																	
2	Ja	1														1												
	Sh	0																										
Total		5									1		1			2												1

Graph : 7.2

Number of People with diverse skills according to the reasons and contexts of their migration

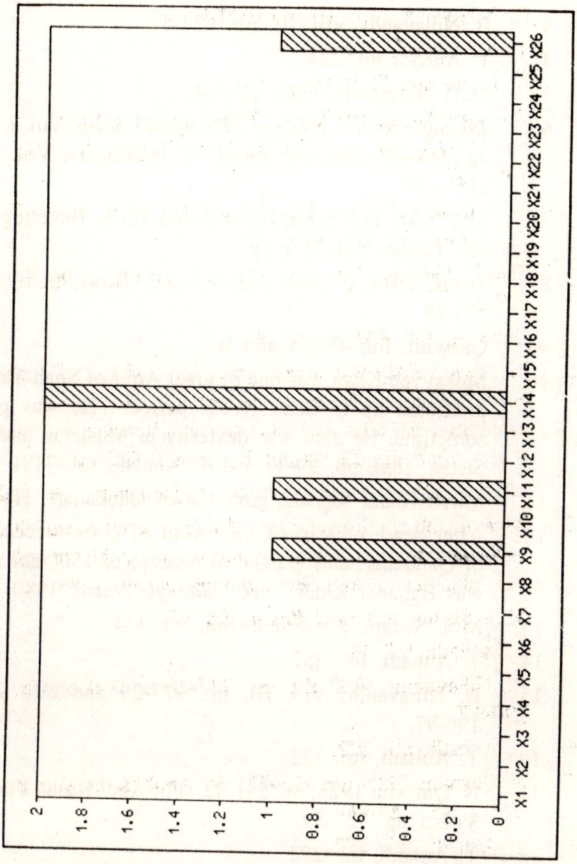

REFERENCES

1. See: Tables: 7.1, 2 and Graph: 7.1.
2. For details see: Tables: 7.1, 2, Graph: 7.1 and text.
3. B. Nihavandi, Vol. III, pp.1027-57.
4. T. Auhadi fol. 224.
5. M.T. Nasrabadi, 1938, p. 304.
6. *Jahangir Nama,* 1980, p. 272. *Amal-i-Salih,* Vol. I, p. 562 and Vol. III, pp. 418-420 also see: *Tuzuk*, Tr by Rogers. Vol. II pp. 29, 30, 179, 195, 197.
7. *M.U.* text, Vol. I, pp. 405-408 and Tr. by Beveridge Vol. I, p. 397 also see: Lahori Vol. II, p.79.
8. *Tuzuk,* 1914, p. 349, and also see; *Tuzuk,* tr. by Rogers, Vol. II pp. 227-28.
9. Qazwini, fol. 430 A and B.
10. Mosayyeb Khan was one of great Amir of Shah Tahmasp. His position promoted up to Shah Abbas period. He was governor of Ray for sometime. He also was dexterity in Musician and history. (See; M.S. Sistan, *Ibid,* pp. 29-30 and T. Auhadi, fol. 713).
11. Mirza Ghazi was the governor of Qandahar. He died in 1021/1612.
12. After death of Mirza Ghazi Abul Bi Uzbek received the governorship of Qandahar, and granted to *mansab* of 1500 *zat* and *sawar*. His title was Bahadar Khan. See: *Jahangir Nama,* 1980, p. 128.
13. M.S. Sistani, *Khairul Bayan*, fol. 374.
14. T. Auhadi, fol. 387.
15. B. Nihavandi; Vol. III, pp. 927-29 and also see; T. Auhadi, fol. 196-97.
16. T. Auhadi, fol. 272.
17. N. Qazwini 1926, pp. 541-42. For Abol Hasan Turbati see; (*M.U.* Text, Vol. I pp. 727-39.
18. T. Auhadi, fol. 272.
19. Probably is four years.
20. *M.S.* Sistani, *Khairul Bayan*, fols: 403-404 also see; M.T. Nasrabadi, 1938, p. 257.
21. T.Auhadi, fol. 272.
22. Farhad Khan Qaramanlu was brave, patriotic and traitor. Shah Abbas I killed him in 1007/1598, because of his defeat from Uzbek army in herat (see; *A.A.A.* 1334 A.S/1955, pp. 574-76.)
23. M.S. Sistani; *Khairul Bayan;* fol. 377.
24. For details see, *Tuzuk,* tr. by Rogers, Vol. I, p. 238.

25. M.T. Nasrabadi; 1938, p. 118.
26. T. Auhadi, fol. 270.
27. M.T. Nasrabadi, 1938, p. 399.
28. T. Kashi, *Khulasatul-Ashar,* manuscript.
29. The Author of *Farhang-i-Sukhanvaran* mentions: Jawahar Raqami died in 1137/1724. See; A.R. Khaiyampur, 1961 p.14, for details about Sayyid Ali. See : M.T. Nasrabadi 1938, pp. 208-209, also see: A.G. Maani, 1969, Vol. II, pp. 603-605, M.H.A. Lucknow, 1951, p.82.
30. *M.S.* Khurasani, *Imtehan-ul-Fuzala or Tazkirat-ul-Khattatin,* Tabriz, 1291/1874, under the name of Jawahar Raqam Tabrizi, see also: G.M.Haft Qalami Dehlavi, 1910, p. 57. For details see: *Amal-i-Salih,* Vol. III p. 445.
31. G.M. Haft Qalami Dehlavi, 1910, p. 57 also see. M.T. Nasrabadi, 1938, pp.208-209 and A.G. Maani, 1969, Vol. II, pp. 603-605.
32. Q.A. Mir Munishi; *Golistan-i-Honar,* ed. by Muhammad Hadayat Husain, Calcutta, 1328/1910 p. 122.
33. See: A.B. Nihavandi, Vol. III, pp. 792-97 also see; T. Auhadi, fol.153.
34. See: M.S. Mina, *Subh-i-Sadiq,* p. 62.
35. The author of *Miratul-Alam* mentions: Mir Abdullah Tarmazi (see: M. Bakhtavar Khan, 1979, Vol.II, p. 483 but it is not correct, because Mir Abdullah Wasfi was from Kerman (see. G.M. Haft Qalami Dehlavi, 1910, pp.101-102 also see: A.G. Maani 1969, Vol. II, pp.783-86.
36. See: G.M.Haft Qalami Dehlavi, 1910, pp.101-102. T. Auhadi, fol.792 also see: A.G. Maani, 1398/1929, Vol. II. pp. 783-86.
37. Mir Abdullah is mentioned in the *Ain* (I,103) as one of the renowned calligraphers of the age.
38. Badauni, Vol III, pp. 383-84 and Tr. by S.W. Haig, Vol. III, p. 518.
39. *Amal-i-Salih,* 1939, Vol. III, p. 444.
40. Badauni, Vol III, p. 384 and Tr. By S.W. Haig, Vol. III, p. 518.
41. About Mir Abdullah Wasfi Kermani See: above under his name.
42. M. Bakhtavar Khan, 1979, Vol. II, pp. 484-85 also see: T. Auhadi, fol.792.
43. *Amal-i-Salih,* Vol. III, p. 444.
44. T. Auhadi, fol. 816.
45. B. Nihavandi, Vol. III, pp. 1354-60.
46. About Muhammad Qasim Siraja *Naqqash* (painter) see: M.T. Nasrabadi, 1938, p. 139.
47. B. Nihavandi, Vol. III, p. 1697.
48. Khwaja Beg Mirza Safavi came to India in 999/1590, he was in the service of Akbar and received *mansab* of 5000. He was *Kotwal* of

Ahmadnagar in the reign of Jahangir (see; *Jahangir Nama,* Tehran Press, pp. 104, 224, 260).

49. *T. Auhadi.* fol. 283.
50. W.Q.B. Shamlu Heravi, MS and also same book, ed. By Sadat Nasiri, 1995, Vol. II, p. 97 and M.T. Nasrabadi, 1938, pp. 332-33.
51. T. Auhadi, fol. 511.
52. B. Nihavandi, Vol. III, pp. 1521-24.
53. N. Qazwini, 1926, pp. 588-89.
54. *Amal-i-Salih,* Vol. II, pp. 229-30.
55. M.S. Mina, Esfahani, *Subh-i-Sadiq,* p. 50-51 - N.Qazwini, 1926 p. 560 also see: M.T. Nasrabadi, 1938, pp. 306-307.
56. M.S. Mina, *Subh-i-Sadiq,* p. 47 for his verses also see: S.A. Hasan Khan Bohpali, 1878, p. 214.
57. M.S. Mina, *Subh-i-Sadiq,* p. 46.
58. M.M. Husain, Lucknowi, 1879, p. 635.
59. M.T. Nasrabadi, 1938, pp. 1, 20.
60. See: Sadiqi Kitabdar, 1948, p. 95, T.Kashi, *ibid,* manuscript and see M. Bayani; *Ahwal va Athar-i-Khushnavisan*, Tehran, 1363 A.A./1984, Vol. III-IV, pp. 818-23.
61. A. Khayampur, *Farhang-i-Sukhanvaran,* Tabriz, 1961, p. 552.
62. Q.A. Mir Munshi, 1921, p.119.
63. N. Qazwini, 1961, pp. 854-55, also see: M.M.H. Lucknowi, 1964, Tehran Press, p. 359; M.M. Mustoufi Bafqi, 1963, Vol. III, pp. 468-69.
64. *Ibid.,* pp. 440-41.
65. M.M.A. Modarres, 1956, Vol. II p. 496.
66. M.T. Nasrabadi, 1938, pp. 454-55.
67. M.M.H. Lucknowi, 1964, p. 65.
68. Zavareh is a city near Ardestan in North-East of Esfahan.
69. W.Q.Shamlu Heravi, MS also see; W.Q. Shamlu Heravi, 1995, Vol. II, p.174-75.
70. M.T. Nasrabadi, 1938, pp. 342-43.
71. M.T. Nasrabadi, 1938, pp. 342-43.
72. W.Q. Shamlu Heravi, *op. cit.*
73. M.T. Nasrabadi, 1938, pp. 388-89 for *Kulliyat* of Rashida; see: Tehran, Malik Library, No. 5266.
74. He was chancellor of Shah Abbas II. He died in 1060/1649.
75. M.T. Nasrabadi, 1938, p. 325.
76. Ethe, II, No. 1604.

77. M.A. Sarkhush, 1951. p. 9.
78. *Ibid.,* also see: M.T. Nasrabadi, 1938, p. 325 and see; M.Q. Gopamavi, 1957, p. 49.
79. T. Auhadi, fol. 513.
80. Maktub Khan was the superinetendent of Jahangir Library. He received *mansab* of 1,500. (See; *Tuzuk*; tr. by Rogers; Vol. I, p. 12, Vol. II, p. 12).
81. Inayat-ullah is not mentioned in the *Ain* nor in the *Tabaqat.*
82. Badauni, *Ibid.*, Vol. III, pp. 283-84 and S.W. Haig translation, Vol. III, p. 391-2.
83. A.A. Razi, *ibid,* Calcutta Press, Vol. I, p. 302.
84. A. Munzavi, *Fihrest-e-Nuskhai Khati,* Farsi, (The list of Persian manuscripts), Vol. IV, p. 3272.
85. For details and Naii's quatrain see: B. Nihavandi, Vol. III, pp. 1689-90.
86. *Jahangir Nama, ibid*, 1980, p. 215, unfortunately it has not mentioned in Rogers' translation of *Tuzuk.*
87. M.T. Nasrabadi, 1938, p. 288.
88. For Nizam Dasghib-i-Shirazi see: N. Qazwini, 1961, pp. 641-60.
89. For Ghiyas Halvai Shirazi, see. A.G. Maani, 1980, pp. 316-24.
90. M.S. Sistani, *Khairul-Bayan,* p. 384.
91. Muhammad Zaman was Iranian Amir of Bengal.
92. M.S. Mina, *Subh-i-Sadiq,* pp.73-74.
93. For details and his verses see: M.T. Nasrabadi, 1938, p. 383-84.
94. For Ibrahim Khan Fath Jang see: *Jahangir Nama,* 1980, Tehran Press, pp. 438, 463 also see: *M.U.* Text, Vol. I, p. 135.
95. N. Qazwini, 1961, pp. 898-99.
96. T. Auhadi, fol. 403 also see; M.T. Nasarabadi, 1938; p. 305.
97. N.Qazwini, 1961, pp. 914-16.
98. For details and Ruzebeh's verses see: L.N. Shafiq Aurangabadi, 1977, p. 95 also see: M.S. Hasan Khan Bahador 1876, p. 178.
99. T. Auhadi, fol.271.
100. B. Nihavandi, Vol. III, pp. 1527-35.
101. About Hakim Davoud Taqarrup Khan see: *Amal-i-Salih*, Vol. II, p. 402 and Vol. III, pp. 395-96.
102. M.T. Nasrabadi, 1938, p. 116.
103. Q.A. Mir Munshi, Qomi, 1910, p. 148.
104. For details and his verses see: B. Nihavandi, Vol. III, pp. 1677-79.
105. T. Auhadi, fol.721 also see: M.T. Nasrabadi, 1938, p. 311.

106. Mirza Fasihi Khurasani was a panegyrist of Shah Abbas I.
107. M.S. Sistani, *Khairul-Bayan,* fol. 382.
108. There is difference of opinion about his name: in *Khairul Bayan* (p. 347) Qulu Khan Beg, in *Ahyaul-Mulk* (p.476) Wali Khan Beg and in *Shame-e-Ghariban* (p. 240) and *Subh-i-Gulshan* (p. 364) Murteza Quli Beg.
109. T. Auhadi, fol. 601-603.
110. The author of *Ahyaul-Mulk* has written Mujrim Shamlu came to India in 1015/1606. (See: M.S. Sistani, *Ahyaul Mulk,* 1965, p. 476.
111. M.S. Sistani, *Khairul Bayan,* fol. 347.
112. *M.U.* Text, Vol. II, pp. 290-91 and Beveridge Translation, Vol. I, pp. 259-60.
113. M.S. Mina, *Subh-i-Sadiq,* p.73.
114. See: Tables: 7.3, 4 and Graph: 7.2
115. For details see: *Ibid.*
116. T. Kashi, *Khulasatul-Ashar,* manuscript.
117. S. Kitabdar, 1948, p. 284.
118. *A.A.A.* 1955, pp. 187-88.
119. For details see: *Z.Kh.,* Vol. III, pp. 38-39, A.G. Maani, 1926, pp. 226-28 also see: A.J. Malikapuri, 1950, pp. 615-16.
120. M.P. Nasrabadi, 1938, pp. 258-59.
121. Don't mistake between Qazi Abul-Barekeh and Foruqi Samarqandi, (his name also was Abul-Barekeh) who was one of poets of 9th/15th century.
122. Qataii Heravi, 1979, p. 136.
123. T. Auhadi, Fol. 816.

8

Iranian Traders and Iranian Travellers

Migration from homeland to an alien country in anticipation of economic betterment and congenial socio-political environment, has been practice of men ever since the ancient times. Religious or political persecution has often compelled people to leave their motherland for better opportunities. In this sense, India has been heaven for the fortune seekers from the adjoining countries, especially Persia and Central Asia. This chapter narrates Persian families and individuals who migrated to India to try their luck in trade and commercial pursuit. Besides in a section of this chapter an attempt is made to survey the Iraninan tourists and travellers who visited different cities of the Mughal territory during our period.

During the 17th century 24 Iranians settled in various cities of the country for trade.[1] 15 of them were also poets, 2 had not in significant positions in administration, while 7 were exclusively men of trade. Further, among them the aim of 21 persons was primarily trade and thus search for better opportunities, two of them like; Qudrati Esfahani and Mir Muhammad Said Mir Jumla fled from Iran chiefly to avoid persecution.With Mir Jumla came also his son Mir Muhammad Amin Khan.The larger number of the 7 traders came to India in the period of Jahangir, except Qurbi Shirazi, who came to India in later days of Akbar.Touri and Johari Tabrizi belonged to west and North-West of Iran, Ghiyas Mashhadi migrated from East and North-East, and the others belonged to central plateau. Three of them returned to Iran, two of them stayed on in India, about the other 2 we have no evidence if they stayed back in India or returned to Iran.

Among fifteen traders who were also known as poets, Shapur Tehrani, Najdi Yazdi and Salahi Esfahani moved to India in the later days of Akbar, five of them migrated during Jahangir's reign.Askari Kashani who was important Irani merchant came to Mughal India via Deccan.Another 6 traders came to India in the reign of Shah Jahan.They migrated from different regions of Iran like west and north-west (3 persons), central plateau (9), and east and north-east, three persons.Among them Shapur Tehrani belonged to a noble family.He was the son of Khwaja Khwajagi, and was the first cousin of Jahangir's minister Itimadud-Daula.

Mir Muhammad said Mir Jumla and his son Muhammad Amin Khan were among the most important Irani nobles in trade.They spent their early life in Esfahan.In the Deccan, Mir Jumla acquired an interest in jewellery trading, and eventually managed to use the profits from the diamond trade to enter into the Golkonda administration by buying a revenue-Farm.By the mid-1650s he entered Mughal service and received the title Muazzam Khan. When he paid his respects to the Emperor in Delhi he received the rank of 6000 *zat* with 6000 *sawar*. On the accession of Aurangzeb he was promoted to the rank of 7000 *zat* with 7000 *sawar,* and was deputed to lead the army against prince Shuja in the East. Mir Jumla is the best example of a noble indulging successfully in sea-borne trade.Besides the reputation of being statesman general and diplomat, he is also known for his frequent business deals with European factories.He was in a real sense a merchant in trade of India, Bengal, Persia and Arabia. Mir Jumla's reason for leaving Iran in said to be escape from the *Zulm* and the grasping instinct of the Persian Shaik-ul-Islam with regard to the property of the orphans and the poor.

Mir Jumla's son, Muhammad Amin also had high business capacity and he was master of the port and bought and sold and loaded and unloaded cargo free of every impost.During Jahangir's reign he was promoted to the rank of 3000 *zat* with 1000 *sawar* and was appointed deputy *Wazir* on his father's behalf at the Court.In 1675 Muhammad Amin, in addition to the office of deputy *Wazir*, was appointed *Mir Bakhshi*, his rank was increased to the rank of 3000 *zat* with 1500 *sawar* and a bejewelled pen-case was granted to him.

Table : 8.1
IRANIAN TRADERS

Name of migrants	Place of Birth	Provinces	Regions	Period of migration	Contexts and Reasons of migration	Position in Iran	Position in India	Place of Death
Touri Tabrizi	Tabriz	Azarbaijan-i-Sharqi	West and North-West	Jahangir 1614	Trade	Trade	Trade	Iran
Johari Tabrizi	Tabriz	Azarbaijan-i-Sharqi	West and North-West	Jahangir	Trade	Trade	Trade	Iran
Ami Esfahani	Esfahan	Esfahan	Central Plateau	Jahangir	Trade	Trade	Trade	India
Amin-i-Kashani	Kashan	Esfahan	Central Plateau	Jahangir	Trade	Trade	Trade	Iran
Tahir Taleqani	Teleqan	Tehran	Central Plateau	Later day of Jahangir	Trade	Trade	Trade	Unidentified
Qurbi Shirazi	Shiraz	Fars	South	Twice-Akbar and Jahangir	Trade	Trade	Trade	Agra
Ghiyas-i-Mashhadi	Mashhad	Khurasan	East and North-East	Jahangir	Trade	Trade	Trade	Unidentified

Table : 8.2
TRADERS AS POET

Name of migrants	Place of Birth	Provinces	Regions	Period of migration	Contexts and Reasons of migration	Position in Iran	Position in India	Place of Death
Salih Tabrizi	Tabriz	Azarbaijan-i-Sharqi	West and North-West	Jahangir	Trade	Trade and poet	Trade and poet	Unidentified
Rahim Tabrizi	Tabriz	Azarbaijan-i-Sharqi	West and North-West	Jahangir	Trade	Trade and poet	Trade and poet	India
Motia-i-Tabrizi	Tabriz	Azarbaijan-i-Sharqi	West and North-West	Shahjahan	Trade	Trade and poet	Trade and poet	Esfahan
Shapur Tehrani	Tehran	Tehran	Central Plateau	Akbar (1587) and Jahangir	Trade	Trade and poet	Trade and poet	India
Najdi Yazdi	Yazd	Yazd	Central Plateau	Akbar and Jahangir	Trade	Trade and poet	Trade and poet	Iran
Askari Kashani	Esfahan	Esfahan	Central Plateau	Jahangir (1613) C.A. Via Deccan	Trade	Trade and poet	Trade and poet	Unidentified
Qasimi Esfahani	Esfahan	Esfahan	Central Plateau	Jahangir 1615	Trade	Trade and poet	Trade and poet	Unidentified

Table Contd..

Table Contd..

Qudrati Esfahani	Esfahan	Esfahan	Central Plateau	Shahjahan	Dissatis-faction of his live	Trade and poet	Trade and poet	Unidentified
Nasib-i-Esfahani	Esfahan	Esfahan	Central Plateau	Shahjahan	Trade	Trade and poet	Trade and poet	Unidentified
Haji Muhammad Makki	Esfahan	Esfahan	Central Plateau	Shahjahan	Trade	Trade and poet	Trade and poet	Iran
Kazim Savoji	Saveh	Markazi	Central Plateau	Shahjahan	Trade	Trade and poet	Trade and poet	Saveh
Aqa Ahmadi	Yazd	Yazd	Central Plateau	Shahjahan	Trade	Trade and poet	Trade and poet	Mecca
Salahi Esfarayeni	Esfarayen	Khurasan	East and North-East	Akbar (1573) and Jahangir	Trade	Trade and poet	Trade and poet	Iran
Taqi Pirzad	Mashhad	Khurasan	East and North-East	Jahangir (1613) C.A.	Trade and travelling	Trade and poet	Trade and poet	Agra (1615)
Mujibi Nehi	Nehbandan of Birjand	Khurasan	East and North-East	Jahangir 1615 C.A.	Trade	Trade and poet	Trade and poet	Unidentified

Table : 8.3
TRADERS AS ADMINISTRATORS

Name of migrants	Place of Birth	Provinces	Regions	Period of migration	Contexts and Reasons of migration	Position in Iran	Position in India	Place of Death
Mir Muhammad Said Mir Jumla	Ardestan	Esfahan	Central plateau	1630 C.A. via Deccan	Trade and Escape the *Zulm*	Trade	Trade and Admiinstrators 6000 *zat* and 6000 *sawar*	India
Muhammad Amin Khan	Ardestan	Esfahan	Central plateau	1630 C.A. via Deccan	Accompany of his father	Trade	Trade and Administrators	Ahmadabad

IRANIAN TRADERS

WEST AND NORTH-WEST IRAN

Touri Tabrizi

His name was Ashraf Beg, was called Touri as he belonged to Tour, a village near Tabriz. He had fascination for travels for trade and loved to be in the company of traders and eloquent and witty people.He then turned out as a successful merchant, visited several places in Iran and outside in Hindustan in connection with trade. Auhadi says: Ashraf Beg came back to Iraq from India in 1025/1616.[2]

Jauhari Tabrizi

Mirza Muqim Jauhari was the son of Ustatd Mirza Ali *Zargar* (goldsmith) Tabrizi and lived in Abbasabad in Esfahan.Mirza Muqim left goldsmithry, his father's job after his death and engaged in trade. He visited India twice for trade during Jahangir and shah Jahan's reigns. It is said that each time during his stay in India he earned enormous wealth, was very close to a number of the Mughal nobles.He died in Iran.Mirza Muquim was also a poet.His pen name was Jauhari.Nasrabadi has recorded some of his verses in his *Tazkira*.[3]

Central Plateau

Maulana Ami Esfahani

He was known *Ami* (commoner) because he did not come from any notable family. He migrated to India for trade when he was still very young and settled in the Deccan where he lived for long time and obtained enormous riches. Ami in connection with his trade also visited Agra, Ahmadabad and Mandu in Jahangir's time. He died in prison.[4] The author of *Sham-e-Ghariban* has mentioned him as *Alimi*, which probably is an error of the *katib*.[5]

Amin-i-Kashani

His name was Khwaja Muhammad Amin Kohsa.He belonged to Kashan. He is reported to have visited different parts of Iran and India. His source of livelihood is reported to be trade.Amin came to India during Jahangir's reign. In 1023/1614 he moved to Agra from Gujarat in connection with trade at an advanced age of seventy. Later Amin returned to Iran.[6]

Tahir Taleqani

Mir Muhammad Tahir Husaini belonged to Taleqan, a city in the north-west of Tehran. He came to India during the later days of Jahangir's reign. He was wealthy and is mentioned as merchant. During Shah Jahan time he joined the service of Zafar Khan and remained associated with him for a long time. He was also a poet. Muhammad Afzal Sarkhush the author of *Kalimat-ush-shuara* mentions some of his verses.[7]

SOUTH OF IRAN

Qurbi Shirazi

His full name was Fetahai Qurbi. He came to India in the later days of Akbar in order to trade. After some time during the Jahangir's reign he left for Iran and then he moved to Mecca where he lived for some time.Later Qurbi came to India again and settled in Agra. He died in Agra in 1025/1616 at the age of seventy.[8] According to Amin Ahmad Razi Fetaha was trader, and his source of livelihood was trade. Besides he composed some verses.[9] Qurbi also served the Mughal emperor in different ways. The author of *Akbar-Nama* says: Qurbi was dispatched to Kashghar by Akbar as ambassador in 1006/1597.[10] He was also given the responsibility of delivering the emperor's letter of invitation to visit Hindustan to Allama Chalabi Beg, Faregh Tabrizi[11] and Allama Mir Taqi-ud-din Muhammad Nisabah[12] Shirazi.[13]

EAST AND NORTH-EAST

Ghiyas Mashhadi

Khwaja Ghiyas Mashhadi was a reputable merchant. He migrated to India in Jahangir's reign in order to trade and he lived as a merchant exclusively.His son Raqim Mashhadi was a poet and was associated with Islam Khan Mashhadi.[14]

TRADERS AS POET

WEST AND NORTH-WEST

Salih Tabrizi

He was born in a family of learned men and passed early life in Qazwin. Trained in religious sciences and juris prudence, he could not imbibe his education into his character and freely amused himself with wine and music.His talents for trade satisfied his lust for seeing the world.After many successful trading missions to Turkey, he turned to India and carried on his business activities in many cities of the sub-continent. On his way Bengal, he halted at Patna and was received by the author of *Mai-Khana* in his house.He was also a poet and Abdun-Nabi "felt very much pleased by hearing his verses". A copy of his divan deposited in the imperial library of the Mughals has survived.[15]

Rahim Tabrizi

Mirza Rahim was son of Muhammad Qasim and brother of Muhammad Husain Chalabi.[16] He lived as a merchant and poet. He came to India for trade. Rahim is mentioned as a man of merit and piety. He died in India. The following verse is by him.

Alam Ze Botan-i-Hend Ziba ast; Chon dida ke Roshan az Siahiist.[17]

Motiai Tabrizi

He was born in Tabriz, but he grew up in Abbasabad of Esfahan. He is described by our authorities as an accomplished person. His source of livelihood was trade, and came to India twice during Shah Jahan and Aurangzeb's reigns. During his second trip his son died in India, and then Motiai returned to Esfahan where he died some time later. He was also a poet.[18]

CENTRAL PLATEAU

Shapur Tehrani

Khwaja Sharaf-ud-din was the son of Khwaja Khwajagi,[19] and was the first cousin of Jahangir's minister, Itimadud-Daula.[20] According to Auhadi the original name of Aqa Shapur Tehrani was Khwaja Arjasp. Shapur was also a poet. His penname was Faribi, but after coming to India he acquired a new penname, Shapur. Shapur visited India many times.[21] Nasrabadi writes that his travels to India were "to explore trade prospects."[22] Iranians, as we know, had vast trading interests in Mughal India and their caravans laden with precious goods passed between the two countries in all seasons of the year. Being a poet as well, Shapur was warmly welcomed by the literary men in Lahore, Agra and other cities of the empire.[23] Talib-i-Amuli, the poet laureate, addressed verses in his praise and copies of his *divan* circulated among the nobles of the court.[24] The author of *Mai-Khana* interviewed him in Lahore, and obtained his verses, 1025/1616.[25]

Abul Fazl Allami writes: Khwajagi Khwaja had a son of the name of Khwaja Shapur, who was likewise a literary man.[26] Sadiqi *Kitabdar* says: Faribi Tehrani was the son of Maulana Omidi.[27] But this is an error. According to A. Razi he was the brother's son of Omidi.[28] The author of *Khairul Bayan* has written: Aqa Shapur Faribi was born and grew up in Ray. He migrated to India in 996/1587 and was welcomed by Asaf Khan,[29] he returned to his homeland after some time, and then again after three years in 1019/1610 hecame to India with Yadagar Ali Sultan, ambassador of Shah Abbas I at the court of Jahangir.[30] According to the author of *Majmaul Fusaha* he died in India[31] in 1048/1638.[32]

Najdi Yazdi

Amir Abdul-Wahab Mir Najdi belonged to a Sayyid family of Yazd. He was a merchant and travelled widely.Early in his life he lived in Yazd and Kerman. He came to India several times to explore better prospects for his trade. Najdi was eloquent, witty and also composed several verses.[33]

Askari Kashani

Mir Hasan was the son of Mir Husain Kashani, one of the notable man of Kashan. Askari was a merchant and went with trading caravans to Rume, where his success encouraged him to explore similar market in the Deccan. Bijapur and Golkonda being the traditional importers of Iranian merchandise, Askari soon established himself and earned a lot of profit. He was also offered government service, but he politely declined the offers, saying, his trade required whole-time attention. But, there was enough time at his disposal to enjoy the company of the literary men; he was a friend of Zuhuri and Malik Qommi. Wealth filled his mind with novel plans: he must perform the pilgrimage to Mecca and return home to spend the rest of life in comfort. Fate decreed otherwise, for, the ship carrying the pilgrims was wrecked by storm and he survived with much difficulty. In a few days, he was a penniless man as he landed at Surat. From Gujarat he travelled via Ajmer to Kashmir and took refuge under the provincial governor, Hashim Khan[34] and his successor, Safdar Khan.[35]

The latter sent Askari on official mission to Tibet and he brought back interesting information about the land of the Lamas. Impressed by his polished manners, prince Khurram enrolled him on his personal staff and his remaining career passed under prince Shah Jahan. Among his friends was the author of *Mai-Khana* who preserved his biographical details together with a piece of *Saqi-nama*.[36]

Qasimi Esfahani

He was the son of Haji Waqif.Qasim was a cloth-seller and his source of livelihood was drapery. In order of his business he travelled to many parts of Iran. He migrated to India in 1024/1615.

Though he was not a professional poet, still he composed some good verses.[37]

Qudrati Esfahani

Mulla Muhammad Ali, known as Qudrati, was the son of Khwaja Nasir-ud-din Esfahani. Qudrati was a poet of Shah Abbas II's time. He was noted for fair-speaking and for his prudence in speech. His source of livelihood was trade.[38] He came to India in Shahjahan's reign because he was not satisfied in Iran. In India he was engaged principally in trade. He died before 1083/1672.[39]

Nasib Esfahani

Haji Talib, well known to Nasib, was the son of Haji Maqsoud *Chitsaz* (Chintz-maker) Esfahani, the headman of his area.Haji Talib after his father's death left his job of Chintz-making and engaged in trade. He migrated to India in Shah Jahan's reign as a trader. He also composed some verses.[40]

Haji Muhammad Makki

Haji Muhammad Makki belonged to Esfahan. He was an agate seller. Haji Muhammad left Iran three times.Two times he went to Macca and lived there in all for twenty-two years, as an agate merchant. He came to India during Shahjahan's reign possibly for trade. After some time he returned to Esfahan. In poetry he followed the style of the *masnavi* of *Maulavi-ye Rum*.[41]

Kazim Savouji

Muhammad Kazim belonged to Saveh, a city in south-west of Tehran, in Markazi province. He came to India in Shah Jahan's time as a trader. After some time he returned to Saveh and died there.He has also left some verses.[42]

Aqa Ahmad

Aqa Ahmad, famous as Nakhuda belonged to Yazd. He was a trader. He visited India ten times during Shah Jahan and Aurangzeb's reigns for trade. During his last visit he left for Mecca via Surat where he died in 1083/1672. He has also left some of verses.[43]

EAST AND NORTH-EAST

Salahi Esfarayeni

He belonged to Esfarayen, a city in Khurasan province. Salahi mentions in one of his *qasidas* that he was born at Murghab, a city in Trans-Oxiana in 1955/1548, but he grew up in Esfarayen. His father's name was Maulana Aqili Hakim, who was born in Esfrayen. Maulana Aqili was in the service of the Uzbek kings for some time.[44]

Hasan Beg Salahi emigrated to India from Esfayan in 981/1573 in pursuit of trade. He travelled to many parts of India, and obtained much money. He visited the holy city of Mecca in 999/1590, and lived there for two years. Afterwords he returned to India.[45]

Taqi Pirzad

His father Pirzad came from Mazandaran to Mashhad and settled there. Taqi was born and brought up there. He was witty with an inventive talent.He had made wit and humour his profession and it was due to this that he had free access to the princes and noble men. But some time his *jokes* were very vulgar that he displeased people. From Mashhad he came to India in order to see the land and travelled over the most part of this sub-continent. He visited princes and noblemen and received many valuable rewards, still he spoke ill of them. He was also endowed with some taste for poetry. He visited Khan-i-Khanan at Burhanpur, wrote a *Saqi nama* and presented it to him.Khan-i-Khanan amply rewarded him for the *Saqi nama*. After staying at Burhanpur for some time, he went to the capital city of Agra and entered the service of Jahangir. He became one of his companions and died in the year 1021/1612.His *Saqi nama* shows his fine taste for poetry, but due to his natural perversion and vulgarity he sometimes pleased and sometimes displeased people.[46] The author of *Reyaz-ush-Shuara*, mentions Taqi Pirzad as a prominent poet and jester of Jahangir's court.[47] Amin Ahmad Razi says: Taqi was a trader, and he served most of his time in the service of noblemen and kings.[48] According to *Arafatul-Ashiqin*, Muhammad Taqi Pirzad had good nature and disposition. He could not pull along with the emperor, was eventully impriosoned in Goliwar Fort. The reasons of his imprisonment however are not clear. After some time he died at Agra in 1024/1615.[49]

Mujibi Nehi

Mir Sayyid Sharif Mujibi[50] belonged to Nehbandan,[51] a city near Birjand in Khurasan province. He lived as a merchant and a poet. Mujibi could compose different kinds of verses. He migrated to India in the reign of Jahangir in pursuit of trade. Baqi Nihavandi met with him at Burhanpur in 1024/1615. He also received a *mansab* and joined the retinue of Khan-i-Khanan, but after some time however he left the service, wore *darvishi* dress and travelled to many parts of India.[52] According to Auhadi he seemed to have spent some time with Khwaja Beg Mirza Safavi and composed a verse in his praise. Auhadi visited him at Agra.[53]

The author of *Khairul Bayan* says: Mir Sayyid Sharif was one of the great and notable men of Neh. Early in his young age he left his hometown because of the unkindness of the governor, and shifted to Sistan. After four years he migrated to India where he was in the service of Mirza Jafar Qazwini for four years. He then moved to the Deccan and entered the service of Qutab Shah. Later five years after he went to Mecca and then returned to Iran. He did not stay in Iran, however, came back to India again after two years.[54]

TRADERS AS ADMINISTRATORS

CENTRAL PLATEAU

Mir Muhammad Said Mir Jumla

Mir Muhammad Said Ardestani, known to history as Mir Jumla and entitled Muazzam Khan, Khan-i-Khanan, *Sipahsalar*, and *Yar-i-Wafahadar* is a well noted Iranian who combined *tijarat* with *imarat*. Jagdish Narain Sarkar has given us a definitive biography of the man, based on the varied original sources available in Persian, English and Dutch, etc.[55] It is, therefore, not necessary here to go over the same ground again, and a summary statement of the main facts, of his life may suffice. Mir Jumla's parents belonged to an extremely indigent Sayyid family, settled, as his name, shows, at Ardestan, a city in Esfahan province. His father, Mirza Hazaru, was a poor oil-merchant of Esfahan in the vicinity of which he was born at Ardestan about 1519. In spite of the poverty of his parents, Mir Muhammad found an opportunity to acquire some knowledge of letters. Probably this helped him to secure the office of a clerk to a diamond merchant, who was ferquently in touch with Golkonda. This early experience about diamond trade stood him in good stead in his subsequent career and proved to be the cornerstone of his future prosperity. On reaching the age of discretion and manhood, Mir Muhammad Said, tormented by growing economic wants, due to a large extent to the financial exactions of a grabbing Shaikh-ul-Islam, and consequent lack of governance in Persia,[56] he left the land of his birth, like many other Persians in search of fortune.As Mir Muhammad himself observed in one of his letters to Nawwab Khalifa-i-Sultan, *Wazir* of Persia, that he had to leave his native country (1) to make our living easy, (2) to send some help to near relations, and the aged and the infirm and members of the family (3), to escape from the oppressions of the Persian *Shaikh-ul-Islam*. The story of the *zulm* and the grabbing instinct of the Persian *Shaikh-ul-Islam* with regard to the property of orphans and the poor, is widely known. The Sunnis who come here complain in Shah Jahan's court and get the reply that 'such a creed deserves such a Shaikh-ul-Islam. Therefore, owing to these defects in administration, some foreign traders stopped the despatch of goods to Persia,[56] others, considering Hindustan a better and more peaceful place than Iran, recalled their goods, already despatched, as far as possible.

Mir Muhammad joined the service of a Persian merchant, who was carrying some horses from Persia for sale to the king of Golkonda which, in those days. The exact date of his arrival in Golkonda is uncertain, but most probably it was earlier than 1630. We are also in the dark about the exact position of Mir Muhammad immediately after his arrival there.[57]

He, however, soon established himself at Golkonda primarily as a great merchant and subsequently entering Qutbshahi service obtained the title of Mir Jumla which denotes his position as the principal minister or general. He was particularly responsible for Qutb Shahi occupation of parts of the Vijayanagar empire (Karnataka), and the Qutb Shahi Karnatak became practically his private kingdom. This was bound to excite jealousy at the Qutb Shahi court; and Mir Jumla in turn turned to the Mughals for protection.[58]

It was in 1656 that Mir Jumla threw himself under the protection of

Shah Jahan who, after the successful invasion of Golkonda by Aurangzeb, granted him initially the rank of 500/5000, while his son Muhammad Amin obtained that of 2000/1000.[59] Subsequently, he was granted the title of Muazzam Khan and the rank of 6000/6000 and he was appointed to the high office of *Wazir* of the Mughal empire.[60] On the accession of Aurangzeb he was promoted to the *mansab* of 7000/7000 and was deputed to lead the army against prince Shuja in the east.[61] After the successful conclusion of the campaign, he was granted the title of Khan-i-Khanan *Sipahsalar*.[62] He then led an invasion of Assam, but on his return, died at Khizrpur in Kuch Bihar in 1663.[63]

Mir Jumla[64] was a very great officer and a princely nobleman. He was unrivalled among the leaders and *Amirs* of his age for judgment, dignity, far sightedness, wisdom, courage, genius and zeal.[65] Mir Jumla is the best example of a noble indulging successfully in sea-borne trade besides holding the reputation of an able statesman, general and diplomat, he is also known for his frequent business deals with European factors, to whom he even advanced loans. In 1642-43, the English factors are reported to have decided to borrow 4 or 5 thousand pagodas from him at Golkonda at an interest of 1½% a month for 4 or 5 months.[66] He also lent the English in Madras 16000 rials of eight or twelve months gratis.[67] Mir Jumla himself occasionally borrowed money from the English factors, apparently to financing his business enterprises.[68] He was in a real sense a merchant prince his, ships carrying on trade between Arakans, southern India, Bengal, Persia and Arabia.[69]

Mir Jumla's extensive and well organised commercial enterprises, both internal and external constituted one of the principal sources of his revenue. He charged monopoly prices and tried to control internal production. His commercial activities, for the sake of convenience, may be studied in two phases, Karnataka and Bengal. In the first phase, as Sar-i-Khail of Golkonda from 1637, Mir Jumla continued his efforts to prevent the loss to customs revenue of the state, arising from the illegal profits of the English by insisting on the strict application the Golden *farman* (of February 26, 1634).[70] His outlook seems to have been legal and rational. But he moulded his policy as suited his own interests even at the cost of those of the state.[71] Consequently, when Mir Jumla emerges as the state rom. *Wazir* of Golkonda, the European factor adopted the policy of appeasement viz-a-viz the Mir Jumla. Hence they offered him presents, lent him personnel pilots, sailors, gunners, and carried his cargoes on their own ships without changing freight and customs. Mir Jumla, in turn helped them on various occasions by lending money, confirming their privileges and allowing them to use his ships and pilots. Thus, he tried to use them as an instrument for the realisation of his commercial and political ambitions.[72]

By 1647, besides his political and administrative engagements in Karnataka, Mir Jumla expanded his sea-borne trade and his junks plied between Masulipatnam, Surat, Gombroon, Mokha, Peru, Pegu, etc.[73] In 1651 Mir Jumla is said to have owned 400 horses, 300 elephants, 400 or 500 camels, and 10000 oxen for transporting his goods to several countries like Golkonda and Bijapur and also into different parts of the Mughal empire. He also had trade relations with Pegu, Tenasserm (Mergui Archipelago), Achin, Arakan (in Burma), Persia, Bengal, Mokha, Peruk, Maldives and Mecassar. His fleet then consisted of ten ships and he intended to build more.[74] For this purpose he appears to have employed an Englishman Thomas Prait for Rs. 500/- per month, whose duty apart from building boats, was to make ammunition for river fighting.[75] He also possessed a large crew of sailors and navigators for his fleet, including both Muslims and Europeans.[76]

In 1656 when Mir Jumla joined the service of Shah Jahan he is said to have made a present to the emperor amounting to Rs. 15 lakhs and other valuables including the famous *Koh-i-Nur.*[77] An idea of his wealth may also be had from the fact that while in Golkonda, he maintained his own army equipped with efficient artillery and many European artillerymen.[78] When he was in Mughal service, he is also said to have declared that he could maintain his entire establishment and thus supplement the expenditure sanctioned by the emperor from his own resources.[79] Much of this opulence of Mir Jumla arose out of Mir Jumla's commercial activities. His diamonds were usually counted in sacks.[80] Thevenot says, that Mir Jumla possessed 20 mounds of diamonds.[81] He preferred selling the best diamonds to the Portuguese. Dom Phelipe Massarhnas, the Portuguese viceroy of Goa, was his friend as well as chief customer.[82] They exchanged presents. Dom Phelipe sent him several kinds of brocade and porcelam from China, together with many curos from Japan, and Mir Jumla sent back gems and diamonds extracted from his Golkonda mines.[83] Two of his diamonds, weighing 57 and 67 1/2 carates, which Dom showed to Tavernier at Goa were probably obtained from the Mir.[84]

Mir Jumla does not seem to have disdained commerce of any sort. He dealt in cloth, bezoar, iron, steel and saltpetre in Karnataka.[85] During his governorship of Bengal (1660-1663) Mir Jumla endeavoured to monopolise all articles of necessity and then sell them at fanciful prices. About 1660, Mir Jumla offered to supply the English factors every year as much saltpetre as they would require. In the opinion of the Madras factors he did so for his personal profit. About the same time the English factors at Patna were indebted to him for supply for 30000 bags (6000 mounds) of saltpetre.[86] Again, sale of grain placed under a strict monopoly. Paddly and other necessaries coming to Madras through his jurisdiction had to pay customs, while paddy was sold to the townspeople at 25% more than the market price. The English at Madras could not sell anything except the articles purchased from the men of Nawab's farmer at prices 50% higher than those prevailing in the neighbourhood. He wanted to establish a monopoly of "all imported goods".[87]

Muhammad Amin Khan

He was the son of Mir Muhammad said Mir Jumla,[88] styled Muazzam Khan, who was a Sayyid of Ardestan in the province of Esfahan. Mir Muhammad Amin came to India with his father. He was the only son of Mir Jumla and was an important noble of Golkanda kingdom, when the latter was at the height of his power. He had a considerable following at court and acted as deputy of his father when he was absent in Karnatak.[89] When Mir Jumla transferred his allegiance to Shah Jahan, Mir Muhammad Amin was imprisoned by Qutb Shah along with his family and his property was confiscated. He was subsequently released under the pressure of Aurangzeb's forces which invaded Golkanda. He waited upon prince Sultan Muhammad (Aurangzeb's son) near Haidarabad.[90] It was in the 30th year of Shah Jahan (1656) that Muhammad Amin, along with his father entered Mughal service. But on account of heavy rains and of his sudden illness he had to stay behind at Burhanpur while his father went to the court. After some time he came to court and received a *khilat* and the title of Khan.[91] He being promoted to the rank of 3000/1000 was appointed deputy *wazir* on his father's behalf at the court.[92] In 1657 Muhammad Amin Khan, in addition to the office of deputy *wazir,* was appointed *Mir Bakhshi*, his rank was increased to 3000/1500 and a bejewelled pen-case was granted to him.[93]

In 1658, Muhammad Amin Khan was imprisoned in Agra by Dara

Shukoh simply on the charge of neglect of duty but actually on the suspicion of Mir Jumla's collusion with Aurangzeb in the Deccan. But shortly afterwards he was released from confinement.[94]

After Aurangzeb's accession Muhammad Amin was appointed to the office of *Mir Bakhshi* and his rank was raised to 4000/3000.[95] In the 2nd year his rank was increased to 5000/4000,[96] and further to 5000/5000[97] in the 5th year. In the 7th year (1664) 1000 of his *sawar* rank was made *do-aspa* and *sih-aspa*.[98]

During the reign of Aurangzeb he also was appointed *subadar* of Lahore,[99] and Kabul.[100] In the 25th year on 16 June 1682 he died in Ahmadabad while still its *subadar*. He was buried within the Bhadra citadel.[101]

Muhammad Amin was proud and self-conceited by his nature[102] but at the same time he was known for honesty and truth. He had a wonderful memory. He memorized the *Quran* in a very short time and attained the privilege of being designated a *Hafiz* by the emperor himself.[103] Muhammad Amin also had high business capacity and he was master of the port and bought and sold and loaded and unloaded cargo free of every impost.[104]

Table : 8.4

IRANIAN TRADERS

Rg	Pr	Nu	Reasons and Contexts of Migration																									
			X1	X2	X3	X4	X5	X6	X7	X8	X9	X10	X11	X12	X13	X14	X15	X16	X17	X18	X19	X20	X21	X22	X23	X24	X25	X26
NO	Ak	0																										
0	Ja	0																										
	Sh	0																										
WNW	Ak	0																										
5	Ja	4																			4							
	Sh	1																			1							
SW	Ak	0																										
0	Ja	0																										
	Sh	0																										
CP	Ak	2																			2							
14	Ja	5																			5							
	Sh	7				1															6							
SO	Ak	1																			1							
1	Ja	0																										
	Sh	0																										
ENE	Ak	1																			1							
4	Ja	3																			3							
	Sh	0																										
SE	Ak	0																										
0	Ja	0																										
	Sh	0																										
UA	Ak	0																										
0	Ja	0																										
	Sh	0																										
Total		24				1															23							

Graph : 8.1

Number of Traders according to the reasons and contexts of their migration

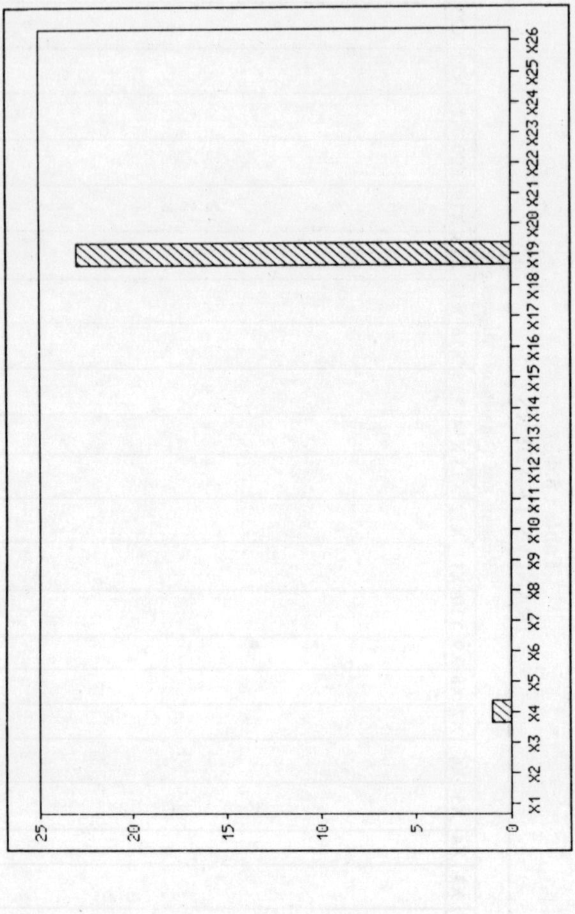

IRANIAN TRAVELLERS

India under Akbar, Jahangir and Shah Jahan created considerable bureaucratic consternation.There is ample evidence to show that persons of professional and bureaucratic skills were always in demand at the Mughal court. Besides India also attracted tourist and travellers, because it was rich, clean and beautiful. Therefore, during Jahangir and Shah Jahan's reigns 22 Iranis came to India as a travellers. All of them migrated to India only for visiting the land of the Mughals. Among these 22 persons, except Muniri Taleqani, came during Jahangir's reign.

Here also our table shows that the travellers came to India from different parts of Iran (north of Iran I, south-west 1,2 from central plateau and 1 from east and north-east). However, nobody came from West and north-west, south and south-east.

Table 8.5
IRANIAN TRAVELLERS

Name of migrants	Place of Birth	Provinces	Regions	Period of migration	Contexts and Reasons of migration	Position in Iran	Position in India	Place of Death
Qasmati Astarabadi	Astarabad	Mazandaran	North of Iran	Jahangir 1612	travelling	tourist	tourist	India
Munesi Shushtari	Shushtar	Khusestan	South-West	Jahangir 1620	travelling	tourist	tourist	Un-identified
Tazeh Resideh Esfahani	Esfahan	Esfahan	Central Plateau	Jahangir 1616	travelling	tourist	tourist	Un-identified
Muniri Taleqani	Taleqan	Tehran	Central Plateau	Jahangir 1632	travelling	tourist	tourist	Un-identified
Nutqi Mashhadi	Mashhad	Khurasan	East and North-East	Jahangir 1614	travelling	tourist	tourist	Un-identified

NORTH OF IRAN

Qasmati Astarabadi

His place of birth and growing up was the town of Astarabad in Mazandaran province. He acquired many of the sciences as a student of Khwaja Husain Saniaii.[105] Besides, Qasmati was in attendance of Mirza Beg Findarski[106] the son of Mir Zia-ud-din.[107]

According to Auhadi, Muhammad Ali Qasmati was a traveller. He fell in love at the early age to Ali Gol, and attracted him with his kindness and affable nature and then they chose travelling for some time together. Auhadi met him in Esfahan. His death occurred within 1022-1024/1613-15 in Golkonda.[108]

SOUTH-WEST IRAN

Munesi Shushtari

Maulana Munesi came to India from his native place Shushtar, a city in Khuzestan province, on a pleasure trip.His residence was in Surat.Taqi Auhadi saw him at Surat in 1030/1620.[109]

Muhammad Sadiq Mina also visited him at Surat in 1037/1627. Munesi was well known for magnanimity and high ambition.[110]

CENTRAL PLATEAU

Tazeh Resideh Esfahani

According to Arafatul-Ashiqin, Mirza *Abdul-Husain* belonged to Esfahan. He was granted by *Shah Abbas* I the title of Tazeh Resideh. He came to India during Jahangir's reign to travel through the Mughal domain. Auhadi saw him at Ajmer in 1025/1616. Tazeh Resideh spent of his time travelling.He was also a poet.[111]

Muniri Taleqani

Mirza Muhammad Tahir Muniri was a learned and an accompolished person.He migrated to India from his native place, Taleqan, a city in Tehran province, for travelling. He visited many cities of India like, Lahore, Burhanpur and Akbarabad.Mirza Muhammad Sadiq Mina met him at Bengal in 1042/1632. Afterwards Muniri as Mina says went to Patna.[112]

EAST AND NORTH-EAST

Nutqi Mashhadi

Maulana Haidar Nutqi Mashhadi was a soft-spoken person. He also served most of his time in travelling. He visited many countries. Nutqi travelled to India in the reign of Jahangir and joined the service of Nur-ud-Din Quli *kotwal*, who was an important Amir of Jahangir. The nature of his service, however, is not clear. He was in Patna in 1024/ 1615.[113]

The following table shows one of Iranian traveller who was also a poet came from West and North-West of Iran, 7 from Central Plateau.A very limited number come from the southern (1) and northern (1) regions. The regions of a further four are unclear.

Table 8.6
TRAVELLERS AS POET

Name of migrants	Place of Birth	Provinces	Regions	Period of migration	Contexts and Reasons of migration	Position in Iran	Position in India	Place of Death
Qaisari Hamadani	Tuysarkan	Hamadan	West and North-West	Jahangir	Travelling	Tourist and poet	Tourist and poet	Gujarat
Razi Esfahani	Esfahan	Esfahan	Central Plateau	Jahangir 1017	Travelling	Tourist and poet	Tourist and poet	Iran
Qasim Esfahani	Esfahan	Esfahan	Central Plateau	Jahangir	Travelling	Tourist and poet	Tourist and poet	Iran
Subhi Esfahani	Esfahan	Esfahan	Central Plateau	Jahangir	Travelling	Tourist and poet	Tourist and poet	Unidentified
Neyazi Esfahani	Esfahan	Esfahan	Central Plateau	Jahangir	Travelling	Tourist and poet	Tourist and poet	Unidentified
Muhsin-i-Razi	Ray	Tehran	Central Plateau	Jahangir	Travelling	Tourist and poet	Tourist and poet	Banaras
Iizadi Yazdi	Yazd	Yazd	Central Plateau	Jahangir	Travelling	Tourist and poet	Tourist and poet	Banaras
Shamkhal Esfahani	Esfahan	Esfahan	Central Plateau	Shahjahan	Travelling	Tourist and poet	Tourist and poet	Iran
Arif Eigi	Darab	Fars	South	Akbar and Jahangir	Travelling	Tourist and poet	Tourist and poet	Bengal

Table Contd...

Table Contd..

Yaqini Mashhadi	Mashhad	Khurasan	East and North-East	Jahangir 1615	Travelling	Tourist and poet	Tourist and poet	Patna
Nami Alikhan	Iran	Iran	Unclear	Jahangir	Travelling	Tourist and poet	Tourist and poet	India
Sulhi	Iran	Iran	Unclear	Jahangir	Travelling	Tourist and poet	Tourist and poet	India
Amir Talib	Iran	Iran	Unclear	Jahangir	Travelling	Tourist and poet	Tourist and poet	Unidentified
Sharif-Rafi-ud-din	Iran	Iran	Unclear	Jahangir	Travelling	Tourist and poet	Tourist and poet	Unidentified

Among the Fourteen travellers as poet, Arif Eigi came to India during Akbar's reign and Shamkhal Esfahani came during shahjahans's period. The other 12 migrated to India during Jahangir's reign.

WEST AND NORTH-WEST

Qaisari Hamadani

Maulana Qaisari Hamadani was born at Sarkan,[114] but he was brought up in Hamadan. He lived as a tourist, and he travelled in many parts of Iran and India. Qaisari was a learned man, was also a poet, composed some verses in old style. He died in 1022/1613 in Gujarat.[115]

CENTRAL PLATEAU

Razi Esfahani

Aqa Razi was from Esfahan. He was also a poet. He left Iran to India in 1017/1608 to journey through the Mughal territory for travelling. He entered Jahangir's service also and stayed there for some time. His verses were fluent and simple.[116]

According to Auhadi Qazi Razi-ud-din Muhsin Esfahani was very clever and intelligent, and he also had good knowledge of religious sciences. Auhadi visited him at Agra and Gujarat with Yadgar Ali Sultan, ambassador of Shah Abbas I. Afterwards Razi planed to return to Esfahan. Auhadi heard the news of his death at Ajmer in 1026/1616.[117]

The author of *Sarv-i-Azad* mentions that Aqa Razi travelled to many parts of India, and then he returned to his native country where he died in 1024/1615.[118]

The author of *Shame-i-Ghariban* mentions his name under the titles: Qazi Razi-ud-Din Mohsin Esfahani and Aqa Razi Esfahani.[119]

Qasim Esfahani

Maulana Qasim Esfahani came to India as a tourist and lived here for a long time. He was a religious person. Auhadi was his neighbour and his classmate in Esfahan. Qasim returned to Iran in 1025/1616. He passed his time as a poet and tourist.[120]

Subhi Esfahani

Subhi belonged to Esfahan, and left his native place for India during Jahangir's reign as a traveller. Subhi Beg travelled to many cities of India. He was also a poet. The fllowing verse is by him:

Gar Koshad qatil-i-man Cheshm mabandid mara;
Zankeh Yek didan ou qimat-i-sad Jan bashad.[121]

Neyazi Esfahani

According to Auhadi Naqi Assar-i-Neyazi was from Esfahan. He and his father and his brother engaged to oil pressing in Esfahan. Neyazi came to India during Jahangir period. He travelled through many parts of India, and then he returned to Iran. Neyazi was also a poet.Auhadi has recorded some of his verses.[122]

Muhsin-i-Razi

According to Malik Shah Sistani, Muhsin Razi[123] was born at Ray and received education in Shiraz. He visited India in Jahangir's reign as a tourist. He was regarded by poets and great men of India as a good poet.[124] The author of *Arafatul-Ashiqin* says: Muhammad Muhsin Razi[125] had high ambition and poetic nature. He lived in Agra and Manikpur[126] for a long time, and died at Benares.He left a *masnavi, Khusrau-Shireen.*[127]

Izadi Yazdi

He was born and grew up at Yazd.Izadi visited India in Jahangir's reign. He lived as a traveller in Iran and India. He was not a professional poet, but he composed several good poems.[128]

CENTRAL PLATEAU

Shamkhal Esfahani

Shamkhal Beg was one of *khaneh zadai* (son of a slave) Nawab Khalifa Sultan.[129] Shmkhal was a wise person. He came to India in the reign of Shah Jahan as a traveller. He travelled to many parts of India, and then he returned to Iran. He also had poetic nature. The following verses are by him:

Dar qid hayat har ke chon man bashad; Karsh hamagi nalih-o-shivan bashad.
Gar zindagi in ast ke man mibinam; Homar abadi nasib doshman bashad.[130]

SOUTH

Arif Eigi

Hakim Sirajud-Din Husain, known with his penname, Arif, was the son of Ghiyasuddin Ali. He came to India in 998/1589 as a traveller at the age of 28.Abdun-Nabi the author of *Mai-khana*, preserved a detailed account of his life in his own words which run as follows: I was born at Eig in 976/1568, the seat of the Shaban-karah Darab Fars between Shiraz and Kerman; and my father was the chief of that area. After his death, my elder brother did not treat me well and I left home. Overwhelmed by the desire to see the world, I came to India and presented a *qasida* in praise of Prince Salim, son of Akbar, at Allahabad, Alas! Jealous tale-bearers spoiled my case and told the prince that I first served his brother, Prince Danyal. Prince Salim ordered that I should be imprisoned in the fortress of Mandu, where I languished for two years. Then, I was pardoned and the prince enlisted me as his courtier. But, I enjoyed wandering, and therefore, slipped away from Allahabad without seeking his permission. In Agra, I easily found a job among the legion of court-poets; and every comfort was available to me for five years till the old Emperor (Akbar) died. As my earlier patron succeeded his father, I avoided him in view of my past conduct and trotted away from Agra towards the Deccan, where Muhammad Quli Qutb Shah, the king of Golkonda, received me kindly. Home-sickness being man's natural weakness, in a few months I voyaged back to Iran. At home, family quarrels made my life hell in five years, and I found myself compelled to take road a second time to India via Qandahar. My hopes were not belied; and the Emperor Jahangir, may God grant him life till eternity, graciously accept me in the circle of his praise-singers. Generally, I spend my regular salary and casual earnings in travelling across this vast country; and there must be hardly an important place on the map of India, which I have not seen. In the maeantime, I was punctual to recite *qasidas* before the minister, I'timadud-Daula. Thanks to his generosity, I possess five hundred bighas of land here in Bihar. Now, as you record my talk, I am fifty-two years old, 1028/1618.[131]

Taqi Auhadi, also his friend, noted down additional reminiscences in his *Tazkira*. Arif left a *divan* containing nine thousand verses, a didactic poem: *Andarz nama*, and *Saqi Nama* composed on Firdawsi's metrical pattern[132] Mirza Muhammad Sadiq Mina-i-Esfahani says: In Patna Hakim Arif Eiji visited my father, He was a notable poet of time and in Akbar's reign migrated to India. For a while Arif was in the service of Jahangir. Finally he settled in Patna, Mirza Muhammad Sadiq saw him in 1031/1621, and in 1035/1625 he went to Bengal, and the same year he died.[133] Arif Rihi (Tarif Eigi) in *Subh-i-Golshan*[134] and Arif Irani in *Qamus ul-Ahlam*[135] and *Rihanat-ul-Adab*[136] is same person.

EAST AND NORTH-EAST

Yaqini Mashhadi

According to Auhadi, Maulana Yaqini Mashhadi migrated to India duriong Jahangir's reign as a tourist.[137] The author of *Sham-e-Ghariban* mentions that Mir Muhammad Sayyid Yaqini died in 1024/1615 at Patna. This verse by him is also mentioned.

Dar kohan Khaneh donya be firaghat maneshin;
Gosh bar Halqa dar bash ke awazi hast.[138]

FROM UNKNOWN AREAS

Nami Ali Khan

He belonged to a Turkish family of Iran. Nami came to India as a tourist, and travelled in many parts of India. He was also poet and composed some verses. He died in 1029/1619.[139]

Sulhi:

According to Auhadi, Sulhi was a traveller.He came to India during Jahangir's reign. Sulhi travelled in many parts of India and died at Malwa.The following lyrical verses are by him:

Maiim ke joz koye bala manzil ma nist; Dar ishq be joz dard, murad dil-i-ma nist.
Goftim ke Sulhi ze ghulaman qadimi ist; Zad khanda ke khub ast vali qabil ma nist.[140]

Amir Talibi

Amir Talibi shifted to India from Iran in the reign of Jahangir to see the country of the Mughals. He visited many parts of India and spent his time as a poet and a traveller.This verse is by him:

Tavafe kaba-o-dor-i-hajar cha dard-i-sar ast in;
Be gard koye to gardam ke kaba degar ast in.[140]

Sharif Rafi-ud-Daula

Sharif came to India from Iran in the reign of Jahangir for travelling. Raf-ud-Daula visited many cities of India. He left some verses.[142]

TRAVELLERS AS ARTIST

Among the Iranian travellers as artist Zain-i-Esfahani came to India twice during the times of Akbar and Jahangir, and the other two come during Jahangir's reign. A list of them is as follows:

Table 8.7
TRAVELLERS AS ARTIST

Name of migrants	Place of Birth	Provinces	Regions	Period of migration	Contexts and Reasons of migration	Position in Iran	Position in India	Place of Death
Rahmati Tabrizi	Tabriz	Azarbaijan Sharqi	West and North-West	Jahangir 1606	Travelling	Traveller, poet and calligraphist	Traveller, poet and calligraphist	Agra 1616
Mahdi Kohkiluyehi	Tabriz	Kohkiluyeh va Buyer Ahmad	South-West	Jahangir	Travelling	Traveller, Musician and poet	Traveller, Musician and poet	India
Zaini-i-Esfahani	Esfahan	Esfahan	Central Plateau	Akbar	Travelling	Traveller, calligraphist and poet	Traveller, calligraphist and poet	Iran

WEST AND NORTH-WEST

Rahmati Tabrizi

According to Auhadi, Rahmati was an important tourist. He also was well versed in calligraphy and could write Naskh and Sols. Auhadi met him in Shiraz. Rahmati visited India in 1015/1616 to see the country. He died at Agra in 1025/1616. He left a *divan* with near 8000 verses.[143]

SOUTH-WEST

Mahdi Kohkiluyehi

He belonged to a great family of kohkiluyeh va Buyer-i-Ahmad province. Mahdi Quli Sultan was the son of Khalil Khan kohkiluyehi. He was a traveller and came to India in the reign of Jahangir. Mahdi Quli was also a poet and a guitar (*Tanbur*) player. He travelled in many parts of India. Auhadi met him in Gujarat in 1021/1612. He died in 1027/ 1617.[144]

CENTRAL PLATEAU

Zain-i-Esfahani

Originally he was from Basnian of Faridan in Esfahan province, but he was born and grew up at Yazd. His ancestor Khwaja Malik Shah and his father Khwaja Muhammad Husain were traders.Hakim Zain-ud-din Mahmud was a calligraphist. He visited India during Akbar and Jahangir's reigns in order to see the country. He was a friend of Auhadi. Zain Esfahani also left some verses.[145]

Table 8.8
IRANIAN TRAVELLERS

Rg	Pr	Nu	Reasons and Contexts of Migration																									
			X1	X2	X3	X4	X5	X6	X7	X8	X9	X10	X11	X12	X13	X14	X15	X16	X17	X18	X19	X20	X21	X22	X23	X24	X25	X26
NO	Ak	0																										
1	Ja	1																			1						
	Sh	0																										
WNW	Ak	0																										
3	Ja	3																			3						
	Sh	0																										
SW	Ak	0																										
1	Ja	1																			1						
	Sh	0																										
CP	Ak	1																			1						
10	Ja	8																			8						
	Sh	1																			1						
SO	Ak	0																										
1	Ja	1																			1						
	Sh	0																										
ENE	Ak	0																										
2	Ja	2																			2						
	Sh	0																										
SE	Ak	0																										
0	Ja	0																										
	Sh	0																										
UA	Ak	0																										
4	Ja	4																			4						
	Sh	0																										
Total		22																			22						

Graph : 8.2

Number of Travellers according to the reasons and contexts of their migration

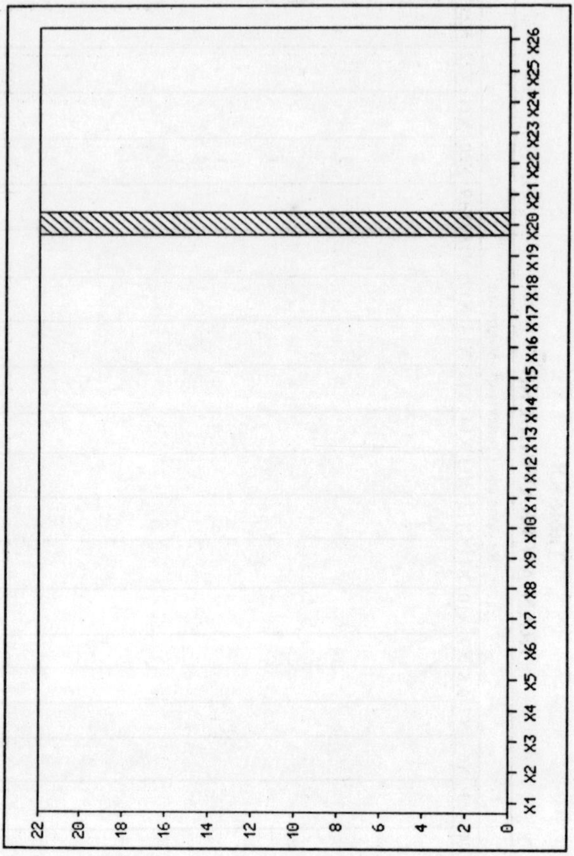

REFERENCES

1. See: Tables: 8.1, 2, 3, 4, and Graph: 8.1.
2. T. Auhadi, fol. 428.
3. M.T. Nasrabadi, 1938, pp.136-37.
4. T. Auhadi, fol. 490.
5. R. Lachmi Narayan, *Sham-e-Ghariban,* edit by Muhammad Akbar-ud-Din Sidiqi, Karachi, 1977, p. 162.
6. T. Auhadi, fol. 127.
7. M.A. Sarkhush, Lahore Press, 1942, p. 70.
8. T. Auhadi, fols: 599-600
9. A.A. Razi, Vol. I, pp. 253-54.
10. *A.N.* Vol. III, p. 732.
11. Kamal-ud-din Chalabi, pen-name Faregh was one of great men of Tabriz. In India he was in the service of Akbar. He died in 1014/1605.
12. Nisaba Shirazi was an expert of Arabian science and Hekmat (philosophy).
13. See: *A.N.* Vol. III, p. 747.
14. G.A Azad Bilgrami, 1871, pp. 238-44.
15. N. Qazwini, 1340, A.S., 1961, pp. 881-82.
16. Muhammad Husain Chalabi went to Rum in 1007/1598, then he shifted to Egypt. After some time he migrated to Mecca, afterwards he came to India and joined Jahangir, and then returned to Iran.
17. M.T. Nasrabadi, *Manuscript,* Yazd, Waziri Library.
18. M.T. Nasrabadi, 1938, pp. 291-92 under the name of Adai Yazdi, and pp. 391-92 also see: M.G.A. Azad Bilgrami, 1913, p. 57; S.A. Hasan Khan Bohapali, *Subh-i-Golshan,* 1878, pp. 424-25, A.R. Khaiyampur, 1961, p. 548.
19. A.A. Razi, Vol. III, pp. 7-78.
20. For details see; G.A. Azad Bilgrami, *Maasir-ul-Kiram* (*Sarv-i-Azad*), 1913, Vol. II, p. 285.
21. T. Auhadi, Fols: 372-75.
22. M.T. Nasrabadi, p. 237 also see: S. Numani, *Sharul-Ajam,* Tr. to Persian by Fakhr Daghi, Gilani, 1334/1955, Vol. III, p. 164 and see: H.L.A.B. Azar Beg Deli, *Atashkada Azar,* Calcutta, 1249 A.H./1833, p. 203.
23. T. Auhadi, Fols: 372-75.
24. R.Q. K. Hadayat, *Majmaul-Fusaha,* ed. Ali Quli Khan Mukhbrod-Daula, writer's son, Tehran, 1962, Vol. II, p. 23.
25. For details See: N. Qazwini, 1926, pp. 379-83.
26. *Ain-i-Akbari*, 1869, Vol. I, p. 318.
27. S. Katibdar, *Majmaul-Khawas*, Tabriz, 1327s/1948, p. 201.

28. A.A. Razi, Vol. III, pp. 73-5.
29. According to "Nasrabadi" Asaf Khan (Jafar Qazwini) was the sister's son of Shapur. (M.T. Nasrabadi, p. 237).
30. M.S. Sistani, Fols: 314-15.
31. R.Q.K. Hadayat, 1962, Vol. II, p. 23.
32. A. Kashmiri, *Tazkira Shuara Kashmir,* p. 164 qouted from *Qamusul-Ahlam*, Vol. IV, p. 2804 but in list of Rieu, p. 404, has written. He died in 1030/1620.
33. T. Kashi, Manuscript also see: S. Kitabdar, 194, pp. 98-99 see also: T. Auhadi, Fol. 766; A.A. Razi, Calcutta Press, p. 187.
34. About Hashim Khan the son of Qasim Khan Mir Bahr see: *Jahangir Nama,* 1980, pp. 45, 114, 357 and also see: *M.U.* text; Vol. III, p. 941.
35. Safdar Khan, the governor of Kashmir was the son of Mirza Yusuf Khan Razavi Mashhadi. He was *subadar* of Kashmir during 1022-1024/1613-15. Shah Jahan gave him title of Saf Shikan Khan. He died in 1055/1645.
36. N. Qazwini, 1961, pp. 719-31.
37. T. Auhadi, Fol. 600.
38. W.Q. Shamlu Heravi, 1995, Vol. II, p. 101.
39. M.T. Nasrabadi, 1938, p. 421.
40. *Ibid.,* p. 360.
41. *Ibid.,* p. 428.
42. *Ibid.,* p. 399.
43. M.M. Mustoufi Bafqui, *Jami'i Mufidi,* ed. Iraj Afshar, 3 Vols. Tehran; 1961, Vol. III, pp. 453-54.
44. T. Auhadi, Fols: 487-88.
45. A.G. Maani, *The Caravan of India,* Mashhad, 2 Vols., 1369 A.S./1990, p. 736.
46. B. Nihavandi, Vol. III, pp. 1057-89.
47. A.Q. Walih Daghistani, *Reyaz-ush-Shuara,* Ms, Tehran, Malik Library, N. 4301, p. 1066.
48. A.A. Razi, *Haft Iqlim,* ed. Jawad-i-Fazil, Tehran, 1961, Vol. II, p. 220.
49. T. Auhadi, Fol. 166.
50. Recent *Tazkira* writers have written different kinds like: Mujibi Behbahani, Mojed Nehandani and Mojed Hamadani, see: M.M.A. Modarres, *Rihant-ul-Adab,* 6 vols. Tehran, 1335 A.S./1956, Vol. IV, p. 94, also see: S. Sami Pasha, *Qamusul-Ahlam,* Stanbul, 1306 A.H./1888, 6 Vols, Vol. VI, p. 446 and S.A. Hasan Khan Bhopali, *Subh-i-Golshan*, Bhopal, Tehran, 1344 A.S./1955, p. 658 also see: A.B. Tehrani, *Azzorrieh,* Tehran and Najaf, 1381/1962, Vol. IX, pp. 969; 1117.
51. *Farhang-i-Geografihai Iran,* Vol. IX, p. 429.

52. B. Nihavandi, Vol. III, pp. 1123-9.
53. T. Auhadi, Fols: 697-98.
54. M.S. Sistani, Fols: 354-55.
55. J.N. Sarkar, *The Life of Mir Jumla,* The General of Aurangzeb, second edition, New Delhi, 1979, p. 2.
56. For Mir Jumla's letters to Khalifa-i-Sultan in Tabrizi's Golkonda letters see: J.N. Sarkar, Mir Jumla-Iran Correspondence in: *Journal of Bihar and Orissa Research Society,* pt. 1, 2, March and June 1943, pp. 87-93.
57. J.N. Sarkar, 1979, pp. 2-3.
58. F. Bernier, *Travels in the Mughal Empire,* 1655-68, Tr. A. Constable, Second Edition, New Delhi, 1968, pp. 18-20 also see: Jean Baptiste Tavernier, *Travels in India,* (1640-67), Tr. V. Ball, ed. W. Crooke, 2 Vols, London, 1889, Vol. I, p. 165.
59. Waris, p. 312 , *M.U.* text; Vol. III, pp. 531-32.
60. Waris, p. 346, 350 and *M.U.* text; Vol. III, pp. 534-35.
61. *Alamgir Nama;* Bib. Ind., Calcutta, 1868-73, pp. 218-19, 233, 266-67 see also, F. Bernier, 1968, pp. 79-80.
62. *Ibid.,* p. 563.
63. *Ibid.,* p. 173 also see: *M.U.* text; Vol. III, p. 554.
64. For a good account of Mir Jumla see: Charles Stewart, *The History of Bengal,* 2nd edition, Calcutta, 1910.
65. *M.U.* Tr. by Beveridge, Vol. II, pt. I, pp. 204-205.
66. *The English Factories in India,* ed. by W. Foster, (1642-45), pp. 69, 79.
67. *Ibid.,* (1646-50), XXVIII, pp. 166-67.
68. J.N. Sarkar, 1979, p. 94.
69. *E.F.I, (1651-54),* p. 12, for details see: J.N. Sarkar, Mir Jumla's overseas commercial activities, in: *Journal of the Bihar and Orissa Research Society,* December 1945, pp. 262-65.
70. As governor of Masulipatam from 1635-6, Mir Jumla viewed with jealousy the commercial concessions enjoyed by the English. By the Golden *farman* the English had secured complete exemption from the customs in the Golkonda kingdom on certain conditions, and the farmers of the Masulipatam customs had been allowed to pay 800 Pagodas (about 400) less a year to the State treasury by way of compensation for the resultant loss. The *farman* was to become invalid as the duties payable by the English exceeded that amount. But Mir Jumla and other officers at Masulipatam viewed these commercial concessions of the English with grave concern, as they involved the state in great loss of customs revenues, owing to unlicensed practices on the part of the English East India Company's traders. Mir Jumla together with the Dutch, therefore, took steps against them and acquainted the sultan of

their violation of the Golden *farman.* The result was that the *Sar-i-Khail.* (Abdullah Khan Mazandarani) and the Dabir (Mulla Wais) of the Golkonda court demanded from the English the excess over 800 pagodas, the stipulated yearly abatement. (See : J.N. Sarkar, 1979, pp. 8, 92).

71. *Ibid,* pp. 92-93.
72. *Ibid.,* pp. 93-94.
73. *E.F.I.,* (1646-50), pp. 98, 139, 273.At that time Golkonda merchants were obliged to carry their own goods to these places on ships mostly owned by Mir Jumla. See: W.H. Moreland, *From Akbar to Aurangzeb,* New Delhi, 1972, p. 86.
74. *E.F.I.* (1651-54), p. 12.
75. N. Manucci, 1907-8, Vol. II, pp. 85-102.
76. J.N. Sarkar, 1979, p. 84.
77. *M.U.* text; Vol. III, p. 535, For *Koh-i-Nur,* see: N. Manucci, Vol. I, pp. 237-38.
78. *Ibid.,* Vol. I, pp. 232-33.
79. S.K. Bhuyan, *Lachat Barphukan and his Times,* Gauhati, 1947, p. 152.
80. F. Bernier, 1968, p. 17.
81. Jean De Thevenot, *The Indian Travels of Thevenot and Careri,* Tr. and ed. S.N. Sen, New Delhi, 1949, pp. 144-45.
82. F. Bernier, pp. 17-18 see also; N. Manucci, Vol. I, pp. 232-33.
83. *Ibid.,* Vol. I, pp. 232-33.
84. J.B. Tavernier, Vol. I, pp. 200, 288.
85. *E.F.I.* (1651-54), p. 12.
86. *E.F.I.* (1661-64), p. 67.
87. *E.F.I.,* (1655-60), pp. 41, 93.Also see: J.N. Sarkar, 1979, pp. 77-78.
88. See: *M.U.* text; Vol. III, pp. 530-55.
89. *M.U.* text; Vol. III, p. 613 also see: Waris, p. 365.
90. Waris, p. 336.
91. *M.U.* text; Vol. III, p. 613 also see: Waris, p. 363.
92. Waris, p. 365.
93. *M.U.* text, Vol. III, pp. 613-14.
94. *Alamgir Nama;* 1868-73, p. 84.
95. *Ibid.,* pp. 111-12.
96. *Ibid.,* p. 426.
97. *Ibid,* p. 762.
98. *Ibid.,* 855.

99. For details see: *Ibid.*, p. 1065, also see: *Maasir-i-Alamgiri,* 1871, pp. 62-63.
100. For details see: *Alamgir Nama,* p. 1067, and *Maasir-i-Alamgiri,* p. 64.
101. Ali Muhammad Khan, *Mirat-i-Ahmadi*, ed. Sayyid Nawwab Ali, Baroda, 1927-28, Vol. I, p. 302.
102. *Maasir-i-Alamgiri,* 1871; p. 219 also see; N. Manucci, Vol. II, p. 179.
103. *M.U.* text, Vol. III, p. 620 also see: *Maasir-i-Alamgiri,* 1871; p. 219. For more information about Muhammad Amin Khan see: *M.U.*, text, *op. cit.*, pp. 618-19, and see; *Amal-i-Salih,* Vol. III, p. 213.
104. For details see: F. Bernier, 1968, p. 195 also see: *E.F.I.* (1655-60), p. 187.
105. A.A. Razi, Calcutta Press; Vol. III, pp. 122-23.
106. Eskandar Beg Munshi says: Mirza Beg Findarski was from great Sayyid family of Astarabad. He was in the service of Safavid Kings.(See: *A.A.A.*, p. 530).
107. S. Kitabdar, 1948; p. 229.
108. T. Auhadi, Fol. 600.
109. T. Auhadi, Fol. 730.
110. M.S. Mina, *Subh-i-Sadiq,* p. 62.
111. T. Auhadi, Fol. 497.
112. M.S. Mina, *Subh-i-Sadiq,* p. 57.
113. T. Auhadi, Fol. 768.
114. The correct name is Tuysarkan, a city near Hamadan.
115. T. Auhadi, Fol. 604 also see: A.A. Razi, 1961. Vol. II, pp. 569-70.
116. M.S. Sistani, *Khairul-Bayan,* Fols. 398-99.
117. T. Auhadi, Fol. 269.
118. M.G.A. Azad-i-Bilgrami, 1913, p. 31.
119. Lachmi Narayan, 1977, pp. 88-89.
120. T. Auhadi, Fol. 596.
121. T. Auhadi, Fol. 403.
122. T. Auhadi, Fol. 782.
123. There is a difference of opinion about his name: Husain Lucknowi mentions Fani Tehrani (See: M.M.H; Lucknowi, 1964, p. 502) and Hasan Khan Bhopali has written Fani Razi (See: S.A. Hasan Khan Bhopali, 1878, pp. 373-74).
124. M.S. Sistani, Fols. 348-49.
125. In *Arafatul Ashiqin,* erroneous copy of Bankipur, *Katib* (Scriber) has written Muhammad Hasan Razi.
126. Manikpur is district between Iskandar Pur and Qunoch near Ganga (See: *A.N.*, Vol. III, p. 109).

127. T. Auhadi, Fols. 708-709.
128. T. Auhadi, Fols. 129-30.
129. Sayyid Ala-ud-din-Husain Khalifa Sultan Mazandarani (d. 1064/1653) was the son of Mir Rafiud-Din Muhammad Sadr, who was the great man of his time. Khalifa Sultan was bridegroom and *Wazir* of Shah Abbas I and Shah Abbas II (For details See: M. T. Nasrabadi, 1938, pp. 15-16).
130. *Ibid.,* p. 147.
131. N. Qazwini, Lahore Press; pp, 420-30 also see: A.A. Razi, 1961; Vol. I, pp. 169-171.
132. For details see: T. Auhadi, fols, 488-89.
133. M.S. Mina-i-Esfahani, *Subh-i-Sadiq,* p. 47.
134. S.A. Hasan Khan Bhopali, Bhopal 1295/1878, p. 267.
135. Sami Pasha, *Qamusul-Ahlam,* Stanbol, 1306/1888, Vol. IV, p. 3039.
136. M.M.A. Modarres, *Rihanatul-Adab,* Tehran Press, Vol. III, p. 47.
137. T. Auhadi, fols. 815-16.
138. L.N. Shafiq Aurangabadi, *Sham-e-Ghariban,* ed. by Muhammad Akbar ud-Din siddiq, Karachi, 1977, p. 271.
139. T. Auhadi, fol. 763.
140. T. Auhadi, fol. 407.
141. T. Auhadi, fol. 421.
142. T. Auhadi, fol. 270.
143. T. Aauhadi, fol. 265.
144. T. Aauhadi, fol. 731.
145. T. Auhadi, fol. 284.

Conclusion

Akbar promoted Iranian nobles to high ranks as a reward for their loyalty when he faced difficulties to his plans because of the inordinate ambitions of the Chaghtais.[1] During the reigns of Jahangir and Shahjahan Iranis are found to have improved their position in number and *mansab*. It appears that the Iranian nobility inherited by Akbar had already formed its nucleus in the court during the period of Humayun's stay in Iran and his restoration of the Indian Empire. In addition to this nucleus a large number of Iranians migrated to India during the 16th and 17th centuries in search of employment and were admitted to the nobility. Together with Mughal King's conscious effort at diversifying the ruling class, his patronage of Persian culture was obviously the principal factor which might have encouraged them to come to India. According to the sources we consulted from amongst the contemporary Persian, later Persian, both Iranian and Indian, European accounts and travelogues, related to the subject, 461 Iranians in different categories migrated to India to live here temporarlily or permanently in the period under our review. Among these 461 mentioned in these sources, 187 persons came from Central plateau, like Esfahan, Qazwin, Yazd, Kashan, Kerman, Qom, Tehran, Zanjan, Damghan and Saveh; 70 from east and north-east, such as Mashhad, Turbat, Qain, Khaf, Gonabod, Sarakhs, Sabzevar, Neishabour and Quchan. It can be said that most of Iranian immigrants came from eastern or central part of Iran. 64 persons came from west and north-west regions like Ardabil, Khalkhal, Tabriz, Hamadan, Tuysarkan, Nihavand and Lurestan, 48 from south such as Shiraz, Neyriz, Kazerun, Jahrum, Darab and Hormuzgan, 28 came from north such as Astarabad, Amul, Sari, Rasht, Rudbar and Lahijan. A very limited number 9 people, came from south-west such as Khusestan and Kohkeyluyeh va Boyer Ahmad provinces, there was only one immigrant from Sistan va Baluchistan province. The homelands of the remaining 54 people are unclear.[2]

It often happened in the eastern Islamic world that due to a lack of expertise in administration, a new dynasty employed bureaucrats of the former dynasty. Thus the Safavid dynasty re-employed administrators of the Aq Qoyunlu, the dynasty they themselves had overthrown. In this context, it is readily understandable that when the Mughal empire was founded in the sixteenth century, many members of the Iranian elite were invited to the Mughal court. The lack of administrative specialists with Persian bureaucratic skills in the newly conquered territory must have been particularly serious. Furthermore, the fact that the second Emperor Humayun was finally able to gain the throne as a result of Safavid military aid must have had something to do with the increase in the Iranian strength at the Mughal court in the middle of the sixteenth century. Therefore, it is interesting and noteworthy that even at the zenith of the dynasty's prosperity in the seventeenth century under Jahangir and Shah Jahan, the Mughals welcomed Iranian immigrants and gave them high positions.

It must be underlined that, although the Mughal emperors were Sunnis, they welcomed Iranian Shia immigrants. The Mughal Empire was certainly much more liberal pragmatic than the Ottoman Empire and Uzbek regime as far as religion was concerned. Iranian migration to Ottoman empire and Central Asia after the rise of the Safavids was limited only to those who were religiously persecuted. In addition, in this context this is also to be noted that Persian was official and court language of Mughal empire, whereas the language of Ottoman territory and Uzbek regime was Turkish. Therefore, the Iranian people who migrated to India were not simply very large in number compared to those who left for Central Asia or the Ottoman lands; they belonged to diverse spheres of intellectual, literary political and commercial pursuits. Among them as we saw above, 201 people were poets, 54 in politics and administration, 47 artists and craftsmen, 37 scholars, 27 poets as administrators, 24 traders, 22 travellers, 19 Shaikhs, *sufis, darvishes* and *qalandars;* 11 scholars, *Waqianavis* and artists in administration, 9 physicians and *qazis,* 5 with diverse skills and 5 Iranian women. As regards the period of their migration, 98 of them came to India in the later days' of Akbar's reign, 256 persons in the reign of Jahangir and 107 during Shah Jahan's reign.[3]

The Iranians made a steady advance in occupying high offices, though they were far from obtaining the monopoly. We have seen that most of Iranians came to India during Jahangir's reign when the

Table : Con.1

REGIONS AND CATEGORIES OF THE MIGRANTS

Rg	Pr	PA	OA	S	AG	DO	SW	PQ	SS	IT	IR	P	IW
NO	Ak	0	2	1	0	0	0	0	0	0	0	3	0
28	Ja	0	0	4	3	0	0	1	0	0	1	7	1
	Sh	0	0	0	0	0	0	0	0	0	0	5	0
WNW	Ak	1	1	2	0	0	0	0	0		0	1	0
64	Ja	1	4	4	5	0	0	0	0	4	3	21	1
	Sh	3	0	0	2	0	0	0	0	1	0	10	0
SW	Ak	0	0	0	0	0	0	2	1	0	0	0	0
9	Ja	0	0	3	0	0	0	0	0	0	1	1	0
	Sh	0	0	0	0	0	0	0	0	0	0	1	0
CP	Ak	14	5	1	4	1	2	1	3	2	1	13	0
187	Ja	7	5	9	11	1	2	1	6	5	8	37	1
	Sh	5	0	1	6	0	0	2	0	7	1	25	0
SO	Ak	1	0	1	1	0	0	1	1	1	0	3	0
48	Ja	1	0	4	8	1	0	0	3	0	1	6	0
	Sh	0	0	2	1	0	0	0	0	0	0	12	0
ENE	Ak	3	3	2	1	0	0	1	0	1	0	6	0
70	Ja	4	1	2	2	0	5	0	2	3	2	19	2
	Sh	0	3	1	0	0	0	0	0	0	0	7	0
SE	Ak	0	0	0	0	0	0	0	0	0	0	0	0
1	Ja	0	0	0	0	0	0	0	0	0	0	1	0
	Sh	0	0	0	0	0	0	0	0	0	0	0	0
UA	Ak	6	1	0	0	1	0	0	0	0	0	3	0
54	Ja	5	0	0	1	1	2	0	3	0	4	15	0
	Sh	3	2	0	2	0	0	0	0	0	0	5	0
Total	461	54	27	37	47	5	11	9	19	24	22	201	5

Graph : con.1

Numer of Iranian migrants in different categories according to the places of their origins

NORTH

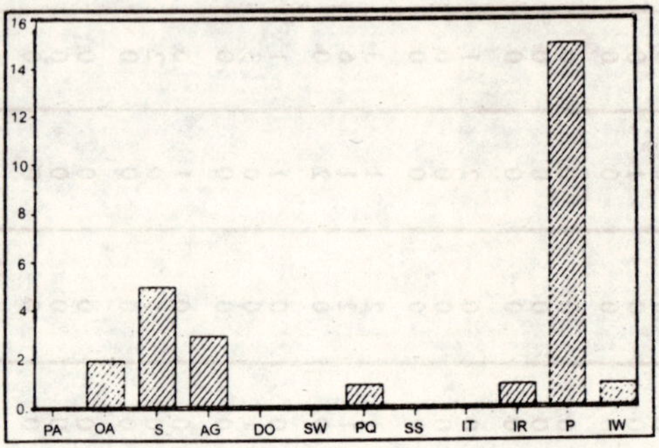

WEST AND NORTH-WEST

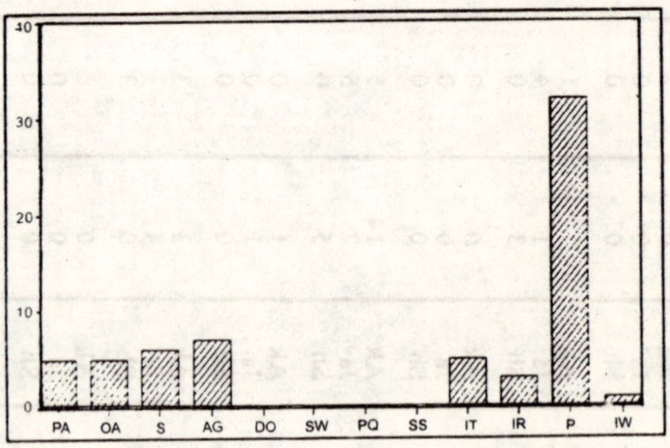

Graph Contd.

SOUTH-WEST

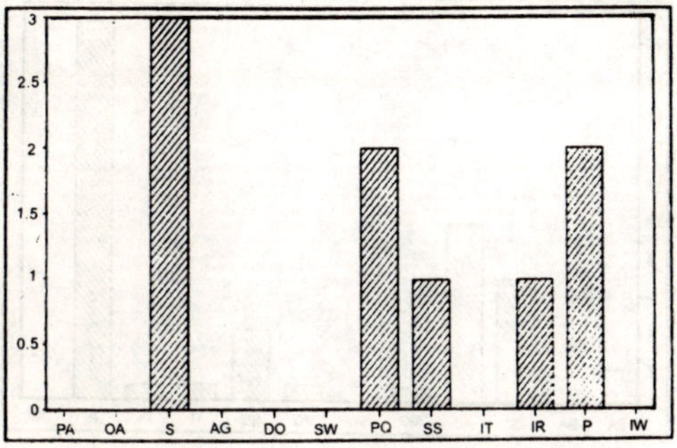

CENTRAL PLATEAU

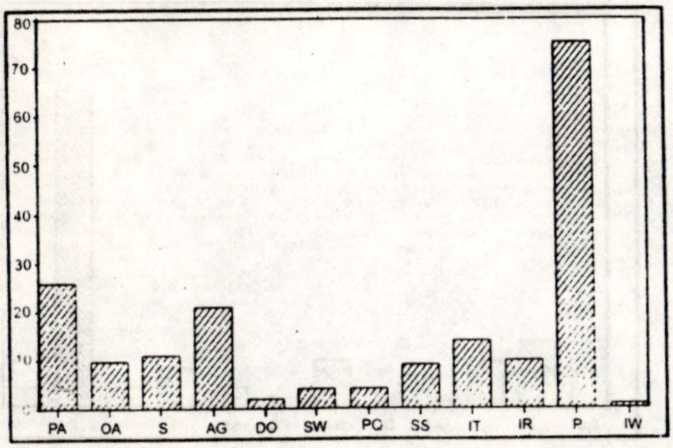

Graph Contd.

SOUTH

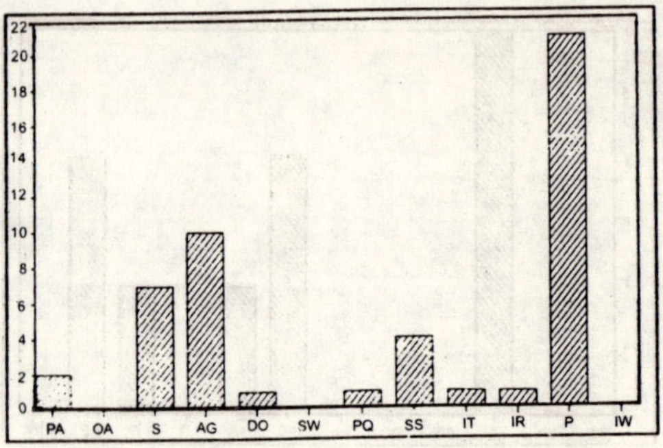

EAST AND NORTH- EAST

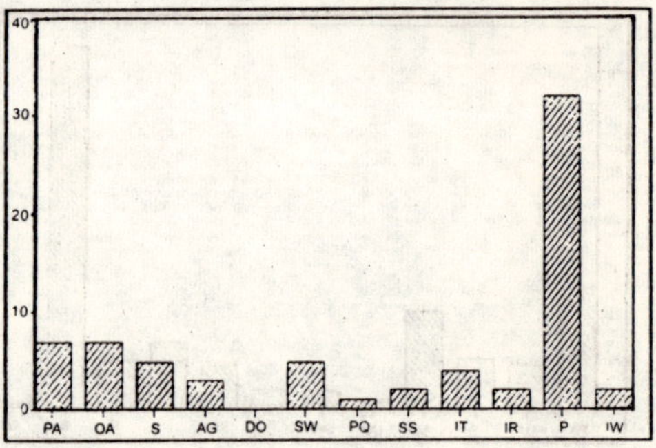

Graph Contd.

SOUTH- EAST

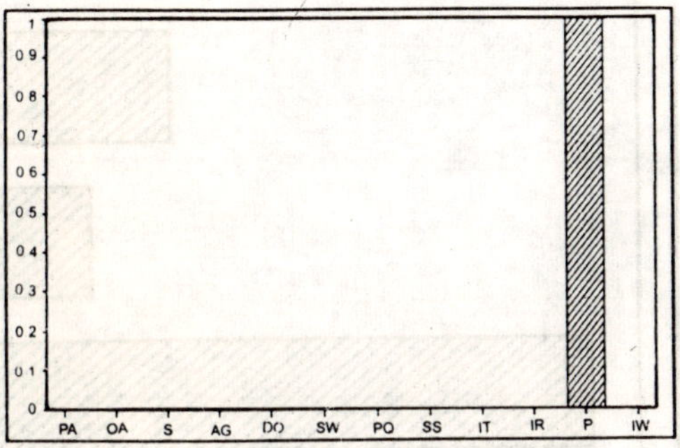

UNCLEAR AREA

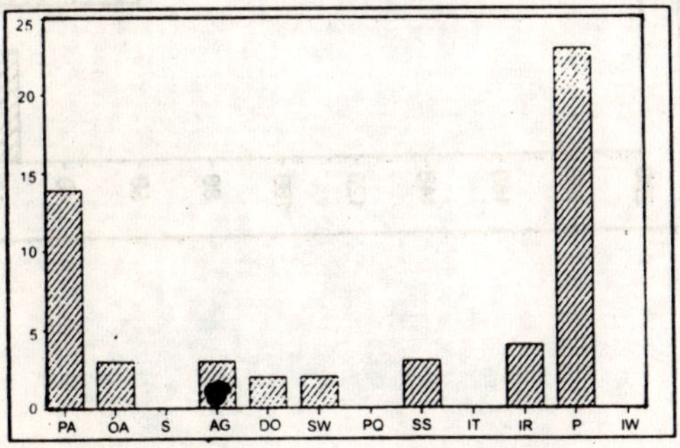

Graph : con.2

Iranians migration in mughal India according to the regions from where the migrants came

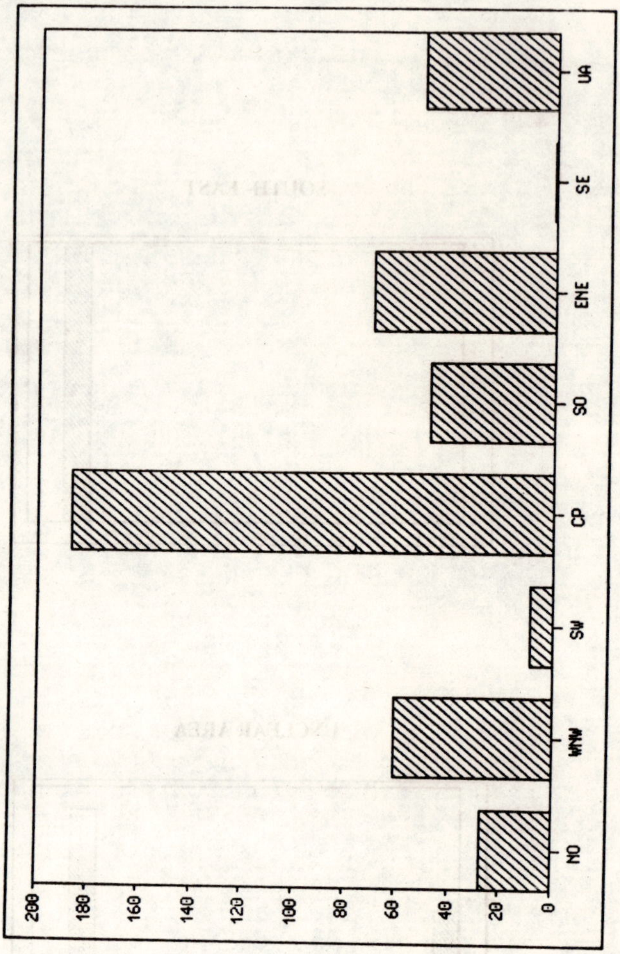

Iranians formed a very important element in the nobility, and this element was constantly replenished by immigration. Changes in the racial composition of ministers are of some interest. It will be seen that Akbar drew his ministers from almost all sections of the nobility: Iranis, Turanis, Hindus and Indian Muslims. But with Jahangir, the complexion changes: all his three wakils were Iranis; so were all his six diwans, except for one *wazir-ul-mulk* who held the office jointly for barely one year at the beginning of the reign. All his *Mir Bakhshis* and *Mir samans* also were Irani. The sadrs formed the sole exception to this process of Iranization, partly because, being a semi-theological office, there was a basic preference for those who were Sunnis, and the Iranis were mostly Shias. Iranian domination continued under Shah Jahan. Asaf Khan was his only wakil. All the thirteen years of the three decades of Shah Jahan's reign. As for sadrs, the sole Irani *sadr* of Jahangir's reign continued under Shah Jahan for fifteen years, but his two successors were Indian Muslims.

Table : Con. 2

CATEGORIES, NUMBERS AND PERIODS OF THE MIGRANTS

Categories	Number	Periods		
		Later Days of Akbar	Jahangir	Shah-jahan
Politics and Administration	54	25	18	11
Poets as Administrators	27	12	10	5
Scholars	37	7	26	4
Artists and Craftsmen	47	6	30	11
People with Divers Skills	05	2	3	0
Scholars, *Waqia Navis*, and Artists in Administration	11	2	9	0
Physicians and *Qazis*	9	5	2	2
Shaikhs, *Sufis*, *Darvishes*, and *Qalandars*	19	5	14	0
Traders	24	4	12	8
Travellers	22	1	20	1
Poets	201	29	107	65
Women	5	0	5	0
Total	461	98	256	107

Graph : con.3

Number of Iranian people according to the periods of their migration

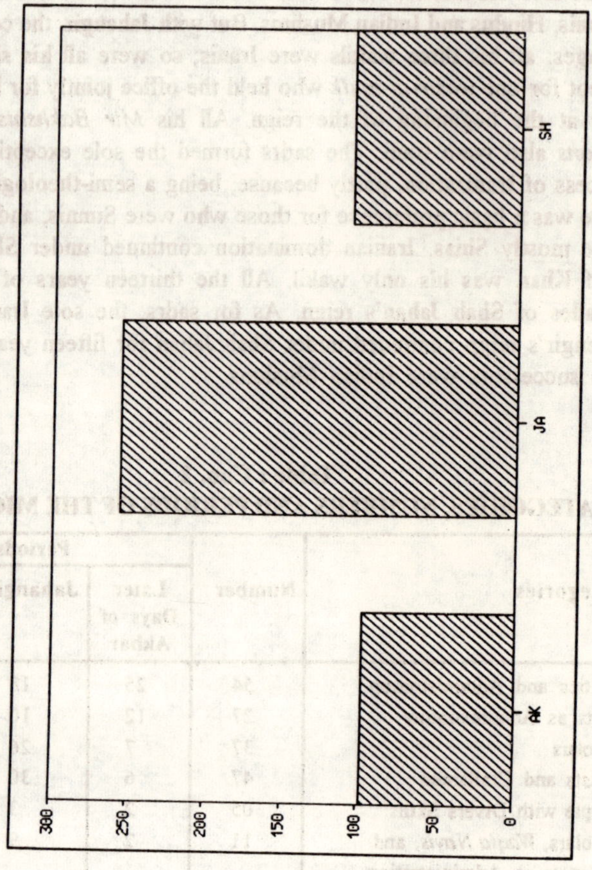

In addition, our sources show 26 reasons[4] and factors responsible for Iranian migration to India. The most important reason was the unfavourable religious atmosphere in Safavid Persia during the sixteenth and seventeenth centuries. Our tables[5] show 21 people having migrated to India because of religious persecution in Iran in the period under review. The most important of them were Naqib Khan Qazwini, who hailed from the family of the Saifi Sayyids of Qazwin. His father Abdul Latif was the first person known to have come to India because of religious persecution in Iran. He was a noted member of the Iranian Sunni community. Abdul Latif's father, Mir Yahya Saifi was a famous philosopher and theologian. He enjoyed the patronage of Shah Tahmasp who used to call him Yahya Masum. The Shah's favours to him excited the jealousy of his enemies the target of whose envy was in particular Masumi's sons Abdul Latif and Alaud Daula. This resulted in the imprisonment of Mir Yahya and his sons. Subsequently, Abdul Latif along with his son Khwaja Ghiyas-ud-din fled to Gilan and then at the invitation of Humayun proceeded to India. After the arrival of Mir Abdul Latif and Ghiyas-ud-din Nqib Khan other members of the family such as Shah Ghazi Khan a cousin of Ghiyas-ud-din Naqib Khan, Alaud-Daula Qazwini and Qazi Isa who had served as *Qazi* of Iran for a very long period came to India and were taken in service. Badauni states that Saifi Sayyids were all orthodox Sunnis and Shah Tahmasp deprived them of their estates in Iran,[6] thus compelling Ghiyas Beg (Itimad-ud-daula Tehrani) and his brother Wasli Tehrani together his son Sharif to come to India.

Table : Con. 3
TOTAL NUMBER OF IRANIAN MIGRANTS

CAT	No.	Reasons and Contexts of Migration																									
		X1	X2	X3	X4	X5	X6	X7	X8	X9	X10	X11	X12	X13	X14	X15	X16	X17	X18	X19	X20	X21	X22	X23	X24	X25	X26
PA	54	4	6	5	2	0	0	1	7	0	0	0	3	0	12	0	0	0	2	0	0	0	2	0	0	2	8
OA	27	1	0	1	0	0	0	0	3	3	0	1	1	0	4	1	2	0	3	1	0	0	0	0	0	0	6
S	37	1	2	0	1	0	0	0	1	0	1	3	0	1	3	8	0	1	0	1	1	1	0	0	0	0	12
AG	47	1	1	1	0	0	0	0	2	0	0	0	2	0	16	4	2	0	2	0	2	0	0	0	0	0	14
DO	5	0	0	0	0	0	0	0	0	1	0	1	0	0	2	0	0	0	0	0	0	0	0	0	0	0	1
SW	11	1	0	1	0	0	0	0	4	0	0	1	1	0	1	0	0	0	0	0	0	0	0	0	0	0	2
PQ	9	1	0	1	0	0	0	0	1	0	0	0	0	0	3	0	0	0	0	0	0	0	0	0	0	0	3
SS	19	1	0	0	0	0	2	0	1	0	0	1	0	0	2	0	0	0	0	0	2	0	0	6	0	0	4
IT	24	0	0	0	1	0	0	0	0	0	0	0	0	0	0	0	0	0	0	23	0	0	0	0	0	0	0
IR	22	0	0	0	0	0	0	0	0	0	0	0	0	0	0	0	0	0	0	0	22	0	0	0	0	0	0
P	201	11	2	1	3	1	0	4	2	4	0	10	1	0	65	11	0	0	7	1	17	2	1	0	1	0	57
IW	5	0	0	0	0	0	0	0	2	0	0	0	1	0	1	0	0	0	0	0	0	0	0	0	0	0	1
Total	461	21	11	10	7	1	2	5	23	8	1	17	9	1	109	24	4	1	14	26	44	3	3	6	1	2	108

Graph : con.4

Total number of Iranian migrants according to the reasons and contexts of their migration

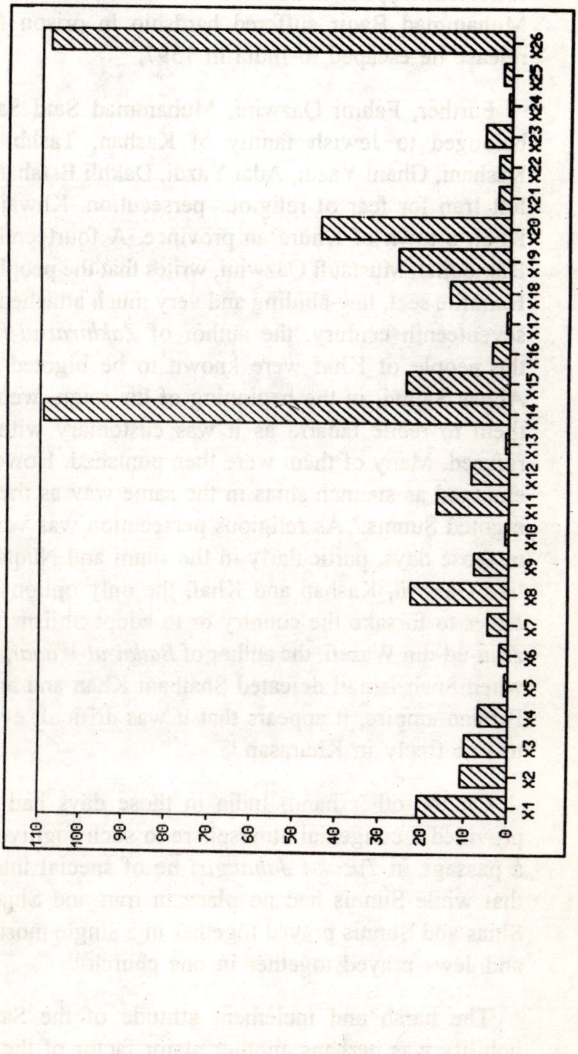

Sharif Amuli, a leader of Nuqtawi sect, is also said to have migrated to India from Amul under similar circumstances of persecution.[7] Muhammad Baqir Khurdah Kashani was accused of heresy because he followed the path of Mahmud Pasikhani, the founder of Nuqtawi sect. Muhammad Baqir suffered hardship in prison for two years. After release he escaped to India in 1597.

Further, Fahmi Qazwini, Muhammad Said Sarmad Kashani, who belonged to Jewish family of Kashan, Tashbihi Kashi, Ebadullah Kashani, Ghani Yazdi, Adai Yazdi, Dakhli Esfahani and Amini Darsani left Iran for fear of religious persecution. Khwaja Jahan belonged to Khaf, a town of Khurasan province. A fourteenth century chronicler, Hamdullah Mustaufi Qazwini, writes that the people of Khaf were of the Hanafite sect, law-abiding and very much attached to their faith.[8] In the seventeenth century, the author of *Zakhirat-ul-Khawanin* states that the people of Khaf were known to be bigoted Sunnis. When Shah Abbas Safavi, in the beginning of his reign, went to Khaf, he forced them to recite tabarra as it was customary with the shias, but they refused. Many of them were then punished. However, the Khafis later emerged as staunch shias in the same way as they had formerly been bigoted Sunnis.[9] As religious persecution was very common in Persia in those days, particularly in the sunni and Nuqtawi dominated areas, like Qazwin, Kashan and Khaf, the only option left with people was either to forsake the country or to adopt Shiism. From the account of Zain-ud-din Wasefi, the author of *Badai-ul-Waqai*, who was in Khurasan when Shah Ismail defeated Shaibani Khan and annexed that region to Persian empire, it appears that it was difficult even for *Tafzili* Sunnis to live freely in Khurasan.[10]

On the other hand, India in those days had liberal environment, provided a congenial atmosphere to such fugitives. In this connection a passage in *Tuzuk-i Jahangiri* be of special interest. Jahangir noted that while Sunnis had no place in Iran and Shias in Turan, in India Shias and Sunnis prayed together in a single mosque just as Christians and Jews prayed together in one church.[11]

The harsh and inclement attitude of the Safavids towards their nobility was perhaps another major factor of the migration. After the death of Shah Ismail Safavi (1524 A.D.) family feuds among princes and factional rivalries among nobles led to instability and anarchy in the Empire which found its culmination in the establishment of a kind of tradition of bloodthirstiness in Persia.[12] The author of *Alam-Ara-i-Abbasi* gives a detailed account of political crisis after Shah Tahmasp's death and before the accession of Shah Ismail II dealing with the execution of leading nobles and assassination of princes.[13] Abul Fazl writes that in the reign of Shah Ismail II which lasted for one year and six months, a large number of important men were killed and deprived of their posts. The Shah stretched out his hand to slay his brothers, other relatives and the grandees. He further adds that in the reign of Shah Muhammad Khudabanda because of the rebellion of Abbas Mirza (later Shah Abbas) a large number of nobles were killed.[14] In his letter to Shah Abbas, Akbar while discussing the critical condition of the Safavid court, particularly advises him that he (Shah Abbas) must practice endurance of burdens and the ignoring of the mistakes of the hereditary servants and new employees and advance the interests of the sincere, and that he must also exercise supreme caution before putting anybody to death.[15]

Shah Abbas had then decided to break the Turkman leader's monopoly of military power by creating a new army. The policy as a result reduced the number of powerful Qizilbash provincial governors who had acted like petty princes in the areas under their jurisdiction and enhanced the prestige of a new element in Safavid Iran, namely, the *Ghulams*. Subsequently, a good number of leading Safavid nobles migrated to India. Mahmud Turkman, Sultan Afshar, Khwaja Beg Mirza Safavi, Imam Quli Beg Shamlu, Hakim Dawud Taqarrub Khan, Ghururi Kashi, Mir Ilahi Hamadani, Tasalli Lurestani and Mir Findarski came to India under such circumstances. Hakim Abul Fath Gilani, son of Abdur Razzaq the *Sadr* of Gilan, fled to India along with his two brothers Hakim Humam and Hakim Nur-ud-din after the imprisonment of Khan Ahamd Karkia the ruler of Gilan. In India they were given employment by Akbar in 1575.[16] Amongst the direct Iranian immigrants the best known was Ali Mardan Khan Zig, a Kurd by origin. His father Ganj Ali Khan Zig was a confidential officer of Shah Abbas I who called him *Arjomand Babai* and appointed him governor of Kerman and Qandahar. After his father's death Ali Mardan Khan was appointed governor of Qandahar and was called *Babai Sani* by the Shah.[17] When he was charged with serious offences by Shah Safi he made over the fort of Qandahar to Shah Jahan in 1638 and came to India where he was awarded the rank of 7000 *zat* and 7000 *sawar* and the titles of *Amir-ul-Umara* and *Yar-i-Wafadar.*[18]

Prof. Athar Ali writes that Shah Abbas I during 31 years of his rule executed no less than 48 prominent officers either on suspicions or on religious grounds. In the Mughal empire, as he remarks, let alone such executions, even dismissals were very rare, and confiscation of nobles property as punishment was practically unknown.[19]

Some of the Iranis (10 people) came to India under the growing pressure of Uzbek invasions on the border povinces and the Safavid subjugation of hereditary chiefs under whom they were serving in important positions. Amini Mashhadi and Wajhi Heravi belonged to such a family. They had to forsake their country under the pressure of Uzbek invasion on Khurasan. The two Safavid brothers, Mirza Muzaffar Husain and Mirza Rustam Safavi, great grandsons of Shah Ismail Safavi, also migrated to India under such condition. They were granted high positions at the Mughal court.

In addition, there were a number of other factors which led to the Iranians settlement in Mughal India. There were some who fell into disfavour, not of the Safavid monarch, but of their *Wazirs* and governors, or were overwhelmed because of their rivalry with others in the field of their activities and therefore left for India. Salim Tehrani, a disciple of *Khalifa Sultan* rose to be *Shaikh-ul-Islam* of Tehran, but felt that he could find peace only in India. Some came in the retinue of Iranian embassy or even in the company of their relatives; some for trade, or travelling, simply in search of job, or to earn fame, on the invitation of friends and relatives, having heard the legendary fame of the Mughal court, or just by chance.[20] Mirza Qawam-ud-din Jafar left Iran in search of fortunes. He was the son of Badi-uz-Zaman, the *wazir* of Kashan in the reign of Shah Tahmasp. Mir Abdur-Razzaq Mamuri, Rahmat Khan Kashani, Sultan Nazr and Saif Khan Mirza Safi left Iran at the instance of their relatives already settled in India.

There are some important Iranian immigrants who had first served in the Deccan before joining the Mughal court. As regards the persons of rank, our sources show that many of the immigrants or their ancestors held important offices under their previous masters too in Iran or in the Deccan, before joining the Mughal service. Mir Fathullah Shirazi, the famous scholar and scientist, first came to the Deccan at the invitation of the Adil Shah of Bijapur. Later Akbar invited him to his court.[21] Mir Muhammad said, Mir Jumla Shahristani was *Wazir* of Golkonda under Muhammad Quli Qutb Shah. When Qutb Shah died,

Mir Jumla returned to Esfahan, where he was ill-treated by Shah Abbas I. Eventually, in a letter to Jahangir he expressed his earnest desire of joining the Mughal service. Jahangir thereupon invited him and appointed him *Mir-i-Saman.*[22] There are some others fled from Iran out of fear from Shah Abbas I. In 1614-15/1023-24 Shah Abbas ordered the massacre of the *Sufis* and *darvishes,* when he feared that their resistance to the new policy may Jeopardize his position. He accused them of hatching or at least being involved in intrigues against him in collaboration with the Ottomans. Thereupon many of *Sufis* and *Qalandars* escaped to India.

In addition to these specific types of immigrants, a large number of Iranis (109 people) came to India during the 17th century to try their luck or as adventurers in search of better opportunities and better prospects. They knew that the Mughal court was open to talented people, where by merit they might be able to achieve distinct positions and high *mansabs*. In this category come a large number of the poets. It is well known that during the seventeenth century Persian poetry blossomed in India rather than in its birthplace in Iran. The Safavids then were more concerned with the propagation of the shia doctrine and the encouragement of divine learning, theological principles and laws, whereas poets and their poetry served as means to promote the ostentation and magnificence of the imperial court. These Iranian poets and their *qasidas* added to the lustre and glamour of the Mughal court. The poets encouragement and fortunes were not limited to the royal court alone. A large number of the nobles and high *mansabdars* also had poets in their entourage. Patronage of poets was a status symbol, and the expense incurred was well-justified in a noble's view. Since a Mughal noble's *mansab* and estate was not hereditary, he tried to spend his wealth as lavishly and as elegantly as possible during his lifetime. Some of the high nobles of Mughal India stand out here as eminent patrons of Persian poetry. The most distinguished of them was Abdur-Rahim Khan-i-Khanan, himself a poet in three languages. His protege Abdul-Baqi Nihavandi has left in his *Ma'asir-i-Rahimi* accounts and specimens of verses of scores of poets, most of them of Persian origin, who enjoyed his patronage. We can mention a large number of Iranian poets in Khan-i-Khanan's literacy circle such as Mulla Nawai, Hayati, Shouqi, Naziri Neishabouri, Shakibi Esfahani, Mahvi Hamadani, Hamzeh Bowanati, Maulana Nizam, Wafai Heravi, Abu-Turab Razavi Mashhadi, Qasim Asiri, Sharari Hamadani and many others.

Next only to Khan-i-Khanan, the most eminent patron of poets in Jahangir's India was Ghazi Beg Tarkhan.[23] During his governorship of Qandahar several Persian poets who came to India tried their fortune first in his service, remained with him permanently and sought other patrons only after his death. Among them were Murshid Bourjerdi, Mahvi Ardabili, Wasli Shirazi, Soruri Yazdi and Ahsani Gilani. Mahabat Khan Zaman Beg, a Shirazi Sayyid, was another such patron of poets. Further, Zafar Khan, the generous patron of Saib, attracted several Persian poets to his entourage; Ziya and Sattar Tabrizi were in the service of Munim Khan in Bengal during the reign of Shah Jahan, and Ibrahim Farsi was in the entourage of Ibrahim Khan Fath Jang, the governor of Bengal.

There were also several Iranian nobles in the Mughal court who patronised and helped other Iranians in India. Among them we can mention. Itimad-ud-daula Tehrani, Asaf Khan, Nur-i-Jahan, Baqir Khan Najm-i-Sani, Mir Muhammad Said Mir Jumla, Mirza Abu Talib Shaista Khan,[24] Muzaffar Husain, Rustam Mirza and Khwaja Beg Mirza Safavi, Nur-ud-Din Quli Esfahani, *Kotwal* of Agra, Mir Muhammad Baqir Savoji,[25] Nazim of Bengal; Mulla Shafia Yazdi well known Danishmand Khan;[26] Islam Khan Mashhadi,[27] Qasim Khan Juwaini[28] Governor of Bengal, Sadullah Khan[29] entitled Nawazash Khan and Mirza Lashkari,[30] entitled Safdar Khan, or Safshikan Khan.

As the immigrants came to India they married in important aristocratic families and some times their daughters were demanded in marriage by emperors, princes, and other nobles. In the reign of Jahangir the family of Itimad-ud-daula emerged as a very important family group. Though previously too the family enjoyed a high status, it is evident that the marriage of Nur-i-Jahan with Jahangir played an important role in furthering the interest of her family and other Iranians.[31] The story of the rise of the family of Rustam Mirza and Muzaffar Husain Mirza Safavi (Qandahari) provides another significant example. They came to India being expelled from Qandahar and Zamindawar. After reaching India they, because of their high lineage, were able to contact matrimonial alliances with the Mughal ruling family and with the families of some other important and influential nobles, and thus they obtained high *mansabs* and appointments.[32]

Whatever the cause of a particular person's migration, his previous status and experience in Iran played an important part in the rank and office assigned to him in the Mughal empire. Only those who had requisite experience and qualifications were taken into state service. In this sense the Safavid empire seems to have provided a training ground for the Mughal bureaucracy. There is ample evidence to show that persons of professional and bureaucratic skills were always in demand at the Mughal court.

Those Iranians who were forced to leave Iran, under the circumstances which created hardships for them, rarely returned back to their homelands. India became their homeland. But many of those who came in search of opportunities better than those available in Iran, returned to Iran, or at least kept in touch with their friends and relatives there.

Our aim in this study was to identify the individuals and the families of the Iranian migrants in Mughal India during the 17th century, the Iranian regions[33] and towns from where they came as well as the reasons and the contexts of their migration. We have tried to achieve our target to the possible extent that our sources helped us, even as we have been aware of our limitations all thorough. We have noticed that these migrants were not distributed over the regions evenly. How can this imbalance and difference be explained? In all there were 461 migrants; of them, for instance, 187 came from central plateau, 9 from regions in south-west, and only one from south-east. This imbalance may be explained in the fact that the people of south-west, (Chahar Mahal va Bakhtiyari, Kohkiyloyeh va Buyer Ahmad and Khusestan provinces and south-east (Sistan va Baluchistan province) were primarily nomadic and tribal. Whatever they did was in a collective form, their move generally was in droves, individual migration was rare among them. Further, it was also difficult for them to leave for India because of the radical difference between the climates of their areas and India. Again these provinces were situated far off from the central seats of the Safavid power. They were thus not as much within the reach of the intolerant princes as, say, the people in Qazwin and Esfahan. Besides, the Central Plateau was more populated than the peripheries and were also the hubs of some bigotted Sunnis and Nuqtawis. Esfahan, Yazd, Qazwin and Kashan were, for example, such cities where from, according to our sources, no less than 130 persons left for India during our period.

Next to the central plateau were the regions in east and north-east (70) whence the migration to India was the most; In these two regions

A Sketch Map of Regional Distribution of the Iranian Migrants Category-wise

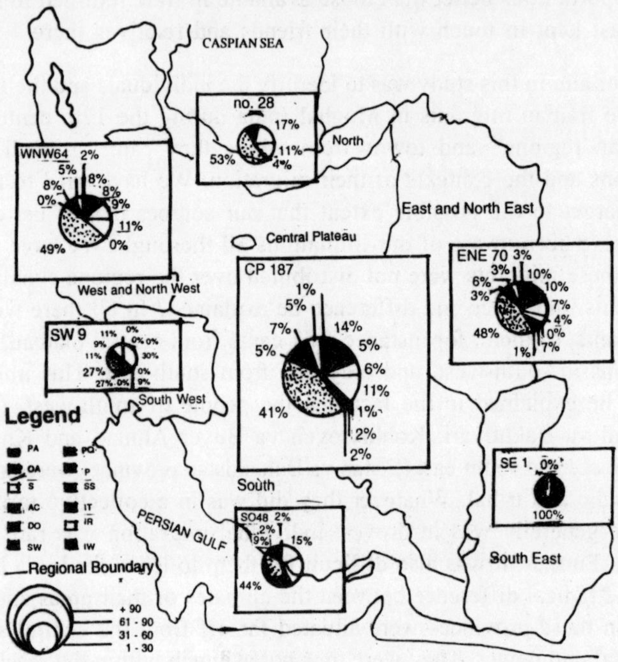

Map No. 5

were located the places like Mashhad (34) and Neishabour (5). Then came west and north-west regions (64) with cities like Tabriz (33) and Hamadan (14). The most pressing factor for migration of north-eastern people appears to have been the rise of Uzbeks and their numerous inroads into this area. In this connection the religion of the residents of a given area or town, as that of the inhabitants of Khaf whom we noticed above, was also a matter of significance. Thus the only option left with the people of this place was either to forsake the country or to adopt Shiism.

A major reason of migration of the people from north-western regions was the constant threat and actuality of the Ottoman raids there. The magnitude of this problem could be gauged from the fact that Shah Tahmasp was faced to move the Safavid capital from Tabriz to Qazwin in 955/1548 primarily under the Ottoman pressure. Later Shah Abbas I moved further and decided to chose Esfahan as his capital in place of Qazwin. The decisive factor in these moves were the fear of the Ottomans. However, it is also true that a certain tendency on the part of the Safavids towards Iranising their empire, together with their mistrust of the Turkmens and a determination to protect the polity from their influence in particular in Azarbaijan and Tabriz also guided these moves.

Tabriz was the first capital of the Safavids and many Qizilbash tribes had settled in this city. But as we saw above when Shah Abbas I ascended the throne he reduced the power of the Qizilbash and broke the Turkman leaders' monopoly of military power by creating a new army under the *Ghulams.* The policy thus proved an added factor for migration of the elite including the Qizilbash from this region to India.

Further, the migration was from the regions where Iranian talent thrived. In this category could be enlisted south where was located the city of knowledge, Shiraz (32) and northern regions, namely Gilan and Mazandaran (28). The province of Fars was enviably rich in talent, from there the people of professional and bureaucratic skills came, who were always in demand at the Mughal court. The areas of Gilan and Mazandaran also abounded in talent, but interestingly from those two areas only 28 Iranians are reported to have migrated to India, less in number than the combined strength of those who came from south, east, Central Plateau and western regions. One significant factor which may have arrested the flow of the people of this area was Khan Ahmad

Karkia the governor of Gilan, a generous patron of poets and scholars. His generosity attracted a number of talented and skilled people to join his entourage. During the governorship of Khan Ahmad Karkia the province of Gilan came to be known to be the *Hindustan-i-Sefid*[34] (white India). We may thus sum up with the submission that for a balanced assessment of the Iranian migration to the seventeenth century Mughal India both the pull and the push factors have to be given due weightage.

REFERENCES

1. For details, Iqtidar Alam Khan, the Nobility under Akbar and the development of his religious policy 1650-80, in: *J.R.A.S.*, pt. 3-4, 1969, pp. 29-36.
2. For origin of Iranian immigrants see: table:Con.1 and graphs:Con.1, 2.
3. For details see, table: Con. 2 and Graph: Con. 3.
4. For details see, table: Con. 3 and Graph: Con. 4.
5. *Ibid.*
6. Badauni, 1868-69, Vol. III, pp. 97-99.
7. *A.A.A.* 1350/1971, Vol. II, p. 476.
8. H. Mustaufi, *Nuzhat-ul-Qulub,* tr. G.LE Strange, London, 1919, p. 152.
9. *Z.kh.* Vol. I, pp. 195-96 see also: *M.U.* text, Vol. I, pp. 664-69.
10. Afzal Husain, Growth of Irani element in Akbar's nobility, in; *P.I.H.C.*, Aligarh, 1975, p. 168, About persecution of Sunnism under Tahmasp and Shah Abbas I see, S.A. Arjomand, 1984, pp. 119-121.
11. *Tuzuk,* 1863-64, p. 16.
12. *A.A.A.* Vol. I, pp. 45-46.
13. *Ibid.*, pp. 192-212.
14. *A.N.*, Vol. III, pp. 590-91, 657-61.
15. *Ibid.*, pp. 657-61.
16. *M.U.* text, Vol. III, pp. 558-562.
17. *A.A.A.* 1955, Vol. II, p. 1041.
18. Lahori, Vol. II, pp. 92, 123-26, 222-23.
19. M. Athar Ali, 'Towards an Interpretation of the Mughal Empire in *J.R.A.S* of Great Britan and Irland', 1978, No. I, p. 44.
20. For details see: table: Con. 3 and Graph: Con. 4.
21. *A.N.*, Vol. III, p. 391.
22. Lahori, I, pp. 258, 279.
23. A comprehensive study of his literary circle see: H. Rashidi, Karachi,

1970. For his official career, see: *Z.Kh.* II, pp. 18-31 and *M.U.* text, Vol. III, pp. 345-48.

24. For Umdat-ul Mulk Shaista Khan See: *M.U.* text, Vol. II, pp. 690-704.
25. For Taqarrub Khan see: *Amal-i-Salih,* Vol II, p. 402, Vol. III, pp. 395-96.
26. For Mulla Shafia Yazdi see: *M.U.* text, Vol. II, pp. 30-32.
27. For Islam Khan see: *M.U.* text, Vol. I, pp. 162-62 also see: *Z.Kh.* Vol. III, pp. 25-27.
28. About Qasim Khan Juwaini see: *M.U.* text, Vol. III, pp. 78-82.
29. For Sadullah Khan see: *Jahangir Nama,* Tehran Press; pp. 113, 163, 252, 409.
30. About Mirza Lashkari see: *M.U.* text, Vol. II, pp. 736-38, also see: *Jahangir Nama,* Tehran Press, 1980, pp. 146-172.
31. Vide see: Irfan Habib *'The Family of Nur-i-Jahan during the reign of Jahangir - A Political Study' Medieval India.* A Miscellany, Vol. I, writes Nur-i-Jahan's family accounts for nearly one twelfth of the *zat mansab* and one tenth of *sawar* in 1621 while in 1605 they had barely held one-fifth of the *zat mansab.*
32. For details about Muzaffar Husain and Rustam-Mirza Safavi see: *Z.Kh.* Vol. I, p. 99, also see: *M.U.* text, Vol. III, pp. 296-302.
33. See: Map. No. 5.
34. For term of *Hindustan-i-Sefid;* see: T. Auhadi, Fol. 575 also see: B. Nihavandi, Vol. III, p. 1684.

Appendix

IRANIAN WOMEN

Besides men a few women also migrated to India because of various reasons. The table[1] shows that of the five women who come to India, two came in later days of Akbar's reign and three during Jahangir's reign. Some women about whom we have some information in our sources are as follows:

Sati Khanum, sister of Talib Amuli, moved to India in order to visit her relatives. She joined the service of Mumtaz-uz-zamani (Nur-i-Mahal) wife of Shahjahan held was teacher of Aurengzeb's eldest daughter. She held office of *muhrdari* (keeper of the seal) in the reign of Shah Jahan. Later she became the head of the imperial *Harem.*

Qurishi Khanum, was another women who migrated from Tabriz to India; but reasons of her migration are unknown. She was a poetess.

Jamileh Esfahani left Iran in search of better prospects. She also was a poetess.

Mehr-un-Nisa (Nur-i-jahan Begum) wife of Jahangir, came to India in the company of her father and brother, Itimud-ud-duala and Asaf Khan. Nur-i-jahan was a poetess and powerful administrator. She also was inventor and designer of several ornamentations for dress and jewellery.

Qandahari Mahal daughter of Muzaffar Husain Safavi was a great grandson of Shah Ismail and governor of Qandahar. She left her native place to visit India in the comanay of her father because of Uzbek pressure on Khurasan and from the fear of losing royal favour. She was prince Khurram's wife.

Table : Appen.1
IRANIAN WOMEN

Name of migrants	Place of birth	Provinces	Regions	Period of migration	Contexts and reasons of migration	Position in Iran	Position in India	Place of Death
Sati Khanum	Amul	Mazan-daran	North	Jahangir	To visit relatives in India	She belonged to learned family of Amul, wife of Nasira, brother of Hakim, Rukna of Kashan, Sister of Talib Amuli.	Service of Mumtaz-uz-Zamani (Nur-Mahal), wife of Shahjahan, *mansab* of *Muhrdari* (sealer) Head of *Harem*, teacher of Aurangzeb's eldest daughter	Lahore
Qurishi Khannum-e-Tabrizi	Tabriz	Azarbai jan-i-Sharqi	West and North-West	Jahangir	Unclear	Poetess	Poetess	Unclear
Jamileh Eshahaniyeh	Esfahan	Esfahan	Central Plateau	Jahangir	In order to better her prospects	Poetess	Poetess	Iran
Mehr-un-Nisa (Nur Jahan Begum)	Qandahar (1576) originally she belonged to Tehran	Khurasan	East and North-East	1590	In company of her father Itimud-du-daula and her brother Asaf Khan because of losing royal favour and in search of fortune.	Her ancestors had high position in Safavid's court.	Wife of Jahangir inventer and designer of several ornament-ations for dress and jewellery, administr-ator, poetess	Lahore 1645
Qandahari Mahal	Qandahar	Khurasan	East and North-East	1595	In company of her father Muzaffar Husain Mirza Safavi, because of Uzbek pressure and also losing royal favour	Her father was governor of Qandahar, and great grandson of Shah Ismail Safavi	Wife of Prince Khurram	India

Sati Khanum

Sati Khanum was from a Mazandaran family, and she was sister of Talib Amuli who in the reign of Jahangir received the title of Malik-ush-shuara. She came to India during Jahangir's reign. After the death of her husband Nasira, the brother of Hakim Rukna of Kashan, she entered the service of Mumtaz-uz-zamani (Nur-Mahal, the wife of Shah Jahan). She was adorned with an elequent tongue, and a knowledge of etiquette, and knew house-keeping and medicine. She was an accomblished woman, achieved position far beyond the ones the other servants did, eventually reached the rank of *muhrdari* (sealer). As she knew[2] the art of reading (The *Qoran*) and was acquainted with Persian literature, she was appointed as instructor to the Begum Sahib (Aurangzeb's eldest daughter) and so attained a high distinction (lit. rose to the sphere of Saturn the seventh heaven). After the death of Mumtaz-uz-Zamani, the emperor in appreciation of her merits, made her head of the *Harem.* As she had no child she adopted[3] her brother's two daughters after his death. The elder one was married to Aqil Khan,[4] and the younger to Zia-ud-din, who was styled Rahmat Khan, and who was the son of Hakim Qutba, the brother of Hakim Rukna. In the 20th year, when the royal residence was at Lahore, the younger daughter, of whom the Khanum was very fond, died in her childhood. The Khanum went home and mourned her death for some days. After that, the emperor sent for her and placed her in the quaters that he had in the palace, and personally came to see her there and offered her consolation. She after discharging the duties connected with the presence[5] of the emperor, went to her appointed dwelling and surrendered her soul to God. The emperor gave from the treasury Rs.10,000 for her funeral and burial, and ordered that her body should be kept in a coffin placed in a temporary grave. After a year and odd it was carried to Agra and buried in a tomb west of the sepulchre of the *Mahad Aliya* (Nur Mahal) in the Jilaukhana Chauk[6] (Taj Mahal).

Qurishi Khanum-e-Tabrizi

Fasiheh Baligheh belonged to Tabriz, and came to stay in India during the reign of Jahangir. She was very affable and kindly and she held a high position in India. The following verses are by her.

Az badah vahdat ast bihoshi man
Vaz talat-i-saqi ast madhoshi man.

Mansur Ke serr-e-haq ayan kard on did:
Asrar nahofta-ast-ze khamooshi man.[7]

Jamileh Esfahaniyeh

Her name was Jamileh, Fasiheh and Maliheh, who was extremely accessible and eloquent. Her origin and birth place was Esfahan. In the early youth she was concubine of Khwaja Habibullah Tarkeh.[8] Some poets attributed Khwaja Habib Ullah's verses to her. After the death of Habib Ullah, she migrated to India in the reign of Jahangir in search of good foretune. The author of *Arafatul-Ashiqin* says: After death of Khwaja Habib Ullah she married Khwaja Ismail-ibn Khwaja Mirak Hal. She passed her life as a poetess. She was very beautiful as was her name and her *takhallus*.[9]

Nur Jahan Begum (Mehrun Nisa)

She was the daughter of Mirza Ghiyas Beg Itimadud-daula and sister of Abul Hasan Asaf Khan, the *Wazir* of both Jahangir and Shah Jahan. She was born in 984/1576, at Qandahar, when her father Ghiyas Beg fled with his two sons and one daughter from Persia. On his arrival at Qandahar, Ghiyas Beg's wife gave birth to another daughter, who received the name of Mirun-Nisa (the Sun of women) a name which her future title of Nur Jahan has alsmost brought into oblivion.

At the death of Ali Quli Beg Istajallu (Sher Afgan Khan),[10] who was an Iranian noble of ordinary rank posted in Bengal, Mihrun-Nisa was sent to court as a prisoner "for the murder of Qutb-ud-Din Khan,[11] and was handed over to Ruqayya Sultan Begum.[12] At the new year's feast of the 6th year, 1020/1611, the old feelings were revived as a result of the emperor Jahangir seeing her again and the unfulfilled desire of old time developed more vigorously. He married her with all pomp. At first she was called Nur Mahal, and later Nur Jahan Begum.[13] Nur Jahan's power over Jahangir is sufficiently known from the histories.[14]

Nur Jahan Begum in addition to her physical charms possessed many intellectual excellencies. She was the unique personality of her age having quick understanding, good sense, penetration and tact. The emperor used to say that until she came to his house, he had not understood domestic pleasures or the spirituality of marriage. She invented and designed several ornamentations for dress and jewellery which are still prevalent in India. For instance *dudami* (flowered muslin) for dress, *panchtolia* for veils, *badla* (silver thread) and *kinara* (silver-thread lace), *atir* (perfumes), rose perfume known as the *atir-i-Jahangiri,* and silvery carpet (*Farash Chandani*) were all her[15] innovations. She exercised such influence over emperor Jahangir that except for the name of emperor he exercised no other powers. In fact, except[16] for the khutba not having been read in her name, she exercised all the prerogatives of royalty, so much so that she sat in the *jharokha*, and received the respects of the royal officers. Coins were struck in her name.

Be hukm-i-Shah Jahangir Yaft Sat Zivar;
Be nam-i-Nur Jahan Padashah Begum Zar.

By order of Shah Jahangir gold was adorned a hundred-fold; By the name of Nur Jahan the Queen Begum.

The *Tughra* (royal grant) decrees also bore the following description. The order of the exalted lady of the sublime touch, Nur Jahan Padshah Begum. The estates assigned to her corresponded to the rank of 30,000. It is stated that the fiefs (*tiyul*) of her relations (*silsila*) amounted to half the estates of the kingdom.[17]

Her influence ceased with Jahangir's death and the capture of Shahryar, fifth son of the emperor, to whom she had given her daughter (by Sher Afgan) Ladli Begum, in marriage. She had no children from Jahangir.

Shah Jahan allowed her a pension of two lacs per annum.[18] She died at Lahore at the age of 72, on 29th Shawwal, 1055/1645, and lies buried in Lahore near her husband in a tomb which she herself had built.[19] She composed occasionally Persian poems, and like Salima Sultan Begum and Zebun-Nisa Begum wrote under the assumed name of Makhfi.[20]

Here are some verses composed by Jahangir and Nur Jahan in reply to each other's. Jahangir once said:

Bulbul neyam ke nara konam darda-sar daham;
Parvana neyam ke soozam-o-dam bar nayavaram.

"I am not the nightingale to fill the air with my plaintive cries; I am a moth that dies without uttering a single moan".

Nur Jahan replied:

Parvana neyam man ke be yek shohla jan deham;
Shamam ke shab besoozam-o-dam bar nayavaram.

"I am not the moth that burns itself instantaneously; I suffer a lingering death like the candle which burns through the night without a murmur".

Once Jahangir said:

Chera kham gashta migardand piran-i-Jahan dida.

"Why do old and experienced people go about with their backs bent?

Nur Jahan at once replied:

Be zir-e-khak mijooyand ayyam-e-javani ra.

They are searching for the days of their youth under dust.

Qandahari Mahal

Qandahari Mahal was the daughter of Muzaffar Husain Safavi. She came to India in the 40th year of Akbar's reign, towards the end of 1003/1595, when, her father and her four brothers, Bahram Mirza, Haidar Mirza, Alqas Mirza and Tahmasp Mirza and 1000 Qazilbash soldiers arrived in India. Qandahari Mahal was married in 1018/1609 to Prince Khurram, and gave birth in 1020/1611, to Nawab Parviz Banu Begum.[21]

Table : Appen. 2
IRANIAN WOMEN

Rg	Pr	Nu	Reasons and Contexts of Migration																									
			X1	X2	X3	X4	X5	X6	X7	X8	X9	X10	X11	X12	X13	X14	X15	X16	X17	X18	X19	X20	X21	X22	X23	X24	X25	X26
NO	Ak	0																										
1	Ja	1												1														
	Sh	0																										
WNW	Ak	0																										
1	Ja	1																										1
	Sh	0																										
SW	Ak	0																										
0	Ja	0																										
	Sh	0																										
CP	Ak	0																										
1	Ja	1														1												
	Sh	0																										
SO	Ak	0																										
0	Ja	0																										
	Sh	0																										
ENE	Ak	0																										
2	Ja	2								2																		
	Sh	0																										
SE	Ak	0																										
0	Ja	0																										
	Sh	0																										
UA	Ak	0																										
0	Ja	0																										
	Sh	0																										
Total		5								2				1		1												1

Graph : Appen. 1

Number of Women according to the reasons and contexts of their migration

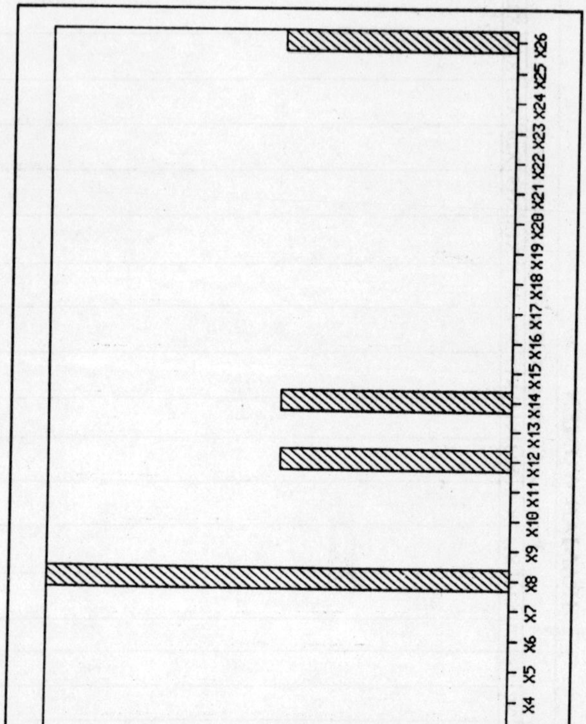

REFERENCES

1. For details see: Tables; appendices.1,2 and graph: appendix 1.
2. Lahori, Vol. II, p. 629.
3. She sent for them from Persia. See; Lahori, Vol. II, p. 630; see also: *M.U.* text, Vol. II, p. 283, notice of Rahmat Khan.
4. For Aqil Khan (Inayat Ullah) see: *M.U.* text, Vol. II, pp. 790-92.
5. The duty of preparing Shah Jahan's breakfast, see : Lahori, Vol. II, p. 630.
6. Ibid., Vol. II, p. 629.
7. T. Auhadi, Fol. 600.
8. Khwaja Habib Ullah belonged to great family of Tarkeh Esfahan. In that time he was *Qazi* of Tarkeh.
9. T. Auhadi, Fol. 200.
10. See: *M.U.* text, Vol. II, pp. 622-25 and see also; *Ain-i-Akbari,* Transl. by Blochmann, Vol. I, pp. 591-92.
11. See: *M.U.* text, Vol. III, pp. 66-68.
12. The *Maasir* has Salima Sultan Begum (*M.U.*, Vol. I, pp. 130-71).
13. See also:B. Prasad,1962, pp.176-182, *Iqbal-nama-i-Jahangiri,* pp. 55, 56.
14. *Ain-i-Akbari,* Tr. by Blochmann, Vol. I, p. 574.
15. *M.U.* Tr. by Beveridger, vol. II, part II, pp. 1076-77 quoted from Khafi Khan. I, p. 274, and B.Prasad, 1962, p. 183 and see also: Blochmann, Vol. I, p. 574.
16. *M.U. Ibid,* quoted from *Iqbal nama-i-Jahangiri,* p. 56.
17. *M.U.* Beveridge Tr. Vol. II, Part. II, p. 1077.
18. Elphinstone has by mistake of lacs per mense. The highest Allaowance of Begums on record is that of Mumtaz Mahal viz 10 lacs per annum vide: *Padshah nama,* I, p. 96.
19. *Padshah nama,* II, p. 475 In the *Padshah nama,* Nur Jahan is again called *Nur Mahall,* viz 10 lacs per annum vide; *Padshah nama*, I, p. 96.
20. Blochmann Tr, *Ain-i-Akbari,* Vol. I, p. 574 for details about Nur Jahan see: *z.kh.* Vol. II, pp. 13-18 and also N. Qazwini,. 1961 pp. 441-442, *Tuzuk,* Rogers Tr, pp. 266, 278, 319-342, 380, 397, 401.
21. *M.U.* text, Vol.I II, pp. 300-302, *A.N*, Vol, III, pp. 668-71, also see: *Tuzuk,* Rogers Tr. p. 80, *Ain-i-Akbari,* Tr.by Blochmann, p. 328 and see: *Amal-i-Salih,* Vol. I, pp. 48-49.

Bibliography

Primary Sources

Unpublished Books

Arzu, Siraj-ud-din Ali Khan: *Majma-un-Nafais,* Tehran MS, 2 vols, University, Central Library, No. 2426.

Auhadi,Taqi: *Arafat-ul-Ashiqin,* MS, Tehran, Malik Library No. 5324.

Azad, Bilgrami, Mir Gholam Ali : *Yad-i-Baiza,* MS, Aligarh, Azad Library, No. 920/46.

Azimabadi, Aqa Husain Quli Khan: *Nishtar-i-Ishq,* MS, Bankipur, Nos. 716,717.

Banaresi, Ibrahim Ali Khan: *Suhuf-i-Ibrahim,* Tehran University Central Library, No. 2976.

Darabi Shirazi, Muhammad Arif: *Lataif-ul-Khayal,* MS, 2 vols in one, Tehran, Malik Library, No. 4325.

Dehlavi Hamadani-ul-Asl, Muhammad Sadiq: *Tabaqat-i-Shah Jahani,* MS, National Museum, No. 68082.

Esfahani, Muhammad Akbar; *Diwan:* MS, Tehran, Majlis Library, No.945.

Hashimi Sandilvi, Ahmad Ali Khan: *Makhzan-ul-Gharaib,* Photo MS, Tehran University, Central Library, No. 1671.

Kashi, Mir Yahya : *Diwan,* Khuda Bakhsh Library, Patna, No. 331.

Kashi, Taqi : *Khulasat-ul-Ashar,* MS, Tehran, Malik Library, No. 4078.

Khushgu, Bindraban Das : *Safina Khushgu,* MS, Tehran, Sipahasalar/ Majlis Library, No. 2724.

Minai Esfahani, Mirza Muhammad Sadiq: *Subh-i-Sadiq,* Aligarh, Azad Library, No. 65415.

Mir Findarski, Abul Qasim: *Sharh-e-Almehareh* (description of Almehareh), Tehran, Majlis Library, No. 4757.

Mir Findarski, Abul Qasim: *Maqtu-al-Harakat Va Tahqiq Fiha,* Najafabad, Shushtari Library.

Mir Findarski, Abol Qasim: *Kashf-ul-Loghat-e-Jukba Shast,* Tehran, Majlis Library, No. 4757.

Mir Munshi Qomi, Q.A: *Kuhlasat-ul-Tawarikh,* MS, Tehran, Malik Library, No. 4067.

Monsif Tehrani: *Diwan,* MS, Public Library of Esfahan No. 11509.

Muhammad Salih: *Majmua-i-Makatib-e-Mukhtalifa,* MS, Tehran, Majlis Library, Catalogue VIII, No. 2665, X. Nos. 2247, 3349, 3455.

Nasrabadi, Muhammad Tahir: *Tazkira Nasrabadi,* MS, Yazd, Waziri Library.

Qazwini, Abdun Nabi: *Terazul Akhbar,* Tehran University, Central Library, No. 325.

Qazwini, Abdun Nabi: *Nawadir-ul-Hikayat-Gharib-ul-Revayat,* Tehran University, Library of Law Faculty, No. 55.

Qazwini, Muhammad Amin: *Padishah Nama,* MS, Br. M. or. 173 (Rotograph) and transcript of the Reza Library, MS, (Rampur) in the Dept. of History, Aligarh.

Rashida-i-Abbasi, *Kulliyat-e-Rashida,* Tehran, Malik Library, No. 5266.

Shamlu Hiravi,Wali Quli Beg: *Qasasul-Khaqani,* MS, Tehran, Majlis Library, No. 2155 and 2156.

Shirazi, Muhammad Arif: *Lataif-ul-Khayal,* MS, 2 Vols in one, Tehran, Malik Library, No. 4325.

Sistani, Malik Shah: *Khairul-Bayan,* Tehran, personal Library of Fakhrud-Din-i-Nasiri.

Shoqi Savoji: *Diwan,* MS, Tehran University, Central Library, No. 32,412.

Sururi Kashani, Muhammad Qasim: *Majmaul-Fors,* Mashhad, Astan-e-Quds-e-Razavi, No.10411.

Tabatabai Ardestani, Jalala: *Majmua Munshat or Kulliyat'* MS, Tehran University, Central Library, Nos. 2591-2592, 2944, Firest.10

Tabrizi, Nizam: *Tazkira Nizam,* Tehran, Malik Library, No. 6456.

Walih Daghastani, Ali Quli: *Reyaz-ush-shuara,* MS, Tehran, Malik Library, No. 4301 also in Asafiyeh, No. 120.

Walih Hiravi, Darvish Husain: *Diwan Walih,* Bankipur, Vol. III, No. 332.

Published Books

Abdul-Ghani, Muhammad, *Takhallus* Ghani: *Tazkira-i-Shuara Ghani,* Aligarh, 1916,

Akbari Savi, M.H: *Tufatul Murad* (Description of Findarski *Qasida*), Tehran, 1372/1993.

Ali Muhammad Khan: *Mirat-i-Ahmadi*, ed. Sayyid Nawab Ali, 2 Vols; Baroda, 1927-29, 1930.

Allami, Abul Fazl: *Ain-i-Akbari*, 3 Vols, Lucknow, 1869, 1882, 1893.

Allami, Abul Fazl: *Ain-i-Akbari,* translated into English by H. Blochmann, Delhi, 1979, Calcutta, 1873.

Allami, Abul Fazl: *Akbar Nama*, 3 vols, Bib. Indica, Calcutta, 1877-86.

Allami, Abul Fazl: *Akbar Nama,* translated into English by H. Beveridge, Bib. Indica, Calcutta, 1897-1921.

Azad Bilgrami, Mir Gholam Ali: *Khazana-i-Amira,* Kanpur, 1871.

Azad Bilgrami, Mir Gholam Ali: *Sarv-i-Azad,* (*Maasir-ul-Kiram*), Lahore, 1913.

Azar Beg Dili, Haji Lotf Ali: *Tazkira Atashkada,* Calcutta, 1249 A.H/ 1833.

Azar Beg Dili, Haji Lotf Ali: *Tazkira Atashkada,* ed. Hasan Sadat Nasiri, 3 Vols, Tehran, 1336/1957.

Babur: *Babur Nama or Tuzuk-i-Baburi,* Transt. by A.S. Beveridge, 3 vols, London, 1912-21.

Badauni, Abdul-Qadir: *Muntakhab-ut-Tawarikh,* 3 Vols., ed. Maulavi Ahmad Ali and W.N. Lees, Bib. Ind. Calcutta, 1864-69.

Badauni,Abdul-Qadir : *Muntakhab-ut-Tawarikh,* translated into English, Vol. I; G.S. Ranking (1898); Vol. II, W.H. Lowe (1898), Vol. III, T.W. Haig (1925), All volumes reprinted in Delhi, 1986.

Bakhshi, Nizam-ud-din Ahmad: *Tabaqat-i-Akbari,* 3 Vols, Nawal Kishore, Lucknow, 1870, 1875, and Bib. Indica, Calcutta, 1931.

Bakhtavar Khan, Muhammad: *Mirat-ul-Alam,* ed. Sajida Alvi, 2 Vols, Lahore, Punjab University, 1979.

Bayat, Bayazid: *Tazkira Humayun Va Akbar,* Bib. Indica, Calcutta, 1941.

Bhakkari,Shaikh Farid: *Zakhirat-ul-Khawanin,* ed. Sayyid Moinul Haq, 3 Vols, Karachi, 1961, 1970, 1974.

Bhakkari, Shaikh Farid: *Zakhirat-ul-Khawanin,* Vol. I, transl. into English by Ziya-ud-Din A. Desai, Delhi, 1993.

Binesh, Sayyid Murtaza: *Tazkira Isharat-i-Binesh,* edit. Sharif Husain Qasemi, Delhi, Indo-Persian Society, 1973.

Fani, Muhsin: *Dabistan-i-Mazahib,* English Tr. D. Shea and A. Troyer, Paris, 1843, Vol I.

Firshta Astrabadi; Muhammad Qasim: *Gulshan-i-Ibrahimi or Tarikh-i-Firshta;* 2 Vols Bombay, 1247/1832 also Nawal Kishore Press, Lucknow, 1863.

Fuzuni Astarabadi, Mir Muhammad Hashim: *Buhairah* (General History), Tehran, 1328 A.H/1910.

Ghaznavi, Sayyid Hasan: *Diwan Sayyid Hasan,* ed. Ustatd Moddarres-e-Razavi, Tehran University, 1328 A.H/ 1910.

Gopamavi, Muhammad Qudratuliah: *Nataijul-Afkhar,* Bombay : 1336/ 1957.

Haft Qalami Dehlavi, Gholam Muhammad: *Tazkira-Khushnavisan,* ed. Muhammad Hadayat Husain, Calcutta, 1328/1910.

Hasan Khan Bahadur, Sayyid Muhammad Siddiq: *Sham-e-Anjuman,* Bhopal, 1293/1876.

Hasan Khan Bhopali, Sayyid Ali: *Subh-i-Golshan,* Bhopal, 1295 A.H/ 1878.

Hidayat, Reza Quli Khan: *Reyazul Arifin,* Tehran, 1305 A.H/1887.

Hidayat, Reza Quli Khan: *Majmaul-Fusaha,* ed. Ali Quli Khan Mukhbrud-daula, writer's son, Tehran, 1341 A.s/1962.

Husaini, Sayyid Ashraf Khan: *Raqaim-i-Karaim,* Epistles of Aurangzeb, ed. S.M.Azizuddin Husain, Idarah-i-Adabiyat-i-Delhi, Delhi, 1990.

Jahangir Padashah; *Jahangir Nama or Tuzuk-i-Jahangiri* (*Memories of Jahangir*) ed. by Sayyid Ahmad Khan, Ghazipure and Aligarh 1863, and Nawal Kishore Press, Lucknow, 1914.

Jahangir Padashah: *Tuzuk-i-Jahangiri,* transl. by A. Rogers and H. Beveridge, 2 Vols. in one, Delhi, 1968.

Jahangir Padashah: *Jahangir Nama,* ed. Muhammad Hashim, Tehran, 1359/1980.

Jazayari, Sayyid Abdullah, Faquir Takhallus: *Tazkira-Shushtar,* ed. Bahadur Maula Bakhsh and Muhammad Hidayat Husain, Calcutta, 1343/1924 and Ahwaz Press.

Kambu Lahori, Muhammad Salih: *Amal-i-Salih,* 3 Vols., ed. Gulam Yazdani, Bib. Indica, Calcutta, 1912-39.

Kanwer Khan, Muhammad Hadi: *Tazkirat-us-Salatin-i-Chaghta,* ed. Muzaffar Alam, Asia Publishing House, Bombay, 1980.

Kashmiri (Aslah) Mirza: *Tazkira Shuara-i Kashmir,* ed. Sayyid Hasam-ud-din-i-Rashidi, Karachi, 1346/1967.

Kashmiri, Inayatullah Khan, *Kalimat-i-Taiyibat,* Collection of Aurangzeb's Orders, ed. S. M. Azizuddin Husain, Idarah-i-Adabiyat-i-Delhi, Delhi, 1982.

Kewal Ram, Ray: *Tazkirat-ul-Umara,* Tranl. into English, by S.M. Azizuddin Husain, New Delhi, 1985.

Khafi, Mir Abdur-Razzaq (Shah Nawaz Khan): *Baharestan-i-Sukhan,* ed. Mir Abdul Wahab Bukhari, Madras, 1958.

Khafi Khan, Muhammad Hashim: *Muntakhab-ul-Lubab,* ed. Maulavi Kabir-ut-din Ahmad, Bib. Indica, Calcutta, 1860-74, 1909-25.

Khan Saheb, Maulavi Abdul Muqtadir: *Catalogue of Arabic and Persian,* Ms; in Oriental Public Library, Bankipur, Vol. III, Persian Poetry, Vol. VII, Indian History, Patna, 1977.

Khuihami, Pir Ghulam Hasan: *Tarikh-i-Hasan,* Srinagar, 1954.

Khurasani, Mirza Sank Lakh: *Imtehan-ul-Fuzala or Tazkirat-ul-khattatin,* Tabriz, 1291/1874.

Lachmi Narain, Shafiqu: *Sham-e-Ghariban,* ed. Muhammad Akbar-ud-din Siddiq, Karachi, 1977.

Lahiji, Hazin: *Tazkirat-ul-Measirin,* Esfahan, 1334/1995.

Lahori-Abdul Hamid: *Padashah Nama,* ed. Maulvi Kabir-ud-din and Maulavi Abdur Rahim, 3 Vols., Bib. Indica, Calcutta, 1876-72.

Lodi, Sheer Ali Khan: *Mirat-ul-Khayal,* Bombay, 1324/1906; and Calcutta, 1831.

Lucknowi, Muhammad Muzaffar Husain: *Tazkira Ruz-e-Raushan,* Tehran, 1343/1964, Bhopal, 1297/1879.

Mashhadi, Muhammad Qasim: *Diwan of Verses,* Lucknow, 1294/1877 and 1809.

Masum Ali Shah: *Taraiqal-Haqaiq,* 3 Vols, ed. By M.J. Mahjub, Tehran, 1339/1960.

Minorsky, Vladimir, ed: *Tazkirat-ul-Mulk,* A Manual of Safavid Administration, London, 1943.

Mir Findarski Abul Qasim: *Resaleh-i-Sanahiya,* Bombay, 1276/1850 under the title of Haqayaq-ul-Sanayeh.

Mir Munshi Qomi, Qazi Ahmad: *Golistan-i-Honar,* ed. Muhammad Hadyat Husain, Calcutta, 1328/191.

Mirza Nathan: *Baharishtan-i-Ghaibi,* transl. by M.I. Borah, 2 Vols, Gauhati, 1936.

Mirza Samia: *Tazkirat-ul-Mulk,* ed. Muhammad Dabir Siaqi, Tehran, 1332/1953.

Modarres, Mirza Muhammad Ali: *Rihanatul-Adab,* 8 Vols, Tehran, 1335/1956, Tabriz, Khaiyam, 1346/1967.

Moris, Herbert: *Muhammad Reza Travellers,* transl. By Abdul Husain Vojdani, Tehran, 1362/1984.

Muhammad Kazim: *Alamgir Nama,* ed. Maulavi Khadim Husain and Abdul Hai, 2 Vols, Bib. Indica, Calcutta, 1868-73.

Muhammad Shah: *Dabistan-i-Mazahib*, Calcutta, 1224/1809.

Munshi Turkman, Eskandar Beg: *Tarikh-i-Alam* Ara-i-Abbasi, ed. by Iraj Afshar, 2 Vols., Tehran 1314/1935, 1334-35/1955-56, 1350/1971.

Mustaad Khan, Muhammad Saqi: *Maasir-i-Alamgiri,* ed. *Agha Ahmad* Ali, Bib. Indica, Calcutta, 1871.

Mustaad Khan, Muhammad Saqi: *Maasir-i-Alamgiri,* transl. by J. Sarkar, Bib. Indica, Calcutta, 1947.

Mustoufi, Hamdullah: *Nuzhat-ul-Qulub,* transl. G. Le Strange, London, 1919.

Mustoufi Bafqi, Muhammad Mufid: *Jami Mufidi,* ed. Iraj Afshar, 3 Vols., Tehran, Vols. 1,2, 1961, Vol. 3, 1963.

Mutmad Khan, M.S. *Iqbal Nama-i-Jahangiri,* Bib. Indica, Calcutta, 1865.

Nasrabadi, Muhammad Tahir: *Tazkira Nasrabadi,* ed. Wahid Dastgardi, Tehran, Armaghan, 1317/1938.

Natanzi, Mahmud Afushteh: *Nuqawat-ul-Asar Fi-Zekral Akhyar,* ed. Ehsan Ishraqi, Tehran, 1350/1971.

Naui Khabushani, Muhammad Reza: *Masnavi Soz-o-Gudaz,* Lucknow, 1284/1867, Tehran, 1348/1969.

Nihavandi, Abdul-Baqi: *Ma'asir-i-Rahimi,* ed. Muhammad Hadayat Husain, 3 Vols, Calcutta, 1924-31.

Qaneh hattavi, Mir Ali Sheer: *Maqalat-ush-Shuara,* ed. by Sayyid Hisama-ud-din-Rashidi, Karachi, 1957.

Qatai, Hiravi: *Majma-Ush-Shuara Jahangir Shahi,* ed. Muhammad Salim Akhtar, Karachi, 1979.

Qazwini, Abul Hasan: *Favayidul-Safaviya,* ed. Maryam Mir Ahmadi, Tehran, 1367/1988.

Qazwini, Abdun-Nabi: *Tazkira Mai-Khana,* ed. Muhammad Shafih, Lahore, 1926.

Qazwini Abdun-Nabi: *Tazkira Mai-Khana*, ed. Ahmad Golchin Maani, Tehran, 1340 A.S/1961.

Ray Lucknowi, Munshi Aftab: *Reyazul Arifin*, ed. Sayyid Hisam-ud-din Rashidi, Rawalpindi, Markaz Taqiqat-i-Iran Va Pakistan, 1974.

Razi, Ahmad Amin: *Haft Iqlim,* ed. Vols. I, II by Jawad-e-Fazil, Tehran, 1340 A.S/1961, Vol. III ed. by Dr. Ishaq, Calcutta, 1939.

Riazul Islam (ed.): *Bahr-al-Asrar Fi Manaqib-ul-Akhyar,* Karachi, 1980.

Rumlu, Hasan: *Ahsan-ul-Tawarikh,* ed. and transl. C.N. Seddon, A Chronicle of the early Safavis, 2 Vols., Vol. I (text) Baroda, 1931, II, (transl) Baroda, 1934.

Sadiqi Kitabdar: *Majma-ul-Khawas,* transl. into Persian by Abdul-Rasoul Khaiyampur, Tabirz, 1327/1948.

Sanbhali, Mir Husain Dost: *Tazkira Husaini,* Nawal Kishore Press, 1875.

Sarkhush-Muhammad Afzal: *Kalimatush-Shuara,* ed. Muhammad Husain Mahvi Lucknowi, Lahore, 1942, and Madras, 1951.

Sayyid Nurul-Hasan: *Nigarestan-i-Sukhan,* Bhopal, 1293/1876.

Shah Kashmiri, Khwaja Muhammad Azam: *Tarikh-i-Azami or Waqeat-e-Kashmir,* Lahore, 1303/1885.

Shah Nawaz Khan Abdul-Razzaq and Abdul-Hayy: *Ma'asir-ul-Umara,* 3 Vols., ed. Molvi Abdur Rahi, Calcutta, Bib. Indica, 1889-91.

Shah Nawaz Khan, Abdur-Razzaq and Abdul-Hayy: *Ma'asir-ul-Umara,* transl. by H. Beveridge and B. Prasad, 2 Vols., Patna, 1979.

Shah Nawaz Khan, Mir Abdur-Razzaq: *Baharistan-i-Sukhan,* ed. Abdul Wahabi-i-Bukhari, Madras, 1958.

Shamlu, Hasan Khan; *Munshaat-i-Hasan Khan Shamlu,* ed. by Riazul Islam, Karachi, 1971.

Shamlu Hiravi, Wali Quli Beg: *Qasasul-Khaqani,* ed. Sayyid Hasan Sadat Nasiri, 2 Vols., Tehran, 1371/1992 and 1374/1995.

Shirazi, Mirza Nizam ud-din Ahmad: *Hadiqat-ul-Salatin,* Haidarabad Deccan, 1961.

Shushtari, Mir Ala-ul-Mulk: *Risalah Ferdus,* ed. Muhadth Armavi, Tehran, Anjuman Athar Melli, 1352A.S./1973.

Sistani, Malik Shah: *Ahyaul-Mulk,* ed. Manucher-e-Sutodeh, Tehran Bonga Tarjuma Va Nashr-i-Kitab: 1344/1965.

Sururi, Kashani, Muhammad Qasim: *Majmaul-Furs,* ed. Muhammad Dabir Siaqi, 3 Vols., Tehran, 1342/1963.

Tabatabai, Jalal-ud-din: *Tauqiat-i-Kisrawiya,* trans. from Arabic to Persian, Calcutta, 1824 and repeatedly lithographed in Lucknow and Kanpore.

Tajalli Shirazi, Maulana Ali Reza: *A Masnavi of Mirajul-Khayal,* Bombay, 1313/1895.

Taqavi, Sayyid Mir Muhammad: *Tarkhan Nama,* ed. S.H. Rashidi, Haidarabad, 1965.

Tarbiat-e-Tabrizi, Muhammad Ali: *Danishmandan-e-Azarbaijan,* Tehran, Majlis Publication, 1314/1935.

Wahid Qazwini, Muhammad Tahir: *Abbas Nama,* ed. Ibrahim Dahgan, Arak, 1329/1950.

Yusuf Mirak: *Tarikh-i-Mazhar-i-Shah Jahani,* ed. Sayyid Hasam-ud-din Rashidi, Karachi, 1962.

Arabic

Tehrani, Shaikh Aqa Buzork: *Azzarrieh,* Najaf and Tehran, 25 Vols., Vols. 6, 15-18, 1961-67.

Urdu

Malikapuri, Abdul Jabbar: *Tazkira Mahabub-Zeman,* Haidarabad Deccan, 1329/1911.

Turkish

Sami Pasha, Shams-ud-din: *Qamus-ul-Ahlam,* 6 Vols., Istanbul, 1306/ 1888.

European Sources:

Bêrnier, Francosi: *Travels in the Mughal Empire (1656-68)*' transl. by A. Constable, Second Edition, New Delhi, 1968.

Denison Ross, Sir. E. (ed.) : *Sir Anthony Sherley and his Persian Adventure,* London, 1933.

Foster, W.: *The English Factories in India,* 13 Vols., Oxford 1914, 1918-21, 1622-23, 1630-33, 1637-40.

Malcolm, Sir John: *The History of Persia from the Most Early Period to the Present time,* 2 Vols., London, 1815.

Manucci, Niccelao: *Storia do Moger,* ed. and tranl. William Irvin, 4 Vols., London, 1906-08.

Roe, Sir Thomas: *The Embassy of Sir Thomas Roe,* ed. by Sir W. Foster, O.U.P. 1929.

Stewart, Charles: *The History of Bengal,* 2nd edition, Calcutta, 1910.

Thevenot, Jean De: *The Indian Travels of Thevenot and Careri,* tranl. and edit, S.N. Sen, New Delhi, 1949.

Tavernier, Jean Baptiste: *Travels in India* (1640-67), transl. by V. Ball, ed. by A. Constable, Second edition, New Delhi, 1968.

Secondary Sources

Persian

Aftab Asghar: *Tarikh navisi dar Hend Va Pakistan* (*Historiography in India and Pakistan*), Lahore, Iran Culture House, 1364/1985.

Ajand, Yaqub: *Hurufis in History,* Tehran, 1369/1990.

Akbari Savi, Muhammad Husain: *Tuhfatul Murad,* Tehran, 1372/1993.

Bastani Parizi, Muhammad Ibrahim: *Ganj Ali Khan,* Kerman, Farhang-i-Honar, 1353/1974.

Bayani, Mahdi: *Ahwal va Athar Khushanavisan,* 4 Vols. in two, Tehran, 1363/1984.

Danish Paju, Muhammad Taqi: *Continuity in Foundation of Iranian Music in Fihrest-i-Kitabhai Chapi,* by Khan Baba Mushar, Tehran, Wizarat Farhang.

Darakh, Mahdi: *Buzurgan-i-Sukhan Sarayan-i-Hamadan,* Tehran, 1341/1962.

Ethe Herman: *History of Persian Literature,* transl. into Persian by Reza Zada Shafaq, Tehran, 1337/1958.

Falsafi, Nasrullah: *Tarikh-e-Ravabet-e-Iran va Orupa dar doreh-Safaviyeh,* Tehran, Ibn Sina, 1939.

Falsafi, Nasrullah: *Zindegani-ye-Shah Abbas-i-Avval,* 4 Vols., Tehran, 1955-61.

Falsafi, Nasrullah: *Chand Maqala-ye-Tarikhi va Adabi,* Tehran, 1342/1963.

Fumani, Abdul Fattah: *History of Gilan,* Tehran, Bunyad-i-Farhang-i-Iran, 1349/1970.

Golchin Maani, Ahmad: *Fihrest-i-Noskhahai Khatti Farsi,* Vol. III, Tus Mashhad, 1340/1961.

Golchin Maani, Ahmad: *Maktab-i-Wuqu,* Tehran, 1348/1969.

Golchin Maani, Ahmad: *Tarikh-i-Tazkireai Farsi,* History of Persian *Tazkiras,* 2 Vols., Tehran, 1348/1969.

Golchin Maani, Ahmad: *Tazkira Pimana,* Mashhad, Firdusi University, 1359/1980.

Golchin Maani, Ahmad: *The Caravan of India,* 2 Vols., Mashhad, Astan-i-Qods Razavi, 1369/1990.

Golchin Maani, Ahmad: *Fihrest-e-Razavi* (*Razavi list*), Vol. VII.

Golchin Maani, Ahmad: *The list of manuscript books of Astan-i-Quds-e-Razavi,* Vol. VII, No. 932.

Hekmat, Ali Asghar: *Naqsh-i-Parsi Bar Ahjar-i-Hend* (*Persian Picture on the Indian Stones*), Tehran, Second Edition, 1337/1938.

Honarfar, Lotfullah: *Ganjina-ye-Athar Tarikhi Esfahan,* Esfahan, 1344/1965.

Husaini, Sayyid Ahmad: *Fihrest-e-Noskhai Khatti* (*List of Manuscript copies*), Qom, Ayatullah Marashi Library, Vols. II, III.

Kiya, Sadiq: *Nuqtawian or Pasikhanian,* Tehran, 1320/1941.

Munzavi, Ahmad: *Fihrest-e-Noskhai Farsi* (*List of Persian Manuscript copies*), Vol. III, IV, Tehran, 1351/1972.

Nafisi, Said: *Tarikh Nazm va Nasr Dar Iran* (*History of Prose and Verse in Iran*), Tehran, 1344/1955.

Nawai, Abdul Husain: *Shah Tahmasp-e-Safavi,* (Documents), Tehran, 1350/1971.

Nawai, Abdul-Husain-i: ed. *Asnad va Makatibat-e-Tarikhi Shah Abbas-e-Avval,* Tehran, 1352/1973, Vol. p. 125, and Vol. II, p. 17.

Nuhmani Shibli: *Sherul Ajam,* transl. into Persian by Muhammad Taqi Fakhr-e-Dahi Gilani, 5 Vols., Tehran, Vol. III, 1334/1955.

Qaraman, Muhammad (ed.): *Diwan-i Kalim*, Tehran, 1367/1988.

Sahb, Abulqasim: *Zindegani Shah Abbas Kabir,* Tehran, 1325/1946.

Thabitiyan, Dh.: *Asnad va Namahai Tarikhi Daura-i-Safaviyeh,* Tehran, 1343/1964.

Urdu

Ansari, Sharif-un-Nisa, *Hayat va Tasnifat-i-Mirza Abu Talib Kalim Hamadani,* Haidarabad Deccan, 1961.

Rashidi, Sayyid Hasam-ud-din: *Mirza Ghazi Tarkhan and Bazm-e-Adab,* Karachi 1971.

English

Ahmad Khan, Shafaat; edit: *John Marshall in India, Notes and Observations in Bengal* (*1668-72*), Oxford, 1927.

Alam, Muzaffar: *The Crisis of Empire in Mughal North India,* Delhi, Oxford, 1986.

Alam, M and S. Subrahmanyam (eds) : *The Mughal State, 1526-1750*, Oxford, 1998.

Ali. M. Athar: *The Mughal Nobility under Aurangzeb*, Bombay, 1966.

Ali M. Athar: *The Apparatus of Empire, Awards of Ranks, Offices and Titles to the Mughal Nobility* (*1574-1658*), Delhi, 1985.

Arjomand, Said Amir: *The Shadow of God and the Hidden Imam*, University of Chicago, 1984.

Ashraf, K.M: *Life and Conditions of the People of Hindustan*, Delhi, 1959.

Askari, Sayyid Hasan: *Mirza Muhammad Baqir Najm-i-Sani*, Arshi presentation volume, eds. Malik Ram and M.D. Ahmad, New Delhi, Majlis-i-Nazr-i-Arshi, 1965.

Alvi, Sajida Sultana: *Advice on the Art of Governance, Mauizah-i-Jahangir of Muhammad Baqir Najm-i-Sani*, New York, 1980.

Ball, Upendranath: *Modern India;* Lahore, 1939.

Banerji, S.K: *Humayun Padashah*, 2 Vols; Oxford, Lucknow, 1938, 1941.

Beni Prasad, Saksena: *History of Shah Jahan of Delhi*, Allahabad; 1932.

Beni Prasad: *History of Jahangir*, Allahabad; 1962.

Bhuyan, S.K: *Lachat Barphukhan and his Times*, Gauhati, 1947.

Brown, Percy: *Indian Painting under the Mughals*, Oxford, 1924.

Brown, E. G: *A Literary History of Persia*, Vol. IV, Cambridge, 1956-59.

Burn, Richard: *The Cambridge History of India*, Vol. IV, Cambridge, 1963.

Boyle, John. A: *Persia, History and Heritage*, London, 1978.

Chaudhuri, K.N: *The European Trading World of Asia and the English East India Company* (*1660-1760*), Cambridge, 1978.

Chopra, P. N: *Life and Letters under the Mughals*, New Delhi, 1976.

Elliot, Sir. H. and J. Dawson: *History of India as told by its own Historians*, Vol. V, London, 1867, Vol. VI, 1990.

Ghani, Abdul: *History of Persian Language and Literature at the Mughal Court*, Vol. III, Allahabad, 1930.

Gorekar, N.S: *Indo-Iran Relations, Cultural Aspects*, Bombay, 1970.

Habib, Irfan: *Agrarian System of Mughal India,* Bombay, 1963.

Habib, Irfan: *The family of Nur Jahan during Jahangir's reign:* A Political Study in; Medieval India, A Miscellancy, Dept. of History, Aligarh Muslim University, 1969.

Habib, Irfan: *The Technology and Economy of Mughal India,* Dev Raj Chanana Lectures (mimeographed) Delhi, 1970.

Haneda, Masashi: *Emigration of Iranian Elites to India during the 16-18th centuries, in: Lheritaage Timouride,* ed. by Maria Szuppe, Paris, 1997.

Hasan, Hadi: *Collection of Articles,* Haidarabad Deccan, 1954.

Howorth, Sir, H: *History of Mongols,* London, 1876-1927.

Ibn Hasan: *The Central Structure of the Mughal Empire,* New Delhi, (Reprint) 1970.

Ishwari Prasad: *A Short History of Muslim Rule in India,* Vol. II Allahabad, 1939.

Jackson, Peter and Lockhart Laurence (eds.): *The Cambridge History of Iran, the Timurid and Safavid periods,* Vol. VI, Cambridge, 1986.

Lambton, A.K. S: *Landlord and Peasant in Persia, A Study of Land Tenure and Land Revenue Administration,* Oxford, 1953.

Lockhart, Laurence: *Persian cities,* London, 1960.

Majumdar, R.C, *The History and Culture of the Indian People, The Mughal Period,* Bombay, 1984.

Marshall, D.N: *Mughals in India, A Bibliographical Survey of Manuscripts,* London and New York, 1967.

Minorsky. V; *Iran opposition, Martyrdom and Revolt, in: G.E. Von Grunebaum (ed) Unity and Varity in Muslim Civilisation, Chicago,* 1955.

Mohiuddin, Momin: *The Chancellery and Persian Epistolography under the Mughals,* Calcutta, 1971.

Moosavi, Shireen: *The Economy of the Mughal Empire,* Delhi, 1987.

Moreland, W.H: *From Akbar to Aurangzeb, A Study in Economic Indian History,* London, 1923, New Delhi, 1972.

Naqvi, Sadiq: *The Iran-Deccan relations,* Haidarabad, 1994.

Nehru, J.L: *The Discovery of India,* Calcutta, 1946.

Pant, D: *The Commercial Policy of the Mughals,* Delhi 1930.

Qanungo, K.R: *Dara Shukoh,* 2nd Edition, Delhi, 1953.

Ray Choudhary, T. and Irfan Habib: *The Cambridge Economic History of India,* Cambridge, 1982.

Ray Choudhary, S.C; *History of Mughal India:* Delhi, 1988.

Riazul Islam: *Indo-Persian Relations,* Lohore, Iran Culture House, 1970.

Riazul Islam: *A Calendar of Documents on Indo-Persian Relations,* 2 Vols, Karachi, 1979, 1982.

Richards J.F: *The New Cambridge History of India, The Mughal Empire,* Cambridge, 1993.

Rieu. Chartes: *Catalogue of the Persian Manuscripts in the British Museum,* 3 Vols, British Museum, 1879-1883.

Rypka, Jan: *History of Iranian Literature,* ed. Karl Jahn, Dordrecht, 1968.

Sarkar, Sir Jadunath, *History of Aurangzeb Northern India* (*1658-81*); Vol. III, New Delhi, 1928.

Sarkar, Jagadish Narayan: *The life of Mir Jumla, The General of Aurangzeb,* (second edition) New Delhi, 1979.

Savory, R.M: *Safavid Persia, in: The Cambridge History of Islam,* ed. P. M. Holt, Part.I, Cambridge, 1970.

Savory, R.M; *Iran under the Safavids,* Cambridge, 1980.

Sharma, S.R; *Mughal Empire in India,* (*1526-1761*), Poona, 1934.

Siddiqi, Abdul Majeed: *History of Golkonda,* Haidarabad, 1956.

Siddiqi, N.A: *Land Revenue Administration under the Mughal,* Bombay, 1970.

Singh, Meera: *Medieval Indian History,* New Delhi, 1978.

Smith, V. A: *Akbar, the Great Mughal,* Oxford, 1917.

Srivastava, A. L: *The Mughal Empire,* Agra, 1989.

Steensguard, Niels: *Carraks, Caravans, and Companies: The Structural Crisis in the European Asian Trade in the early 17th Century,* Copenhagam, 1972, Republished as the Asian Trade Revolution of the Seventeenth Century, Chicago, 1974.

Storey, C.A: *Persian Literature, A Bio-bibliographical Survey,* 2 Vols, London, 1970-71.

Sykes, P.M: *A History of Persia,* London, 1915.

Tripathi, R.P: *Rise and Fall of the Mughal Empire*, Allahabad, 1956.

Encyclopaedias

Bosworth, C. E. and E. Wan Donzel, (ed): *Encyclopaedia of Islam*, Vol. I. 1960, Vol. VII, VIII, New York, 1993, 1995.

Gwnn, R.. *The New Encyclopaedia Britannica,* Vol. VII, XXI, Chicago, 1968.

Houtsma and Arnold (ed): *The Encyclopaedia of Islam,* Vol. I, Leyden, 1913, p. 168.

Yarshater, Ehsan: *Encyclopaedia Iranica,* Vol. I, London, 1985.

Zafar Ali, S. M: *The Cyclopaedia of India,* Vol. II, Delhi, 1992.

Dictionaries

Persian

Abdur Rashid. S: *Farhang-i-Rashidi,* ed. Maulavi Zulfiqar Ali and Azizur Rahman, 2 Vols, Calcutta, 1875.

Dahkhuda, Ali Akbar: *Loghat Nama Dahkhuda,* section Alef under the name of Abulqasim Mir Findareski, Tehran University, 1325 AH/ 1907.

Khaiyampur, Abdul, Rasoul: *Farhang-i-sukhanvaran,* Tabriz, 1340/ 1961.

Moin, Muhammad, *Farhang-i-Moin*, Vol. VI, Ahlam, Amir Kabir, 1371 AS/1922.

Razm Ara, H: *Farhang-i-Geographia-i-Iran,* Tehran, Artesh (Army) Publication. 1330 AH/1912.

English

Beale, Thomas: *An Oriental Biographical Dictionary,* London, 1894.

Hadi, Nabi: *Dictionary of Indo-Persian Literature,* New Delhi, 1995.

Periodicals Literature

Abdur Rahim: Mughal Relations with Persia, in: *Islamic Culture,* Vol. VIII, July, Oct, 1934, Vol. IX, Jan, 1935.

Abidi, S.A. H; Life and poetry of Qudsi in; *Islamic Culture,* Vol. XXXVIII, No. 2, April, 1964.

Ahmad, Nazir: Muhammad Sadiq Esfahani: An Official of Bengal of Shah Jahan's time in: *Indo-Iranica,* Vol. XXIV, Nos. Three and four, Calcutta, 1971.

Ahmad, Aziz: Safavid Poets and India, in: *Journal of the British Institute of Persian Studies:* Vol. XIV, London, 1976.

Ahmad, Imtiaz; Mahabat Khan, Khan-i-Khanan: A case study of Indian cultural influences on the Mughal nobility in: *Islamic Culture,* Vol. III, No. II, 1978.

Alam Khan Iqtidar: The nobility under Akbar and the development of his religious policy (1650-80); *Journal of the Royal Asiatic Society*, pt: 3-4, 1969.

Alam, Muzaffar: Eastern India in the early eighteenth century crisis, in; *India Economic and Social History Review I,* January, March, 1991.

Alam, Muzaffar: Trade, Politics and Regional Change: Aspects of Commercial Relations between Mughal India and Central Asia, 1550-1750, *Journal of Economic and Social History of the Orient,* No. 2, 1994.

Alam, Muzaffar; State Building under the Mughals: Religion, Culture and Politics: *Cahiers D'Asie Centrale No. 3-4, 1997.*

Alam, Muzaffar; The Pursuit of Persian: Language in Mughal Politics, *Modern Asian Studies,* June, 1998.

Ali, M, Athar; Towards an Interpretation of the Mughal Empire, in; *Journal of the Royal Asiatic Society of Great Britain and Ireland*, No. I, 1978.

Alvi, Sajida Sultana; Shiism in India during Jahangir's Reign some Reflections, in; *Journal of the Pakistan Historical Society,* 27, No. I, 1979.

Banani, Amin; The social and economic structure of the Persian Empire in its heyday: A paper submitted to the Harvard Colloquium on tradition and change in the *Middle East,* December, 1967.

Banani, Amin; Reflections on the social and economic structure of Safavid Persia at its zenith in; *Iranian Studies,* Vol. XI, 1978.

Edwards, Clara Cary; Relations of Shah Abbas the Great of Persia, with the Mughal Emperors, in; *Journal of the American Oriental Society,* Vol. 35, Nos. 1-3, 1915, New York.

Golchin Maani, Ahmad: Majma-ul-Furs (fourth writing) in; *Majalleh Danish Kadah Adabiyat va Hulum-i-Ensani,* Mashhad No. I, year 10.

Golchin Maani, Ahmad: Hemasehai Dini (Religious epic) in; *Nama Astan-i-Quds,* Vol. VI.

Gorekar, N. S; Indo-Iranian Relations during the Mughal Period, in; *Indica,* 12, 1975.

Hidayat Husain, M: Contemporary historian during the reign of the Emperor Shah Jahan, in; *Islamic Culture,* Jan, 1941.

Husain, Afzal: Growth of Irani element in Akbar's nobility, *Proceedings of the Indian History Congress,* 36th session, Aligarh, 1975.

Husain, Afzal: Mahabat Khan and court politics during Jahangir's reign in; *Proceedings of the Indian History Congress,* Mysore, 1993.

Jarfi, Abdul Amir; Iran and India: Age old friendship, in; *India Quarterly,* Vol. L, No. 4, Oct. Dec. 1994, New Delhi.

Juwani, Qasim Khan: Diwan, ed. Muhammad Shamon Israili, in; *Index Islamica,* June, 1962 and December, 1963.

Kanwar, H.I.S: Ali Mardan Khan in; *Islamic Culture,* Vol. XLVII No. 2, April, 1973.

Khan, Muhammad Afzal: The Mamuris: An unexplored clan in the Mughal nobility in; *Indian History Congress,* 1981.

Kiya, Sadiq: Nuqtaviyan ya Pasikhaniyan, *Iran Kudeh,* Vol. XIII, Tehran, 1332/1953.

Murtada-Al-Musavi, Mustafa: Persian Trade under the Safavids, in; *Sumer*; Vol. XXV, Baghdad, 1969.

Nasr, Sayyid Husain: Religion in Safavid Persia: in; *Iranian Studies,* Vol. VII, 1974.

Riazul Islam: Iran and the Mughal frontier provinces in; *Farhang-i-Iran Zamin,* Vol. XXI, Nos. 1-4, Tehran 1976.

Sarkar, Jagadish Narayan: Mir Jumla, Iran correspondence, in; *Journal of the Bihar and Orissa Research Society,* Pts. 1and 2, March and June 1943.

Sarkar, Jagadish Narayan: Mir Jumla's overseas commercial activities, in; *Journal of the Bihar and Orissa Research Society,* Dec. 1945.

Sarkar, Ashok Kumar, Itimad-ud-daula: A sketch of his life and career, in: *The Quarterly Review of Historical Studies,* Vol. X, No. 3, 1970-71.

Savory, R.M : The principal offices of the Safavid state during the reign of Tamasp (930-984/1524-76) in; *Bulletin of the School of Oriental and African Studies,* Vol. XXIV, 1961.

Index

Abbas I, 205, 207, 240
Abbas II, 204, 209
Abbas Mirza (Later Shah Abbas), 383
Abdul Aziz, 102
Abdul Baqi, 240
Abdul Baqi Nihavandi, 149, 252, 385
Abdul Haq, 314
Abdul Latif, 72-73, 94
Abdul Latif Qazwini, 94, 95, 379
Abdul Qadir, 253
Abdul Qadir Basinani, 97, 98
Abdul Wahhab, 152
Abdullah Beg, 103
Abdullah Khan Uzbek, 76, 158
Abdullah Qutb Shah, 55-56
Abdun Nabi, 85
Abun Nabi Qazwini, 179
Abdur-Rahman, 92
Abdur-Rahim, 105, 110, 117
Abdur-Rahim Farahani, 75, 118
Abdur-Rahim Khan, 119
Abdur-Rahim Khan-i-Khanan, 28, 46, 75, 85, 90, 109, 113, 115,-16, 138, 146-48, 182, 205-206, 240, 249, 252-56, 277, 291, 301, 306, 308, 385
Abdur Razzaq, 264, 383
Abu Said Mirza, 116
Abu Talib Kalim Kashani, 28-29
Abu Turab Razavi, 385
Abul Baqa Abar Quii, 313
Abul Bi, 300
Abul-Bi-Uzbek, 292
Abul Fazl, 250, 383
Abul Fazl Allami, 338
Abul Hasan, 89, 96
Abul Həsan Asaf Khan, 396
Abul Qasim, 118
Abul Wali, 313
Adai Yazdi, 205, 382
Adil Khan, 45, 113
Adil Shah, 46, 49, 56, 384
Afghanistan, 21, 31
Afshar Tribe, 25, 275
Afzal Khan, 49, 109, 119, 255
Afzal Khan Shirazi, 75
Agha Mulla, 87
Agra, 146, 152, 155, 157, 179, 190, 210, 250, 255, 257, 258, 262, 264, 279, 306-307, 335-36, 340-41, 355, 357
Ahadi Khurasani, 264
Ahmad Beg Khan, 178
Ahmad Beg Lang, 100
Ahmad Beg Qurchi, 56
Ahmad Razi, 100
Ahmadabad, 276
Ahmadnagar, 46-47, 114
Ani-i-Akbari, 21, 145-46, 152, 273-74
Ajmer, 75, 85, 94. 98, 105, 108, 145, 188, 189, 247, 256, 261, 275, 305, 355, 338
Ajmer and Mandu, 93
Akbar, (Jalal-ud-din Muhammad Akbar) 21-22, 25, 27, 29, 35-39, 45-46, 55-56, 72-73, 75-76, 85, 87, 89, 91, 94-97, 107, 110-11, 114-15, 117, 137-38, 146-48, 150-53, 156, 161, 171-73, 176, 185, 188, 189, 192-94, 204, 206-208, 239, 247, 250, 254,

255, 257, 261, 263, 269-73, 276, 292, 304-5, 310, 312, 329, 330, 337, 349, 357, 360, 369, 377, 384, 393, 394
Akbarabad, 155
Akbarnagar, 178
Akbar-nama, 115, 273, 336
Al-Muzaffar Dynasty, 172
Alam Ara Abbasi, 43-44, 47, 379
Alam Khan, 176
Alaud daula, 379
Alaud daula Qazwini, 73
Alexander, 109
Ali Ajri Tabbakh, 307
Ali Esfahani, 291-92
Ali Esfahani Musannef, 306
Ali Mardan (Khan), 51, 73, 101-104, 209, 263
Ali Mardan Khan Zig, 383
Ali Quli, 110
Ali Quli Khan Shamlu, 150
Ali Reza Esfahani, 307
Ali Turkman Khurasani, 75, 110
Alladad, 85
Alladad Khan, 261
Allahabad, 171, 176, 357
Allama Chalabi Beg, 336
Allami Afzal Khan, 105
Alqas Mirza, 398
Aman Ullah, 108
Amanat Khan, 117-18, 314,
Amani Esfahani, 274, 331, 335
Amin Kashani, 30, 331, 334
Amini Darsani, 205
Amini Mashhadi, 292, 313, 384
Amir Abdul Wahab Mir Najdi, 338
Amir Khusrau, 146
Amir-ul-Umara, 73
Amir Taqi-ud-din Muhammad, 252
Amir Yar Muhammad Khan Najm-i-Sani, 176
Amul, 145
Aqa Ahmad, 340
Aqa Baba Julaki, 251
Aqa Beg, 43
Aqa Khizra, 251, 255
Aqa Muhammad Bakhshi, 306
Aqa Muhammad Mustaufi-i-Ghulaman, 45
Aqa Mulla, 99
Aqa Mulla Tahir, 74
Aqa Razi, 355
Aqa Shapur Tehrani, 337
Aqa Tahir, 188
Aqa Zaman, 161
Aqidat Khan, 161
Aqil Khan, 395
Aqil Khan Inayat Ullah, 119
Arab Khans, 343
Arab Poets, 255
Ardabil, 24, 369
Arghuns, 115
Arjumand Babai, 101
Arjumand Banu Begum (Mumtaz Mahal), 89
Arif Darabi Shirazi, 262
Arif Eigi, 356
Arif Shirazi, 192
Arsalan Beg, 52-53
Arz-i-Mukarrar, 75
Asad Beg, 138
Asad Beg Qazwini, 150
Asad Qissa Khan, 181
Asaf Beg Qazwini, 138
Asaf Khan , 89-93, 96, 99, 102, 115, 117, 137, 150, 207, 257, 338, 377, 386, 393
Asaf Khan Malika Banu, 117
Asaf Khan Muhammad Salih, 96
Asaf Khan Tehrani, 74, 89,
Asaf Qomi, 310
Ashraf Beg, 335
Asir, 145
Asirgarh, 38
Asiri Shirazi, 312
Askari Kashani, 338
Asri Damghani, 255
Astarabad, 85

Atai Cherudi Shirazi, 313
Atga Khan, 157
Aurangzeb, 22, 54, 86, 92-93, 102-106, 113, 145, 159-60, 172-73, 178-81, 188, 190, 205, 208, 303, 330, 337, 339, 343, 345, 346, 393
Autar Khan, 53
Awadh, 104
Azam Khan, 98, 100, 108, 112
Azerbaijan, 24, 72, 93, 147, 389
Azerbaijan-i-Gharbi, 24
Azerbaijan-i-Sharqi, 24

Baba-i-Sani, 73, 101
Babur, 26, 34, 46, 57
Badakhshan, 35, 37
Badi--uz-Zaman, 137, 384
Baghdad, 21, 39, 45, 51
Bahadur Shah, 104
Bahram, 92
Baharam Mirza, 114, 115, 398
Bahram Sultan, 102
Bahri Beg, 48
Bahari Kashani, 292, 307
Bairam Beg Khan-i-khanan, 34
Bairam Khan, 35
Balkh, 37, 52-53, 102, 158, 259, 265
Badakhshan, 102
Baluchistan, 76
Banda-Reza, 86
Bandar Abbas, 55
Bandar Lahiri, 189
Baqai Khurasani, 207
Baqi Nihavandi, 85, 240, 251-53, 262, 311
Baqir Kashani, 304
Baqir Khan, 90, 207
Baqir Khan Najm-i-Sani, 28, 171, 176-77, 386
Baqir Khurdah, 304
Baqir Shirazi, 263
Baqiyai Naini, 307
Barlas, 41
Basra, 277
Bastam, 53-54
Bebadal Khan, 300
Beg Oghli, 102
Beglur Begi of Khurasan, 74
Begum Sahib (Aurangzeb daughter), 395
Bengal, 155-56, 161, 171, 292, 308, 315, 322
Bidar, 95
Bidil, 203
Bijapur, 47, 55, 95, 113, 138, 150, 155, 208, 304, 338
Bijapur Court, 208, 251
Bijapur and Ahmadnagar, 46
Birjand (Khurasan), 341
Bukhara, 102
Bundela Jujhar Singh, 98
Burhan Nizam Shah, 255, 277, 304
Burhanpur, 49, 104, 109
Bushehr, 24

Central Asia, 21, 23, 26, 33, 34, 50, 203, 329, 370
Chaghtais, 369
Chahar Mahal Bakhtiyari, 24
Chak Rulers, 256
Chalabi Tabrizi, 302
Chand Bibi, 206, 255
Chardin, Jean, 139
Chausa Battle, 34
Chehginian Oimaq, 85
Chinigiz Khan, 119
Chirag Beg, 315

Dabail Port, 252
Dakhli Esfahani, 205
Danishmand Khan, 106, 206, 386
Daniyal, 114
Dara, 54
Dara Shukoh, 16, 51, 102, 104-106, 203, 205, 346
Darab Khan, 262
Dar-ul-Insha, 309
Dar-ul-Saltanat of Lahore, 292

Darogh-i-Imarat, 179
Darvishes, 23, 29, 47
Das Bishen, 41
Dastour Qazwini, 257
Daulat Khan, 53, 96
Daultabad Fort, 95, 100, 160
Dawar Bakhsh (Prince), 152
Deccan, 26-27, 30, 42, 44-47, 49, 54, 55, 71, 73-75, 85, 95, 98, 100-101, 104, 107, 108, 111-113, 138-39, 146-47, 149, 152-53, 156, 161, 181, 188, 203, 207-208, 250, 252, 255, 259, 265, 275, 277, 307, 313, 329-30, 338, 341, 346, 357
Delhi, 30, 34, 39, 53, 56, 90, 108, 110, 152, 171, 309, 330
Delhi and Agra, 34
Din-i-Ilahi, 150
Din Muhammad Uzbek, 85
Diwan-i-Buyutat, 87, 105
Diyanat Khan, 87

East India Company, 90
Ebadullah Kashani, 205
Esfahan, 22, 24, 30, 41, 51, 53, 57, 72-74, 87, 94, 96-98, 110, 139, 151-53, 153, 158, 171, 176, 179, 185, 204, 209, 239-40, 248-51, 257, 259, 274, 275, 303-310, 313, 330, 337, 339-41, 345, 355, 369, 385, 389, 396
Esfandeyar Khan, 86
Eshik Aqasi Bashi, 38
Eskandar Qissa Khan, 182
Etibar Khan, 36

Fahmi Qazwini, 73, 99, 382
Fakhr-uz-Zamani, 256
Fani Gilani, 249
Fani Shirazi, 276-77
Farah Sistani, 76
Faregh Tabrizi, 336
Farhad, 102
Farhad Khan, 302
Faridun, 102
Faribi Tehrani, 338
Fars, 24
Fars-i-Hamadani, 253
Farzana Begum (Bibi Jiu), 92
Fatehpur Sikri, 87, 138, 145-46, 155, 258
Fathi Ardestani, 275
Fathul Qulub, 304
Fayeq-i-Lahijani, 292, 300
Fayez Gilani, 188
Fidai Khan, 156
Firdausi (Shah-Nama), 312
Forsi Shidani, 310
Furouqi Qazwini, 318
Fuzuni Astarabadi, 249
Fuzuni Qomi, 255
Fuzuni Tabrizi, 250

Ganges, 178
Ganj Ali Khan Zig, 73, 101, 383
Ghaiyur Beg Kabuli, 107
Ghani Yazdi, 205, 382
Ghayur Beg, 75
Ghayuri, 254
Ghazi Beg, 148
Ghazi Beg Tarkhan, 207, 386
Ghazi Shaikh Ali, 35
Ghaznin, 76
Ghiyas Beg, 74
Ghiyas Beg (Itimad-ud-daula Tehrani), 86-87, 204
Ghiyas Mashhadi, 329, 332, 336
Ghiyas-ud-din Naqib Khan, 73, 379
Gilan, 24, 43, 72, 147, 204, 390
Gilan and Mazandaran, 389
Girami Shamlu, 138, 161
Golivar Fort, 341
Golkonda, 30, 46-47, 55, 85, 95, 139, 150, 153-54, 188, 207-208, 250, 255, 270, 276, 293, 312, 330, 338, 342-45, 357, 384
Golshan, 269
Golshani Shirazi, 277
Gujarat, 148, 152, 155, 157, 171, 176, 273, 277, 335

Gulshan-i-Asrar, 304

Habsh Khan, 47
Haidar Beg, 44
Haidar Beg Hamadani, 257
Haidar Khisali, 138
Haidar Mirza, 115, 398
Haidar Safavi, 117
Haji Beg, 43
Haji Ismail Neyrizi, 311
Haji Maqsoud Chitsaz Esfahani, 339
Haji Muhammad jan Qudsi Mashhadi, 29, 159
Haji Niamat, 43
Haji Rafiq, 41
Haji Talib, 339
Haji Waqif Qasim, 339
Hajib, 86
Hakim Abul Fath Gilani, 146, 383
Hakim Ali, 192
Hakim Ali Gilani, 191
Hakim Arif Eigi, 354
Hakim Dawud, 185, 189-90
Hakim Dawud Taqarrub Khan, 383
Hakim Fakhr-ud-din, 191
Hakim Humami, 383
Hakim Jamala-i-khan, 179
Hakim Masih-al-Zaman, 189
Hakim Mashhadi, 192
Hakim Mirza Muhammad, 189
Hakim Nizam-ud-din Ali Kashani, 188
Hakim Nur-ud-din, 383
Hakim Qutba, 105
Hakim Rukna, 188, 189, 263, 395
Hakim Rukna of Kashan, 105
Hakim Rukna kashi, 145
Hakim Rukn-ud-din, 252
Hakim Rukn-ud-din Masih, 145
Hakim Sadra, 191
Hakim Shah Reza, 277
Hakim Shifai, 155, 307
Hakim-ul-Mulk, 56
Hamadan, 24, 148, 204, 240, 251, 253, 310, 369, 387
Hamzeh Bowanati, 206, 385
Hanafiti Sect, 172
Harem, 395
Hasan Beg Hamadani, 253
Hasan Beg Rafi Mashhadi, 138, 158-59
Hasan Beg Salahi, 340
Hasan Beg Takallu Itabi, 205
Hasan Safavi, 116
Hasan Sultan, 314
Hashim Khan, 111, 138, 155-56, 338
Hasil Mashhadi, 265
Hayati, 385
Hayati Gilani, 137, 145-46
Hayati Shawqi, 206
Herat, 21, 38, 41, 138, 150-51, 157-58, 179, 239, 259, 263, 292
Herat and Qandahar, 24
Hindustan, 34, 36-37, 87, 92, 98, 102, 111, 145, 336-37, 342
Humayun, 21, 26, 46, 56, 57, 72, 94, 239, 263, 369
Husain Beg, 39, 119
Husain Beg Quaichaji Tabrizi, 47
Husain-i-jami, 269, 277
Husain Khan Ziyad Oghli Qajar, 85
Hormuz, 275
Hormuzgan, 24
Hozni Alvi, 269, 278

Ibrahim Adil Shah, 208, 259, 304
Ibrahim Adil Shah II, 47, 251
Ibrahim Beg, 103
Ibrahim-i-Farsi, 292, 312
Ibrahim-i-Husain Bakhshi, 161
Ibrahim Khan, 103
Ibrahim Khan Fath Jang, 177-78, 207, 292, 312
Ibrahimabad Sodhra, 104
Ikhtisas Khan, 112
Iksir Esfahani, 292, 309
Ilam, 24
Imam Ali Ibn Abi Talib, 302
Imam Ali Reza, 209, 292

Imam Quli, 55
Imam Quli Beg, 383
Imam Quli Beg Shamlu, 119, 383
Imam Quli Khan, 56
Imam Reza, 292, 313
Imamiya Sect, 192, 248
Inayat Esfahani, 152
Inayatullah, 310
India, 21-31, 33, 37, 39, 40-44, 46, 48, 50, 57, 71-75, 85-87, 89, 91, 93-94, 96, 98, 99, 103-106, 109, 112, 114, 117, 137-39, 145-50, 153, 155, 157, 161, 171, 176, 179-181, 185, 188, 190, 194, 204-205, 208-210, 239-41, 247-55, 257, 259, 261-65, 268-70, 273, 275, 277-79, 291, 292, 301-305, 337-41, 343, 349, 352, 355-358, 360, 369-70, 379, 382-87, 393, 385, 398
Indian culture, 208
Indian Empire, 369
Indian Mughal Rulers, 23
Indian Music, 308
Indian Muslims, 27, 71, 377
Indian Rulers, 22, 25
Iradat Khan, 92, 100
Iran, 23-30, 33, 35-42, 45, 48-50, 53, 56-57, 71-75, 85, 89, 93, 98, 106, 137-39, 145, 149, 153, 155, 189, 204-208, 210, 239, 240, 247-49, 252, 255, 258, 262, 264-65, 268-70, 275, 291, 301, 305, 312, 329, 335-36, 341-42, 349, 355-56, 379, 384
Iranians, 21-31, 35, 37-39, 43, 71, 73, 85, 137, 139, 309, 329, 338, 341, 337-70, 377-79, 384-85, 387-89, 395
Iranis, 21, 72, 74, 110, 377, 384-85
Iranologists, 203
Iraq, 21, 23, 85, 302
Irevan, 38
Irij Shahnawaz Khan, 90
Isa Khan Beg Qurchi Bashi, 155
Ishaq Beg, 103
Ishaq Beg Yazdi, 45
Ishrat Khan, 292
Islam Khan, 118, 154
Islam Khan Chishti, 156
Islam Khan Mashhadi, 75, 112-13, 180, 336, 386
Islamabad (Mathura), 100
Islamic World, 370
Ismail I, 26, 34
Ismail Mirza, 115
Ismail Nasrabadi, 292
Isna-Ashari Shiism, 109
I'timad Khan Khwaja Idrak, 178
Itimad-ud-daula, 74, 88-91, 101, 107, 110, 112, 156, 205, 276, 307, 312, 329, 337, 357, 393
Itimad-ud-daula Jahangir-i-Tehrani, 86, 188, 386
Itiqad Khan Mirza Shapur, 90-91
Itizad-Daula Farhad Khan, 302
Izadi Yazdi, 356

Jafar Heravi, 157
Jafar Khan, 92-93
Jafar Qazwini, 149
Jahan Ara Begum, 159
Jahangir, 25, 27, 29, 38, 39, 40-48, 50, 55, 72-75, 85, 87-92, 94-100, 107, 109-12, 114-19, 137-39, 145-57, 171, 176-82, 185, 189, 192, 204-210, 239-40, 247, 250, 254-58, 261, 264-65, 269, 271, 273, 276-77, 279, 291-94, 302, 305-306, 308, 310-15, 329-30, 335, 338, 340, 349, 355-56, 358-60, 369-70, 377, 385-86, 393-94, 396-97
Jahangir Nama, 161
Jahangirnagar (Dacca), 311
Jahangir's Tomb, 89
Jalal Khan Afghan, 261
Jalal-ud-din, 76, 85
Jalal-ud-din Nakhash, 249
Jam-i-Esfahani, 154
Jamileh Esfahani, 393, 395
Jami Masjid (*Atga Bazar Agra*), 157
Jannat Makani (Jahangir), 109

Jan Nisar Khan, 52-53, 178
Jaswant Singh (Raja), 265
Jaunpur, 100
Javid Qazwini, 275-76
Jawahar Raqam Tabrizi, 303
Jesmi Hamadani, 152, 291, 301
Johri Tabrizi, 329, 331, 335
Julak, 240

Kabul, 33-35, 51, 50, 53-54, 73, 75, 87, 101-103, 107-109, 112, 118, 139, 145, 150, 209, 263, 273, 346
Kachhwaha, Man Singh, 97
Kaifi Sabzvari, 264
Kalantar or Magistrate, 87
Kalbi Zul Qadr, 278
Kalim Hamadani, 208
Kamil Jahromi, 261
Kangra Fort, 88
Karbala, 262
Karbala-i-Maulla, 299
Karkiraq Khana, 105
Kashan, 204-206, 239, 251-52, 264, 270, 304, 307-308, 335, 338, 369, 382, 384, 387
Kashi, Mirza Ziad-ud-din, 38
Kashmir, 33, 51, 72-73, 88, 90, 93, 99, 101-104, 111, 119, 156, 159, 179, 180-81, 192, 205, 207-208, 249, 255-57, 262, 264-65, 269-70, 273-74, 276, 338
Kashmiri, Mohsen Fani, 41
Kaukab, 95
Kazim Savoji, 30, 339
Kerman, 73, 369
Kermanshah, 24
Kerman and Sistan, 101
Khadija Begum, 176
Khadim Heravi, 314
Khaf, 172-73, 180, 382- 389
Khafi Khan, 36
Khairat Khan, 55
Khairul Bayan, 314
Khalaf Beg, 256
Khalifa Sultan, 205, 384
Khalil Khan Afshar, 86
Khalilullah Khan, 103
Khalissa and Khwajgi Khwaja, 74
Khalkhal, 369
Khalqi Shushtari, 254
Khan Ahmad Karkiya, 147, 389-90
Khan Alam, 39, 41, 42, 44, 117
Khan Dauran Nusrat Jang, 112
Khan-i-Jahan Lodi, 98, 100, 107-108, 112, 118, 149, 151
Khan-i-Khanan, 36, 89, 107-108, 110, 114, 137, 151, 157, 160, 192, 206-207, 240, 248, 252-55, 269-70, 276, 292-93, 299, 301, 306, 311, 313, 340-41, 343, 385-86
Khan Mirza, 34
Khan Saman, 89, 109, 181
Khan, Shah Beg, 39
Khan, Shaibani, 34
Khan Zaman, 97, 108
Khanzada Begum, 34
Khavari Gilani, 299
Kheirat Khan, 41
Khisali Heravi, 179-80
Khosla, 22
Khuld-i-Barin 50
Khurasan, 23-24, 36-37, 39, 50, 101-111, 138, 151-52, 158, 172, 179, 264, 269, 292, 313, 340, 383-84, 393
Khurasan and Iraq, 34
Khurasani Nobles, 39
Khurram (Prince), 89, 107-108, 138, 156
Khurram Shahr, 73
Khusrau, 39, 107-108, 119
Khusrau Bagh, 305
Khuzestan, 24
Khwaja Abul Hasan Turbati, 75, 111, 302, 308
Khwaja Abdul Karim Gilani, 40
Khwaja Abdul Samad, 35
Khwaja Afzal, 150
Khwaja Afzal Esfahani, 138

Khwaja Ahmad, 74
Khwaja Amin Razi, 87
Khwaja Beg Mirza, 114, 307
Khwaja Beg Mirza Safavi, 341, 383, 386
Khwaja Burj Ali Nakh Chiwani, 40
Khwaja Darya Dle Raushan, 302
Khwaja Ghiyas, 158
Khwaja Ghiyas Itimad-ud-daula Tehrani, 74
Khwaja Ghiyas-ud-din, 72
Khwaja Habibulla Tarkeh, 396
Khwaja Haji, 45
Khwaja Ismail-Ibn Khwaja Mirak Hal, 396
Khwaja Jahan, 96-97, 172, 258
Khwaja Jahan Khafi, 28, 171-72, 180
Khwaja Jalal-ud-din Mahmud, 35
Khwaja Maghsud Ali Heravi, 148
Khwaja Mirza Ahmad, 87, 100
Khwaja Moin-ud-din Chishti's Tomb, 254
Khwaja Muhammad Baqir, 40
Khwaja Muhammad Murad Qazwini, 150
Khwaja Muhammad Sharif, 74, 86-87
Khwaja Muhammad Tahir Wasli Tehrani, 92
Khwaja Nasir-ud-din Esfahani, 339
Khwaja Nizam-ud-din Ahmad Heravi, 145
Khwaja Qasim, 49
Khwaja Qasim Khurasani, 114
Khwaja Qasim Mustaufi Esfahani, 272
Khwaja Qasim Sayyid Atai, 111
Khwaja Shapur, 87, 338
Khwaja Sharaf-ud-din, 337
Khwaja Wais Hamadani, 312
Khwaja Zahir-ud-din Abdullah Imami, 151
Khwajigi Khwaja, 87
Koh-i-Nur, 344
Kohkiluyeh va Buyur Ahmad, 24, 86
Kokrah, 178
Kordestan, 24
Kurd Tribe, 73, 251
Kurdish Clan of Zig, 101
Kurdish Tribe, 269
Kurds, Imgadiya, 274

Ladli Begum, 107, 397
Lahiri Sind (Port), 138, 148
Lahore, 33-34, 38, 43, 45, 73, 85, 89-99, 101, 103-104, 109, 111, 156, 179, 188, 192-94, 256, 259, 261, 264, 277-78, 307-308, 337, 346
Lashkar Khan, 90, 106, 160
Likraj, 41
Lur, 25
Lurestan, 24, 72, 148
Lutfi Tabrizi, 138, 148

M. Athar Ali, 22-23
Ma' asir-ul-Umara, 23, 107, 152, 171
Mahabharat, 94
Mahabat Khan, 75, 97-98, 107, 109, 111, 118, 138, 149, 151-52, 161, 273, 309
Mahabat Khan Zaman Beg, 207
Mahdi Kohkiluyehi, 359-60
Mahmud Beg Turkman, 72, 85
Mahmud Pasikhani Gilani, 25, 292, 382
Mahmud Turkman, 383
Mahvi Hamadani, 206, 385
Majlesi Esfahani, 307
Makramat Khan, 172, 179
Makki Shirazi, 277
Malaki Qazwini, 150
Mali Shirazi, 261
Malik Ambar, 44, 275
Malik Banu, 118
Malik Ghiyas-ud-din Muhammad, 41
Malik Husain Sistani, 155
Malik Mahmud, 76
Malik Masud, 87
Malik Qomi, 304, 338
Malik Shah Sistani, 155, 356
Malik-ul-Shaura, 208-209

Malwa, 74-75, 92, 97, 108, 273, 358
Ma'mura (Kabul), 73
Mamuri Sadat of Esfahan, 171, 179
Mandu, 42, 47, 179, 273, 335, 357
Manija Begum, 156
Man Singh, 145
Manoucher Beg, 38
Markazi, 24
Maryam Makan Begum
(Hamida Banu Begum), 38
Masanavis,
Asman-i-Hashtum, 154
Gulistan-i-Naz, 154
Khusrau-Shireen, 154
Laili-va-Majnun, 154
Mashhad, 206, 293, 340, 389
Mashhad and Turbat, 72
Masih Kashani, 188
Masjid -i-Hakim, 185
Masud Masihi, 252
Masum Begum, 307
Maulana Ali Reza Sufi Mahmur, 307
Maulana Aqili Hakim, 340
Maulana Haidar Khisali Herati, 157
Maulana Haidar Qissa Khan, 181
Maulana Haidari Tabrizi, 147-48
Maulana Jalal-ud-din, 181
Maulana Ismail Mufti, 253
Maulana Kamal-ud-din Jesmi, 301
Maulana Nizam, 206, 385
Maulana Naziri, 279
Maulana Omidi, 340
Maulana Raqimi, 305
Maulana Sahifi, 312
Maulana Sahvi Khushnavis, 303
Maulana Sharari Hamadani, 302
Maulana Urfi, 110
Mazandaran, 24, 48, 204, 249, 292, 300, 311, 340, 394
Mazandaran and Gilah, 239
Mecca, 53, 189, 191, 251, 261, 263, 277, 299, 302, 208, 311, 314, 338-40
Mecca and Medina, 37, 180, 189
Mehdi Quli, 86
Mihr-un-Nisa or Nur Jahan, 87, 393-96
Mir Abdul Karim Mamuri Esfahani, 28, 171, 179
Mir Abdul Latif, 93-94
Mir Abdul Wahab Khan, 96
Mir Abdul Wahab Mamuri, 138, 152
Mir Abdullah Wasfi, 304-305
Mir Abdur Razzaq Mamuri, 73, 96, 152-53, 384
Mir Abd-us-Salam, 112
Mir Abul-Qasim Findarski, 240, 248, 257
Mir Abdur-Rahman, 113
Mir Abu Turb-i-Turabi, 257
Mir Afzal Sarkhush, 159
Mir Aziz-ud-din, 43, 52
Mir Bakar, 48
Mir Bakhshi, 27, 92, 99
Mir Barka, 48
Mir Fakhr-ud-din Samaki, 153
Mir Fathullah Shirazi, 384
Mir Findarski, 383
Mir Ghiyas-ud-din Ali, 93
Mir Hashim, 100
Mir Hasti, 148
Mir Hisam-ud-din, 43
Mir Husain, 50
Mir Husain Kashani, 338
Mir Husaini, 56
Mir Ibrahim Hamadani, 109
Mir Ilahi Hamadani, 29, 205, 207, 383
Mir-i-Saman, 385
Mir Jalal-ud-din Husain, 153
Mir Jumla, 153-54, 207, 329, 341-46, 384-85
Mir Jumla Ardestani, 30
Mir Jumla Sharistani, 258
Mir Khalilullah Khushnavis, 46-47
Mir Masum Bakhri, 38, 205
Mir Muhammad, 30
Mir Muhammad Amin, 138-39
Mir Muhammad Ashraf, 181

Mir Muhammad Baqir Savoji (Azam Khan), 99
Mir Muhammad Ghiyas, 180
Mir Muhammad Hashim, 249
Mir Muhammad Mumin, 292
Mir Muhammad Mumin Akbarabadi, 305
Mir Muhammad Mumin Shamimi Yazdi, 308
Mir Muhammad Said Mir Jumla, 265, 329, 341-42
Mir Muhammad Salih, 292, 305
Mir Muhammad Sharif, 94, 180-81
Mir Muiz-ud-din Muhammad Kashani, 304
Mir Mumin Astarabadi, 153
Mir Muqim, 303
Mir Murad, 155
Mir Murad Juwaini, 156
Mir Muzaffar, 304
Mir Nizam-ud-din Ahmad, 305
Mir Reza, 154
Mir Saman, 27, 35, 45, 99
Mir Sayyid Ali, 35, 303
Mir Sayyid Husain Khing-Suwar, 94
Mir Sayyid Sharif, 341
Mir Shahmir, 303
Mir Taqi-ud-din Muhammad Shirazi, 109
Mir Yahya, 93
Mir Yahya Saifi, 72, 379
Mir Zahir-ud-din Ilmi, 150
Mir Ziya, 309
Mirat-ul-Alam, 152, 159
Mirza Abu Said, 91
Mirza Abu Talib Shaista Khan, 90, 386
Mirza Abu Turab Turkman, 252
Mirza Abul-Hasan, 74, 89
Mirza Ahsan, 300
Mirza Ala-ud-daula, 87
Mirza Ali Quli, 110
Mirza Ali Zargar, 334
Mirza Aziz Kuka, 115, 157
Mirza Badi-uz-Zaman, 93, 149
Mirza Barkhordar Khan, 41
Mirza Beg Ibin Sadr-ud-din Musavi Astarabadi Findarski, 248
Mirza Darab Beg Juya-i-Kashmiri, 147
Mirza Darab Khan, 147
Mirza Fasihi, 307, 314
Mirza Ghazi, 26, 181, 182
Mirza Ghazi Beg Tarkhan, 97, 115, 138, 273
Mirza Ghazi Khan, 292, 300-301
Mirza Ghiyas Beg, 307
Mirza Ghiyas Beg Itimad-ud-daula, 396
Mirza Ghiya-ud-din Ali Asaf Khan II, 90
Mirza Ghiyas-ud-din Muhammad, 86
Mirza Ghiyas Itimad-ud-daula, 177
Mirza Habibullah Sadr, 310
Mirza Hakim, 36, 75, 107, 116
Mirza Hasan Safavi, 100
Mirza Hazaru, 341
Mirza Isa Tarkhan, 138, 155, 261
Mirza Ibrahim Hamadani, 301
Mirza Ibrahim Rafati Tabrizi, 303
Mirza Jafar Asaf Khan, 248
Mirza Jafar Qazwini, 207, 341
Mirza Jalal, 260
Mirza Jani Beg, 115, 149
Mirza Kamran, 34-35, 119
Mirza Kamran Beg Guya-i-Kashmiri, 147
Mirza Mahmud Bazil, 138, 160
Mirza Malik Mashriqi, 307
Mirza Muhammad Hakim, 145
Mirza Muhammad Husain Sirati Ghaffari, 308
Mirza Muhammad Qazwini, 203
Mirza Muhammad Sadiq Mina, 308, 311, 357
Mirza Muhammad Tahir Wasli, 91
Mirza Mumin, 208
Mirza Muqim, 335
Mirza Murad, 116
Mirza Muzaffar Husain, 38

Mirza Muzaffar Husain Safavi, 76, 117
Mirza Nizami, 256, 311
Mirza Qawam-ud-din Jafar Beg, 137, 384
Mirza Qawam-ud-din Jafar Asaf Qazwini, 99
Mirza Rashid, 160-61
Mirza Razi, 139
Mirza Rustam, 37, 76, 115
Mirza Rustam Safavi, 97, 114, 115, 189
Mirza Safdar Khan, 256
Mirza Safi, 117
Mirza Safavi, 38
Mirza Sayyid Ali Tabrizi, 292
Mirza Shah-Rukh bin Amir Taimur, 43
Mirza Yadgar, 255
MirzaYusuf Khan Razvi, 94
Mirza Zain-ul-Abidin Qazwini, 93
Mohsin Shirazi, 311,
Moin-ud-din Farahani, 160
Moreland, 21,
Mosayyeb Khan Takllu, 300
Motiai Tabrizi, 337
Muazzam Khan, 30, 92, 330, 341, 345
Mughal(s), 21-23, 25-29, 33-34, 37-38, 43, 45-46, 49-53, 55-56, 71-72, 76, 101, 117, 138, 150, 160, 171-72, 176, 188, 204, 206, 208-209, 249-50, 252, 255-57, 261, 265, 275, 291, 304, 312, 329, 335, 337, 343-45, 355, 369-70, 384-85, 387
Administration, 22, 26, 27
Armies, 149
Bureaucracy, 387
Court, 29, 38, 40, 42-43, 48, 54, 73-74, 101-102, 117, 139, 151, 172, 185, 206-207, 239, 291, 345, 370
Culture, 29, 57, 176, 203
Custom, 43
Diplomacy, 41
Empire, 21, 33
Forces, 115
Historiography, 71
History, 21
Indian Society, 21
Kings, 25
Life Style and Culture, 23
Nobility, 2, 7
Policy, 23
Polities and Administration, 26, 71
Polity, 22
Rulers, 26, 57
Society, 312
State, 23, 27
Troops, 51
Mughal India, 21-22, 25, 27, 29, 56-57, 203, 252, 256, 304, 318, 329, 337, 384-85, 387, 389
Mughal Religious and Political Culture, 26
Mughal Kingship, 22
Mughal-Safavid Relations, 33
Mughal-Uzbeks Invasion, 37
Muhammad Adil Shah, 5
Muhammad Afzal Khan, 172
Muhammad Afzal Sarkhush, 336
Muhammad Ali, 75, 103
Muhammad Ali Beg, 48-49
Muhammad Ali Beg Afshar, 104
Muhammad Ali Esfahani, 104
Muhammad Ali Khan, 190
Muhammad Amin, 343
Muhammad Amin Khan, 106, 345-46
Muhammad Baqir Khurdah Kashani, 292, 382
Muhammad Farukh Siyar, 113
Muhammad Husain, 254
Muhammad Husain Chalabi, 40
Muhammad Khurshid Nazar, 112
Muhammad Munem, 161
Muhammad Naii Neyrizi, 292, 311
Muhammad Nisabah Shirazi, 336
Muhammad Qasim Beg, 40, 42
Muhammad Quli Beg, 54, 55
Muhammad Quli Khan, 148
Muhammad Quli Qutab Khan, 188

Muhammad Quli Qutab Shah, 153, 310, 357, 384
Muhammad Quli Qutbul-Mulk, 153
Muhammad Quli Salim, 207, 210
Muhammad Qutb Shah, 250
Muhammad Reza, 151
Muhammad Reza Beg, 251
Muhammad Reza Beg Shamlu, 40, 42
Muhammad Rustam Safavi, 100
Muhammad Sadiq, 105
Muhammad Sadiq Mina, 149, 162, 315
Muhammad Salih, 96
Muhammad Salih Beg, 147
Muhammad Salih Lunbani, 279
Muhammad Salim Tehrani, 29
Muhammad Sharif, 83
Muhammad Shuja, 90, 100
Muhammad Sufi Mazandarani, 247
Muhammad Tanbureh, 312
Muhammad Taqi, 119
Muhammad Yahya, 118
Muhammad Zaman, 311
Muhibb Ali, 43
Muin-i-Chishti, 94
Muizz yazdi, 308
Mujibi Nehi, 340
Mujrim Shamlu, 314
Muklis Tabrizi, 86
Mukhlis Husain Tabrizi, 86
Mulkash Sultan Istajllu, 299
Mulla Abdul Hakim, 106
Mulla Ahmad, 150
Mulla Ali Reza, 209
Mulla Hazini, 160
Mulla Jamal-ud-din Washat, 309
Mulla Kalab Tabrizi, 86
Mulla Muhammad, 247
Mulla Muhammad Ali, 339
Mulla Murshid Shirazi, 179
Mulla Nawai, 206, 385
Mulla Qazwini, 99
Mulla Rajab Ali Tabrizi, 269
Mulla Shafia-i-Yazdi, 74, 386
Mulla Shukrullah Shirazi, 75, 109
MullaTughra, 264-65
Multan, 33
Mumin Gonabadi, 313
Mumin Taleqani, 255
Mumtaz Mahal, 45
Mumtaz-uz-Zamani (Nur-i-Mahal), 393, 395
Munhi Zavarehi, 152-53
Muniri Taleqani, 349
Munshi, Eskandar Beg, 41
Munshi-ul-Mamalik, 94
Muntakhab-ul-Lubab, 36
Muqim Tabrizi, 303
Murad (Prince), 102
Murad Bakhsh, 102, 104,105, 181
Murad Safavi, 116
Murshid Borujerdi, 148
Murshid Khan, 148-49
Murshid Shirazi, 172
Murtaza Nizam Shah, 47
Murtaza Quli Khan, 148
Musin-i-Razi, 356
Muslim, 33, 45, 157, 344
Mustafa Beg, 42
Mustafa Khan, 85
Mustafa Turkman, 71, 85
Mustaid Khan, 209
Mutamid Khan, 172, 179
Mutaqid Khan, 48
Muttalib, 179
Muzaffar Husain, 386
Muzaffar Husain Mirza, 114-115, 138
Muzaffar Husain Mirza Safavi, 157, 179, 393-98
Muzaffar Khan, 96

Nabi Qazwini, 256
Najaf, 73, 96
Najdi Yazdi, 329, 338
Naji Servani, 262
Nami Ali Khan, 358

Nami Forahi, 319
Naqdi Khan, 103
Naqib Khan, 93
Naqib Khan (Mir Ghiyas-ud-din Ali), 94
Naqib Khan Qazwini, 72, 94-95
Nasab-nama-shahr Yari and Nasab nama-i-Qutb Shahi, 310
Nasib Esfahani, 339
Nasira-i-Hamadani, 250
Nasiruddin Muhammad Humayun (Humayun), 34-36
Nawwab Khalifa Sultan, 356
Nawwab Parviz Banu Begum, 398
Nazar Muhammad Khan, 52-53, 102, 158-59
Nazim Tabrizi, 251
Naziri Neishabouri, 206, 301
Nazri Qomshehi, 275
Neishabour, 73, 369, 387
Neyazi Esfahani, 356
Nikhati Shushtari, 254
Nizam Dasghib-i-Shirazi, 261
Nizam Shah, 46-47, 100, 292, 304
Nizam Shahis, 45
Nizam-ul-Mulk, 45, 111
Nizam-ul-Mulk Deccan, 98
Nizami Qazwini, 178-79
Nuqtavis, 25, 239, 387
Nuqtavi Sect, 137, 205, 247, 292, 304, 382
Nur-nama, 137
Nur-i-Jahan, 44-45, 88-89, 107-108, 156, 171, 176, 178, 205, 207, 386, 393, 397
Nur Jahan Begum (Mehrun Nisa), 396
Nur Mahal, 396
Nur Manzil, 156
Nur Nama, 150
Nur-ud-din, 98-99
Nur-ud-din Jahangir, 137
Nur-ud-din Quli, 352
Nur-ud-din Quli Esfahani, 98, 386
Nutqi Mashhadi, 352

Oimaq Mosulo Tribe, 279
Omidi, 338
Ottoman, 24, 27, 33, 36-37, 51, 53, 147, 268, 370, 385, 389
Ottoman Army, 147
Ottoman Emperor, 38, 208
Ottoman Turks, 37, 55

Par Pahiz Banu Begum, 115
Parviz (Prince), 45
Peacock Throne, 208, 300
Persia, 26, 33-34, 37, 39-42, 45, 47-50, 52, 55-56, 76, 87, 101-102, 154, 172, 329, 330, 342-43, 382-83
Persion(s), 23, 25, 28, 33, 37, 38, 39, 41, 42-47, 49, 51-55, 94, 101, 117, 176, 203, 204, 208, 239, 263, 265, 268, 318, 341, 342, 369, 370
    Ambassador, 39
    Artists, 34
    Court, 53
    Poetry, 385
    Poets, 204, 207, 209, 386
    Immigrants, 29
Peshawar, 103
Pietro Della Valle, 41
Plato, 109
Poets,
    Baqi Nihavandi, 148
    Helaki, 148
    Mayeli, 151
    Mir Aqil Bazmi, 148
    Mir Razi Artimani, 148
    Mudriki, 148
    Musa Reza, 148
    Rashki, 148

Sanai, 151
Shukohi, 148
Wali Dasht Bayazi, 151

Ports,
Broach, 95
Surat, 95

Portugese, 157
Prince Khurram, 149, 262, 307, 311, 338, 393
Prince Murad Bakhsh, 265, 268
Prince Parvez, 110, 138, 147, 252, 308,
Prince Parwiz, 151
See Also Parvez
Prince Salim, 188
Prince Shuja, 343

Qaisari Hamadani, 35, 355
Qalandar, 29
Qamar Khan, 95
Qamus-ul-Ahlam Or Rihanat-ul-Adab, 358
Qandahar, 26, 33, 34, 35-38, 39, 42, 43, 44, 47-57, 73, 75, 76, 85, 87, 101, 103, 104, 113, 114-116, 152, 181, 205, 207, 209, 256, 261, 292, 299, 300, 311, 357, 386, 393, 396
Qandahari Mahal, 115, 393, 398
Qannauj, 34
Qasim Deylami, 189
Qasim Asiri, 385
Qasim Beg, 43, 47
Qasim Esfahani, 355
Qasim Khan, 156-57
Qasim Khan Juwaini, 86, 100, 138, 386
Qasim Khan Mir Bahr, 111
Qasim Siraja, 306
Qasimi Esfahani, 339
Qatii Heravi, 263
Qazaq Khan, 74, 87
Qazi Ahmad Mir Munshi, 313
Qazi Isa, 73
Qazi Najm-ud-din Ali, 174, 185
Qazi Nurullah Shushtari, 185, 192-93, 264, 272
Qazi Razi-ud-din Muhsin Esfahani, 355
Qazilbash, 72, 75, 110, 299, 313, 389
Qazilbash Tribe, 38, 299
Qazilbash Tripal Warfare, 268
Qazilbash Amir, 117
Qazi Zada Kashani, 138, 155
Qazwin, 24, 34, 37, 41, 72, 93, 189, 239, 257, 308, 312, 336, 369
Qazwin and Esfahan, 387
Qilij Khan, 51, 119
Qom, 24, 41, 100, 110, 204, 239, 369
Qudsi Gilani, 249
Qudrati Esfahani, 329, 339
Quli Beg, 56
Quli Khan Beg Mujrim Shamlu, 257, 314
Qunduz, 34
Quran, 346
Qurbi Shiraji, 329, 332, 336
Qureshi Khanum, 393
Qureshi Khanum-e-Tabrizi, 393
Qutb Shah, 47, 56, 341, 345
Qutb Shah Family, 46
Qutb Shah Service, 342
Qutb Shahis, 46-47
Qutb-ud-din Khan, 396
Qutb-ul-Mulks, 45, 49
Qutlu Lohani, 97
Qutluq, Muhammad Sultan, 102

Rafi-ud-din Haidar, 252
Rahim Khan, 104

Rahim Muhammad, 56
Rahmat Khan, 105, 395
Rahmat Khan Kashani, 73, 384
Rahmati Tabrizi, 359, 360
Rajputs, 27, 71, 109
Rajputs Geneology, 109
Rana Amar Singh, 109
Rana of Mewar, 107
Rana Sisodia, 97
Raqim Sad-ud-din, 158
Rashida Abbasi, 309
Rasmi Qalandar Yazdi, 151, 276
Rathore, Jaswant, 99
Raunaqi Hamadani, 301
Raushan Zamir Salabat Khan, 92
Raushanaiyah Movement, 85
Razavi Sayyid, 75, 109
Razi Esfahani, 355
Reza Hamadani, 253
Reza Quli Khan Hadayat, 261
Rezai Farsi, 269
Roe, Sir Thomas, 42
Roshan Rai Begum, 105
Rudsar of Gilan, 299
Ruhul-Amin-i-Shahristani, 153
Rukn-us-Saltanat, 108
Ruqayya Sultan Begum, 396
Rustam Khan, 54
Rustam Mirza, 114, 157, 386
Rustam Mirza Safavi, 179
Ruzbeh Shirazi, 312-13

Sabari Esfahani *(Darvesh)*, 302
Sabir-i-Esfahani, 318-19
Sabzevar, 264, 369
Sadat Mamuri, 73
Sadiq Khan, 49, 91, 92
Sadiq Khan Mir Bakhshi, 91
Sadr, 27
Sadullah Khan, 54, 102, 386,
Safavid, 24, 25, 26, 27, 29, 33, 34, 41, 45, 50, 55, 57, 71, 73, 86, 101, 114, 137, 139, 147, 150, 158, 176, 185, 203, 204, 205, 208-09, 239, 248, 258, 301, 306, 308, 314, 370, 382-85, 387, 389
  Brothers, 384
  Court, 29, 41, 49, 101, 147, 185, 306, 383,
  Dynasty, 139, 176, 370
  Empire, 73
  Iran, 25, 56, 208, 203, 383
  Kings, 86, 114,
  Monarchy, 33
  Persia, 33, 379
  Poets, 209
  Rulers, 26, 50, 71
  Society, 25
Safdar Khan, 49, 50, 111, 249, 338
Saf Shikan, 116
Saf Shikan Khan, 75, 111
Saf Shikan Khan Mirza Lashkari, 110
Safi Esfahani, 270
Safi Khan, 113
Safi Mirza, 48
Saib Tabrizi, 29
Said Khan, 50, 51
Saida-i-Gilani, 292, 293, 299-300
Saif Khan, 118
Saif Khan Mirza Safi, 75, 117, 118, 384
Saifi Sayyids, 72, 93, 95, 204
Saifi Sayyids of Qazwin, 379
Saifi Zulqadr, 312
Salahi Esfarayeni, 340
Salamullah Arab, 39, 117
Salih Azadani, 98
Salih Tabrizi, 137, 147, 332, 336
Salim, 40

Salim (Prince), 86, 107
Salim Tehrani, 205, 384
Salima Sultan Begum, 397
Sam Mirza, 48
Samandar Shamlu, 292, 314
Sameri Tabrizi, 138, 146-47
Samugarh Battle, 104
Sanjar Mirza, 76, 114, 116
Saqi-nama, 304, 340, 357
Sar-i-Khail of Golkonda, 343
Sarmad, 203
Saru Taqi, 51, 52
Sati Khanum, 105, 393-94
Sattar Tabrizi, 207
Sayyids, 153, 241, 338, 345
Sayyid Husain, 42
Sayyid Jalal-ud-din Ashtiyani, 248
Sayyid Safavi Beg, 36
Sayyids of Esfahan, 153
Sayyids of Saveh, 99
Sea
    Caspian, 145
Semnan, 24
Shabankareh, 148
Shabankareh Darab Fars, 357
Shaikhs, 23
Shaikh Abul Fazl, 150, 273
Shaikh Abu Nasr Frahi, 263
Shaikh Farid Murtaza Khan, 177
Shaikh Husain Jami, 278
Shaikh Khatan, 257
Shaikh Muhammad Khatan, 47
Shaikh Nizami, 150, 304
Shaikh-ul-Islam, 205, 342, 384
Shaikh Wajih-ud-din, 91
Shah Abbas, 29, 38, 39, 40-48, 53, 72, 86, 101, 110, 117, 147, 153, 185, 188, 240, 249, 251, 257, 259, 268, 304, 311,
Shah Abbas I, 37, 38, 44, 46, 48, 55, 73, 75, 85, 101, 110, 139, 153, 248, 251, 252, 311, 314, 338, 355, 383-85, 388
Shah Abbas II, 52, 53, 54, 56, 103, 189, 269, 309, 339,
Shah Abbas Safavi, 147, 172, 382
Shah Abul Fath, 313
Shaharyar, 107, 397
Shah Beg Arghun, 85
Shah Beg Khan 107
Shah Ghazi Khan, 73, 379
Shah Ghiyas, 305
Shah Husain, 41
Shah Ismail, 34, 57, 76, 139, 171, 240, 248
Shah Ismail II, 36, 46, 153, 311, 383
Shah Ismail Safavi, 56, 114, 157, 176, 251, 384
Shahjahan, 25, 29, 30, 40, 43-46, 48-56, 72, 73, 75, 86, 89, 90-93, 95, 96, 98, 99, 100-106, 108-113, 115-117, 137-38, 145, 149, 154, 157-58, 160-62, 171-73, 176-181, 185, 188-91, 204-205, 207, 208-209, 239-41, 250, 258, 260-61, 263, 265, 269, 291-92, 300, 303-304, 308-309, 313-14, 330, 336-37, 339-40, 342-45, 349, 356, 369-70, 393-94
Shahjahanabad, (Delhi), 92, 93, 106, 113
Shah Mirza, 101
Shah Muhammad Khudabanda, 76, 383
Shah Nama, 254
Shah Nawaz Khan, 138, 147
Shah Nawaz Khan Safavi, 116
Shah Nawaz Khan Shirazi, 208
Shah Quli Beg, 53
Shah Safi, 48, 49, 50, 51, 52, 56, 73,

75, 101, 103, 104, 119, 248,
Shah Shuja, 90, 117, 265,
Shah Sulaiman, 209, 308
Shah Sulaiman Safavi, 138, 158, 306
Shah Tahir Husain, 46
Shah Tahmasp, 46, 56, 57, 72, 74, 87, 93, 114, 153, 248, 257, 308, 318, 321, 379, 383-84, 389
Shah Tahmasp Safavi, 153, 254
Shah Verdi Beg, 54
Shahzada Buland Iqbal, 51
Shalimar Garden, 103
Shakibi, 206
Shakibi Esfahani, 151, 206
Shamkhal Esfahani, 356
Shamlu Tribe, 161, 314
Shamsai Zarrin Qalam, 300, 301
Shamlu Turk of Iran, 138
Shanawaz Khan Shirazi, 251
Shapur Tehrani, 329-30, 337
Sharari Hamadani, 385
Sharif Amuli, 137, 145, 205, 382
Sharif Kashi, 76, 270
Sharif Rafi-ud-daula, 358
Sher Afghan Khan, 396
Sher Khan Afghan of Fushang, 50
Sher Khan Tonvar, 112
Sherly, Robert, 42
Shia, 25, 55, 172, 207, 382
Shia State, 26
Shiakhs, 29
Shibani Khan, 177
Shiism, 25, 172, 203, 389
Shiite, 46
Shiraz, 109, 148, 369
Shirazi Kitabdar, 310
Shirazi Sayyid, 207
Shouqi, 385
Shrine of Najaf, 40
Shuja, 116, 330
Singh, Jagat, 91
Sistan, 41, 204, 254, 276, 292, 300, 341, 369
Siraja, 291
Siraj-al-Menhaj, 176
Sirati Qazwini, 38
Sistan Va Baluchistan, 24
Suhhan Quli Sultan, 102
Subhi Esfahani, 355
Subhi Hamadani, 149
Sufi, 240, 247, 256, 275, 276, 277, 279
Sufi Poets, 203
Sufis, 23, 29, 145, 268-69, 305, 370, 385
Sufism, 181, 203, 269
Suhrab Khalifa Mosului Turkman, 85
Sulhi, 358
Suliman Khalifa, 85, 110
Suliman Khalifa Turkman, 110
Sulaiman Shukoh, 103, 181, 305
Sultan Afshar, 73, 86, 383
Sultan Haidar Mirza , 153
Sultan Ibrahim, 53
Sultan Khusrau, 87, 102
Sultan Mahmud, 36
Sultan Mahmud Khudabanda, 36, 268
Sultan Muhammad Qutb Shah, 47
Sultan Nazr, 75, 118, 384
Sultan Quli Chandan Oghli, 36
Sultan Parviz, 152
Sultan Salim, 97
Sunni and Nuqtavi Creeds, 24
Sunnis, 25, 56, 93, 204, 206, 208, 370, 379, 382
Sunnis Community, 72, 379
Surat, 106, 109

Suri, Sher Shah, 33, 56
Sururi Kashani, 259
Suti Yazdi, 292, 309

Tabaqat-i-Akbari, 146, 207
Tabatabai Sayyids, 309
Tabatabai Sayyids of Ardestan, 259
Tabhi Kandu Sulqani, 138, 155
Tabriz, 72, 369, 387
Tahir Nasrabadi, 158, 265
Tahir Taleqani, 332, 336
Tahmasp (shah), 26, 34, 35, 36, 204
Taj Mahal, 172, 179, 395
Tajalli Gilani, 291, 293
Takllu, 25
Takllu, Walad Beg, 35
Takhta Beg Yuzbashi Ustajlu, 45
Talib Amuli, 29, 105, 307, 337, 382, 393-94
Talib Amuli (Peot Laureate), 337
Talib Esfahani, 269, 271
Talib Kalim, 112
Talibi, Beg Oghli, 47
Talish, Yadgar Sultan Ali, 39
Taqarrub Khan, 189, 190, 313
Taqi Auhadi, 257, 258
Taqi Kashi, 146, 303
Taqi Khurasani, 114
Taqi Murwarid Kashi, 258
Taqi Pirzad, 340
Taqi Shushtari, 253
Taqi-ud-din Muhammad, 253
Taqiya of Balban, 254
Tardi Ali Qatghan, 102
Tarkhan, Mirza Ghazi, 39
Tasalli Shirazi, 317, 319
Tashbihi Kashi, 205
Tatar Khan, 74
Tatar Sultan, 86
Tazkira Nasrabadi, 308
Tehran, 24, 72, 204, 239, 255, 369
Tehran and Qazwin, 155
Tehran University, 256
Telang (Hydarabad and Golkonda), 153
Thatta (Sind), 92, 96, 97, 151, 154, 181, 250, 273
Tibet, 338
Timorids, 26, 102
Title of
  Amir-ul-Umara, 101, 102
  Aqidat Khan, 138
  Danishmand Khan, 74
  Iradat Khan, 99
  Itimad Khan, 181
  Itiqad Khan, 89
  Khan-i-Khanan, 75
  Mahfuz Khan, 182
  Masih-uz-Zaman, 188, 191
  Masti Avar, 148
  Mauzun-ul-Mulk, 138, 148
  Mir Jumla, 153
  Muzaffar Khan, 73-74, 97
  Rukn-us-Sultanat, 111
Touri Tabrizi, 331, 335
Trans-Oxiana, 340
Tughluq-Nama, 146
Tun and Tabas, 85
Turan, 49, 52, 53
Turanians, 21
Turanis, 27, 71, 377
Turanis and Iranis, 21, 22
Turbat, 111
Turkey, 40, 50
Turkish Language, 21
Turkman, 25
Turkman and Takllu Tribes, 85
Turks, 36, 37

Tuzuk, 48
Tuzuk-i-Jahangiri, 302

Ujjania, Raja, 107
Ulama, 145
Ulugh Beg, 35, 40, 43
Urfi, 208, 302
Urfi Shirazi, 306
Ustad Ghazanfar Tabrizi, 40
Uzbek, 27, 33, 37, 38, 44, 53, 55, 56, 71, 76, 101, 102, 110, 115, 116, 117, 138, 179, 205, 270, 292, 340, 370, 384, 387, 393
Uzbek Raids, 157
Uzbek, Abdullah Khan, 37, 38
Uzbek, Abdul Mumin Khan, 38
Uzbekistan, 52

Vijaynagar Empire, 342

Wafai Esfahani, 269, 274
Wafai Heravi, 206
Wahshat Ardestani, 309
Wajhi Heravi, 157, 384
Wakil-i-Kul, 88
Wakils, 27
Wali Beg Dharogha Shotar Khan, 44
Wali Quli Shamlu Heravi, 275
Walih Shirazi, 311
Wasfi Kermani, 292, 304
Wasli Shirazi, 26, 85
Wasli Tabrizi, 303
Wasli Tehrani, 204, 379
Wazir Zafar Khan, 92
Wisal Beg, 43

Yadgar Ali, 338
Yadgar Ali Sultan, 75, 117, 338, 355
Yadgar Beg, 49, 51
Yadgar Sultan Rumlu, 37-38
Yadgar Tukariya, 102
Yahya Masum, 72, 93, 379
Yahya Qomi, 73
Yamani Gurji, 318-19
Yamin-ud-daula, 91, 92, 99, 117
Yaqini Mashhadi, 358
Yaqub Khan, 104
Yaqub Zargar Bashi, 306
Yar-i-Wafadar, 73
Yar Quli Beg Anisi, 151
Yazd, 74, 239, 369
Yazd and Kerman, 24, 338
Yusuf Aziz Esfahani, 291, 306
Yuzbashi, 119

Zabardast Khan, 90, 104, 112
Zafar Khan, 157, 207, 209
Zafar Khan Turbati, 208
Zahid Beg, 44, 45
Zain Khan Kokultash, 148
Zain Khan Kuka, 157, 274
Zain-i-Esfahani, 359-60
Zainal Beg, 42, 43, 44
Zakhirat-ul-Khawanin, 23, 155, 382
Zaman Beg, 75
Zaman Beg Mahabat Khan, 256
Zaman Esfahani, 307
Zamani Esfahani, 307, 264, 277
Zamin-Dawar, 53
Zanjan, 24
Zargar Khaneh, 100
Zavareh, 309
Zib-un-Nisa, 397
Ziya-ud-din, 105, 395
Zoroastrian, 240
Zoroastrian and Hindu in Huences, 240
Zubdat-ul-Tujjar, 40
Zuhuri, 29, 338
Zul-Faqar Khan Nusrat Jang, 90
Zul Qadr Khan, 51